*Cross-Cultural Research
at Issue*

Cross-Cultural Research at Issue

Edited by

LEONORE LOEB ADLER
Institute for Cross-Cultural and Cross-Ethnic Studies
Department of Psychology
Molloy College
Rockville Centre, New York

ACADEMIC PRESS 1982
A Subsidiary of Harcourt Brace Jovanovich, Publishers
New York   London
Paris San Diego San Francisco São Paulo Sydney Tokyo Toronto

ACADEMIC PRESS, INC.
111 Fifth Avenue, New York, New York 10003

United Kingdom Edition published by
ACADEMIC PRESS, INC. (LONDON) LTD.
24/28 Oval Road, London NW1 7DX

Library of Congress Cataloging in Publication Data
Main entry under title:

Cross-cultural research at issue.

"A continuation or a follow-up of many of the studies
that were presented ... in the Annals of the New York
Academy of Sciences (1977, volume 285, pp. 753) under the
title, Issues in cross-cultural research"--Pref.
    Includes bibliographies and index.
    1. Cross-cultural studies--Addresses, essays, lectures.
2. Ethnopsychology--Addresses, essays, lectures.
I. Adler, Leonore Loeb. II. Issues in cross-cultural
research.
GN345.7.C755   301   82-3918
ISBN 0-12-044280-9   AACR2

PRINTED IN THE UNITED STATES OF AMERICA

82 83 84 85   9 8 7 6 5 4 3 2 1

To the memory of my parents,

Leo and Elsie Loeb

who instilled in me an appreciation and a respect for
the great variety of individual ways, the manners, and
the customs in which people behave.

Contents

List of Contributors   xiii
Preface   xvii

I   THEORETICAL ISSUES IN COGNITIVE RESEARCH

1   *Developmental Theories Applied to Cross-Cultural Cognitive Research*   3
MICHAEL COLE and SYLVIA SCRIBNER

2   *Developmental Theories in Cross-Cultural Perspective*   13
JOHN W. BERRY, PIERRE R. DASEN, and HERMAN A. WITKIN

3   *Indigenous versus Construct Validity in Cross-Cultural Research*   23
MARC IRWIN, ROBERT E. KLEIN, and JOHN W. TOWNSEND

4   *The Ponzo Illusion among the Baganda*
         of Uganda: Implications for Ecological
         and Perceptual Theory   31
         PHILIP L. KILBRIDE and H. W. LEIBOWITZ

II   ISSUES IN DEVELOPMENTAL RESEARCH

5   *The Infant's Niche in Rural Kenya*
         and Metropolitan America   47
         CHARLES M. SUPER and SARA HARKNESS

6   *Role of Nonverbal Maternal Behavior*
         in the Learning Process   57
         LORRAINE KIRK

7   *Children's Drawings as an Indicator of Individual*
         Preferences Reflecting Group Values:
         A Programmatic Study   71
         LEONORE LOEB ADLER

8   *Father Absence Cross-Culturally: A Review*
         of the Literature   99
         REGINA C. SPIRES and MITCHELL W. ROBIN

III ISSUES IN APPLIED PSYCHOLOGICAL
         RESEARCH

9   *Caregivers and Children Learning Together:*
         A Cross-Cultural View   113
         ALICE STERLING HONIG

10 *The Rhode Island Pupil Identification Scale (RIPIS) in Cross-Cultural Perspective* 125
PETER F. MERENDA

11 *Constancy of WISC IQs of Puerto Rican, White, and Black Children* 137
ANN M. MARMORALE and FRED BROWN

12 *Why African Children Are So Hard to Test* 145
SARA HARKNESS and CHARLES M. SUPER

13 *Quranic Pedagogy in Modern Morocco* 153
DANIEL A. WAGNER

14 *Cross-Cultural Aspects of Piaget's Theory: The Competence-Performance Model* 163
PIERRE R. DASEN

15 *Teachers' and Students' Instructional Strategies* 171
HUGH MEHAN and MARGARET M. RIEL

IV MODERNIZATION AND STEREOTYPES

16 *Ideologies of Sex: Archetypes and Stereotypes* 193
ELEANOR LEACOCK and JUNE NASH

17 *Advertising as a Basis for Cross-Cultural Comparisons* 209
FAIRFID M. CAUDLE

18 *Attitudes Accompanying Modernization in Advanced and Developing Societies* 231
ROBERT C. WILLIAMSON

19   *Sociopsychological Correlates of Traditionalism*
          in Values: Cross-National Findings   243
          PAULINE A. JONES

20   *A Comparison of Women in the Soviet Union*
          and Israel   253
          FLORENCE L. DENMARK, NIRA WEINBERG,
          and JOYCE BLOCK

21   *Ego Identity Status of Married Couples*
          and Their Interactions on Structured
          and Unstructured Tasks   263
          USHA KUMAR and URMIL ARORA

22   *A Comparison of Ideal Self-Ratings between*
          American and German University Students   275
          UWE P. GIELEN

V   ASSESSMENT AND EVALUATION

23   *Selection for Intercultural Living:*
          The Peace Corps Experiment   291
          GORDON F. DERNER

24   *Interdisciplinary Conflict in Fieldwork:*
          A Case of Ideological Shock   303
          JOHN CAWTE

25   *Who Are We? Who Are They?*
          And What Is Going on Here?   311
          JOHN BEATTY and JUNICHI TAKAHASHI

26   The United States-United Kingdom
        Cross-National Project: Issues in
        Cross-Cultural Psychogeriatric Research   323
        BARRY J. GURLAND and JOSEPH ZUBIN

27   Attitudes toward Stigma-Related and
        Stigma-Free Stimuli: A Cross-National Perspective   335
        JEAN G. GRAUBERT and LEONORE LOEB ADLER

28   War Bereavement in the United States
        and Israel   349
        VICTOR D. SANUA

29   Epilogue: An Exaltation of Cross-Cultural
        Research: The Nature and Habits of
        the Hyphenated Elephant   361
        KURT SALZINGER

Index   367

List of Contributors

Numbers in parentheses indicate the pages on which the authors' contributions begin.

LEONORE LOEB ADLER (71, 335), Institute for Cross-Cultural and Cross-Ethnic Studies, Department of Psychology, Molloy College, Rockville Centre, New York 11570

URMIL ARORA (263), Department of Applied Psychology, University of Bombay, Bombay 98, India

JOHN BEATTY (311), John Beatty Enterprises, Brooklyn, New York 11234

JOHN W. BERRY (13), Department of Psychology, Queen's University, Kingston, Ontario, K7L 3N6 Canada

JOYCE BLOCK (253), Graduate School and University Center, City University of New York, New York, New York 10021

FRED BROWN (137), The Mount Sinai School of Medicine, City University of New York, New York, New York 10028

FAIRFID M. CAUDLE (209), Department of Psychology, The College of Staten Island, City University of New York, St. George Campus, Staten Island, New York 10301

JOHN CAWTE (303), The School of Psychiatry, The University of New South Wales, Prince Henry Hospital, Little Bay, N.S.W. 2036, Australia

MICHAEL COLE (3), Laboratory of Comparative Human Cognition, University of California, La Jolla, California 92093

PIERRE R. DASEN (13, 163), Faculté de Psychologie et des Sciences de l'Éducation, Université de Genève, CH-1211 Geneva, Switzerland

FLORENCE L. DENMARK (253), The Graduate School and University Center, Graduate Center, City University of New York, New York, New York 10036

GORDON F. DERNER (291), Institute of Advanced Psychological Studies, Adelphi University, Garden City, New York 11530

UWE P. GIELEN (275), Department of Psychology, St. Francis College, Brooklyn, New York 11201

JEAN G. GRAUBERT (335), Department of Psychology, Adelphi University, Garden City, New York 11530

BARRY J. GURLAND (323), The Center for Geriatrics and Gerontology, The Faculty of Medicine, College of Physicians and Surgeons, Columbia University, New York, New York 10032

SARA HARKNESS (47, 145), Judge Baker Guidance Center, Boston, Massachusetts 02115 and Department of Psychiatry, Harvard Medical School, Boston, Massachusetts 02115

ALICE STERLING HONIG (113), Department of Child and Family Studies, College for Human Development, Syracuse University, Syracuse, New York 13210

MARC IRWIN[1] (23), Greenwell Springs Hospital, Department of Health and Human Resources, State of Louisiana, Greenwell Springs, Louisiana 70739

PAULINE A. JONES (243), Institute for Research in Human Abilities, Memorial University of Newfoundland, St. John's, Newfoundland, A1B 3X8 Canada

PHILIP L. KILBRIDE (31), Department of Anthropology, Bryn Mawr College, Bryn Mawr, Pennsylvania 19010

LORRAINE KIRK (57), Department of Sociology and Anthropology, University of Missouri, St. Louis, Missouri 63121

ROBERT E. KLEIN (23), Division of Human Development, Institute of Nutrition of Central America and Panama (INCAP), Carraterra Roosevelt, Guatemala City, Guatemala, Central America

USHA KUMAR (263), Department of Humanities and Social Sciences, Indian Institute of Technology, Kanpur, 208016, U. P., India

ELEANOR LEACOCK (193), Department of Anthropology, The City College, City University of New York, New York, New York 10031

H. W. LEIBOWITZ (31), Department of Psychology, Pennsylvania State University, University Park, Pennsylvania 16802

ANN M. MARMORALE (137), Department of Psychology, The College of Staten Island, City University of New York, Staten Island, New York 10301

HUGH MEHAN (171), Department of Sociology, University of California, San Diego, La Jolla, California 92093

---

[1] *Present address:* New Mexico Psychological Services, P.C., Farmington, New Mexico 87401

PETER F. MERENDA (125), Department of Psychology, University of Rhode Island, Kingston, Rhode Island 02881

JUNE NASH (193), Department of Anthropology, The City College, City University of New York, New York, New York 10031

MARGARET M. RIEL (171), Division of Social Sciences, University of California, Irvine, Irvine, California 92717

MITCHELL W. ROBIN (99), Department of Social Sciences, New York City Technical College, City University of New York, Brooklyn, New York 11201

KURT SALZINGER (361), Social Psychiatry Research, The New York Psychiatric Hospital, New York, New York 10032 and Department of Social Sciences, Polytechnic Institute of New York, Brooklyn, New York 11201

VICTOR D. SANUA (349), Department of Psychology, St. John's University, Jamaica, New York 11439

SYLVIA SCRIBNER[2] (3), Center for Applied Linguistics, Washington, D.C. 20007

REGINA C. SPIRES (99), Department of Social Sciences, New York City Technical College, City University of New York, Brooklyn, New York 11201

CHARLES M. SUPER (47, 145), School of Public Health and Department of Nutrition, Harvard University, Boston, Massachusetts 02115 and Judge Baker Guidance Center, Boston, Massachusetts 02115

JUNICHI TAKAHASHI (311), Graduate Center, City University of New York, New York, New York 10036

JOHN W. TOWNSEND (23), Division of Human Development, Institute of Nutrition of Central America and Panama (INCAP), Carraterra Roosevelt, Guatemala City, Guatemala, Central America

DANIEL A. WAGNER (153), Graduate School of Education, University of Pennsylvania, Philadelphia, Pennsylvania 19104

NIRA WEINBERG[3] (253), Graduate Center, City University of New York, New York, New York 10036

ROBERT C. WILLIAMSON (231), Department of Social Relations, College of Arts and Sciences, Lehigh University, Bethlehem, Pennsylvania 18015

HERMAN A. WITKIN[4] (13), Educational Testing Service, Princeton, New Jersey 08540

JOSEPH ZUBIN (323), University of Pittsburgh Medical School and Research Career Scientist, Highland Drive VA Medical Center, Pittsburgh, Pennsylvania 15206

---

[2] *Present address:* Developmental Psychology Program, The Graduate Center, City University of New York, New York, New York 10036

[3] *Present address:* Ferkauf Graduate School, Yeshiva University, New York, New York 10033

[4] Deceased.

Preface

With the proliferation of cross-cultural activity in academic departments, scientific journals and books, as well as in new areas of specialization, interest in cross-cultural research is booming. Many of the salient issues in cross-cultural research that were under consideration and discussion a few years ago are still of crucial importance. Therefore there existed a need to follow up the initial investigations detailed in an earlier volume, a need that is met here in the following chapters. As was the case previously, these issues fall under specific topics that are clearly important to the understanding of cross-cultural research. In fact, frequently they are identical to those that arise in other psychological studies, which, however, do not include the cultural variables.

The present book, itself not a conference volume, represents, at least in part, a continuation or a follow-up of many of the studies that were presented at a conference, the proceedings of which were published in their entirety, in the Annals of the New York Academy of Sciences (1977, Vol. 285) under the title *Issues in Cross-Cultural Research*, with myself as editor. The conference served to bring together an illustrious assembly of cross-cultural scientists from different disciplines, including psychology, anthropology, sociology, education, linguistics, and medicine.

Many of the contributors to the present book were involved in the initial volume, and are represented here by their most recent work. The newly added contributors are not newcomers to the field, however; many have been active and productive researchers for some time. The inclusion of their work greatly enhances the value of the present volume. The issues, which primarily involve practical aspects of cross-cultural research, include several comparatively new areas of investigation. The major areas remain the same for the most part, however, though with expanded coverage and exciting additions to each topic.

The many authors who contributed shared my enthusiasm about the prospect of preparing this volume. I would like to take this opportunity to thank each author for that enthusiasm and, above all, for contributing so much valuable information about the state of the art. Special notes of thanks, for his continual cooperation, are due to Bill Boland, executive editor of the Annals of the New York Academy of Sciences, in which a number of these articles appeared in earlier form. I am most indebted to Helmut E. Adler, Yeshiva University, and to Beverly S. Adler, Hofstra University, for their continual support in innumerable ways and for their great tolerance and consistently sympathetic understanding. All their helpful suggestions are most gratefully acknowledged, as both of them made my task much easier.

LEONORE LOEB ADLER

Theoretical Issues in Cognitive Research

The first section of this book on cross-cultural research deals with important theoretical issues in developmental psychology, including cognition and perception, for example, visual illusions. Some of these have been "hot" topics for a long time, going back several years before I organized the New York Academy of Sciences Conference entitled Issues in Cross-Cultural Research. This section includes chapters that feature different approaches to resolving the same old question: What are the influences that the cultural environment exerts on the development of the individual's behavior? The value and the advantages of different methodologies and theoretical issues in cross-cultural research are discussed in the two lead-in chapters. In the first, coauthors Michael Cole and Sylvia Scribner seek to discover the relationships that exist between culture and cognition; in the second, John W. Berry, Pierre R. Dasen, and Herman A. Witkin discuss the effects of cultural and ecological factors on socialization patterns. The next chapter, by Marc Irwin, Robert E. Klein, and John W. Townsend, deals with those environmental factors, such as socioeconomic status, influencing mental development and behavioral complexity that may be due, all or in part, to the consequences of malnutrition. Then follows a chapter by Philip L. Kilbride and H. W. Leibowitz concerning a controversial issue in visual space perception and its effectiveness with regard to testing illusions on "two-" and "three-dimensional" observers. The results pose a dilemma for current ecological and perceptual theory of visual illusions, as well as for our understanding of visual mechanisms.

MICHAEL COLE
SYLVIA SCRIBNER

1

Developmental Theories Applied to Cross-Cultural Cognitive Research[1]

ABSTRACT

This chapter examines criteria of adequacy in evidence used to support ascription of developmental status to children and adults. Leading theories of cognitive development assume, and require evidence for, intertask consistency within and across behavior domains. Cross-cultural research has frequently failed to yield evidence for such consistency and calls into question the appropriateness of developmental interpretations applied to mature individuals on the basis of limited experimental evidence.

Almost from the outset, psychologists engaged in cross-cultural research seemed to realize that their work posed methodological problems different from, and probably in addition to, those that faced their colleagues in other branches of their science. It has been generally understood that it is one thing to observe a difference in behavior across cultural groups and quite another to interpret it.

This realization is reflected in the continuous concern of cross-cultural psychologists with problems of methodology, dating from Rivers (1901) and Titchener (1916) to contemporary investigators such as Campbell (1961), Berry (1969), Goodnow (1969), Glick (1974), and others. We, too, have been concerned with questions of method and the special difficulties of

[1] Support for the preparation of this chapter was provided by the Carnegie Corporation and the Ford Foundation.

CROSS-CULTURAL RESEARCH AT ISSUE

3

inference from observation to psychological process that are endemic to the cross-cultural enterprise. Some of our work has been concerned with the problems of specifying the culturally determined independent variables that relate to the dependent variables we study (Cole, Gay, Glick, & Sharp, 1971). Following the lead of Campbell and many others, we have sought to use the opportunities offered by different cultural settings to deconfound theoretically promising causal factors that are ordinarily "packaged" in modern, technological societies (Whiting, 1973). This work has engaged us in a companion issue that has been of great concern to us: What significance can we attach to our dependent variables? Here we enter the perennial debate between anthropologists and psychologists as to the proper methods for studying cognitive behavior, a debate that has centered around deciding what inferences about psychological processes of individuals are warranted on the basis of experimental and naturalistic observations (cf. Cole & Scribner, 1975, Scribner, 1975).

Like most anthropologists, we are committed to the view that observations of intelligent behavior in everyday life are an important source of information about culture and cognitive processes. But we also believe experiments to be important and probably necessary tools for disentangling the complex relationships among culturally determined experiences and specific intellectual skills. To use Scribner's (1975) term, this position requires us to "situate" the psychological experiment as one of many contexts in which to sample behavior. This approach to "behavior-in-context" leads us to question the generality of inferences from experiments that are not corroborated by nonexperimental data. At the same time, it leads us to attempt a more precise characterization of the cognitive demands of nonexperimental situations (Cole & Scribner, 1975).

The distinctions that we have in mind can be briefly illustrated by our research on free recall. In several studies (see Cole & Scribner, 1974, for a summary), our concern was with specifying population characteristics correlated with performance differences in multitrial free recall of categorizable nouns. Age, educational status, and exposure to a modern cash economy were some of the variables found to be associated with improved recall performance in some of these studies. But finding such differences held no magic key to explaining them in terms of the variations in memory processes that underlay the performances we were observing. To approach an explanation at that level required a program of experimentation in which there was systematic variation of different aspects of the task—the items to be recalled, the contexts in which the items were presented, the incentives for good performance, and others. Even when much of that work was done, we were left with the question of how we could generalize from performance in our experiments to memory tasks that our subjects faced daily but that we were not observing. This question was particularly pertinent in the case of memory, because the lore of anthropology had led us to expect fine performance in our experimental task, but such outcomes were rare and restricted to special task formats.

In this entire line of work, our range of inference and interpretation was restricted to generalizations about one particular set of skills—memory skills. We were not attempting to make inferences about intellectual performance or cognitive status *in general*. When cross-cultural research attempts such global assessment within the framework of some general developmental theory, a host of new conceptual and methodological problems are superimposed on those we encountered. The enterprise is broadened. The investigator has not only the task of interpreting the relationship between particular performances and the operations accounting for them, but also that of characterizing those operations according to some hypothesized developmental sequence. An entirely new chain of inference is involved in moving from an analysis of performance to an assessment of what that performance represents in developmental terms.

It is our impression that cross-cultural cognitive research would profit from a better understanding of the conditions under which it is legitimate to draw developmental conclusions on the basis of differences in cognitive performance. As our contribution toward this goal, we would like to examine the requirements that developmental theories themselves prescribe for making inferences about "developmental status," and consider whether these have been satisfied in cross-cultural research.

At the risk of inviting misunderstanding through oversimplification, we will try to characterize the main features of the two developmental theories that have been applied most widely in cross-cultural research: the theories of Piaget and those of Witkin. Setting aside for the moment the radically different approaches they take to cognition, we believe they share certain common characteristics:

1. Both theories characterize development in terms of an orderly progression in the organization of systems composing the individual's psychological structure. They postulate, so to speak, one developmental process, in terms of which psychological changes occurring from infancy to adulthood are to be understood.

2. This developmental progression is conceived of as characterizing the person as a whole—that is, the individual's entire intellectual and social functioning. Within both theories, therefore, it is possible to speak of a "level of development" that a given individual has attained (although it is acknowledged that individuals may not always operate at the highest level they have attained). These levels of development are generally ordered with reference to age.

3. Within this conceptual framework, tasks in various domains of performance are often used in the manner of diagnostic instruments to assess where the person stands in the developmental sequence.

Although this line of theorizing has been dominant for some time, it has encountered increasingly strong challenges in recent years. Without taking sides, we would like to suggest that some of the debates that appear in the cross-cultural literature are similar to (and, we would argue, might be formally identical to) debates that are currently emerging around the proper interpretation of age-related differences in performance on various cognitive tasks investigated within *one* culture. Controversies surrounding the general set of propositions characterized as Piagetian theory can serve as a case in point.

Investigators have found, in a whole host of instances, that changes in performance related to modifications in experimental procedures (Bryant, 1974; Gelman, 1972; Marastsos, 1973; Turiel, 1974) and contexts (Shatz & Gelman, 1973) suggest a characterization of young children's competence different from that originally proposed by Piaget. The thrust of this work is to make problematic the interpretation of performance on tasks that have been widely assumed to be diagnostic of developmental level. Neither *presence* of a particular performance nor *absence* of that performance is clearly interpretable with respect to a child's development level—a general point clearly stated by Werner (1937) nearly 40 years ago. Although we still find differences that are generally correlated with age, evidence of variability related to task modifications suggests a line of theorizing about development that emphasizes not only basic competencies but also the operational skills that children acquire and employ in different ways, depending upon specific features of the task and situation. This point of view is exemplified in the seminal paper by Flavell and Wohlwill (1969), which distinguishes between formal and functional subcomponents in the developing competence of the child, and in the current work of Pascual-Leone (1975) and Case (1974).

The import of this line of work is that characterization of a person's developmental status on the basis of experimental performance is debatable even when the research is entirely intracultural.

Nonetheless, the problems raised by this evidence do not have to be interpreted as fundamentally damaging to Piaget's theoretical position. Although it is possible to find variability on almost every Piagetian task and it is also possible to provide alternative interpretations of performance on any single task, the general theory is bolstered in the face of local difficulties by the enormous range of correlated phenomena that it accounts for. Essentially, it is the interweaving of evidence from performance in many different domains of children's activities that gives credence to Piaget's interpretation of performance in localized contexts. Piaget himself is quite explicit on this point:

We have just described the cognitive aspects of the developmental process which connect the structure of the initial sensori-motor level with those of the level of concrete operations. . . . The affective and social development of the child follows the same general process, since the affective, social and cognitive aspects of behavior are in fact inseparable [Piaget & Inhelder, 1969, p. 114].

His general point is illustrated in Goodnow's particularly lucid discussion of cross-cultural Piagetian research, in which she emphasizes that the transfer of the same underlying operations across the range of tasks that presumably require them is the necessary condition for making judgments about the child's developmental level (Goodnow, 1969, pp. 443ff.).

The importance of this general point of "domain consistency" to the support of general developmental theory is also made explicit by Witkin and Berry (1975):

Progress toward greater differentiation during development involves the organism as a whole, rather than proceeding discretely in separate domains. Hence, a tendency toward more differentiated or less differentiated functioning in one domain should 'go with' a similar tendency in other domains, making for self-consistency [p. 6].

What happens when this debate is moved to the cross-cultural arena? All the specifications of the theory that apply intraculturally should also apply interculturally, keeping in mind the added methodological difficulties of cross-cultural research that we talked about earlier.

Does the cross-cultural research evidence meet the criteria of adequacy that the theories themselves prescribe for intracultural validation? When we examine the evidence from this perspective, we are led to conclude that in spite of the many sound developmental studies that have been carried out, neither Piaget's nor Witkin's theories has ever actually been tested in cross-cultural research. As so much has been written on culture and cognitive development, and as the impression seems so widespread that developmental theories have been tested extensively, we must take some space to justify this conclusion.

We are led to this position not because of methodological problems with individual studies but because it is our reading of the literature that: (a) there has not been a single nonwestern culture in which investigators have made the wide range of observations necessary to demonstrate that behaviors across tasks and domains go together in the way required by the theory; and (b) in the few instances where more than one task and one domain have been investigated simultaneously, the evidence is ambiguous, if not negative, with respect to such consistency.

We will try to support this position by an examination of cross-cultural research on Witkin's theory of psychological differentiation. We select Witkin rather than Piaget because Witkin and Berry (1975) have stated the theory and its testing requirements so clearly, and have reviewed the research evidence so thoroughly, that we can best illustrate our position with respect to this work.

As we have already stated, Witkin and Berry (1975, p. 5) characterize psychological development in terms of a "differentiation theory," which maintains that "the typical progression in psychological development is from less to more differentiation." More differentiation implies greater specialization and separation of individual functions; perception is differentiated from feeling, thinking from action. It implies as well "specificity in the manner of functioning *within* an area." Although differentiation thus proceeds in many psychological subsystems, Witkin and Berry maintain that it is an organismic, and not a subsystem, process. Research requirements are relatively clear. It is necessary to find precise and valid indicators of differentiation appropriate to the various psychological domains; to demonstrate that these indicators are highly interrelated *within* any one domain; and then to demonstrate that they are highly interrelated *across* domains.

The first issue, and a critical one, concerns the "indicators" of psychological differentiation. Witkin and Berry review these with heavy emphasis on the perceptual domain. The most widely used perceptual tests have been the rod and frame test, the embedded figures test, and the body adjustment test. Consistency in the degree of "differentiation" measured by these tests, at least by adolescence, has been widely reported for studies in the United States. Once we move beyond the perceptual domain, both the question of indicators and the problem of consistency become much more problematic. Witkin and Berry conclude that self-consistency has been demonstrated within the United States in such additional domains as cognition, body concept, and the nature of the self. There are two problems here. To begin with, it is not clear that the indicators in these hypothetically separate domains are separate in the way claimed. The tests in the cognitive domain that correlate with perceptual tests consist mainly of such tasks as block design, picture completion, and the like, for which we can assume heavy perceptual involvement. Similarly, the indicator of a developed body concept is often some form of a draw-a-man test in which perceptual skills related to pictorial representation clearly must play a part. (This problem has been discussed by Vernon, 1969.)

If we go further afield to indicators of differentiation in the social sphere, the problem is somewhat different. To take an example: Witkin and Berry (1975, p. 9) tell us that reliance on external sources of information for self-definition is a good indicator of lack of differentiation in the social domain; field dependent people (as measured in the perceptual domain) are more sensitive to the social content of their surroundings. But in the social domain, who is to say what is figure and what is embedding context? If problem solution depends upon the adequacy of manipulating other people it may not be adequate to treat others as "context," distinguished from the "self" as figure. The central problem in these important extensions of the differentiation notion is the difficulty of assessing the adequacy of the metaphors that suggest the connection between social and physical events.

None of these problems is inherently insurmountable, and we do not intend to denigrate the serious efforts that have been made to come to grips with these issues in the work of Witkin and many others. We only want to suggest that real problems exist *intraculturally* in establishing the main tenets discussed so far.

When we move from the intracultural to the intercultural arena, even the problematic canvas that we have been discussing is not adequately represented. With only a few exceptions, research is centered squarely in the perceptual domain, and even here some significant problems are evident in the uneven levels of differentiation or field independence that have been found in some studies between sensory modalities. We can do no better than to quote Witkin and Berry's (1975) careful summary evaluation of their review of cross-cultural research on self-consistency:

> We find that many studies have investigated and found evidence of self-consistency within the perceptual domain and between the perceptual and body-concept domains. Relatively little has yet been done in non-Western settings to extend the study of self-consistency, as a function of level of differentiation, to the domains of separate identity and defenses. The few studies on record hardly provide substantial evidence of the self-consistency to be expected from differentiation theory and from results of many Western studies on record [pp. 29–30].

When the authors turn, however, to a consideration of studies testing hypotheses about the role of ecological-cultural factors and socialization practices in differentiation, they no longer confine their theorizing to the limited domains to which their test batteries apply. Rather, they revert to the use of the general concept of overall psychological differentiation, and come to conclusions about the developmental status of the individuals studied. Not only individuals within cultures but entire populations and ways of life are assessed in terms of the global characteristic of field independence or dependence. For example, the authors speak of social arrangements in different types of society that "influence development toward greater or more limited differentiation [p. 57]" and reach the conclusion that agricultural and hunting and gathering societies foster different modes of functioning, which can be characterized in terms of the unitary psychological dimension of "field dependence."

It is our contention that this kind of speculation cannot be warranted in the absence of prior demonstrations of domain consistency.

The status of cross-cultural Piagetian research is not dissimilar. Although there have been extensive studies covering a small set of tasks (cf. Dasen, 1974), there have been none meeting Piaget's own requirements for the range of observations, tasks, and spheres of activity necessary to support generalizations about developmental levels. Again, important inconsistencies within psychological domains crop up in the cross-cultural literature, such as those reported by Otaala (1973), Heron and Dowel (1974), and Holos (1975).

We believe, although we cannot document the statement here, that the same problems exist for other general developmental formulations as well. Although it is unpalatable, we have been led to conclude that we simply cannot assess the general significance of a great deal of cross-cultural research that is nominally in the developmental mode. The problem is that deprived of the consistencies in performance across tasks, psychological functions, and behavioral domains which carry the interpretive power of the theory, we do not know how to generalize beyond the performances reported in individual studies. When the studies do not hang together in the theoretically prescribed way, each individual study is of very limited value in serving either as a test of the general theory or as a measure of the developmental status of people in different cultures. This is not to say that such studies can be of no theoretical or practical interest in and of themselves. If they are designed to discover variations in performance associated with features of the task (nature of the material used or response mode analyzed, for example) or with the specialized experiences of different groups (occupation, schooling, and the like), such studies can move us toward a more precise characterization of both the independent and dependent variables related to performance in cognitive investigations.

Nor do we mean to imply that researchers must abandon the effort to generate and test general developmental hypotheses cross-culturally. Several strategies are available.

One is to follow the path so clearly outlined by Witkin and Berry (1975). This involves investigation of the systems defined by the theory in many areas of cognitive activity and many domains of behavior. The great value of the research inspired by Witkin is that it does demonstrate culture–cognition relations, even if the generality of the results is in dispute.

With respect to this approach, we would like to suggest that an extremely useful course to follow might be the involvement of anthropologists in helping to gather data from behavioral situations which are typically inaccessible to psychologists. We thus have in mind here involving anthropologists not only in making psychological test instruments culture sensitive, but also in obtaining observational data of the sort that psychologists usually eschew.

It seems at least an interesting possibility that the consistency observed in Euro-American studies of development is in fact a characteristic of the cultures studied rather than a universal characteristic. If so, a cross-cultural strategy based on the assumption of consistency in performance among various cognitive operations and in various behavioral domains may be going at the task of identifying culture–cognition relations in exactly the wrong way. If cognitive performance is often and importantly specific to a given domain, we ought to be *looking* for variability and its cultural sources rather than explaining it away when we find it. Paradoxically, we may find that, just as the pursuit of consistency has made an important contribution in exposing unexpected variability, the search for variation may lead us to consider the uniformities of cognitive development from a fresh perspective.

In either event, if we are correct in our analysis, the evidence of cross-cultural psychology is silent with respect to the "developmental status" of various third world peoples.

References

Berry, J. W. On cross-cultural comparability. *International Journal of Psychology,* 1969, *4,* 119–128.

Bryant, P. *Perception and understanding in young children.* New York: Basic Books, 1974.

Campbell, D. T. The mutual methodological relevance of anthropology and psychology. In F. L. K. Hsu (Ed.), *Psychological anthropology.* Homewood, Ill.: Dorsey Press, 1961.

Case, R. Structures and strictures: Some functional limitations on the course of cognitive growth. *Cognitive Psychology,* 1974, *6,* 544–573.

Cole, M., Gay, J., Glick, J., & Sharp, D. (Eds.). *The cultural context of learning and thinking.* New York: Basic Books, 1971.

Cole, M., & Scribner, S. *Culture and thought.* New York: Wiley, 1974.

Cole, M., & Scribner, S. Theorizing about socialization of cognition. *Ethos,* 1975, *3*(2), 250–268.

Dasen, P. R. The influence of ecology, culture and European contact on cognitive development in Australian aborigines. In J. W. Barry & P. R. Dasen (Eds.), *Culture and cognition.* London: Meuthen, 1974.

Flavell, J. H., & Wohlwill, J. F. Formal and functional aspects of cognitive development. In D. Elkind & J. H. Flavell (Eds.), *Studies in cognitive development.* New York: Oxford University Press, 1969.

Gelman, R. The nature and development of number concepts. In H. W. Reese (Ed.), *Advances in child development and behavior* (Vol. 7). New York: Academic Press, 1972.

Glick, J. Cognitive development in cross-cultural perspective. In J. Horowitz (Ed.), *Review of child development research* (Vol. 4). New York: Russell Sage, 1974.

Goodnow, J. J. Problems in research on culture and thought. In D. Elkind & J. H. Flavell (Eds.), *Studies in cognitive development.* New York: Oxford University Press, 1969.

Heron, A., & Dowel, W. The questionable unity of the concrete operations stage. *International Journal of Psychology,* 1974, *9,* 1–10.

Holos, M. Logical operations and role-taking abilities in two cultures: Norway and Hungary. *Child Development,* 1975, *46,* 638–649.

Marastsos, M. Nonegocentric communication abilities in preschool children. *Child Development,* 1973, *44,* 697–700.

Otaala, B. *The development of operational thinking in primary school children: An examination of some aspects of Piaget's theory among the Itseo children of Uganda.* New York: Teachers College Press, 1973.

Pascual-Leone, J. A view of cognition from a formulist's perspective. In K. Riegel (Ed.), *Current issues in developmental psychology.* Basil and New York: S. Kazgu, 1975.

Piaget, J., & Inhelder, B. *The psychology of the child.* New York: Basic Books, 1969.

Rivers, W. H. R. Introduction and vision. In A. C. Haddon (Ed.), *Reports of the Cambridge anthropological expedition to the Torres Straits.* (Vol. 2, Pt. 1.). Cambridge, England: The University Press, 1901.

Scribner, S. Situating the experiment in cross-cultural research. In K. F. Riegel & A. Meacham (Eds.), *The developing individual in a changing world* (Vol. 1). Chicago: Aldine, 1975.

Shatz, M., & Gelman, R. The development of communication skills: Modifications in the speech of young children as a function of the listener. *Monographs of the Society for Research in Child Development,* 1973, *38,* 1–38.

Titchener, E. B. On ethnological tests of senstion and perception. *Proceedings of the American Philosophical Society,* 1916, *55,* 204–236.

Turiel, E. Conflict and transition in adolescent moral development. *Child Development,* 1974, *45,* 14–29.

Vernon, P. E. *Intelligence and cultural environment.* London: Meuthen, 1969.

Werner, H. Process and achievement—a basic problem of education and development psychology. *Harvard Educational Review,* 1937, *7,* 353–360.

Whiting, H. *Comparative studies of social and cognitive development.* Paper delivered at the biennial meeting of the International Society for the Study of Behavioral Development, Ann Arbor, 1973.

Witkin, H. A., & Berry, J. W. Psychological differentiation in cross-cultural perspective. *Journal of Cross-Cultural Psychology,* 1975, *6,* 4–87,

JOHN W. BERRY
PIERRE R. DASEN
HERMAN A. WITKIN

2

Developmental Theories in Cross-Cultural Perspective[1]

ABSTRACT

When ontogenetic developmental theories are employed in cross-cultural research, differences in individual behavior which are found in the cultural groups
studied may be interpreted as implying that individuals in some cultures are more
or less "developed" than others. Thus the cross-cultural use of developmental
theories should be accompanied by special consideration and analyses, in order
to avoid the danger of ethnocentrism.

In considering the theories of psychological differentiation and genetic epistemology, two distinctions are made. First, individual differences may be conceived as lying upon some absolute value dimension, or they may be considered
as culturally relative, in functional adaptation to the ecological and cultural context
of the individual; the cross-cultural use of developmental theory should be within
the latter framework. Second, there are frequent confusions made among value
dimensions; it is not necessary to construe cultural differences as developmental
differences. It is concluded that there is no inherent ethnocentrism in developmental theories, but only in their use in ways that do not take into account the
functional adaptation of behavior to its cultural and ecological context.

---

[1] This chapter is a condensed version of a paper entitled "The Use of Developmental
Theories Cross-Culturally" delivered at the Fourth International Conference of the International
Association for Cross-Cultural Psychology, Münich, August 1978, and published in the volume
Cross-Cultural Contributions to Psychology, 1979, edited by L. Eckensberger, Y. Poortinga,
and W. Lonner. It is republished by kind permission of Swets and Zeitlinger B. V., Lisse. This
condensation was undertaken by Berry and Dasen after the death of Hy Witkin in July 1979.

The General Question

This chapter attends to the question of the cross-cultural use of developmental theories with respect to the two developmental theories that are most widely used in cross-cultural work—differentiation theory and genetic epistemology, of H. A. Witkin and J. Piaget respectively. In neither case will there be an attempt to review the theory or the cross-cultural evidence (for reviews, see Berry, 1981; Dasen, 1972, 1973, 1977a, b; Okonji, 1980; Witkin, 1978; Witkin & Berry, 1975). Rather, the focus will be directly on the issue of ontogenetic development, and potential difficulties faced by developmental theory when employed across cultures.

Psychological Differentiation

We wish to make two fundamental points: One is that when we employ differentiation theory (Witkin, Dyk, Faterson, Goodenough, & Karp, 1962; Witkin, Goodenough, & Oltman, 1979) to guide a research program, even though there is a developmental component to the theory, *we are not bound to interpret group differences as developmental differences;* and the other is that *even where a developmental interpretation is made, it need not be in terms of a directional and unilinear development.*

Before tackling these two points, it is necessary to distinguish between them. A useful starting point is the distinction made by Sahlins and Service (1960) between general and specific evolution in the debate about cultural evolution: *Specific evolution* refers to the emergence of new cultural forms in adaptation to new situations; *general evolution* refers to some ordering of these forms in a progressive arrangement—"higher forms arise from and surpass lower" forms (1960, p. 13). It should be clear that differences may be documented and accounted for without any value judgments being made about relative merits. Indeed, as Sahlins and Service argue: "Adaptive improvement is relative to the adaptive problem; it is so to be judged and explained. In the specific context each adapted population is adequate, indeed superior, in its own incomparable way [p. 15]."

Alternatively, one may seek to order the differences according to some dimension, and make judgments about each form relative to each other form, and relative to the end points of the dimension. By analogy, in psychology, differences may be observed and accounted for in nonevaluative terms (an individual *difference* approach) or they may be ordered on a dimension of chronology (a *developmental* approach).

Looking at the *difference* approach first, we may make two points: First, there are frequent *confusions about the dimensions of difference* being employed; and, Second, there is an established paradigm for considering differences—both individual and group—as *adaptive to ecological setting*, rather than in evaluative or developmental terms.

1. Differential studies have traditionally employed three dimensions of difference, all based upon chronology: phylogenetic, ontogenetic, and cultural evolutionary. Despite their common ordering of phenomena by time of appearance, there is no basis whatsoever for identifying an "early" appearance on one dimension with an "early" appearance of another. We maintain that these are conceptually independent dimensions, and that transfers between dimensions based solely upon chronology are unwarranted.

2. From the point of view of *adaptation*, we note that in anthropology the approach of *cultural ecology* permits the analysis and interpretation of cultural differences as specifically adaptive to habitat. As we have seen, this formulation in terms of *specific evolution* has permitted anthropology a "nonevolutionary" option. So too in psychology we have employed such an ecological orientation (Berry, 1976; Witkin & Berry, 1975) and we may claim a right to a "nondevelopmental" option. This option chooses to consider both psychological and cultural change as a function of ecological requirements, which vary from place to place, rather than as a function of some absolute or universal sequence. People become as they are to meet recurrent problems they encounter; such behaviors are to be judged valuable if they permit successful adaptation, not simply if they match some preconceived chronology or other evaluative dimension.

Turning to our second fundamental point, we note that *developmental* conceptions characteristically lead to the ordering of people as being of higher or lower status, according to their standing on a given developmental progression. A possible consequence of exporting a developmental dimension worked out in one culture to other cultures may be to introduce a too easily applied yardstick for labeling at least some of these other cultures as "inferior." We would like to suggest that such a danger is not as great in the case of the *multilinear* conception of development which differentiation theory proposes as it may be in the case of unilinear dimensions (Witkin, 1978).

To the extent that the differentiation dimension, as expressed in field dependence–independence, involves, toward one pole, greater cognitive restructuring skill, and, toward the other pole, more of interpersonal competencies, it may appropriately be regarded as bipolar. That is, with regard to level, it has no clear "high" or "low" end. Relatively more differentiated people do better at tasks which require restructuring; relatively less differentiated people seem to do better in the interpersonal competencies involved in getting along with others.

Relatively less differentiated people are particularly invested in the interpersonal domain during growth, encouraging the development of interpersonal competencies. Relatively more differentiated people make a greater investment in the cognitive domain, leading to the development of cognitive restructuring skills. The proposal is that the field-dependent and field-independent cognitive styles, which are process variables, influence the development of patterns of abilities—in this instance, cognitive restructuring skills and interpersonal competencies, combined in an inverse relationship (Witkin, 1977; Witkin & Goodenough, 1977, 1981).

Among relatively more differentiated and relatively less differentiated people psychological growth thus proceeds along different pathways. In neither case can we speak of an arrest in development. Genuine development takes place along both routes. It is in this sense that differentiation theory is a multilinear conception of development. The bipolarity emphasized in our treatment of differentiation at an individual differences level may be conceived of as the product of multilinearity in development. In an ontogenetic perspective there is certainly no basis for considering the constellation found at one or the other pole as reflecting greater progress in development, and hence as being of higher status.

This is equally true from the perspective of cross-cultural comparisons. Cultural groups, whether western or nonwestern, whose members are, modally, more differentiated or less differentiated, cannot be pegged as being at a higher or lower level of development, compared to each other. In the case of differentiation theory, there seems to be no basis for the concerns expressed by Cole and Scribner (1977) about the cross-cultural application of developmental theories. Cole and Scribner ask for an "explicit admission on the part of cross-cultural psychologists that their data are silent with respect to the developmental status of various Third World peoples [p. 372]." Because of its multilinear conception of development, differentiation theory is not only silent on the ordering of western and nonwestern peoples according to developmental status, but in fact takes an active stand against such an ordering. On the same grounds, differentiation theory provides no basis for the concern of Cole and Scribner about its ascription of childlike status to nonwestern adults, compared to westerners. In fact, nonwestern groups examined to date run the full gamut from field dependent to field independent. We thus see that when the developmental sequelae of differentiation are worked out in detail, a simplistic ordering of individuals' or groups with regard to *developmental status* is hardly possible.

As we noted earlier, differentiation theory is equally clear in its stand against a simplistic ordering of individuals or groups on a *value* dimension. To the extent that the field dependence–independence cognitive style component of differentiation is bipolar, characteristics that are adaptive in particular ecological and cultural circumstances can be found at both poles. On these grounds the cognitive style dimension may be considered value neutral. The dimension carries no inherent definition of value status. What determines the value of the characteristics at one pole or the other is their usefulness in specified contexts.

The multilinear conception of the development of differentiation allows for the possibility that development may follow different progressions in contexts that have different adaptive requirements (Witkin, 1978). To illustrate, whereas the progression during ontogeny is from lesser to greater differentiation, there are grounds for believing that the progression during the course of development of cultural forms may have been in a reverse direction. This proposal is consistent with the view that early appearance on one of the main dimensions of differences based on chronology—ontogenetic, phylogenetic, and cultural—need not necessarily go with early appearance on the others.

We conclude for differentiation theory, first, that cross-cultural research that employs what is in part an ontogenetic developmental theory need not make any developmental interpretations of group differences; and, second, that with ontogenetic development being multilinear, there can be no simplistic ordering of peoples, whether individuals or groups, on some single value dimension.

Genetic Epistemology

From the point of view of genetic epistemology, the development of knowledge about the world we live in occurs in a sequentially ordered series of stages, the structural properties of which are qualitatively different, with an increasing differentiation and integration at each level. Development occurs through interaction with the physical and social environment, but at such a general level that different environments are not expected to produce structural differences. Cultural variations are expected to influence not the operations themselves, but the situations in which they are applied, and the speed or rate of development through the sequence of stages (Piaget, 1966).

If we look at the cross-cultural data collected so far, how do Piaget's predictions fare? This question has to receive a different answer for different levels in the developmental sequence. The universality of the first stage, that of *sensorimotor intelligence,* is extremely likely, although the number of cross-cultural studies is not yet very large (Dasen, Inhelder, Lavallée, & Retschitzki, 1978). Already at this early age, however, environmental factors are found to influence the rate of development.

At the other end of the sequence, the universality of the stage of *formal operations* is questionable. Piaget's developmental end point is really the reasoning of a western scientist, and, because western science does not necessarily represent the form of thought valued in other cultures, this end point is likely to be ethnocentric (Greenfield, 1976). Piaget (1972) has acknowledged the possibility of "new . . . structures that still remain to be discovered [p. 11]," and Greenfield (1976) draws on this suggestion to propose a position of extreme cultural relativism, or, in other words "a Piagetian psychology to each culture, now on an emic rather than etic basis [Dasen, 1977b, p. 336]." These are clearly future directions; for the moment, there is little empirical evidence to go on.

The middle stage in Piaget's sequence, that of *concrete operations,* is the one that has received most attention. Here again, the succession of substages has been very generally confirmed, but marked cultural differences appear in the rate of development. These quantitative variations may be dismissed as unimportant to Piaget's theory, which is certainly a reasonable stance when the time lags are small: What is the importance of attaining a particular stage 1 or 2 years earlier or later? However, when this time lag becomes larger, say 4 to 5 years, or in the case of "asymptotic" development curves (Dasen, 1973, 1979), these differences have important practical as well as theoretical implications.

One possible interpretation of these time lags is that they are due to a western conceptual bias. However, if the whole sequence were culturally specific to the west, why should at least some individuals in each culture (as far as we know) follow the same sequence of substages? If the time lags were only due to methodological difficulties encountered by western experimenters, why do they also occur in studies carried out by nonwestern psychologists studying children of their own culture (e.g., Mureria & Okatcha, 1977; Za'rour & Khuri, 1977)? More importantly, why should the differences observed follow a systematic pattern? For example, Dasen (1975) demonstrated that spatial concepts, as measured by some of Piaget and Inhelder's (1956) tasks, show a much more rapid development in nomadic, hunting and gathering societies than in sedentary, subsistence agricultural societies. According to Berry's (1976) model, this is because spatial skills and concepts are more highly adaptive and valued in nomadic than in sedentary societies. On the other hand, concepts of conservation of quantity, weight, and volume show a more rapid development in sedentary, agricultural societies than in nomadic, hunting and gathering societies, presumably because such concepts are more highly adaptive and valued if food is to be stored and exchanged on markets. This finding has important theoretical implications, for it shows that the "structure d'ensemble," or domain consistency, posited for the western child (although hardly substantiated by empirical evidence) is not universal: If such a domain consistency exists at all, it takes specific forms in each culture, according, for example, to ecocultural demands. This implies that any single task cannot be used as a "diagnostic instrument" to determine the individual's general "level of development" or his "developmental status," to use Cole and Scribner's (1977) terms. A fortiori, it implies that it is not possible to ascertain the "developmental status" of a whole population and to ascribe a "childlike status" to some, as Cole and Scribner (1974) seem to think is generally done.

Cole and Scribner's (1977) demands for domain consistency seem excessive even if the theory is restricted to western children. The consistency over the wide "range of observations, tasks and spheres of activity" which they ask for has not been tested intraculturally, and those who have attempted to do so in developing psychometric scales based on Piaget's concrete and formal tasks have met with serious difficulties.

To summarize our discussion, we have rejected the hypothesis that Piaget's theory is entirely specific to western culture, as well as the hypothesis that it is absolutely universal. We have argued that cultural differences found in the rate of development of concrete operations follow a predictable pattern [such as Berry's (1976) ecocultural dimension]. We have examined some implications of such cross-cultural findings, in particular those which highlight some difficulties of the theory which also occur intraculturally, such as the lack of domain consistency, and we have pointed out that it is impossible to speak of an individual's "level of development" on the basis of single task performance, and quite nonsensical to ascribe a "developmental status" to a whole population.

Because systematic cultural differences do occur, it seems worthwhile to explore further the nature of the development curves. In some cases at least, the asymptote seems to reflect functional rather than structural differences (i.e., performance rather than competence). Evidence for this, based on training studies in several cultures, is presented by Dasen, Ngini, and Lavallée (1979), but much more research is needed on this competence–performance distinction.

Conclusion

In this chapter we have been able to deal only very briefly with a complicated issue. Moreover, the complexity has been compounded because the issue has not been treated identically for the two theoretical positions, except for two basic points. First, we jointly reject the automatic ascription of any "deficiency" (be it childlike, underdevelopment, or retardation) to populations on the basis of variation in task performance. Second, we find that an ecological orientation provides a value free context for the interpretation of differences as unique adaptations, rather than as differential developments. Beyond these communalities lie numerous differences and other similarities which will be taken up in future papers.

References

Berry, J. W. *Human ecology and cognitive style: Comparative studies in cultural and psychological adaptation.* New York: Wiley, 1976.

Berry, J. W. Developmental issues in the comparative study of psychological differentiation. In R. Munroe, R. Munroe, & B. B. Whiting (Eds.), *Handbook of cross-cultural human development.* New York: Garland, 1981.

Cole, M., & Scribner, S. *Culture and thought: A psychological introduction.* New York: Wiley, 1974.

Cole, M., & Scribner, S. Developmental theories applied to cross-cultural cognitive research. In L. L. Adler (Ed.), *Issues in cross-cultural research.* Annals of the New York Academy of Sciences, 1977, *285*, 366–373.

Dasen, P. R. Cross-cultural Piagetian research: A summary. *Journal of Cross-Cultural Psychology,* 1972, *3*, 23–39.

Dasen, P. R. Biologie ou culture? La psychologie interethnique d'un point de vue Piagetien. *Psychologie Canadienne,* 1973, *14*(2), 149–166.

Dasen, P. R. The influence of ecology, culture and European contact on cognitive development in Australian Aborigines. In J. W. Berry & P. R. Dasen (Eds.), *Culture and cognition.* London: Methuen, 1974.

Dasen, P. R. Concrete operational development in three cultures. *Journal of Cross-Cultural Psychology,* 1975, *6*(2), 156–172.

Dasen, P. R. Are cognitive processes universal? A contribution to cross-cultural Piagetian psychology. In N. Warren (Ed.), *Studies in cross-cultural psychology* (Vol. 1). London: Academic Press, 1977(a).

Dasen, P. R. Cross-cultural cognitive development: The cultural aspects of Piaget's theory. In L. L. Adler (Ed.), *Issues in cross-cultural research.* Annals of the New York Academy of Sciences, 1977, *285*, 332–337. (b)

Dasen, P. R. Cross-cultural data on operational development: Asymptotic development curves. In T. Bever (Ed.), *Dips in learning and development curves.* Hillsdale, N.J.: Lawrence Erlbaum, 1979.

Dasen, P. R., Inhelder, B., Lavallée, M., & Retschitzki, J. *Naissance de l'intelligence chez l'enfant Baoule de Côte d'Ivoire.* Berne: Hans Huber, 1978.

Dasen, P. R., Ngini, L., & Lavalée, M. Cross-cultural training studies of concrete operations. In L. Eckensberger, Y. Poortinga, & W. Lonner (Eds.), *Cross-cultural contributions to psychology.* Amsterdam: Swets and Zeitlinger, 1979.

Greenfield, P. Cross-cultural research and Piagetian theory: Paradox and progress. In K. Riegel & J. Meacham (Eds.), *The developing individual in a changing world* (Vol. 1). The Hague: Mouton, 1976.

Mureria, M., & Okatcha, F. M. Conservation of concepts of length, area and volume among Kikuyu primary school children. In F. M. Okatcha (Ed.), *Modern psychology and cultural adaptation*. Nairobi: Swahili Language Consultants and Publishers, 1977.

Okonji, M. O. Cognitive styles across cultures. In N. Warren (Ed.), *Studies in Cross-Cultural Psychology* (Vol. 2). London: Academic Press, 1980.

Piaget, J. [Need and significance of cross-cultural studies in genetic psychology.] In J. W. Berry & P. R. Dasen (Eds.), *Culture and cognition*. London: Methuen, 1974. (Reprinted from *Journal International de Psychologie*, 1966, *1*(1), 3–13.)

Piaget, J. Intellectual evolution from adolescence to adulthood. *Human Development*, 1972, *15*, 1–12.

Piaget, J., & Inhelder, B. *The child's conception of space*. London: Routledge & Kegan Paul, 1956.

Sahlins, M., & Service, E. (Eds.) *Evolution and culture*. Ann Arbor: University of Michigan Press, 1960.

Witkin, H. A. Theory in cross-cultural research: Its uses and risks. In Y. H. Poortinga (Ed.), *Basic problems in cross-cultural psychology*. Amsterdam: Swets & Zeitlinger, 1977.

Witkin, H. A. *Cognitive styles in personal and cultural adaptation. The 1977 Heinz Werner Lectures*. Worcester, Mass: Clark University Press, 1978.

Witkin, H. A., & Berry, J. W. Psychological differentiation in cross-cultural perspective. *Journal of Cross-Cultural Psychology*, 1975, *6*, 4–87.

Witkin, H. A., Dyk, R. B., Faterson, H. F., Goodenough, D. R., & Karp, S. A. *Psychological differentiation*. New York: Wiley, 1962.

Witkin, H. A., & Goodenough, D. R. Field dependence and interpersonal behavior. *Psychological Bulletin*, 1977, *84*, 661–689.

Witkin, H. A., & Goodenough, D. R. Essence and origin of cognitive styles: Field dependence and field independence. *Psychological Issues*, 1981 (Monograph No. 51).

Witkin, H. A., Goodenough, D. R., & Oltman, P. K. Psychological differentiation: Current status. *Journal of Personality and Social Psychology*, 1979, *37*, 1127–1145.

Za'rour, G. I., & Khuri, G. A. The development of the concept of speed by Jordanian school children in Amman. In P. R. Dasen (Ed.), *Piagetian psychology: Cross-cultural contributions*. New York: Gardner Press, 1977.

MARC IRWIN
ROBERT E. KLEIN
JOHN W. TOWNSEND **3**

Indigenous versus Construct Validity in Cross-Cultural Research[1]

ABSTRACT

The special problems of measurement validation in cross-cultural behavioral research are discussed. It is argued that conventional construct validation methods cån supply important information regarding the meaning of measures in the cultural context. Also suggested are tests of indigenous validity of measures, which require the demonstration that cultural group members both identify the dimension of behavior under scrutiny, and place individuals along that dimension similarly to the investigator's placements. Both techniques are illustrated by validation studies performed for tests of intellectual development created for use in the Institute of Nutrition of Central America and Panama's 8-year longitudinal study of the effects of chronic protein-energy malnutrition on mental development in Guatemala.

Introduction

The study of the mental processes of nonwestern peoples has been greatly enriched by the combination of ethnographic techniques with those of experimental psychology (e.g., Cole, Gay, Glick, & Sharp, 1971; Irwin & McLaughlin, 1970; Price-Williams, 1962, 1969). By adapting their measures to the cultural context, such studies have increased the credibility of cross-

---

[1] This research was partially supported by Contract No. NO1-HD-5-0640 from the National Institute of Child Health and Human Development, by National Science Foundations Grants BNSF6-82639 and SOC77-01063, and by a grant from the Grant Foundation.

CROSS-CULTURAL RESEARCH AT ISSUE

cultural research. Nevertheless, systematic efforts to establish the validity of cross-cultural measurements (Irwin, Klein, Engle, Nerlove, & Yarbrough, 1977) have been few and relatively unsophisticated.

Such efforts include the use of checks for absurd responses by Campbell and his co-workers (Campbell, 1964) in their studies of susceptibility to visual illusions among various cultural groups, Cole, Gay, Glick, & Sharp's (1971) comparisons of the learning performances of subgroups within the Kpelle tribe of Liberia, and Angelini's (1966) demonstration among Brazilian subjects of increased need achievement test scores following experimentally manipulated failure experiences. Though each of these efforts has been useful, none is sufficient in itself, as the demonstration of construct validity of behavioral measurements requires multiple predictions of performance.

An entirely different form of validation of measurements of mental processes among a nonwestern group is also possible. This is the demonstration of indigenous validity, or the extent to which cultural group members both identify the dimension of behavior under scrutiny and place individuals along that dimension similarly to the investigator's placements.

This chapter illustrates the processes of establishing both conventional construct validity and indigenous validity of measurements of mental processes of a nonwestern group. It does so by describing the validation efforts carried out in conjunction with an 8-year longitudinal study of malnutrition and mental development conducted by the Institute of Nutrition of Central America and Panama (INCAP) in Guatemala (Klein, Irwin, Engle, & Yarbrough, 1977).

Method

Study Setting

The INCAP longitudinal study was conducted in four subsistence agricultural villages in the department of El Progresso, an arid region located in the eastern portion of Guatemala. These communities ranged in size from about 500 to about 850 inhabitants in 1968, when the study began. Although Guatemala's population is roughly split between Ladino (or Spanish-speaking) and Indian subpopulations, the four villages participating in the study were entirely Ladino. Most families in the study communities were engaged in subsistence agriculture, the major crops being corn and beans. A brief ethnography of life in the study villages is found in Nerlove, Roberts, Klein, Yarbrough, and Habicht (1974), and a full ethnography is provided by Mejía-Pivaral (1972).

Subjects and Cognitive Testing

Subjects in the INCAP study were the over 1500 children who were under 7 years of age and present in the study villages during at least part of the longitudinal study. Over 1200 of these children were administered cognitive tests on at least one occasion. These tests comprised a heterogeneous battery which was administered yearly from ages 3 to 7, within 2 weeks of a child's birthday. Test data described in this chapter are for 7-year-old scores on seven tests for which most complete coverage is available. The cognitive battery employed in the INCAP study was developed over a period of 2 years through a collaborative effort of bilingual North American psychologists, Guatemalan psychologists, and a Guatemalan cultural anthropologist. During this period, tests in the battery underwent as many as ten revisions in an effort to adapt items and testing procedures to the study setting (Klein, 1971).

Other Measures

Other measures employed in the INCAP study and described here include a simple and stable assessment of family socioeconomic status (SES) based upon the size and construction of the family's house. This measure is particularly useful because of the considerable annual fluctuations of income measures and their difficulty of interpretation in the study setting. Also assessed was amount of intellectual stimulation available in the child's home, here indexed by the quantity of toys, reading materials, pictures on the walls, and other objects found in the home.

In addition to these data, primary school performance data based on the average of year-end grades in the two major subjects, language and arithmetic, averaged across all years of school attendance, are described for those children who attended school. Many children do not attend even primary school, and the average length of attendance in these communities is less than 2 years (Irwin, Engle, Yarbrough, Klein, & Townsend, 1978).

Finally, data from two substudies of a small ($N = 61$) subgroup of study children are also presented. These children participated in a study of free behavior in 1971, when they ranged in age from 5 to 8 years old (Nerlove et al., 1974), and a villager ranking study in 1973 when they were 7–10 years old (Klein, Freeman, Spring, Nerlove, & Yarbrough, 1976). In the first of these studies, one dimension assessed was the complexity of behavior in terms of the number of observations that could be characterized as complex self-managed sequences involving either work or play. Work activities included those not easily supervised and involving transformation of objects and systematic movement through space, and those performed alone and requiring going outside the community or gathering, transforming, and relocating objects. Play activities included were those involving rule games, interactive role play, joint or systematic construction, or play that involved going outside the community.

In the second study involving this sample, village women were asked to make pairwise comparisons of study children, with the help of photographs, in terms of each child's degree of "listura" (Klein et al., 1976). "Listura" is an indigenous concept most often translated to English as smartness. The concept closely resembles what is commonly referred to as "brightness" or "quickness" in the United States; the behavioral characteristics used by villagers in describing children who are "listo" include alertness, verbal facility, a good memory, independence, and a high level of physical activity.

Additional information regarding the concept of listura has recently been gained in an unpublished study of villager perceptions of the similarity of several adjectives commonly used to describe children in the study villages. Multidimensional scaling of adjective similarity judgments produced dimensions identifiable as the evaluative, activity, and potency dimensions repeatedly found by Osgood and his co-workers (e.g., Osgood, 1977). Listura emerged in these analyses as highly positive, very active, and neither strong nor weak.

Results

Correlations between cognitive test performances at 7 years and measures of SES, intellectual stimulation, behavioral complexity, school performance, and listura are presented in Table 3.1.

Table 3.1
Correlations between 7-Year-Olds Cognitive Test Performances, and Construct Validity and Indigenous Validity Indicators

Cognitive test	Construct validity				Indigenous validity
	SES	Intellectual stimulation	Behavioral complexity	School performance	Listura
Picture vocabulary naming	.19**	.33**	.15	.27**	.48**
Verbal inferences	.14**	.21**	.06	.32**	.19
Incidental learning	.01	.05	.25*	.23**	.27*
Memory for digits	.13**	.15**	.11	.20**	.30**
Memory for designs	.13**	.21**	.20	.27**	.22
Embedded figures	.12**	.18**	.33*	.16**	.50**
Matching familiar figures	.10*	.12**	.40**	.19**	.36**
	$N \approx 600$	$N \approx 600$	$N = 61$	$N \approx 300$	$N = 61$

$*\ p < .05.$
$**\ p < .01.$

Conventional Construct Validity

The first four columns of Table 3.1 provide information regarding the construct validity of tests in the cognitive battery. As family socioeconomic status is known to be a proxy measure reflecting many factors that may affect intellectual development (e.g., Hess, 1970), it was predicted that test scores would, in general, correlate positively with family SES scores, even in this setting characterized by a very limited range of wealth and opportunity. As Table 3.1 indicates, this was indeed the case. Though correlations are modest in size, scores on every test excepting incidental learning are seen to be significantly positively related to SES.

A positive relationship is also seen in Table 3.1 between test scores and amount of intellectual stimulation available in the home. For this more direct measure of environmental forces impinging on the intellectual development of study children, correlations with test scores are higher than those involving family SES. The highest correlation is that for picture vocabulary naming ($r = .33$, $p < .01$). Once again, incidental learning performance is seen to be unique in showing no significant relationship with intellectual stimulation available in the home.

It was also predicted that children performing relatively better on tests in the cognitive battery would show greater behavioral complexity when observed during their normal daily activities. As Table 3.1 indicates, a significant positive relationship between behavioral complexity and test performance is seen for the incidental learning, embedded figures, and matching familiar figures tests (and a marginally significant one for the memory for designs test). The strongest of these relationships is that for the matching familiar figures test ($r = 40$, $p < .01$), followed by the embedded figures test ($r = .33$, $p < .01$). Lower, nonsignificant, relationships with behavioral complexity are seen for the picture vocabulary naming test, verbal inferences test, and memory for digits test.

Additionally, it was predicted that children who performed well on tests in the cognitive battery at 7 years of age would subsequently do well in school (for which the legal enrollment age is 7). As Table 3.1 indicates, scores on all seven tests are significantly positively correlated with school grades in language and arithmetic. The highest correlation is seen for the verbal inferences test ($r = .32$, $p < .01$), followed by the picture vocabulary naming and memory for designs tests (r for each $= .27$, $p < .01$). That it is indeed intellectual potential, as measured by the INCAP cognitive tests, which predisposes good school performance, rather than factors such as family SES which covary with preschool test performance, is indicated by regression analyses which have been performed on these data (Irwin et al., 1978). These analyses indicate that 7-year cognitive test scores continue to predict school grades even after controlling for family SES, intellectual stimulation available in the home, and other variables.

Indigenous Validity

Indigenous validity information regarding tests in the cognitive battery is provided by the correlations in Table 3.1 between test scores and rankings generated by asking village women to make paired comparisons of a subgroup of study children in terms of their listura. As Table 3.1 indicates, these correlations are consistently positive, and significant for five of seven tests, notwithstanding the small size of the sample. These correlations are in fact the highest for any validation variable in Table 3.1, with some 25% of the variance in test scores accounted for in the case of picture vocabulary naming ($r = .48$, $p < .01$) and embedded figures ($r = .50$, $p < .01$).

Discussion

In this chapter, we have described efforts to establish the measurement validity of tests in a cognitive test battery administered to a large sample of rural Guatemalan children. Though correlations are generally modest in size, test scores are seen to relate as predicted to measures of family SES level, intellectual stimulation available in the home, free behavioral complexity, and later school performance. Furthermore, where wide discrepancies between the general predictions and correlations involving individual tests are seen (e.g., the absence of a relationship between incidental learning test performance and SES or intellectual stimulation available in the home measures; the failure of verbal measures to correlate with behavioral complexity), these discrepancies appear intuitively reasonable.

In addition to this evidence of conventional construct validity of tests in the cognitive battery, several tests also correlate with rankings by village women on the indigenous dimension of listura, which translates as smartness, and closely resembles the concept of "brightness," or "quickness." This evidence of indigenous validity of the INCAP measurements of intellectual ability is particularly important, as it provides information not contained in assessments of conventional construct validation. This is the case as the cultural recognition of a category of behaviors as distinct, and the accompanying interpretation put on those behaviors (such as the highly positive connotation of "listo" for villagers which we have previously noted), is a significant determinant of both their development and their consequences. A vivid demonstration of this function of culture is provided, for example, by the behaviors labeled as psychopathological in western culture and indicative of shamanistic powers among such peoples as the aborigines of Central Australia (Róheim, 1967).

In the INCAP longitudinal study we have had a particular need to establish the indigenous validity of our measurements, as the purpose of the study has been to increase understanding of the effects of malnutrition on people's lives. Information concerning the relationship of nutritional status to mental development, as that concept is defined in terms of socioeconomic causes, behavioral complexity, and school performance, undoubtedly furthers our knowledge of the consequences of malnutrition. Nevertheless, it omits important information about those consequences for people who are likely to spend most of their lives within a village setting that is a world apart from the life most of us know.

References

Angelini, A. L. Measuring the achievement motive in Brazil. *Journal of Social Psychology,* 1966, *68*, 35–40.

Campbell, D. T. Distinguishing differences of perception from failures of communication in cross-cultural studies. In F. C. S. Northrup & H. H. Livingston (Eds.), *Cross-cultural understanding: Epistemology in anthropology.* New York: Harper & Row, 1964.

Cole, M., Gay, J., Glick, J., & Sharp, D. *The cultural context of learning and thinking.* New York: Basic Books, 1971.

Hess, R. D. Social class and ethnic influences on socialization. In P. H. Mussen (Ed.), *Carmichael's manual of child psychology* (Vol. 2). New York: Wiley, 1970.

Irwin, M., Engle, P. L., Yarbrough, C., Klein, R. E., & Townsend, J. W. The relationship of prior ability and family characteristics to school attendance and school performance in rural Guatemala. *Child Development,* 1978, *49*, 415–427.

Irwin, M., Klein, R. E., Engle, P. L., Nerlove, S. B., & Yarbrough, C. The problem of establishing validity in cross-cultural measurements. In L. L. Adler (Ed.), *Issues in cross-cultural research.* Annals of the New York Academy of Sciences, 1977, *285*, 308–325.

Irwin, M., & McLaughlin, D. Ability and preference in category sorting by Mano school children and adults. *Journal of Social Psychology,* 1970, *82*, 15–24.

Klein, R. E. Some considerations in the measurement of the effects of food supplementation on intellectual development and social adequacy. In N. S. Scrimshaw & M. Altschul (Eds.), *Amino acid fortification of protein foods.* Cambridge, Mass.: MIT Press, 1971.

Klein, R. E., Freeman, H. E., Spring, B., Nerlove, S. B., & Yarbrough, C. Cognitive test performance and indigenous conceptions of intelligence. *Journal of Psychology,* 1976, *93*, 273–279.

Klein, R. E., Irwin, M., Engle, P. L., & Yarbrough, C. Malnutrition and mental development in rural Guatemala. In N. Warren (Ed.), *Advances in cross-cultural psychology.* New York: Academic Press, 1977.

Mejía-Pivaral, V. Características económicas y socio-culturales de cuatro aldeas ladinas de Guatemala. *Guatemala Indígena,* 1972, *8*(3). (Monograph)

Nerlove, S. B., Roberts, J. M., Klein, R. E., Yarbrough, C., & Habicht, J.-P. Natural indicators of cognitive development: An observational study of rural Guatemalan children. *Ethos,* 1974, *2*, 265–295.

Osgood, C. E. Objective indicators of subjective culture. In L. L. Adler (Ed.), *Issues in cross-cultural research.* Annals of the New York Academy of Sciences, 1977, *285*, 435–450.

Price-Williams, D. R. Abstract and concrete modes of classification in a primitive society. *British Journal of Educational Psychology,* 1962, *32*, 50–61.

Price-Williams, D. R., Gordon, W., & Ramirez, M. Skill and conservation: A study of pottery-making children. *Developmental Psychology,* 1969, *1*, 769.

Róheim, G. The role of the shaman in primitive culture. In L. Endelman (Ed.), *Personality and social life.* New York: Random House, 1967.

PHILIP L. KILBRIDE
H. W. LEIBOWITZ

4

The Ponzo Illusion among the Baganda of Uganda: Implications for Ecological and Perceptual Theory[1]

ABSTRACT

A series of studies in which the magnitude of the Ponzo perspective illusion was determined among the Baganda of Uganda are described. For college-educated observers, the magnitude of the illusion increases systematically with additional monocular depth cues. For observers with less formal education, illusion magnitude is related to verbal interpretations of photographs. For those observers whose responses are classified as "three-dimensional," illusion susceptibility is highly similar to the college group. However, observers classified as "two-dimensional" do not demonstrate the Ponzo illusion. With respect to the ecological hypothesis, these data raise the possibility that testing illusions with two-dimensional materials is not appropriate for these observers. Alternatively, the lack of illusion sensitivity may accurately reflect the role of these cues in everyday adjustment. However, even in this case it is unlikely that visual space perception or the adequacy of visual adjustment is substantially altered in view of the redundancy of cues under normal viewing conditions. The absence of this illusion among adult observers presents a dilemma for the tuned channel theory of vision which predicts some illusion magnitude regardless of ecological or educational differences.

[1] The field research and analysis for this study were supported by Grants MH22538 and MH08061 from the National Institute of Mental Health. Preparation of the revision was supported by Grant EY03276 from the National Eye Institute.

This chapter is a revised version of material previously published in *Issues in Cross-Cultural Research* (Kilbride & Leibowitz, 1977). Revisions herein include some additional data and incorporation of several relevant articles which appeared after the original publication. The authors are grateful to Robert B. Post for valuable assistance in the preparation of this revised version.

CROSS-CULTURAL RESEARCH AT ISSUE

Numerous cross-cultural studies, dating back to Rivers (1901; see also Segall, Campbell, & Herskovits, 1966), have demonstrated that individuals from various cultural groups differ in their susceptibility to visual illusions. Some of the illusions that have been reported to be affected by cultural factors are the trapezoidal illusion (Allport & Pettigrew, 1957), the Müller-Lyer and horizontal–vertical illusions (Davis & Segall, 1971; Jahoda, 1966; Pollnac, 1977; Segall *et al.*, 1966), and the Ponzo perspective illusion (Brislin, 1974; Brislin & Keating, 1976; Kilbride & Leibowitz, 1975; Kilbride & Leibowitz, 1977; Leibowitz, Brislin, Perlmutter, & Hennessy, 1969; Leibowitz & Pick, 1972; Wagner, 1977). To date, however, no satisfactory explanation for group differences in illusion susceptibility enjoys universal support among researchers in this field. The most commonly discussed possibility is the "ecological hypothesis," which assumes that illusions reflect the influence of monocular depth cues on perceived size, and that cultural groups vary in illusion magnitude because they differ in their histories of exposure to particular cues. For example, exposure to "carpentered" stimuli such as street corners, square rooms, or other angular material artifacts is thought to be responsible for the illusory effect with the Müller-Lyer figure. Environments rich in perspective (e.g., roads, railway tracks) and those that contain broad open vistas are hypothesized to be responsible for the Ponzo and the horizontal–vertical illusions, respectively.

One of the oldest explanations offered for the Ponzo illusion (Figure 4.1) is that it represents the misapplication of depth cues that normally operate in three-dimensional space (Gregory, 1963). According to this theory, the perspective cue represented by railway tracks or sides of roads is typically associated with depth in three-dimensional space, and is inappropriately activated while viewing the two-dimensional Ponzo figure. As we normally "correct" the retinal image size of distant objects in the interest of size constancy on the basis of distance cues, this same correction mechanism is misapplied in a two-dimensional presentation, thereby producing an illusory enlargement of the object located "far away" near the point of convergence of the figure. Evidence for the "inappropriate constancy" hypothesis is provided by both developmental and cross-cultural research. It has been determined that both the Ponzo illusion (Leibowitz & Judisch, 1967) and size constancy for distant objects (Leibowitz, Pollard, & Dickson, 1967; Zeigler & Leibowitz, 1957) increase as a function of chronological but not mental age. If one assumes that one of the monocular cues involved in size constancy is perspective, then it would follow that development of the strength of this cue through perceptual learning resulting from exposure to the environment is responsible for the similar age trends reported for the Ponzo illusion and the size constancy data.

For this reason, it should theoretically follow that individuals reared in an

Figure 4.1. *The stimuli used in the main experiment. The extent of the horizontal lines in these examples is the same. (After Leibowitz et al., 1969.)*

environment with fewer converging lines would exhibit a reduced Ponzo illusion as compared with those whose environment offered many opportunities to associate converging lines with distance. Cross-cultural projects in Guam and Uganda designed to test whether populations with different histories of exposure to perceptual cues also vary in illusion magnitude have produced results consistent with the ecological hypothesis (Brislin, 1974; Leibowitz *et al.*, 1969; Leibowitz & Pick, 1972). Guam has no railroads; vistas on land are comparatively short due to hilly terrain; and roads are winding rather than straight. Guamanian University students produced significantly lower illusion magnitudes than did Pennsylvanian and Ugandan college students. The latter, like their American counterparts, have experienced exposure to straight roads, railway tracks, and comparatively "open" vistas.

In a follow-up study, Brislin and Keating (1976) found predicted cultural differences in the extent to which perspective cues influenced perceived size when tested in a natural world setting. Pacific Islanders showed less utilization of perspective information than individuals from urbanized areas in the Philippines and in the United States. The authors consider this research to be a better test of the ecological hypothesis because previous cross-cultural Ponzo research had been based on two-dimensional pictorial stimuli. However, it is reasonable to assume that university students everywhere respond to pictorial depth cues so that previously reported cross-group differences among educated Guamanians, Americans, and Ugandans probably do reflect exposure to their natural world environment.

Unfortunately, empirical findings do not always lend support to a simple causal relationship between environmental experience and perception. Such factors as mode of presentations, cognitive style, childrearing patterns, retinal pigmentation, and sex are related to illusion susceptibility (Stewart, 1971). In particular, the problem of pictorial depth perception is crucial when less educated groups are studied. Leibowitz and Pick (1972) have reported that the Ponzo illusion is essentially nonexistent among a group of rural Baganda in Uganda. These data were particularly puzzling because the rural Ugandan environment is rich in perspective cues. Leibowitz and Pick suggested that "flatness cues" (absence of binocular disparity, surface reflections, presence of the border of the photograph, etc.) inherent in two-dimensional line drawings and photographs might have dominated the response of the rural Ugandans whose exposure to two-dimensional reproductions is limited. An alternative interpretation is that individuals from cultures where exposure to reading materials, photographs, and representational art is limited or nonexistent are not as affected by symbolic cues that in our culture serve to indicate depth or distance on a two-dimensional pictorial surface (Hudson, 1960, 1967; Miller, 1973). Growing up in a "picture-less environment" typically results in a tendency to view pictures in only two dimensions although perception of the "real world," of course, is three-dimensional. Whatever the basis for the lack of illusion susceptibility, the implications of these data for cross-cultural research involving visual illusions are profound for the following reasons: (a) the *spatial* cues of perspective, or, more broadly, cues to "distance," are theoretically assumed to be responsible for several illusions (e.g., Ponzo, Müller-Lyer); (b) visual illusions are often presented in a pictorial mode; and (c) pictorial depth perception is not a cultural universal. It follows, therefore, that individuals who are not sensitive to symbolic depth cues in pictures would *not* be expected to demonstrate an illusion even though their history of exposure to the relevant cues may be extensive. Many writers have, in fact, pointed out that pictorial depth perception "should be" an experiential factor of importance in illusion research (Jahoda, 1966; Segall et al., 1966).

The assumption that monocular depth cues may not be effective in two-dimensional presentations is technically different from the "flatness cues" argument of Leibowitz and Pick (1972). The former emphasizes the lack of appreciation of cues used to symbolically indicate depth in photographic portrayals (e.g., overlap, converging lines, object size) rather than domination of responses by "flatness" cues. In any case, both interpretations would suggest a two-dimensional bias in the rural Ugandan sample which could explain the lack of an illusion in the data reported by Leibowitz and Pick (1972).

Previous research in Uganda does, in fact, show that rural, traditional Baganda tend to perceive pictures in two dimensions. Kilbride and Robbins (1969) administered the Hudson Pictorial Depth Perception Test (Hudson, 1960, 1967) to 104 adult Baganda living in a rural area of Uganda. These individuals had limited experience with pictorial content and three-dimensional representation in photographs, magazines, and motion pictures. Their exposure to formal education in schools, where the conventions of pictorial representation are learned, was also not extensive. Moreover, traditional Baganda art is generally nonrepresentational. Baskets and woven mats containing two-dimensional geometric designs are widely used by these rural Baganda. When asked to identify a road (linear perspective cue) appearing in Hudson's test, 87% of the Baganda reported a predominantly two-dimensional object (e.g., hill, ladder, house, camera tripod, pitchfork). In the same study 118 urban Baganda were also shown the Hudson pictures. The mean of 7.5 years of schooling per urban subject, although not high, is nevertheless double that of the rural sample. Whereas most rural Baganda are farmers, 29% of the urban sample are teachers, engineers, nurses, clerks, and secretaries. These occupations provide considerable exposure to printed matter. The higher educational level and greater participation in modern occupations of the urban group are reflected in their response to the Hudson "road." Of the urban sample, 35% responded "road," in contrast to 13% of the rural sample. These data show that (a) most rural Baganda perceive pictures in two dimensions; and (b) pictorial depth perception is increased with exposure to western conventions of pictorial representation, for example, in schools and modern jobs.

A recent study in Uganda was designed to analyze the basis for the lack of illusion susceptibility among the rural observers. The data demonstrate the importance of pictorial perception as a factor in the magnitude of the Ponzo illusion and also show that the lack of effectiveness of monocular depth cues may be more salient than domination by flatness cues. This study utilized the same stimuli and procedures as did the previous experiments, and was carried out in the same geographical area of Uganda. The illusion was evaluated by means of a series of stimuli which present increasing amounts of context, including a plain background, a background consisting of two converging lines (classical Ponzo figure), a photograph of a plowed field, and a photograph of railroad tracks (Figure 4.1). For educated observers, a progressively larger illusion effect has been observed as the richness of the background depth cues is increased in this series (Leibowitz et al., 1969).

Experiment 1

Method

The original sample consisted of 105 Baganda. For reasons to be mentioned later, only 82 Baganda—53 males and 29 females—are included in the present analysis. These subjects ranged in age from 16 to 80 years, with a mean of 31 years. Formal education varied from none to 12 years, with a mean of 5.5 years. The subjects were selected from the same rural Ugandan population as in the previous study. However, an effort was made to include subjects who varied in the amount of their formal education as well as in whether they had two-dimensional reproductions in their homes. Most of these subjects were full- or part-time cultivators, with some working in clerical or commercial occupations. Therefore, the sample varied in terms of both education and exposure to mass media. Many homes, for example, contained photographs and printed materials, and in a few cases there were also television sets. The subjects' visual environment typically consisted of small hills no more than 500 ft. in height separated by valleys. Human settlement was usually confined to the higher elevations, with the homes dispersed and embedded among plantain gardens. Numerous roads and paths transversed the area, offering vistas with perspective, sometimes for several miles. The Baganda tend to reside on or near roads, which are important in their daily commerce and communication.

Before administration of the Ponzo figures, each subject was shown the track stimulus and a photograph of a local road (Figure 4.2) and was asked, "What do you see?" While asking the question, the experimenter traced his finger over the railroad tracks or the borders of the road. The purpose of this procedure was to classify subjects as "two-" or "three-" dimensional perceivers, following the distinction made by Kilbride and Robbins (1969). The subjects were classified as "three-dimensional" if responses to both photographs corresponded to three-dimensional objects, such as a road, track, river, or bridge. "Two-dimensional" perceivers were so classified if their responses in both cases corresponded to objects that are predominantly not extended in depth, for example, a house, ladder (most frequent), hill, roof, or a hill with ladder. Those subjects who gave a two-dimensional response to one stimulus and a three-dimensional response to the other were classified as "mixed." A description of the three groups by age, sex, and education is given in Table 4.1. Table 4.2 shows the range of object identification considered to be "two-dimensional."

Administration and scoring methods of the Ponzo test were identical to

Figure 4.2. *Photographs of a rural road in Uganda. This photograph, along with that shown in Figure 4.1A, was utilized in the preliminary experiment to classify the subjects as "two-" or "three-" dimensional perceivers. (After Kilbride & Leibowitz, 1975.)*

those followed in the previous studies.[2] Twenty-three subjects were eliminated because they failed to produce correct judgments for both extreme conditions in one or more series of stimuli.

---

[2] Test administration was in Luganda. Instructions were translated into Luganda through the technique of back translation. Each subject was told (for 10 cards in each of the four series): "On each of these pictures there are two horizontal lines. I want you to tell me which of the two lines is longer than the other. If it is the top, say 'top.' If it is the bottom, say 'bottom.' " (*Ku buli bifaananyi bino, kuliko ennyiriri biri ez'obukiika. Njagala ombulire kunyiriri ezo ebiri luluwa olusinga lunalwo obuwanvu. Bweruba nga lwawaggulu 'gamba nti lwawagullu' bweruba nga lwawansi 'gamba nti lwawansi.'*) In all stimulus cards, the upper line was constant in length whereas the length of the lower lines was presented in random order. For all observation conditions, the equality value was determined by interpolation as the midpoint of the region at which the subject's responses changed. The magnitude of the overestimation, or illusion, is the percentage overestimation of the upper line.

Table 4.1
Sex, Age, and Educational Data for Each Subgroup

Subgroup	Male	Female	Mean age	Mean educational level
2-D	11	8	36.2	4.4
Mixed	8	3	39.2	4.1
3-D	34	18	27.4	6.2

Table 4.2
Two-Dimensional Object Identifications

Road stimulus	N	Railtrack stimulus	N
House	14	Ladder	15
Hill	3	House	4
Roof	1	Roof	2
		Hill	2
		Hill with ladder	1
		Poles	1

Results

The magnitude of the Ponzo illusion, expressed as the percentage over-estimation of the upper line for the four backgrounds is presented for the various background conditions in Figure 4.3. The data for the subjects are plotted separately depending upon whether they were classified in the "two-," "three-," or "mixed-" dimensional categories. For comparison, the data from the previous study for the villagers and for the college students are also reproduced. It will be noted that the data for the three-dimensional perceivers are similar to those of the college students in the previous Ugandan (as well as Pennsylvanian) study. The general trend of the data is the same for the mixed perceivers, but the absolute values are lower.

A two-way analysis of variance with repeated measures and an analysis of the simple main effects for the series of four stimuli confirm the interpretation that Baganda whose verbal responses correspond to predominantly two-dimensional objects do not demonstrate the illusion. An analysis of the simple main effects for the group factor indicates that there was no significant group effect for the control and geometric viewing conditions, but for both the phototexture and the phototrack series the effect was significant. This analysis also indicates a significant difference among "two-dimensional," "mixed," and "three-dimensional" groups in the photographic viewing contexts only.

In effect, the classification of the subjects, based on the results of the

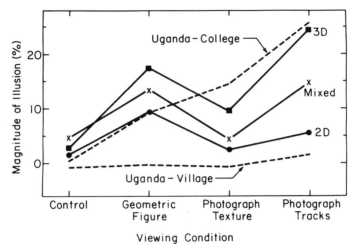

Figure 4.3. *The magnitude of the Ponzo illusion for the principal stimuli reproduced in Figure 4.1. The subjects have been separated into groups based on their responses to the preliminary test. For comparison, the data from the previous study are indicated by the dotted lines. (After Kilbride & Leibowitz, 1975.)*

preliminary tests, reveals that the results for the rural Ugandans classified as three-dimensional perceivers are strikingly similar to those for the groups of college students previously tested. However, the two-dimensional perceivers show no illusion magnitude for any of the background conditions as reported previously for a group of rural Ugandans. The mixed group produced intermediate illusion values. In agreement with the present experiment, Wagner (1977) reports that among Moroccans three-dimensional pictorial perceivers were significantly more susceptible than two-dimensional pictorial perceivers to the photographic stimuli. He also found that mode of pictorial perception has no effect on the control and geometric viewing conditions.

Experiment 2

Experiment 2 was designed as a direct test of the hypothesis that flatness cues may have been responsible for the lack of illusion magnitude in the previous study (Leibowitz & Pick, 1972) as well as for the similar results for the two-dimensional perceivers in Experiment 1 of the present investigation. To this end, the same stimuli were presented in a viewing box designed to minimize flatness cues. The stimuli were mounted vertically at a distance of 63 cm and viewed against an opaque background. This viewing distance was chosen because it represented the "ortho" viewing position, that is, the distance at which the angular dimensions of the stimuli are identical to those in the original scene from the camera position. This distance has been shown to maximize the "reality" or "plastic" depth in photographs (Hardy & Perrin, 1932, pp. 465–469; Schlosberg, 1941). This arrangement also minimizes cues to flatness, such as the familiar background against which the stimuli are ordinarily viewed, borders, and reflections from the surface.

The subjects were 26 rural Baganda, selected and tested in the same manner as the subjects in Experiment 1. The data, separated into two-dimensional and three-dimensional perceivers (there were no mixed responses among this group), are plotted in Figure 4.4.

An analysis of the simple main effects for the series of four stimuli indicates that for the "three-dimensional" group there was a significant series effect whereas the "two-dimensional" group showed no significant effect of series. These findings are interpreted to support the cognitive style interpretation, as Baganda who do not interpret depth (e.g., perspective) in pictures do not display the Ponzo illusion in a viewing situation even when flatness cues have been markedly reduced.

An analysis of the simple main effects for the group factor showed that for both the control and geometric viewing conditions there was no significant group effect, whereas for both the phototexture and the phototrack series there was a significant group effect, indicating that there is a difference between "two-dimensional" and "three-dimensional" groups only in photographic viewing contexts.

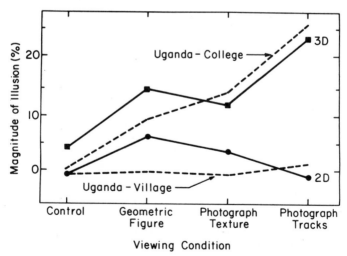

Figure 4.4. The magnitude of the Ponzo illusion under presentation conditions designed to eliminate or minimize cues to flatness. Classification as 2D or 3D is based on the preliminary test. For comparison, the data from the previous study are indicated by the dotted lines. (After Kilbride & Leibowitz, 1975.)

Discussion

Data from college-educated observers are consistent with and provide support for the ecological hypothesis (Leibowitz et al., 1969). The more extensive the exposure to depth cues in the environment, the larger the magnitude of the Ponzo perspective illusion. For less educated observers, a critical factor in predicting illusion magnitude is verbal responses to photographs (Kilbride & Leibowitz, 1975). For those observers whose verbal responses are classified as "three-dimensional," illusion magnitudes are similar to the college-educated groups. Although no data were obtained in this study for three-dimensional observers with different exposure histories, it may reasonably be assumed that their illusion magnitudes would reflect their previous history of exposure to environmental depth cues.

However, it is difficult to evaluate the lack of illusion susceptibility of those lesser educated subjects whose verbal responses are classified as "two-dimensional." In terms of a strict interpretation of the ecological hypothesis, it follows that the strength of the depth cues in question is small or absent even though the subjects have had extensive exposure to monocular depth cues in their environment. However, it is possible that this reduced cue strength is manifested only with two-dimensional materials. In this case, cue strength in everyday life might be the same as for three-dimensional observers and the lack of cue effectiveness is limited to the viewing of two-dimensional materials. Several implications would follow this assumption. With respect to the implicit assumption in the ecological hypothesis that illusion magnitudes reflect the quantitative contribution of cues or perceptual mechanism in everyday life, testing with two-dimensional materials must be considered as inappropriate. The implications of this possibility for cross-cultural methodology in perception are profound and would also be relevant to any situation in which two-dimensional pictorial materials are involved, for example, education.

If, alternatively, the reduced cue strength of the two-dimensional observers does in fact reflect the strengths of static monocular cues in everyday life, illusion magnitude data would be relevant to the ecological hypothesis. However, it must be kept in mind that visual space perception is based on multiple cues. In fact, the original thrust of the present series, and specifically the use of photographs, was motivated by an attempt to increase the number and variety of cues in cross-cultural perceptual research. However, any two dimensional stimulus, even photographs, present only *some* of the cues available in real life. Thus, the lack of cue strength of some of them, which would be accurately reflected in illusion magnitudes, does not necessarily imply that the appearance of the world or the ability of the observer to adjust visually is substantially altered. It simply means that those particular cues play a lesser role for the two-dimensional than for the three-dimensional observers. In the light of our knowledge of the redundancy of perceptual mechanisms, it is quite conceivable that other cues could mediate space perception quite adequately in everyday life.

The lack of illusion among the two-dimensional observers is of major significance with respect to the basis of the geometric optical illusions. The classical explanation of illusions is that they represent the manifestations of cues or mechanisms that normally serve to mediate perception in everyday life. For example, in the Ponzo illusion it is assumed that converging lines are normally associated with distance and influence the perceived size of distant objects in the interest of size constancy. Other depth cues, such as texture and familiar size, which are present in the photographs used in the present study, serve the same function. Experience with these cues increases their strength which in turn is reflected in the magnitude of the illusion. This approach to illusions has played a major role in perceptual theory and is the basis of the ecological hypothesis.

Recently, a new theory of geometrical illusions has emerged from optical linear systems analysis. This approach, which follows from the research of Arthur Ginsburg (1977), has demonstrated that a number of geometrical optical illusions are present in images from which the high frequency Fourier components have been optically eliminated. This point of view assumes that the visual system functions as if it consisted of a discrete number of channels, each sensitive to a limited range of spatial frequencies. Distortion in the illusion configuration follows from the inherent nature of the processing in the low frequency channels.

It is unnecessary to assume that only one monocular depth cue subserves illusions. Indeed, the data that indicate increased illusion magnitude as a function of the richness of depth cues would argue strongly that multiple cues are involved, particularly in photographs. Some of the illusory effect could result from low spatial frequency visual processing and some would be related to previous experience with relevant depth cues. However, the present observation that some individuals demonstrate no illusion is apparently incompatible with the spatial frequency processing approach. Given that stimuli containing low frequencies are abundant in all environments, and appear to play a dominant role in most visually guided behavior, the possibility that the two-dimensional observers have not developed such tuned channels is highly unlikely.

The present data offer a dilemma for perceptual theory. The tuned channel approach is receiving increasing support in the visual community and must be considered as a major advance. One of the most appealing aspects of this approach is its ability to integrate and explain diverse visual phenomena, including many illusions (Ginsburg, 1977). All theories, of course, have limitations and it is not surprising that these are apparent when applied to illusions. In a real sense, illusions are "illusory" because one is tempted to try to explain them with relatively simple ideas and concepts. In fact, as has frequently been pointed out, illusions are helpful in evaluating our understanding of visual mechanisms in that they represent special cases of more general principles. Although the present analysis is unsatisfactory because it presents a dilemma with no obvious solution, it does reaffirm the value of illusion experiments in defining critical gaps in our understanding.

Acknowledgments

The senior author would like to express his gratitude to colleagues at the Makerere Institute of Social Research, Makerere University College, Kampala, Uganda, for their assistance during his tenure there as a senior research associate from June 1972 to May 1973. Various phases of the field research were greatly facilitated by Clive Davis and Michael C. Robbins, who offered invaluable assistance, and Joseph Busuulwa, who served as our Muganda colleague.

References

Allport, G. W., & Pettigrew, T. F. Cultural influences on the perception of movement: The trapezoidal illusion among Zulus. *Journal of Abnormal Social Psychology*, 1957, *55*, 104–113.

Brislin, R. W. The Ponzo illusion, additional cues, age, orientation, and culture. *Journal of Cross-Cultural Psychology*, 1974, *5*, 139–161.

Brislin, R. W., & Keating, C. F. Cultural differences in the perception of a three-dimensional Ponzo illusion. *Journal of Cross-Cultural Psychology*, 1976, *7*, 397–413.

Davis, C. M., & Segall, M. H. Effect of relative positions of segments on strength of the Mueller-Lyer illusion. *Perceptual and Motor Skills*, 1971, *33*, 1051–1058.

Ginsburg, A. P. *Visual information processing based upon spatial filters constrained by biological data.* Unpublished doctoral dissertation, Cambridge University, 1977.

Gregory, R. L. Distortion of visual space as inappropriate constancy scaline. *Nature*, 1963, *199*, 678–680.

Hardy, A. C., & Perrin, F. H. *The principles of optics.* New York: McGraw-Hill, 1932.

Hudson, W. Pictorial depth perception in sub-cultural groups in Africa. *Journal of Social Psychology*, 1960, *52*, 209–219.

Hudson, W. The study of the problem of pictorial perception among unacculturated groups. *International Journal of Psychology*, 1967, *2*, 90–107.

Jahoda, G. Geometric illusions and environment: A study in Ghana. *British Journal of Psychology*, 1966, *57*, 193–199.

Kilbride, P. L., & Leibowitz, H. W. Factors affecting the magnitude of the Ponzo perspective illusion among the Baganda. *Perception and Psychophysics*, 1975, *17*, 543–548.

Kilbride, P. L., & Leibowitz, H. W. The Ponzo illusion among the Baganda of Uganda. In L. L. Adler (Ed.), *Issues in cross-cultural research.* Annals of the New York Academy of Science, 1977, *285*, 408–417.

Kilbride, P. L., & Robbins, M. C. Pictorial depth perception and acculturation among Baganda. *American Anthropologist,* 1969, *71,* 293–302.

Leibowitz, H. W., Brislin, R., Permutter, L., & Hennessy, R. Ponzo perspective illusion as a manifestation of space perception. *Science,* 1969, *166,* 1174–1176.

Leibowitz, H. W., & Judisch, J. The relation between age and the magnitude of the Ponzo illusion. *American Journal of Psychology,* 1967, *80,* 105–109.

Leibowitz, H. W., & Pick, H. Cross-cultural and educational aspects of the Ponzo illusion. *Perception and Psychophysics, 1972, 12,* 403–432.

Leibowitz, H. W., Pollard, S. W., & Dickson, D. Monocular and binocular size-matching as a function of distance at various age levels. *American Journal of Psychology,* 1967, *80,* 263–268.

Miller, R. J. Cross-cultural research in the perception of pictorial materials. *Psychological Bulletin,* 1973, *80,* 135–150.

Pollnac, R. B. Illusion susceptibility and adaptation to the Marine environment: Is the carpentered world hypothesis seaworthy? *Journal of Cross-Cultural Psychology,* 1977, *8,* 425–435.

Rivers, W. H. R. Vision. In A. C. Hadden (Ed.), *Reports of the Cambridge anthropological expeditions to the Torres Straits* (Vol. 2, Pt. 1). Cambridge: The University Press, 1901.

Schlosberg, H. Stereoscopic depth from single pictures. *American Journal of Psychology,* 1941, *54,* 601–605.

Segall, N. H., Campbell, D. T., & Herskovits, M. J. *The influence of culture on visual perception.* New York: Bobbs-Merrill, 1966.

Stewart, V. M. *A cross-cultural test of the "carpentered environment" hypothesis using three geometric illusions in Zambia.* Unpublished doctoral dissertation, Northwestern University, 1971.

Wagner, D. A. Ontogeny of the Ponzo illusion: Effects of age, schooling, and environment. *International Journal of Psychology,* 1977, *12,* 161–176.

Zeigler, H. P., & Leibowitz, H. W. Apparent visual size as a function of distance for children and adults. *American Journal of Psychology,* 1957, *70,* 106–109.

II

Issues in
Developmental Research

In Part II specific issues in developmental psychology focus on the behavior and attitudes which are important for the cognitive and social development in children. The first chapter, by Charles M. Super and Sara Harkness, compares the similarities and differences in the "difficult infant syndrome" in rural Kenya and urban America. The concept of "infant's niche" is useful for both within and between group analyses. Moreover, studies of the structure of the infant's niche may lead to as much information about adult culture as has been provided by studies of, for example, traditional ceremonies. This is followed by Lorraine Kirk's chapter, which deals with the relationship between mothers' nonverbal teaching behavior and children's rates of cognitive development. The author analyzes specific maternal behaviors that were observed on the filmed teaching interactions, such as "single-hand movements" and "single-finger movements," among others. Both of these variables were good predictors of the children's performances on several cognitive tests. Next follows a chapter by Leonore Loeb Adler, which presents an example of the programmatic progress of a series of cross-cultural studies. The most recent of this research evaluated the familiarity hypothesis versus the value hypothesis. This investigation also shows how the pictures of schoolchildren reflect the value systems of parents, family, community, and culture. The last chapter in this section, contributed by Regina C. Spires and Mitchell W. Robin, reviews the cross-cultural literature on the effects—especially to boys—of father absence during childhood.

The Infant's Niche in Rural Kenya and Metropolitan America[1]

ABSTRACT

Developmental and anthropological perspectives are applied to the "difficult infant syndrome" in rural Kenya and metropolitan America. In middle-class American homes an infant who is irregular in habits, not adaptable to changes in the environment, and negative in mood is difficult to care for; this constellation of troublesome dispositions has been related to a variety of clinical problems. Maternal interviews and observations of naturally occurring behavior in samples from rural Kenya and metropolitan America establish similarity in several of the dimensions of individual difference. Because the Kipsigis infant must adapt to a different patterning of flexibility and constraints in the physical and social environment, however, a different set of traits coalesce to make a difficult infant for the Kipsigis caretakers. Regulation of sleep–wake behavior to adult patterns, for example, is not an issue, but adaptability to care by older siblings in addition to the mother is of critical importance, as is the effectiveness of culturally available methods of soothing in case of distress. The concept of an infant's niche, defined initially by culturally regulated factors, is suggested as a useful concept for analysis within as well as between social groups.

Infancy and early childhood have been a focus of interest shared by psychology and anthropology since their earliest collaborations in psychological anthropology. The anthropological interest grew largely from a the-

---

[1] The work reported here and preparation of this chapter were supported in part by grants from the William T. Grant Foundation, the Carnegie Corporation of New York, the National Institute of Mental Health (Grant No. MH33281), and the Spencer Foundation. All statements made and views expressed are the sole responsibility of the authors.

CROSS-CULTURAL RESEARCH AT ISSUE

oretical concern with linking typical or "modal" adult behavior in a variety of societies to culturally patterned methods of childrearing. In pursuit of this goal, anthropology looked to contemporary theories of personality development in psychology. During the formative years of psychological anthropology, the most attractive option was psychoanalytic theory with its strong emphasis on experience in infancy and early childhood. Psychological theory, on its side, stood to advance its interest in the effects of early experience through study of the "natural experiments" offered by nonwestern societies. The results figured significantly in writings on personality and mental health.

However, with a few notable exceptions, the theoretical use of comparative infant studies stagnated at mid-century, as a result of shifting interests and outlooks within the separate disciplines. In the succeeding decades both fields of study have matured. The anthropological perspective has maintained its holistic emphasis on the integrative aspects of culture; at the same time it has become increasingly aware of behavioral variations within cultures and the social "organization of diversity" (Wallace, 1961). Evolutionary considerations have also gained recognition, including the process of adaptation and selection in infancy (e.g., Konner, 1977). In psychology, there has been a fundamental shift toward quantitative, microscopic analysis of infant behavior (e.g., Fantz, 1958). More recently psychologists have grappled with the formal realization that infants are active agents in their own development. This recognition can be seen in both reformulation of the study of direction of influence between infant and caretaker (e.g., Bell, 1968) and appreciation of the role of early differences in temperament (e.g., Thomas & Chess, 1977).

A rejoining of the disciplines seems promising once again, and in this chapter we will attempt to show the value of such a dual perspective on the "difficult infant syndrome," a concept of both theoretical and clinical importance. In middle-class American homes, an infant who is irregular in habits and not adaptable to changes in the environment is difficult to care for. Such a baby may also have intense reactions, withdraw from new experiences, and be negative in mood. Clinical research has related this constellation of troublesome behavioral dispositions to a variety of problems such as colic, night waking, and injuries. As with other aspects of temperament, there is thought to be an inborn component to elements of this pattern (see Thomas & Chess, 1977).

The central point we wish to draw from the observations presented here is that the syndrome more correctly describes, not the *infant,* but the relationship between an infant and his or her immediate environment of care, or niche. Although the relativity of the syndrome has been acknowledged by a number of authors, it has not been given a cultural focus, which might prove useful. The niche that an infant is born into and subsequently modifies is structured both initially and in its adaptive constraints by the culture, that is, the economic activities, social and family structure, physical ecology, and the value and belief systems of the caretakers. The points of pressure and flexibility in mutual adaptation will be patterned by the niche as well as the infant.

Our illustrations come from two communities. One is Kokwet, a farming and herding community in the western highlands of Kenya. The people of Kokwet are Kipsigis, a Highland Nilotic group that arrived in their present location about a century ago. Kokwet is a new community, having been organized as a settlement scheme by the Kenyan government at the time of national independence (1963). The land was purchased from a departing white settler and distributed to indigenous citizens. The surrounding communities had never been taken by Europeans, and thus the people of Kokwet moved in from nearby areas. The Kipsigis of Kokwet are relatively prosperous, producing maize, milk, and pyrethrum as cash crops. Nutrition is good, and because of the altitude (over 6000 ft.) many of the most ravaging tropical diseases are absent. Despite economic modernization, however, the people of Kokwet maintain many traditions of family and community life, as indicated, for example, by the still nearly universal practice of initiation rites at adolescence for both boys and girls.

The infant's day in Kokwet is spent outside, like everyone else's, around the mud and wattle houses and in the gardens and pastures. The mother is the central caretaker, but she is aided, especially after the infant is 3 or 4 months old, by one of her older children, typically a girl of about 7 years of age. Other children, a co-wife and her children may also help out at times. The younger infants tend to be carried along where the caretaker's chores take her. From the caretaker's hip, back, or lap, the baby may watch the surrounding activities—cooking, harvesting, washing, weeding—or, when convenient, crawl around and play with others.

For a relatively familiar point of reference, we are using comparative data from families in metropolitan Boston. They are predominantly upper middle class in background, and live in comfortable suburban homes or urban apartments. Most of an infant's day is spent with only the mother, at home, where the baby is usually free within a limited physical space, such as a single room or a playpen. On most days, the baby is taken on short trips to shop, pick up a sibling at school, or other errands.

Beyond ethnographic observation, we have five sources of quantitative information about the way infants interact with their physical and social niches: (a) the Neonatal Behavior Assessment Scale developed by Brazelton (1973) and his associates; (b) an adaptation of the Carey Infant Temperament Survey (Carey, 1972), which asks the mother about her baby's typical reaction to a number of specific situations, such as having a bath or hearing a loud noise; (c) "spot observations" of where the infants are, what they are doing, etc., over a large sample of times and days; (d) 24-hour observations of infant sleep–wake behavior; and (e) detailed records of naturally occurring caretaker–infant interaction at 4 and 10 months.

To establish a common basis of comparison, we examined the structure of individual differences in infant temperament and found it to be similar to the two samples. That is, by inspecting the clusters of behaviors that emerge from the maternal interview, for example, one can recognize in both groups dimensions of rhythmicity (e.g., does the baby usually wake up around the same time?), intensity of reaction (e.g., strong reaction to being dressed), quality of mood (e.g., cheerful during baths), and adaptability to new situations (e.g., accepts new foods). Preliminary analysis of relationships among the quantitative measures indicates validity of several of the temperament constructs. For example, babies who were reported by their mothers to be generally happy, compared to less cheerful babies, were found in the spot observations to be less frequently subject to quieting procedures such as back carrying and breast-feeding. In the interaction observations, they were seen to engage more in happy, face-to-face interaction. These results lay the groundwork for the comparison to follow in that they establish common dimensions of variation. They are also important in their own right, for the structure of behavior found in a monocultural study may be an artifact of the structure of the niche (Super & Harkness, 1981); the present results indicate this is not true for at least some dimensions of infant temperament.

It does not follow from this finding of common dimensions, however, that the individual variations have similar consequences in the two samples. The two niches differ not so much in the amount of pressure for socialization as in the patterning of pressure around behavioral clusters with cultural salience.

The clearest example of this patterning centers on sleep–wake behavior. Once some method of feeding is established in the opening 2–4 days of life, the major issues of negotiation for the American baby and family concern the disruptions caused by night wakings and the incompatibility of some parental activities with care of an active, awake infant.

Figure 5.1 presents various measures derived from the 24-hour sleep–wake recordings on 10 babies. (The American data in this case come not from our Boston sample, but from a Los Angeles sample studied by Parmelee, Wenner, & Schulz, 1964.) All the measures start out at similar levels in the two groups, and some of them, such as the longest period of wakefulness during a 24-hour period ("maximum awake") and the day–night sleep ratio, remain similar for at least several months. There are, however, two divergent developments. First, the American babies gradually come to sleep more than

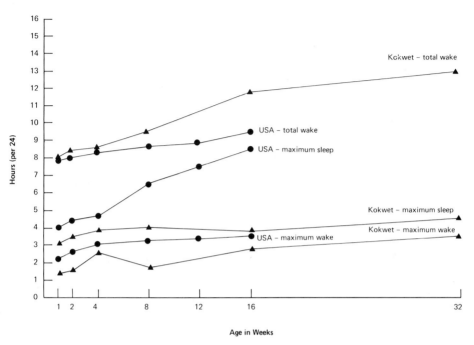

Figure 5.1. *Results from 24-hour sleep recordings.*

their peers in Kokwet. This is true both over the full 24-hour period ("total wake" is significantly lower for the United States sample at 16 weeks, $p < .05$), and separately during the day and night (Figure 5.2 presents daytime estimates derived from over 1700 spot observations). American parents make substantial modifications in their living quarters and family life to facilitate sleeping—they provide a quiet room and arrange special nap times. In addition, care of an infant who is awake is less compatible with the American mother's daily tasks and pleasures than is true for Kokwet. There is some motivation on the part of American parents, therefore, to encourage sleeping.

The second cultural divergence is seen in the measure "maximum sleep," that is, the longest single episode of sleep during the 24-hour recordings (averaged over the 10 cases). In Kokwet, this measure remains stable during at least the first 8 months of life; but the American data show a sharp increase. American babies rapidly concentrate their sleeping into fewer, longer bouts, so that by 4 months the average longest sleep episode is almost 8 hours, just about the amount of time the parents want to sleep themselves during the night. Night waking can be a major annoyance in urban America, especially as it often involves the complex and highly struc-

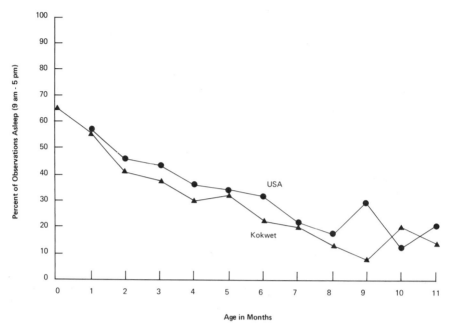

Figure 5.2. *Daytime sleep observed in spot observations.*

tured behavior called "getting the baby a bottle." In Kokwet, the baby sleeps side-by-side with the mother, and the father is probably in another room, if not another house. When the infant wakes up, the mother only has to make sure her breast is within the child's reach. (Recent studies of American infants, using nonintrusive techniques of sleep monitoring, suggest that brief periods of quiet infant wakefulness often go unnoticed by parents, even when they are keeping "sleep logs" for research purposes. See, for example, Anders, 1979. The monitoring studies, however, still show large increases with age in measures of the longest duration of sleep, compared to the relatively flat results for Kokwet in Figure 5.1.)

The amount of attention paid in American families to getting the baby to sleep through the night, and the amount of advice on this topic proffered by family, friends, and professional advisors, suggests that the babies cannot always meet family demands. That is, the environmental pressures may be pushing the limits of the infant's adaptability. If night waking persists beyond 6 or 8 months, concern may be raised about something being seriously wrong, usually with the parents. It may not be coincidental that Sudden Infant Death Syndrome (SIDS)—a residual category for unexplained crib deaths—rises in frequency throughout the first 3 or 4 months in urban America. The syndrome apparently involves a number of medical factors, including mechanisms for physiological regulation that are central to maintaining vital functions during sleep. Although it is evident that childrearing patterns do not cause SIDS, it seems possible that techniques of infant care might contribute to its frequency and pattern of occurrence (Konner & Super, 1979).

It should be noted that these Kenyan data argue for a modest revision in current theories of the development of state behavior (sleep–wake). It is sometimes proposed that the increase in longest sleep episode seen in American data constitutes a good behavioral index of neurological maturation in the brain. The Kenyan data in Figure 5.1 suggest that this is true only when the maturing brain is being asked by the environment to carry out behaviors that tax it to the limits.

Similar contrasts of temporal organization can be drawn in the domains of feeding, elimination, and even social intercourse. In each case, American babies come to concentrate their behaviors into longer, less frequent episodes. For sleep, elimination, and feeding, the American parents' behavior is to some extent deliberate, and the three domains form a cluster of regularity that is familiar to us. To find the same contrast in social behavior suggests a level of either ecological or behavioral organization that is relatively unconscious. Specifically, the overall rate of infant–caretaker interaction seen in the behavior observations is generally similar in the two samples, but the American sample is characterized by more frequent extended episodes of interchange. It is not yet clear in our analysis to what extent this difference in temporal patterning of interaction results from personal differences in the caretakers or from the physical organization of daily life. In any case, the parallel with other domains is intriguing and further emphasizes the adaptive significance, in America, of some infants' ability to regulate their circadian flow of behavior.

It is of course possible to be a difficult infant in Kokwet, but the relevant dimensions of individual variation are different. Wakefulness itself does not unduly interfere with the mother's work and social life, as long as the baby is adaptable to care by siblings and amenable to mediation of distress by nursing and riding on the caretaker's back. A baby's insistence on being cared for or comforted only by the mother, however, can become a source of conflict. A few infants, in addition, refuse to ride on anyone's back, either while awake or asleep, thus depriving the cadre of caretakers of a major stratagem.

The clusters of behavioral dispositions that make a difficult infant in the two samples have pervasive cultural connections. The American infant must learn, in effect, to accept impersonal, externally imposed regularity, whereas the Kipsigis baby is required to adapt to the needs and behaviors of a small number of particular people. A related contrast holds for adult members of the community and their niches. In Kokwet, the difficult deviant refuses to cooperate with family and neighbors and defies the personal mediation involved in local dispute settlement (Harkness, Edwards, & Super, 1981). In America, the adult who is never on time, misses appointments, or chafes at schedules is the troublesome one. More speculatively, the American baby may be learning about external, invariant, impersonal principles, whereas the rural Kipsigis infant learns to adapt in particular and personalized contexts. Such a contrast, in one form or another, is frequently drawn in comparing patterns of habitual thought and cognitive performance in rural Africa and urban America (Super, Harkness, & Baldwin, 1977). These parallels, it should be noted, do not necessarily imply an inherent stability of psychological traits; the point is rather that cultures may provide a continuity of developmental niches supporting particular dispositions.

We argue, in conclusion, that the developmental perspective is as important for the anthropological study of infancy as the anthropological perspective is for the study of child development in our own society. The present synthesis suggests a modification of previous anthropological characterizations of infancy as a period of general indulgence in sub-Saharan Africa, in favor of a more differentiated picture. In addition, it can be seen that the structure of the infant's niche in different societies may contain as much information about adult culture as do the more obvious manifestations, such as ceremonial forms, which have traditionally interested anthropologists. Just as children learn their cultures through the way the environment is structured for them, so may we observers find underlying dimensions of cultural meaning in these patterns. At the same time, we note that recognition of the cultural component in the structuring of an infant's niche is necessary for interpretation of the "difficult infant syndrome" and for the developmental significance of specific behaviors.

The concept of an infant's niche as a source of structure for development is not frequently applied in either of the two professional disciplines. The reason for this, we think, is that the identification and study of the infant's niche require both the developmental perspective, with its recognition of the infant as an active participant in the learning process and its use of quantitative analysis, and the anthropological perspective, which focuses attention on the integrated uniformities as well as the individual variations in culturally specific childrearing practices.

References

Anders, T. F. Night-waking in infants during the first year of life. *Pediatrics*, 1979, *63*, 860–864.
Bell, R. Q. A reinterpretation of the direction of effects in studies of socialization. *Psychological Review*, 1968, *75*, 81–95.

Brazelton, T. B. *Neonatal behavioral assessment scale.* London: William Heinemann, 1973.

Carey, W. B. Clinical applications of infant temperament measures. *Journal of Pediatrics,* 1972, *81,* 823–828.

Fantz, R. L. Pattern vision in young infants. *Psychological Record,* 1958, *8,* 43–47.

Harkness, S., Edwards, C. P., & Super, C. M. Social roles and moral reasoning: A case study in a rural African community. *Developmental Psychology,* 1981, *17,* 595–603.

Konner, M. Evolution of human behavior development. In P. H. Leiderman, S. R. Tulkin, & A. Rosenfeld (Eds.), *Culture and infancy: Variations in the human experience.* New York: Academic Press, 1977.

Konner, M., & Super, C. M. Sudden infant death: An anthropological hypothesis. Unpublished manuscript, 1979.

Parmelee, A. H., Jr., Wenner, W. H., & Schulz, H. R. Infant sleep patterns: From birth to 16 weeks of age. *Journal of Pediatrics,* 1964, *65,* 576–582.

Super, C. M., & Harkness, S. Figure, ground, and gestalt: The cultural context of the active individual. In R. Lerner & H. Bush-Rossnagel (Eds.), *Individuals as producers of their development.* New York: Academic Press, 1981.

Super, C. M., Harkness, S., & Baldwin, L. M. Category behavior in natural ecologies and in cognitive tests. *Quarterly Newsletter of the Institute for Comparative Human Development,* The Rockefeller University, 1977, *1,* 4–7.

Thomas, A., & Chess, S. *Temperament and development.* New York: Brunner/Mazel, 1977.

Wallace, A. F. C. *Culture and personality* (2nd ed.). New York: Random House, 1961.

Role of Nonverbal Maternal Behavior in the Learning Process[1]

ABSTRACT

Five body motion variables of maternal teaching behavior are evaluated for their usefulness in predicting the rate of cognitive development in $5\frac{1}{2}$–$6\frac{1}{2}$-year-old Kikuyu children. Through zero order correlation analysis and canonical correlation analysis, four of the nonverbal material behavior variables are found useful in predicting the children's performance on several of a battery of 10 cognitive tests. The *nonverbal specificity* of the mother seems to be particularly interesting as a predictor of cognitive performance. This is consistent with a study in Ghana (Kirk, 1976, 1977) which isolates the mother's *verbal specificity* as a predictor of cognitive performance among Ga children.

This chapter examines maternal nonverbal behavior in teaching dyads among the Kikuyu of Kenya. A motion film record of mother–child teaching interaction is analyzed in order to demonstrate relationships between the mother's nonverbal communicative behavior and the child's rate of cognitive development.

Method

To examine the effects on child cognition of nonverbal behavior in the mother, three kinds of data were collected. The child's rate of cognitive

[1] The research on which this study is based was supported by a grant from the Carnegie Foundation to the Child Development Research Unit of the University of Nairobi.

CROSS-CULTURAL RESEARCH AT ISSUE

development was measured with a battery of 10 cognitive tests; the mother's nonverbal behavior was measured in terms of five body motion variables derived from analysis of a motion film record of mother–child interaction. Several demographic and educational variables of the child and nuclear family were also included as controls. These data were subjected to a multivariate analysis using zero order correlation and canonical correlation.

In 1973 a battery of cognitive tests was administered by Streeter, Landauer, and Whiting to approximately 500 children in Ngecha, a Kikuyu community in the Central Province of Kenya. For the present purposes we are concerned with the 10 tests listed in Table 6.1.[2] From the sample of children tested by Streeter, Landauer, and Whiting, a subsample was selected in which the children's ages were estimated to be between $5\frac{1}{2}$ and $6\frac{1}{2}$ years. Age was estimated using a technique outlined by Kirk (Kirk, 1975; Kirk & Burton, 1977), which involves observation of the children's total dental eruption patterns. The resulting subsample of 42 children and their mothers was observed in pairs during teaching interaction.

To make possible analysis of the mother's nonverbal behavior within the mother–child teaching interaction, mothers were taught to construct a puzzle in the absence of their children and subsequently were asked to teach their children to construct the puzzle. While each mother was teaching her child, the interactional behavior of the pair was recorded on motion film and sound tape. A series of indices of nonverbal maternal behavior was constructed. From observation of the mother's behavior on silent film, each mother was given a score on each nonverbal index:

1. *Proportion of single-finger movement.* This index is a ratio of the number of frames in which an isolated finger is in motion to the total number of usable frames[3] in the sample. Finger movement is defined as a change in angle at the knuckles of the finger or thumb. This index is intended as a measure of the mother's nonverbal specificity in communicating with her child.[4]

---

[2] For a description of these tests, see Kirk and Burton (1977).

[3] Usable frames are defined here as the number of frames in which the mother is not involved in assembling the puzzle herself, timed from the beginning of the film to either completion of the teaching session or the end of the film, whichever occurs first.

[4] Nonverbal specificity in the communication of the mother with her child can be seen in a number of body parts, but is easiest to perceive and count in the fingers and hand, where motions such as pointing, pinching, grasping, pressing firmly, rotating, and pushing convey specific information from mother to child about manipulations or the spatial organization of the puzzle. When the mother is being specific, she is usually referring to a single part of a structure; this is generally more easily done with a single hand. Addition of the second hand would often make the referent more ambiguous. A positive association is predicted between maternal specificity and the child's cognitive test performance, as mothers who are more specific will provide the child with more information about contrasts and congruencies in the environment.

Table 6.1
Correlations between Cognitive and Independent Variables[a] (N = 41)

	Proportion of single-finger movement	Predominance of single-hand movement	Mother's task relatedness	Amount of construction by mother	Inter-actional synchrony	Age of child	Age of mother	Education of mother	Education of father	Birth sequence	Sex of child
Auditory integration	-.03	.13	.15	-.32	.09	.35	.19	-.09	-.01	.03	-.12
Conservation (correct choices)	.16	.19	.07	-.15	-.26	.21	.24	-.21	-.08	.13	-.04
Conservation (reasons)	.43	-.04	.06	-.18	.14	.32	.12	-.21	-.25	.04	-.10
Checker diagonal	-.03	-.04	.11	-.14	-.16	.10	.44	-.05	-.05	.28	.07
Serial pointing	.13	.43	.17	-.33	.07	.12	.29	-.25	.00	.11	.05
Rank order recall (positions)	-.01	.18	.23	-.26	.05	-.02	.00	.06	.10	-.10	.15
Rank order recall (lists)	.11	.07	.14	-.34	-.11	.20	.06	-.07	-.16	.12	.11
Bender Gestalt	.12	.49	.45	-.06	.40	.16	.01	.07	.01	.02	.11
Face and hands	-.10	-.09	-.05	-.26	-.04	.00	-.01	.18	.20	.02	.05
Body parts (subtest A)	.08	.32	.43	-.12	.04	.13	.26	-.18	-.18	.08	-.09
Body parts (subtest B)	-.03	.03	.00	-.08	-.26	.28	.37	-.23	.05	.04	-.06
Embedded figures	.36	.42	.36	-.04	.07	.19	.28	-.08	-.03	.26	.10
Animal listing	.28	.13	.16	.14	.32	.15	.11	-.14	-.12	-.08	-.06

[a] Significance levels are as follows (one-tailed t test):

$p \leq .05$ $r \geq .20$

$p \leq .01$ $r \geq .27$

$p \leq .005$ $r \geq .33$

$p \leq .001$ $r \geq .44$

2. *Predominance of single-hand movement.* This is a binary variable that contrasts mothers who predominantly use one hand only (coded 2) with mothers who predominantly use both hands (coded 1). This index is another measure of the mother's nonverbal specificity.

3. *Task relatedness.* This is an index of the proportion of time in which the mother is focused on the construction or teaching process rather than on other stimuli in the room. It is computed as the number of frames in which the mother is relating to the task divided by the number of usable frames in the interaction.

4. *Amount of construction of the puzzle by the mother.* This is a measure of the degree to which the mother fails to follow the instruction to refrain from touching or assembling the puzzle during the filmed session of teaching interaction. It is computed as the number of frames of the mother's body motion which are involved in or necessary to touching the puzzle, divided by the total number of frames of teaching interaction.

5. *Interactional synchrony.* This index, unlike the preceding four indices, does not involve systematic counts of objective physical events. It is based, rather, on judgments on a 5-point scale of the degree to which the mother and child are in interactional synchrony; that is, the degree to which they parallel each other in body positioning (positional iso-morphism) and/or rhythm (rhythmic synchrony). This index is in part a test of the intuitive faculty as a yardstick in the measurement of microinteractional events.

For all 42 mother–child pairs, information was recorded on the age of the child and mother, mother's and father's education, the position of the child in the birth sequence of the mother, and the sex of the child.

Analysis

This chapter uses two alternative modes of data analysis.[5] A first is zero order correlation analysis, which examines relationships among pairs of individual variables. A second is canonical correlation analysis, which examines relationships among sets of variables, demonstrating overall relationships between cognitive test scores and measures of nonverbal maternal behavior. The second analysis is used to cross-check the patterns emerging from the zero order correlation analysis.

---

[5] A third approach, multiple linear regression analysis, is presented in Kirk and Burton, 1977.

Correlation Analysis

This section presents correlations (a) between the cognitive and independent variables; (b) among the independent variables; and (c) among the cognitive variables.

RELATIONSHIPS BETWEEN COGNITIVE AND INDEPENDENT VARIABLES

Table 6.1 presents correlations between the cognitive and independent variables. Among the nonverbal variables, task relatedness stands out as the best predictor of cognitive performance, having a number of strong positive correlations (maximum $r = .45$, $p < .001$) with scores on the cognitive tests. There are, further, no substantial negative correlations between task relatedness and any of the cognitive tests.

Predominance of single-hand movement is also a good predictor of cognitive test performance, having a number of high positive correlations (maximum $r = .49$, $p < .001$), but also having some weak negative correlations.

Amount of construction of the puzzle by the mother is useful in predicting performance on rank order recall (lists), serial pointing, auditory integration, and tactual perception on face and hands, with correlations ranging from $-.34$ to $-.26$ (significance levels ranging from $p < .005$ to $p < .05$). All but one of the cognitive tests correlate negatively with amount of construction by the mother.

Proportion of single-finger movement is useful in predicting scores on conservation of area (reasons), embedded figures, and animal listing, with correlations of .43, .36, and .28, respectively (significance levels ranging from .005 to .01). This nonverbal behavior index shows some weak negative correlations, but all substantial correlations are positive.

Interactional synchrony as here measured is an unreliable predictor of cognitive test performance.

Of the cognitive tests considered, five have strong associations with the nonverbal teaching behavior of the mother. Performance of the child on the Bender Gestalt Test shows high correlations with the task relatedness of the mother's movement, predominance of single-hand movement, and synchrony. Embedded figures is highly correlated with task relatedness, predominance of single-hand movement, and proportion of single-finger movement. Body parts, subtest A, is highly correlated with task relatedness and predominance of single-hand movement. Serial pointing has high correlations with predominance of single-hand movement and amount of construction by the mother. Conservation (reasons) is highly correlated with proportion of single-finger movement.

RELATIONSHIPS AMONG INDEPENDENT VARIABLES

Table 6.2 lists correlations among the independent variables (nonverbal, demographic, and educational). Several strong patterns can be seen from the correlations among the independent variables.

1. *Nonverbal variables.* Among the nonverbal variables, the predominance of single-hand movement correlates .45 with the proportion of single-finger movement. These two indices are both measures of the mother's nonverbal specificity. Both measures of specificity are highly associated with interactional synchrony ($r = .59$ and $r = .32$, respectively).

Amount of construction by the mother is negatively correlated with all of the other four nonverbal indices. Mothers who construct part or all of the time for their children tend to exhibit less single-hand movement, less single-finger movement, less synchrony, and less task relatedness.

Task relatedness is positively associated with predominance of single-hand movement and synchrony, but the association between task relatedness and single-finger movement is close to zero.

2. *Demographic and educational variables.* Educational opportunities in Ngecha have been increasing rapidly for many years. Consequently older people have less education than younger people, and the correlation between mother's age and mother's education is $-.71$. There is a negative correlation between mother's age and father's education, and a positive correlation between mother's education and father's education. It can be assumed that age is a mediating factor in the latter correlation. In addition to having less education, older women have more children. Consequently children of older mothers in the sample have more older siblings: There is a correlation of .69 between mother's age and the position of the child in the birth sequence.

RELATIONSHIPS AMONG THE COGNITIVE VARIABLES

Table 6.3 presents intercorrelations among the cognitive variables. The highest correlations are between rank order recall (subtest A) and tactual perception on face and hands (.55), between body parts subtest A and body parts subtest B (.59), and between Bender Gestalt and embedded figures (.54).

Canonical Correlation Analysis[6]

Canonical correlation analysis is designed to study the relationships between two sets of variables. In the present study this mode of analysis is

---

[6] Malcom Dow provided valuable assistance in this analysis.

Table 6.2
Correlations among Independent Variables[a] (N = 41)

	Proportion of single-finger movement	Predominance of single-hand movement	Mother's task relatedness	Amount of construction by mother	Interactional synchrony	Age of child	Age of mother	Education of mother	Education of father	Position in birth sequence	Sex of child
Proportion of single-finger movement	X	.45	.05	−.19	.32	.12	−.02	−.08	−.36	.00	−.10
Predominance of single-hand movement		X	.32	−.38	.59	.13	−.15	.25	.04	−.23	.13
Mother's task relatedness			X	−.20	.22	−.08	.02	.10	−.09	.15	.24
Amount of construction by mother				X	−.24	−.05	.01	−.14	−.24	−.05	−.14
Interactional synchrony					X	−.11	−.30	.21	.11	−.36	−.07
Age of child						X	.15	.05	−.18	−.07	−.03
Age of mother							X	−.71	−.26	.69	−.33
Education of mother								X	.46	−.51	.43
Education of father									X	−.22	.43
Position in birth sequence										X	−.09
Sex of child											X

[a] Significance levels are as follows (one-tailed *t* test):

$p \leq .05 \quad r \geq .20$

$p \leq .01 \quad r \geq .27$

$p \leq .005 \quad r \geq .33$

$p \leq .001 \quad r \geq .44$

Table 6.3
Correlations among Cognitive Variables[a] (N = 41)

	Auditory integration	Conservation (correct choices)	Conservation (reasons)	Checker diagonal	Serial pointing	Rank order recall (A)	Rank order recall (B)	Bender Gestalt	Face and hands	Body parts (A)	Body parts (B)	Embedded figures	Animal listing
Auditory integration	X	.26	.41	−.08	.39	.12	.35	.44	.05	.50	.43	.10	.30
Conservation (correct choices)		X	.42	.09	.47	.11	.33	.21	−.03	.34	.54	.17	.17
Conservation (reasons)			X	.07	.19	.17	.19	.21	.05	.24	.39	.09	.47
Checker diagonal				X	.06	.21	.08	.06	.00	.07	.03	.13	−.05
Serial pointing					X	.17	.50	.44	−.18	.45	.29	.41	.13
Rank order recall (A)						X	−.07	.14	.55	.42	.29	.12	.27
Rank order recall (B)							X	.34	−.31	.23	.21	.17	.15
Bender Gestalt								X	−.12	.36	.23	.54	.40
Face and hands									X	.10	.12	−.14	.19
Body parts (A)										X	.59	.36	.34
Body parts (B)											X	.30	.38
Embedded figures												X	.14
Animal listing													X

[a] Significance levels are as follows (one-tailed t test):

$p \leq .05$	$r \geq .20$
$p \leq .01$	$r \geq .27$
$p \leq .005$	$r \geq .33$
$p \leq .001$	$r \geq .44$

used to examine the relationships between measures of nonverbal maternal behavior and children's cognitive test scores.

Canonical correlation analysis does a simultaneous factor analysis of both sets of variables. This form of analysis yields one or more factors among the independent variables (measures of maternal behavior) and one or more factors among the dependent variables (cognitive test scores). A correlation coefficient is computed between the first factor of the independent variables and the first factor of the dependent variables. The first factors are rotated so as to maximize this first canonical correlation. Hence the canonical correlation analysis describes the best linear relationship between the two sets of variables.

There are 37 mother–child pairs for which there is complete information on all of the variables. For a sample size of 37 it is not advisable to include more than 10 variables in the canonical correlation analysis. The present analysis includes 9 variables: the five measures of nonverbal maternal behavior and four cognitive tests. The four cognitive tests of Streeter, Landauer, and Whiting's cognitive development quotient were chosen here for research comparability and because the cognitive development quotient has been found to be a good summary measure of cognitive development in Ngecha. These four tests are auditory integration (3 second delay), body parts naming, embedded figures, and animal listing.

Canonical correlation analysis of the Ngecha data produces only one factor among the nonverbal maternal behavior variables and only one factor among the cognitive test variables.

Loadings for the single nonverbal maternal behavior factor are listed in what follows. The nonverbal maternal behavior factor can be characterized by the three variables that have highest factor loadings: single-finger movement, single-hand movement, and task relatedness. The nonverbal maternal behavior factor can be interpreted as a measure of nonverbal maternal specificity and of maternal task attention, which is in turn a precondition for specificity.

Factor Loadings for Measures of Nonverbal Maternal Behavior

Variable	Loading
Interactional synchrony	.337
Single-finger movement	.603
Task relatedness	.740
Single-hand movement	.559
Proportion of construction by mother	.118

Loadings for the single cognitive test factor are listed in what follows. The cognitive test factor can be characterized by the two cognitive tests that have highest factor loadings: embedded figures and body parts naming. The cognitive test factor emphasizes nonverbal–spatial cognitive skills (found in

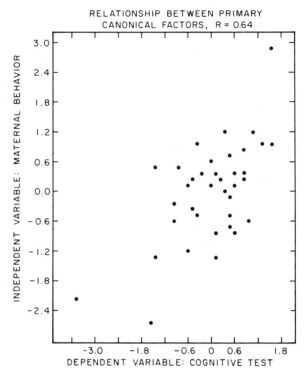

Figure 6.1. Relationship between two canonical factors.

embedded figures and body parts naming) as opposed to more purely verbal cognitive skills (found in auditory integration and animal listing).

Factor Loadings of Cognitive Test Scores

Variable	Loading
Auditory integration	.186
Body parts naming	.702
Embedded figures	.763
Animal listing	.446

The correlation between the nonverbal maternal behavior factor and the cognitive test factors is .64.[7] This strongly linear relationship is depicted in Figure 6.1. The correlation obtained with canonical correlation analysis is higher than any of the individual correlations between cognitive test scores and nonverbal maternal behavior measures, and supports the overall pattern that emerges from the zero order correlation analysis.

---

[7] Similar results have been obtained using linear regression analysis (Kirk & Burton, 1977).

Conclusion

This study evaluates the usefulness of nonverbal maternal behavior in predicting the cognitive development of $5\frac{1}{2}$–$6\frac{1}{2}$-year-old Kikuyu children. For this purpose 10 cognitive tests were used as measures of the children's cognitive performance, and 5 body motion variables were used as indices of nonverbal behavior in analysis of a motion film record of 42 mothers in teaching interaction with their children. The indices of nonverbal maternal behavior are found useful in predicting the cognitive test performance of the children.[8]

Zero Order Correlation Analysis

The nonverbal indices of maternal behavior play an important role in predicting scores on eight of the cognitive tests. The two indices that show consistently strong correlations with cognitive test performance are task relatedness and predominance of single-hand movement. Proportion of single-finger movement and amount of construction by the mother are also good predictors of cognitive performance. Mother–child interactional synchrony is a less adequate predictor, having inconsistent and indirect correlations with cognitive performance.

---

[8] The results of this study raise the question of causal inference. For the background variables such as mother's age, this question is easily resolved. There is no plausible way to argue that mothers become older because their children are more proficient on cognitive tests. We must conclude that mother's age is either a direct cause of said proficiency, or an indirect cause through some intermediate variables which we have not measured. In the case of nonverbal variables, however, we find it more difficult to make such secure causal inferences. The nonverbal indices are intended to measure the mother's proficiency as a teacher. A more proficient teacher should produce a higher rate of cognitive development in the child. However, one might argue that successful children elicit from their mothers the nonverbal behaviors which we have measured in this study; that mothers with receptive children are motivated to be more specific in their reference to the task; that mothers who are low on task relatedness have lost interest in the task because their children are doing poorly; and that mothers construct the puzzle for their children because they feel that the children are unlikely to be able to do it by themselves. This counterhypothesis, however, would imply that mothers adapt to the children's behavior more than the children adapt to the mother's behavior. This would dubiously attribute disproportionately high control and low adaptation to the least powerful and most rapidly developing figure in this small group interaction. Be that as it may, the process of mother–child interaction might also be seen as a feedback system in which mothers influence children and children influence mothers (not necessarily with equal strength). In this ecological model the two actors are interdependent; a circular system of causation holds. An exogenous infusion (deliberate or coincidental) of a new set of habitual behaviors into the cycle by the mother should alter the dynamics of the interaction. If we assume this ecological model to be accurate, a change in the mother's behavior should lead to a change in the child's behavior.

Among the battery of cognitive tests, the Bender Gestalt, embedded figures, body parts, and serial pointing tests are the most accessible to prediction using the nonverbal indices of maternal interactive behavior.

The age of the mother shows strong and uniformly positive correlations with the child's cognitive performance. Other demographic and educational variables, such as child's age and parental education, have much weaker correlations with cognitive performance.

Canonical Correlation Analysis

Canonical correlation analysis was done using the five nonverbal maternal behavior variables and four cognitive tests selected for their salience in an overall index of cognitive development. The results of this analysis produce a picture comparable to that yielded by the zero order correlation analysis. Only one factor emerges among the nonverbal maternal behavior variables: This factor can be characterized as maternal specificity and maternal task relatedness. Similarly, only a single factor emerges among the four cognitive variables: This factor can be characterized by the embedded figures and the body parts naming tests, the two most nonverbal–spatial of the four cognitive tests. A strong linear relationship ($r = .64$) is seen between the maternal specificity–task relatedness factor and the nonverbal–spatial cognitive test factor.

Viewing the nonverbal–spatial emphasis of the cognitive test factor together with the nonverbal nature of the maternal behavior factor, it can be concluded that nonverbal maternal behavior bears a closer relationship with the more nonverbal–spatial cognitive behavior of the child than with the more strictly verbal cognitive behavior of the child.

Summary

Four measures of nonverbal maternal behavior have emerged here as good predictors of the child's cognitive performance. These are task relatedness, predominance of single-hand movement, proportion of single-finger movement, and amount of construction of the puzzle by the mother. Task relatedness accounts for the greatest amount of the variance within the total set of cognitive tests. Specificity of communication, however, as measured by the predominance of single-hand movement and by proportion of single-finger movement, is of greatest theoretical interest. In a previous study across three Ga subcultures in Ghana [Fitzgerald (Kirk), 1970; Kirk, 1976, 1977] where verbal specificity was measured, strong positive associations have been found between the specificity of the mother's communication with the child in teching interaction and the prior cognitive test performance of the child.

The present study has established that the rate of cognitive development in the child can be predicted from three nonverbally measured features of the mother's behavior: (a) her specificity in communication; (b) her attention to the experimental problem; and (c) her tendency to allow the child to perform operations for himself.

This study of *nonverbal* maternal behavior, coupled with a previous study [Fitzgerald (Kirk), 1970; Kirk, 1976, 1977] of *verbal* maternal behavior has established that (a) both the verbal and nonverbal teaching styles of the mother can be used independently to predict the child's rate of cognitive development; and (b) verbal and nonverbal communicative specificity of the mother have parallel relationships with the child's cognitive growth rate.

The specificity of the mother's communication with her child seems to be a relevant variable in the development of cognitive ability. This variable may be both cross-cultural and cross-channel in its association with cognitive growth: It has appeared associated with the child's rate of cognitive growth in two African cultures, and in both verbal and nonverbal channels of communication.

References

Fitzgerald (Kirk), L. Cognitive Development among Ga Children: Environmental Correlates of Cognitive Growth Rate within the Ga Tribe. (Doctoral dissertation, University of California, Berkeley, 1970). *Dissertation Abstracts International,* 1970, *32*(2, Section B). (University Microfilms No. 71–20, 807)

Kirk, L. Estimating the ages of children in non-literate populations: A field method. *Journal of Cross-Cultural Psychology,* 1975, *6*(2), 238–249.

Kirk, L. Cross-cultural measurement of maternal behavior in mother–child teaching interaction. *Quality and Quantity: European–American Journal of Methodology,* 1976, *10,* 127–143.

Kirk, L. Maternal and subcultural influence on cognitive growth rate: The Ga pattern. *Piagetian psychology: Cross-cultural contributions.* In P. R. Dasen, (Ed.), New York: Gardner Press, 1977.

Kirk, L., & Burton, M. Age estimation of children in the field: A follow-up study with attention to sex differences. *Journal of Cross-Cultural Psychology,* 1976, *7*(3), 315–324.

Kirk, L., & Burton, M. Maternal kinesic behavior and cognitive development in the child. In L. L. Adler, (Ed.), *Issues in cross-cultural research.* Annals of the New York Academy of Sciences, 1977, *285*, 389–407.

Children's Drawings as an Indicator of Individual Preferences reflecting Group Values: A Programmatic Study

ABSTRACT

This chapter traces the programmatic progress of cross-cultural research investigating different sources that exert an influence on the preferences of fruit trees as expressed in children's drawings. In a previous study, 4314 children were told by their teachers to "draw a picture—any scene—with a fruit tree in it." The boys and girls were between the ages of 5 and 12 years and came from 24 countries on 6 continents. Although they drew 77 different fruit tree varieties, they pictured more apple trees than any other fruit tree. In fact, this category was larger than the next seven categories combined. A test–retest procedure was then undertaken in 7 countries to establish the reliability of the fruit tree experiment. Several other variables were also tested in this program. For example, a short unfamiliar story about a fig tree harvest (with baboons) was told to groups of American children—both emotionally disturbed and normal—without further comment before the fruit tree drawing session. The responses of the normal and emotionally disturbed children were very similar. However, this similarity did not hold in another study, in which preferences of mentally retarded and normal children were compared after the children had been restricted to the use of specific colors: The retardates' responses showed the same trends as those of normal children, but to a lesser degree. This investigation was then extended to schoolchildren on 3 continents. Although regional differences were noticeable, the children responded in a similar way to the lack or availability of specific colors. From the children's pictures, it was also obvious that the "scenes" represented much that was familiar to the children. This then led to another investigation, involving an evaluation of the familiarity hypothesis versus the value hypothesis. Although the pictures may mirror the environment, they also reflect existing value systems. Given that the apple tree can grow only in a temperate climate and that most of the countries in the temperate zones are "modern" or "westernized," the apple tree could be representative of the desirability of modernization.

CROSS-CULTURAL RESEARCH AT ISSUE

The study of children's drawings has been a standard technique not only with "primitive children" (Mead, 1954), but also in the practice of clinical psychology, when it was desirable to eliminate the language barrier and gain access to nonverbal patterns of behavior. Dennis (1966, 1970) found that children's drawings were useful for the investigations of group values, intellectual functioning, and degrees of westernization. However, no specific information was available about the processes that prompted children to respond with a specific picture.

In previous cross-cultural "fruit tree experiments," I found (Adler, 1965, 1967, 1968) that when children were asked to "draw a picture—any scene—with a fruit tree in it," the majority of the children responded with a graphical representation of an apple tree. This was so even in tropical countries where no apple trees grow, for example, Zaïre and the Netherland Antilles. It was also true for such arctic locations as Greenland where no fruit trees grow.

The results of the children's drawings suggested explanations related to the alphabet, and to the Bible. In the English and German languages the first letter of the alphabet, A, is usually introduced to schoolchildren by a picture of an apple. In Latin languages, however, such as in Zaïre where French is spoken, *apple* is translated as *pomme;* and thus the first letter, *p,* appears in the middle of the alphabet. Although it was also proposed that the Bible story of Adam and Eve, traditionally pictured with an apple, exerted an influence on the children, the Pidgin English editions of the Bible circulated in Zaïre featured the native mango or orange as the forbidden fruit (Adler, 1967).

The boys and girls who participated in the "fruit tree experiment" (Adler, 1968) ranged in ages from 5 to 12 years. They attended regular classes at either public, community, or missionary schools where their teachers administered the fruit tree tests. In this study, 4314 children residing in 24 countries on 6 continents contributed one picture each. More than 40% of these were graphic representations of apple trees. This category was larger than the next seven highest ranking categories combined. Altogether the children had pictured a total of 77 different types of fruit trees. However, the apple tree was their top choice in 17 of the 24 countries. There were 5 countries where apple trees ranked in second place, and in the remaining 2 they held the third highest rank. Interestingly, the 7 countries were located in two geographical areas: 4 (Greece, Israel, Italy, and Yugoslavia) bordered on the Mediterranean, the other 3 (Japan, the Philippines, and South Korea) were Asian countries bordering on the Pacific. In all 7 countries, apple trees are now found but are not indigenous, and in the children's drawings indigenous trees were in first place.

In an extensive test—retest procedure, the reliability of the previous results was studied (Adler, 1968). It was conducted in Argentina, Australia (Fullabo tribe), Chile, Germany, Greenland, Peru, and the United States. These countries represented a range in terms of their history and culture, the languages spoken, and their geographical location and climate. In each country the same children were retested either after 1 month or 3–4 month intervals. Regardless of the length of time interval, more than one-third of the subjects—178 out of 465 children—repeated the same fruit tree variety. Of these, more than half ($N = 103$) pictured apple trees both times.

It had been suggested by some teachers that the time of the year would influence responses. However, the results of the retests with 3 or 4 months delay did not bear out this assumption.

In order to attain a simple measure of the importance of language on the perception of bilingual Aboriginal children in Central Australia, Cawte and Kiloh (1967) and Cawte (1974) used the fruit tree study. On the basis of the children's drawings, they compared the effects of the introduced western cultural environment with those of the native environment. They used a counterbalanced procedure, in which the instructions were given once in the vernacular and once in English, with a 3-day interval between the two sessions. The results showed that when the children were asked in English they drew pictures with "introduced fruit trees," the highest ranking variety being apple trees. However, when the children were instructed in their native language, their first preference was the bush banana, an indigenous shrublike tree which has edible leaves and green, banana-shaped fruits.

A similar fruit tree study in New Britain by Veness and Hoskin (1968) tested the effect of language on the association processes. The results showed that pineapples were consistently associated with apples in the childrens' drawings. The investigators concluded: "English and Tolai or Walbiri are languages that subserve vastly different and contrasting realities. In such transcultural circumstances it might be reasonable to conclude, on the basis of the fruit-tree experiment, that trains of association set in motion by a stimulus in one language will differ from those set in motion by a stimulus in the other. . . . The 'fruit-tree experiment' appears to provide a convenient practical measure of this effect in given transcultural situation [p. 422]."

These studies with bilingual children gave rise to the question, can a new stimulus in a monolingual situation also set a new train of association in motion? Two successive fruit tree experiments in the United States were undertaken to find an answer to this question. The first study dealt with normal public schoolchildren (Adler, 1969, 1970a), the second with emotionally disturbed children, whose IQs ranged from dull normal to borderline (Adler & Berkowitz, 1976). The latter group of subjects resided in a private residential treatment center and attended a school that was part of the city's educational system. In both experiments the effects of a brief, one-time exposure to a short unfamiliar story were analyzed. The same two stories were read to the classes by the teachers immediately before the second fruit tree drawing session (i.e., the second of three sessions, spaced 1 week apart). The experimental groups heard a story about a fig tree harvest that was undertaken with the help of baboons in ancient Egypt. This story was selected because no child in the native region of these schoolchildren had ever pictured a fig tree in previous experiments. The control groups were told about the domestication of the dog by Stone Age man. This story was considered "neutral," because it did not mention any trees. Each story had about 150 words; the focal words *fig* and *dog* were mentioned 12 times each and *monkey* and *man* 6 and 5 times each in the respective stories. Of course, the instructions for the fruit tree drawing sessions were always the same as in previous studies and no mention was made of the story. The results showed strong responses to the unfamiliar stories in both the experimental and control conditions. In other words, this brief one-time exposure gave a new direction to the thought association and imagery to a significant number of children. A comparison between the normal children and the emotionally disturbed children showed that the children in both experiments responded in similar ways.

These studies demonstrated that the content of stories could indirectly influence children to draw a new and different variety of fruit tree than that which they had previously pictured. It was probable that other conditions such as availability of colors could exert a similar influence. It was therefore decided to analyze the fruit tree preferences of children who had only a limited range of colors or no colors available.

Accordingly, two further fruit tree experiments were carried out in the United States (Adler, 1970b, c). The first study was with normal children from three elementary schools in different geographical locations. And the second study was with mentally retarded children, with an IQ range of 31–77, who resided in a state institution. In these studies, as in the previous experiments, the subjects ranged in age from 5 to 12 years. In both of the experiments, the children were divided into four groups: Group I had all colors available; Group II could only use red, blue, and yellow; Group III was restricted to green, brown, and orange; and Group IV had no colors available and was limited to either a blue pen or a black pencil. The results of the normal children showed that apple tree preferences ranked highest in Groups I, II, and especially IV. However, apples were in second place in Group III, and orange trees ranked in first place; though in Group II no child had pictured an orange tree. A comparison of these results with those of the retarded children showed a striking similarity in trends. For the retarded children, again the highest percentage of apple tree pictures occurred in Group IV and the lowest in Group III; however, in Group III orange tree pictures tied with apple tree representations for first rank.

These two experiments showed that the availability of certain colors such as orange—and the unavailability of other colors, such as red—gave new directions of thought associations and imagery for a significant number of normal and of retarded children, even though the latter's responses were not as strong as those of the normal children. Adler (1970c) proposed that

> while it could be possible that the lessened effects with the retarded children might reside in the lack of attentiveness alone, one might wonder whether it is not appropriate to advance, in addition, a parallel to Zeaman and House's (1963) "attention deficiency theory of retardate discrimination learning," namely, to expand it to include "association deficiency theory of retardate imagination." This (broadened theory) would also involve a two-stage process: First, the child has to attend to or be aware of the relevant stimulus dimension (let us say the orange color); and second, the child has to make an appropriate association with the relevant stimulus cue (for instance, think of/imagine an orange tree, when asked to draw a fruit tree). Perhaps the retarded child is defective (slow), not only in the attentional phase, but in the associational phase of the process as well [p. 221].

In this way, the data of the two fruit tree experiments could explain the greater change in responses of the normal children when compared to the retardates under the same conditions.

The ranking of fruit tree varieties (18 for the normal children and 13 for the retardates) corresponded very closely not only between these two groups of children, but also when compared to the worldwide survey of a previous cross-cultural study (Adler, 1968), with apple in first, orange (tangerine) in second, and cherry in third place.

One other aspect was important to follow through, namely, the effects of the different age levels. In an earlier cross-cultural study (Adler, 1967), where children could use all colors, the "younger" age group (5–8 years) had significantly more responses of apple trees than did the "older" age group (9–12 years). It was suggested that this might be a sign of more stereotyped thinking of the "younger" group, as a significant number of "older" children were more readily influenced by the new and unfamiliar story than the "younger" age group (Adler, 1970a). However, under varied conditions of color availability, children in the United States responded in the same manner, regardless of age: "It appeared that color exerted the same influence regardless of age group, to effect a change in content of fruit-tree drawings [Adler, 1970b, p. 194]."

Another study was conducted by Thomas and Osgood (1971) and was designed to examine college students' (ages 18–22) preferences of fruit trees under the same conditions of varied color availability, using the same procedure, and, in addition, to compare these findings with those reported by Adler (1970b). These investigators also extended their fruit tree experiment and examined the apple tree responses in a word association test with "fruit tree" as one of the stimulus words. It was found from the pictures produced that, although the trends remained stable, the degree of the fruit tree preferences was significantly stronger with college students. This can be seen by comparing the percentages of apple tree responses for the various groups: in Group I, college students: 75%, schoolchildren: 53%; Group II, college students: 83%, schoolchildren: 53%; Group III, college students: 21%, schoolchildren: 16%; Group IV, college students: 68%, schoolchildren: 60%. Orange tree responses for Group III were for the college students 74% and for the schoolchildren 67%. In the word association test given the college students, *apple tree* represented 71% of the responses. Thomas and Osgood offered no explanation for these results although they felt that "in view of the current collegiate emphasis on 'doing your own thing,' it was surprising to find the college students' preferences so homogeneous and conforming. This conformity (or uniformity) was again reflected in the number of different trees selected: Ten varieties for the college students compared to 18 varieties for the schoolchildren [p. 255]."

Given that the experiments under varied conditions of color availability were all undertaken in the United States, it remained to do a cross-cultural study to see whether children in other geographical locations would respond in the same manner. It was hypothesized that children in various parts of the world would respond with different fruit tree preferences, depending on the colors associated with the type of fruit tree represented. Therefore a cross-cultural fruit tree experiment was undertaken (Adler & Adler, 1977) to compare responses of children from 7 countries on 3 continents: North America, Central Europe, and East Asia. All 2675 participants were normal schoolchildren attending regular classes and were 5–12 years old. The ages of the children (9–12 years for the "older" and 5–8 years for the "younger" groups) were tabulated, as was the sex distribution for each geographical region. Each child contributed one graphic representation of a fruit tree to this study.

In order to measure the environmental effects, the children were grouped by geographical areas based on continent. Schoolchildren from Canada ($N = 83$) and the United States ($N = 494$) made up the "North American Group" ($N = 577$). Four countries in Europe were chosen, where the native language was something other than English. The children in this "Central European Group" ($N = 396$) resided in Denmark ($N = 38$), France ($N = 121$), Germany ($N = 209$), and Switzerland ($N = 28$). Children in 3 of these countries had drawn apple trees as their first preference in a previous study (Adler, 1968); the fourth country was added for this experiment. It seemed, however, more meaningful and conclusive to test children from a country where the first preference was any other than an apple tree. A glance at the results of previous fruit tree experiments in which children from 24 countries participated showed that in 17 of these apple tree preferences ranked highest. Of the 7 countries where apple trees were either in second or third place, 4 were on the Mediterranean. The results showed that in Greece the children's first preference was the olive tree; both in Israel and in Italy, the children's top choice was the orange–tangerine tree; and in Yugoslavia the cherry tree was in first place. The other 3 were Asian countries on the Pacific Ocean. In all these countries, indigenous trees were in first place. In the Orient, the coconut palm was in first place in the Philippines, the persimmon tree in Japan and South Korea. But whereas Japanese children had predominantly pictured persimmon trees (34%), in South Korea, persimmon trees (28%) barely beat out apple trees (25%). In the color availability experiments, Group III was allowed to use only green, brown, and orange; and, in the United States, it was the orange color that had exerted the greatest influence on students. Because of the availability of brown color in Group III, it would be difficult to analyze the brown coconut responses of the Philippine children. Therefore, it was deemed best to test Japanese children's fruit tree responses in this study. The persimmon fruit falls between red and orange in color, and thus provides an opportunity to test the influence of the orange and of the red colors separately on the responses. The Japanese children ($N = 1702$) were designated the "East Asian Group."

The same procedure was used that had been adopted previously. In order to avoid disruption of the general classroom routine by unfamiliar visitors, the fruit tree test was administered by each teacher to the class as a group during a regular class period. The method used replicated those of Adler's (1970 b, c) fruit tree experiments with varied conditions of color availability.

The results of the cross-cultural research (Adler & Adler, 1977) showed that the children on the 3 continents responded in similar ways to the unavailability, as well as to the accessability, of specific colors. Furthermore, it was shown that local fruits, specific to the geographical areas, seemed to exert an influence on the preferences of fruit trees in children's drawings.

For example, in the East Asian Group the effects of color on the imagery and associative thinking in schoolchildren were very significant. Although the color of the top preference in Groups I, III, and IV, the persimmon, was a shade between red and orange, the results revealed that the availability of the red color without orange (Group II) increased the apple tree responses, and the orange color when red was not available (Group III) did the same for the orange–tangerine tree preferences. In the Central European Group, apple trees were in first place in all four groups. Although here there were fewer apple tree responses in Group III than in the other three conditions, the difference was not significant. Yet there was a significant increase in plum tree responses due to the access to blue in Group II; and in Group III there was a significant increase in orange tree responses, influenced by the orange color, though the number of apple tree drawings decreased insignificantly. For the North American children in Group III, increases in orange tree preferences reached the highest level for any variety of fruit trees; whereas apple tree drawings ranked highest in Groups I, II, and IV, and orange trees were omitted altogether in Group II where the color orange was unavailable. In other words, schoolchildren, who pictured local fruit trees under conditions when either all or no colors were available, were influenced to respond with different fruit trees when they were limited to the use of only a few specified colors. This cross-cultural fruit tree experiment showed that different associations and imagery resulted due to the relevant stimulus of the available colors, regardless of the social or cultural background of the children.

In the current phase of the programmatic research, we set out to investigate the influence of cultural background and social setting, as reflected in the pictorial representations in terms of group value. The question of *values*— those of individuals, as well as those of their society—was broached previously by Dennis (1966). His cross-cultural investigations of children's drawings started before World War II, but reached their peak with the publication of his book *Group Values through Children's Drawings* in 1966. Dennis tried to show that it was really "values or preferences" that children depicted in their drawings ("draw a man"/"draw a woman"), rather than "frequencies of experiences" (p. 172). He felt that two hypotheses—the value hypothesis and the familiarity hypothesis—were often equally applicable with regard to the interpretation of many of the drawings. The *value hypothesis* proposes children will draw scenes in which the themes have culturally desirable qualities and are socially acceptable. The *familiarity hypothesis,* on the other hand, suggests that children in their drawings reflect their environment, or that which they have knowledge of or have experienced. Yet not everything with which the children are familiar is drawn. What then is pictured? Dennis pointed out his own point of view when he stated that "in all instances in which the familiarity hypothesis and the value hypothesis are in conflict, the latter wins [p. 172]." As an example of weakness of the familiarity hypothesis, Dennis pointed out that most city children generally, and teenage boys specifically, were familiar with policemen, dentists, and doctors personally, as well as through advertisements, movies, and television, and thus, "the familiarity hypothesis cannot account for the comparative absence of such men in drawings. Their unpopularity with teen-age boys, not the unfamiliarity, must be responsible for their low per cent of occurrence in drawings [p. 172]."

A parallel can be drawn with regard to the graphic representations pictured in response to the fruit tree experiment. The number of fruit tree varieties pictured by the various groups of subjects is only an indicator of the children's familiarity with the fruits, rather than a complete assessment of their knowledge of the different types of fruits. It was no problem for the New York children who had never seen a fig tree to draw one. None of these children had drawn a fig tree before they had heard the story of the fig tree harvest (Adler, 1970a; Adler & Berkowitz, 1976). However, not knowing what a fig tree looked like, the children generalized and drew it in the shape of an apple tree with brown apple-shaped fruits. The responses suggested that the children were familiar with the dried brown figs that are often sold on a string. A case in point is Figure 7.1, a picture of an imaginary banana tree, drawn by an 11-year-old American girl, who, obviously, had never seen how bananas grow.

As the children were asked to draw "any scene," the results showed a variety of scenes and themes. Most frequently pictured were a harvest, a residential view, or a landscape, all of which were readily associated with a fruit tree. In most of these cases the familiarity hypothesis could apply. Contrary to Dennis (1966) though, my own inclination is to favor a state of harmony between the familiarity hypothesis and the value hypothesis.

Figure 7.1. United States, girl, 11 years, banana tree.

Although the children's drawings may mirror their environment, they also reflect existing value systems by presenting preferences. Take as an example the apple tree, which can only grow in a temperate climate. It so happens that most of the countries in the temperate zones are "modern" or "westernized." Therefore it could be that the apple is representative of the spread of westernization, as well as of the desirability of modernization. In other words, for many children the apple is a prestige fruit. It was Dennis who, as a fervent proponent of the value hypothesis, suggested (in personal communication) that "if you asked children to draw a woman cooking, it would be on a stove, even if the family does not have a stove" (which would show that the children are familiar with such an object).

Explaining the value hypothesis in terms of social desirability, one can readily point to the powerful goal qualities of a prolific harvest, as well as to the attractiveness of leisure hours in a family setting, or enjoying unspoiled nature. Similarly Zaïdi (1979) noticed in his study of Nigerian children's drawings ("draw a whole man"/"draw a whole woman") that women were depicted as inactive and not engaged in any work. As this was in opposition to the traditional customs, such a change in the value system may have occurred as a result of the increased urbanization in Nigerian society. Because cultural values and social roles are undergoing changes, in modern or

Figure 7.2. Japan, girl, 10 years (western age), orange tree.

Figure 7.3. Japan, girl, 6 years (western age), banana tree.

Figure 7.4. Japan, girl, 9 years (western age), grape tree.

"westernized" countries as well as in traditional societies, children's drawings are a good method to assess the existing or shifting value systems. Only one topic, namely that of sex role stereotypes, can be briefly discussed here. (Unfortunately, space limitations do not permit extensive explanations for each picture.)

In modern societies there is a striving for change in social roles. A common

Figure 7.5. United States, girl, 5 years, apple tree.

goal among women in modern countries is to achieve equal status with men in jobs and professions. Men, on the other hand, are content with their higher status. Of course, in any transitional stage a certain amount of conflict is created between the old and the new value systems. And these two sides of the coin (i.e., old and new values), so to speak, are represented in the children's drawings. To begin with, there are different emphases observable in the pictures by girls compared to boys. Figures 7.2–7.10 are pictures drawn by girls; Figures 7.11–7.21 are pictures drawn by boys. Note that cross-culturally although the style of the drawings and the emphasis of what is shown in the "scene" is different, there are remarkable similarities noticeable in the "themes." Another important point to note is that girls represent spontaneously more women than do boys. This effect is lost when children are asked to follow instructions to either "draw a man" or to "draw a woman."

Figure 7.6. Canada, girl, 7 years, apple tree.

Figure 7.7. Germany, girl, 8 years, apple tree and cherry tree.

Here, then, are some selected examples: The goal qualities of the value hypothesis are most accurately depicted in the Japanese girls' pictures. Figure 7.2 shows a scene with a prolific harvest where oranges are picked by two women in traditional clothing and backpacks, and in Figure 7.3 the leisure goal of a tea party in a garden is represented by two women in long dresses, while a girl looks on from a window. Figure 7.4 shows the leisure theme in a family setting. In this figure, all persons represented wear modern clothes, though the woman of the household wears the traditional apron. The father carries his daughter on his shoulders; he wears a long-sleeve shirt but no tie. The young girl is clad in jeans/pants and has a barrette in her hair. Figure 7.5, drawn by a 5-year-old American girl, shows a girl in a dress with a pretty bow in her hair holding an apple. Figure 7.6, drawn by a 7-year-old Canadian girl, pictures a girl picking apples from a tree, while a boy collects the apples. Both figures wear jeans and long-sleeved tops; the only sex differences are seen in the length of their hair.

The next four pictures have a European origin. Figures 7.7 and 7.8 are contributed by two German girls, 7 and 8 years old. One shows a female in a traditional nurturing role, strolling with a baby carriage. The other drawing is a combination of harvest and leisure; the woman stands on the ladder where she picks and eats the cherries. She has long hair and wears

Figure 7.8. Germany, girl, 7 years, cherry tree.

Figure 7.9. France, girl, 10 years, apple tree.

a dress. The man, on the other side of the tree, has a suit on and wears
a hat; he smokes a pipe. The picture shows that he says "Au Au Au"
(*Ouch*), when the cherry falls on his head, though he smiles nevertheless.
The next two pictures are from two French girls, ages 10 and 12. Figure
7.9 represents a barn yard where a smiling woman with long hair, dressed
in pants and a coverall-apron feeds the chickens, while her child watches
and holds an apple. Of course, this theme is not classified as "leisure,"
though it portrays an unrushed and unharried domestic activity. Figure 7.10
sets a "romantic" mood, possibly a date; a young man relaxes, sprawled

Figure 7.10. France, girl, 12 years, pear tree.

Figure 7.11. Japan, boy, 9 years (western age), banana tree.

Figure 7.12. Japan, boy, 9 years (western age), grape vine.

Figure 7.13. United States, boy, 8 years, apple tree.

Figure 7.14. United States, boy, 12 years, apple tree.

Figure 7.15. Denmark, boy, 12 years, pear, apple, and plum trees.

on the grass, and a girl beats the tree with a stick to knock off the pears. Both figures wear similar outfits (long pants and long-sleeved tops), but the length of the hair identifies the sexes.

Now to the boys' pictures: Figures 7.11 and 7.12 are drawn by two Japanese 9-year-olds. The former shows a man, with a moustache and a well-trimmed beard, who wears a modern suit with a tie and has a watch in his breast-pocket. He has on a hat and holds an attaché case in one hand and a walking cane in the other. Obviously he is walking off (to work?) while a boy waves to him from the window; this boy and the boy in traditional clothes, who is standing in the road, are both just "sprouting" moustaches, as shown by the "dots" over their mouths. The latter figure shows the garden of a house where a boy/man (the one wearing glasses) can relax/ study and read a book, or just spend time. Two American boys, 8 and 12 years old, represented themes that are of special interest to boys. The younger one drew a picture of two boys in a tree. One of the boys sits on a swing hanging from the tree, the other boy stands up in the tree and is pecked on the head by a big bird. Nearby are two bicycles (drawn in more detail than the rest of the picture), ready and waiting for the boys in Figure

Figure 7.16. Germany, boy, 9 years, apple tree.

7.13. The older boy showed two race cars with two stick figures in the driving seats (Figure 7.14). Both of these drawings certainly depict leisure goals for boys. Figure 7.15, which successfully combines a working "tool" and leisure, was drawn by a 12-year-old Danish boy. It depicts a man with a pot belly lying in a hammock and smoking his pipe; another man who is also smoking a pipe as he stands up on a ladder harvesting fruits; and a third man who is driving a tractor but not actually working—in that the

Figure 7.17. *Germany, boy, 10 years, apple tree.*

tractor is more like a "man's toy." Two German boys, 9 and 10 years old, contributed some interesting views of coexistence of the modern and the traditional ways of life. In Figure 7.16 there is a horse drawn hay wagon and a tractor pulling a trailer; presumably both drivers are men, though there are no identifying features as to gender on these stick figures. Figure 7.17 portrays a hiker with a knapsack who holds an apple in one hand as he walks along the road, supported by a walking cane in the other hand,

Figure 7.18. France, boy, 12 years, apple tree.

as a modern car (the driver's sex is not distinguishable) passes him by. The next two drawings, made by French boys, 12 and 10 years old, also show effects of modernization, albeit different effects. With the help of mechanized farm equipment, such as the tractor in Figure 7.18, the farmer can enjoy leisure hours in which he can sit by a brook and fish or, whenever the game appears, hunt with the gun leaning up against the tree. However, a negative side of modernization is portrayed in Figure 7.19: Because of an oil (*huile*) spill on the lonely road, a car with two passengers crashes into the only tree in the picture.

Inspection of the boys' pictures revealed that they drew men and boys, whereas the girls portrayed both sexes, with a majority of females being represented. However, there were a few—very few—scenes that boys drew, in all populations, in which women were included. Figures 7.20 and 7.21, which were drawn by two 10-year-olds, are among these rare pictures. The

Figure 7.19. France, boy, 10 years, apple tree.

Figure 7.20. France, boy, 10 years, apple tree.

first of these, an example of a "tongue-in-cheek" humor, was made by a French boy and shows how "chivalrous" the man is, who shoots the little animal with a gun to "protect" the woman. The second picture was made by an American boy, who, obviously, was not quite sure about his affectionate feelings toward the "(girl) Jeanette" and the "(dog) Freckles," since he showed only the upper part of their bodies.

As a whole, the pictures show a certain uniformity of themes cross-culturally. By depicting the socially desirable activity of producing large crops (and sometimes displaying some expensive farm equipment, in the case of the boys' pictures, and equality in the division of labor, in the case of the girls' drawings), as well as various phases of leisure hours or an unrushed life in stereotypic representations (sports for boys, including hunting, fishing, or cars and bikes; nurturing or domestic activities for girls), the pictures were in agreement with the value hypothesis, though the familiarity hypothesis would also apply.

The cultural struggle by women for equality with men can be observed in many of the American and European pictures where feminine figures can often only be identified by the length of their hair, as the androgynous effect of the clothing covers up the gender characteristics. Yet more important is

Figure 7.21. United States, boy, 10 years, apple tree.

the fact that females execute "men's jobs"—for example, they engage in the nontraditional activity of standing on a ladder (in some cases wearing a skirt). This is different in the Japanese pictures (see, as an example, Figure 7.2) where women are shown in the traditionally accepted manners of picking fruits. Of course, the "basic" activity of women is nurturing, and is demonstrated in all geographical areas, regardless of other ongoing women's issues.

In summary, then, it can be said that drawings, as a projective technique, provide children with a good opportunity not only to reflect their personal feelings and their attitudes toward people and situations, but also to express the group values that are prevalent within their cultural environment. The present findings support the contention that children picture admired persons in socially desirable or culturally acceptable conditions. The results of the present cross-cultural fruit-tree experiment are in agreement with the value hypothesis, though they do not exclude the familiarity hypothesis. Analyses of the pictures revealed that these two hypotheses cannot be separated and therefore work in harmony all the time. It was suggested that the apple tree was representative of western culture and that apple tree pictures thus portrayed the positive goal qualities and the desirability of modernization.

The overall findings of this extensive research program showed that 5–12-year-old children, living in different cultures and environments, all responded with similar reactions. Under different experimental conditions, which included verbal and nonverbal stimuli, the children's thought processes were directly or indirectly influenced to set a new train of association in motion. This imagery found expression in the children's graphic representations. The results of this cross-cultural programmatic study have shown not only that the discovery of differences is important, but that the finding of similarities may provide even more meaningful information.

Acknowledgments

The author wishes to express deep appreciation to Beverly S. Adler, for her continued encouragement, as well as sincere thanks for her helpful suggestions with this research project. The author also acknowledges with grateful thanks the help and effort extended by Machiko Fukae with this research.

References

Adler, L. L. *Cross-cultural study of children's drawings of fruit-trees.* Paper presented at the First New York City Psi Chi Psychological Convention, New York, 1965.

Adler, L. L. A note on the cross-cultural preferences: Fruit-tree preferences in children's drawings. *Journal of Psychology,* 1967, *65,* 15–22.

Adler, L. L. A note on the cross-cultural fruit-tree study: A test–retest procedure. *Journal of Psychology,* 1968, *69,* 53–61.

Adler, L. L. The fruit-tree study as a measure of associative thinking and imagery in children of different ages. *Developmental Psychology,* 1969, *1,* 444.

Adler, L. L. Influencing associative thinking and imagery as measured by the "Fruit-Tree Experiment" in children's drawings. *Social Science and Medicine,* 1970, *4,* 527–534. (a)

Adler, L. L. The "Fruit-Tree Experiment" as a measure of children's preferences of fruit trees under varied conditions of color availability. *Journal of Genetic Psychology,* 1970, *116,* 191–195. (b)

Adler, L. L. The "Fruit-Tree Experiment" as a measure of retarded children's preferences of fruit trees under varied conditions of color availability. *Journal of Psychology,* 1970, *76,* 217–222. (c)

Adler, L. L., & Adler, B. S. The "Fruit-Tree Experiment" as a cross-cultural measure of the variations in children's drawings due to regional differences. In L. L. Adler (Ed.), *Issues in cross-cultural research*. Annals of the New York Academy of Sciences, 1977, *285*, 227–281.

Adler, L. L., & Berkowitz, P. H. Influencing associative thinking and imagery in emotionally disturbed children. *Psychological Reports*, 1976, *39*, 183–188.

Cawte, J. E. *Medicine is the law*. Honolulu: The University Press of Hawaii, 1974.

Cawte, J. E., & Kiloh, L. G. Language and pictorial representations in Aboriginal children. *Social Science and Medicine*, 1967, *1*, 67–76.

Dennis, W. *Group values through children's drawings*. New York: Wiley, 1966.

Dennis, W. Goodenough scores, art experience and moderization. In I. Al-Issa & W. Dennis (Eds.), *Cross-cultural studies of behavior*. New York: Holt, Rinehart & Winston, 1970.

Mead, M. Research on primitive children. In L. Carmichael (Ed.), *Manual of child psychology* (2nd ed.). New York: Wiley, 1954.

Thomas, G., & Osgood, S. W. College students' performance on the "Fruit-Tree Experiment" under varied conditions of color availability. *Journal of Psychology*, 1971, *77*, 253–256.

Veness, H., & Hoskin, J. O. Psychiatry in New Britain: A note on the "Fruit-Tree Experiment" as a measure of the effect of language on association processes. *Social Science and Medicine*, 1968, *1*, 419–424.

Zaïdi, S. M. H. Values expressed in Nigerian children's drawings. *International Journal of Psychology*, 1979, *14*, 163–169.

Zeaman, D., & House, B. J. The role of attention in retardate discrimination learning. In N. R. Ellis (Ed.), *Handbook of mental deficiency*. New York: McGraw-Hill, 1963.

REGINA C. SPIRES
MITCHELL W. ROBIN

8

Father Absence Cross-Culturally: A Review of the Literature

ABSTRACT

This chapter deals with the problem of father absence from a cross-cultural perspective and attempts to look at sex role behavior, masculine protest behavior, achievement motivation, and cognitive development. Within the framework of the cross-cultural perspective an attempt has been made to expand the research that has been done in this area on western populations and to attempt to look at other forms of father absence in nonwestern traditions and to ascertain the relationship between such diverse ideas as polygynous marriage, couvade, and strict puberty rituals.

Fathers and fathering have recently received renewed attention in the popular literature of the social sciences. More father involvement in the labor room and the delivery room has brought the father into closer contact with the total process of parenting. This is not necessarily a new phenomenon in cultural history. Margaret Mead's (1935) research on the Arapesh made us aware that many preliterate tribes have looked on fathering as quite a strenuous role. The Mountain Arapesh often pointed out a man looking quite old, "but no wonder, look at all the children he has borne." Within this cross-cultural framework, one might ask what societies stress fatherhood, what societies ignore the role, and what difference does it make anyway. In this chapter, the focus will be on the effects of father absence as it has been discussed, measured, researched, and speculated about over several decades and across many societies. Although the great bulk of father-absent research presumes the nuclear family to be the norm, it is profitable to look

CROSS-CULTURAL RESEARCH AT ISSUE

at those cultures which are not bound by the western notion of appropriate values and family patterns to see if one can discern any specific directions toward compensating behavior for father absence. This chapter concerns itself with the family structures that accept father absence as the norm, that see no social stigma attached to minimal father–child interaction. To this end, material will be drawn from both traditional western subcultures as well as polygynous and matrifocal households in nonwestern cultures. Three major areas will be discussed in terms of the hypothesized impact of living in fatherless homes: (a) sex-role behavior; (b) masculine "protest" behavior; and (c) achievement motivation and cognitive development.

Sex-Role Behavior

In the book, *I the Aboriginal,* Waipuldanya, an Australian Aborigine, gives a graphic and dramatic account of his initiation into the adult male role. From the moment he is taken from his mother at age 9, through the embarrassment of sexual contact with his sisters-in-law and his painful separation in the boys hut, he is aware that his mother mourns him as dead, for he will never return to her hut to eat or sleep as a child. Through the painful ritual of subincision and the 2-year period of controlled silence that follows, Waipuldanya learns the rules of being a man. Here in a single case history, we can see acted out the hypothesis of several cross-cultural researches.

From the time Freud published *Totem and Taboo* (1938), anthropologists and psychologists have speculated about the meaning of initiation rites, couvade, ritual war behavior, and other esoteric cultural practices. In the fifties, the work of Whiting (1958) and Barry, Bacon, and Child (1957) brought renewed interest in the connection between psychology and anthropology. In the Whiting material, there appeared to be a significant association between "status envy," mother–child sleeping arrangements, and severe initiation rites. The logic presented was that "status envy" caused the child to identify with the adult who controlled the resources of food and affection. In essence, the argument went something like this:

1. The mother is the mediator of resources for the child.
2. If the father is absent, the male child will develop a primary cross-sex identity as he strongly identifies with the mother.
3. This process occurs in early infancy.
4. There is more likely to be such cross-sex linkage in polygynous societies where the father has little to do with the day-to-day socialization.

From this logic system, it is not difficult to see why many researchers turned to a comparison of father-present and father-absent males in our own society to see if the same cross-sex identity would be found in one-parent households.

In a study testing the status envy hypothesis, D'Andrade (1973) used both black Americans and Barbadians who were first to third generation Americans. He found strong feminization among father-absent children of both sexes. Contrary to expectation, however, the expected male "protest" behavior was not present. By protest behavior is meant exaggerated violence and physical force sometimes found in relation to negative feelings of masculinity. An interesting finding in this study is the fact that daughters of "masculine" mothers do see themselves as more feminine and less potent.

In a study of children living in Barbados, Burton (1972) hypothesized that because there is no stigma to father absence, there ought not to be any negative effects on the children. The pattern of male identity was studied through the draw-a-person test. In the United States, most children draw the same sex figure first but father-absent boys draw female figures first. In Barbados, both males and females draw women first, reflecting, no doubt, the matrifocal nature of the culture. The average size of the male drawing was directly related to the degree of father presence during the boy's infancy. In contrast, the conditions of sex role conflict are not present for girls regardless of father absence.

Lecorgne and Laosa (1976) in studying low income Mexican-American families found the same high correlation between father absence and the drawing of significantly more feminine attributes in the Goodenough–Harris Drawing Test.

Periodically, researchers attempt to use the status envy hypothesis to explain male sexual orientation, arguing that identification with the female produces the homosexual male. Freund, Langevin, Zajac, Steiner, & Zajac (1974) have again shown that there is no conclusive relationship between father absence and either transsexual or homosexual behavior. Cross-culturally, this issue has rarely been raised due to the fact that most cultures have a wider acceptance of a variety of sexual patterns and assume bisexuality to be the norm. When the recently discovered Tasaday were being interviewed, they overcame their nervousness by mutual penis play but they certainly did not label each other as homosexual.

Sex Roles and Initiation Rituals

The most important work done in terms of the cross-cultural relationship between father absence and sex-role identity was initiated by John Whiting. Building on earlier work by Kardiner (1939), Whiting and Child (1953) put forth a modified version of Kardiner's chain which looked like this:

$$\text{Maintenance systems} \rightarrow \text{Child training practices} \rightarrow \text{Personality variables} \rightarrow \text{Projective systems}$$

This diagram has been further refined and expanded by LeVine (1973) to include biological components. Within both frameworks the recognition exists that ecological and environmental factors determine not only the economic aspects of getting a living but the childrearing practices as well. The !Kung of the Kalahari Desert do not use the same techniques as the Jivaro of the Amazon Jungle. The differences in childrearing practices greatly affect the adult personality which in turn can be studied via the projective systems. The concept here refers not to the psychological processes of displacement, etc., but to the unique cultural patterns of sorcery, magic, rituals, art, and folk tales.

Within this framework, Whiting showed that exclusive mother–infant sleeping arrangements are strongly associated with intense male initiation rites at puberty, especially circumcision subincision. Although several alternate hypotheses have been offered (Whiting, Kluchhorn, & Anthony, 1958) for the association, the majority of the research focuses on the initiation rite as an efficacious way of counteracting the strong identification with the mother. The genital operation serves as a dramatic learning experience that resolves the conflict of sex identity for young males. Interesting to note is the finding of Brown (1963) that traumatic initiation rites for females occurred only where father absence and patrilocality were *both* present.

Munroe and Munroe (1971) investigated the consequences of sex-role identity in societies with strong mother–child ties and yet *no* initiation rituals for males. They hypothesized that males in sex-role conflict will not behave in grossly effeminate ways but that there would be elements in the behavioral repertoire that would be feminized. Because pregnancy confers special status on females, it would not be unexpected to find males exhibiting female pregnancy symptoms. In the general anthropological literature, there are numerous examples of male symptomatology and couvade (male birth pains). This interesting cultural phenomenon is found in diverse groups such as the Wageo of New Guinea, the Chagga of East Africa, and several South American Indian groups. Munroe studied four contiguous African societies all of which reported frequent pregnancy symptoms. Of these four—two Bantu-speaking, one Kalenjiin, and a Nilotic group—only the Nilotic failed to have male circumcision and initiation rituals. Interestingly, not only did these males experience more symptoms (4.7 as compared to 1.5 for the other groups) such as vomiting, lassitude, food cravings, but more than half experienced something akin to labor pains during the wife's parturition. In another study, Munroe and Munroe (1973) tested the hypothesis concerning covert feminization and male pregnancy symptoms on three diverse groups:

American white lower class males, Black Caribs, and the Logoli of Africa. In a sample of 200 white American males, the researchers found that 41% experienced female symptomatology. The researchers used two separate measures for covert feminization—the Franch Drawing Completion Test and preferred T.V. viewing. This latter measure was obtained by comparing general female television choices with the choices of the group. Whereas the control group tended to pick more violent shows as well as variety and panel shows, the research males and general female population tended to pick "Doctor" type shows, shows involving the intricacies of human relations, and the less violent detective shows. In terms of early experience, there was a significant association ($p < .05$) between early father absence and the presence of symptoms.

The Black Carib of British Honduras practice the couvade as a cultural given. About 92% of the males interviewed reported severe pregnancy symptoms. Even in that society which demands male symptomatology as a cultural pattern, there is a high correlation between male father absence and the severity of symptoms.

The Logoli, a Bantu-speaking people, also practice the couvade, but for this group there is no statistical association between father absence and the presence of symptoms. Two factors may affect this finding: (a) there was a very small sample of males interviewed; and (b) there is a rather low level of interaction between father and son as a cultural norm.

In all of the cross-cultural data, there must necessarily arise certain methodological problems. Certainly, the Whiting material has been severely criticized, for example, by LeVine (1973), Harris (1968), and Parker, Smith, and Ginat (1975). This last article is a counterstudy which attempts to show that there is in fact no relationship between father absence and sex-role identification. Although the article offers an extensive and comprehensive review of the theory as well as relevant literature, the authors, by selective editing, leave one with the impression that the major works in the area of father absence have been repudiated by their authors.

Nevertheless, Parker et al. cite an interesting study conducted in a polygynous Mormon community in the Southwest, which shows early and consistent sex-role identity even within a father-absent polygynous household. One might argue, however, that these boys cannot really be considered "father absent." Parker et al. point out that when the father is absent, the other males serve as father surrogates. More importantly, the total thrust of the mother's home life is to impress on the children the importance of their father, to learn songs to please him on his return, and in general to reiterate that in all things men are more important than women. Among the group, it is said that "if a man earns $1.00 and a woman earns $1,000.00 then the man is richer because he now has $1001.00." In such a society, one would not be amazed to find a high degree of consistent sex-role identity for males. What we see functioning here is the concept of psychological presence. MacCubben (1976) in studying children separated from the father in war found that the psychological presence of the father fostered by the mother (e.g., by discussing him, writing letters to him, drawing pictures for him, telling children what the father would or would not approve of) remarkably reduced the effects of father absence during wartime.

One other finding that Parker et al. hypothesized would not be present in the Mormon community was the male "protest" behavior. This is not surprising, and if one returns to Whiting's paradigm one would suppose that a culture that elects a highly theocratic, male-dominated pattern of life would not at the same time produce excessive delinquency patterns. However, this is not to say that there is a dearth of material linking sex-role conflict and masculine protest behavior; recent work indicates that there are very real associations between these variables (Montare & Boone, 1980).

Deviant Behavior and Father Absence

Much has been hypothesized about the relationship between father absence and delinquency. The studies dealing with the United States population have not really found consistent significant correlation between actual deviance leading to arrest and conviction and father absence. Barry, Bacon, and Child (1957), on the other hand, found that the rate of personal crime such as assault, murder, rape, suicide, sorcery, and the making of false accusations is highest in societies with exclusive mother–infant sleeping arrangements. Again, these data may be one of the weakest arguments in trying to link father absence with aggression as the total cultural factor of crowded quarters has also been used to show that where aggressive behavior would be overly destructive to the total group, it is more rigidly controlled. The most important finding in the area of father absence and deviance seems to be in the study done by Hoffman (1971) on the correlation between father absence and the development of conscience. Presenting Kohlbergian tasks to seventh graders in the United States, Hoffman discovered that boys lacking close paternal contact also scored lower on all the moral indices. They were significantly lower for internal moral judgment, guilt following transgression, and acceptance of blame than were father-present boys. Such a pattern of behavior could clearly lead to antisocial behavior although it has not been determined that it in fact does (Parikh, 1980). However, such studies lead one to wonder about what happens when societies with high father–son interaction suddenly reverse that relationship (Moffitt, 1981; Shill, 1981). The psychological literature is full of reports of the effect of even relatively short-term military-induced separations. In a discussion of Nazism, Selzer (1976) reviews an interesting theory put forth by Wangh immediately after World War II. Using some biographical data, he suggests that Hitler's political movement attracted young men who had suffered the psychological effect of double father loss: that is, the initial loss of the male figure when the father went off to fight World War I and the psychological loss when the father returned a defeated soldier incapable of solving the economic problems facing him. Although the data are sketchy, it is one more attempt to offer new insights into what produced this bizarre event in our own time. A close look at family structure in wartime certainly does show that father loss seems to be quite traumatic for all concerned but maybe slightly more so for young girls. Hetherington (1972) found that the effect on girls in adolescence depended on the type of father loss: Loss through divorce tended to lead to more promiscuous behavior and unwanted pregnancy, whereas loss through death resulted in girls with poor heterosexual relations and unrealistic expectations of males. None of the Hetherington data show early traumatic effects on females. However, Marberg and Susz (1972) present the case of a 2-year-old girl living in a kibbutz who lost her father in the Six Days' War. Anath was a well-adjusted, happy child, reared primarily with parent surrogates and interacting with her 30-year-old parents for the typical few hours at bedtime. The loss of the father completely traumatized the child for 4 years, she frequently referred to herself as crippled by the loss of the father and had serious difficulties with the entire oedipal stage. Stolorow and Lachmann (1975) report on a young woman who lost her father in a concentration camp at age 4. The long-term effect of this disruption of the oedipal phase resulted in malfunctioning of the ego and superego formation, libidinal development, self-image, and sexual identity in previously hypothesized directions. Needless to say, both case histories are probably extreme and certainly aggravated by the surrounding social disruption of war, yet other studies on mental illness, suicide, and emotional disturbances suggest that father absence plays a significant role in precipitating these behaviors (e.g., Lange & Trubsbach, 1969; Tseng, 1973). Recent studies further point up the problems faced by father-absent girls in terms of their own mothering ability (Elrod & Crase, 1980; Parish & Dostal, 1980; Uddenberg & Englessen, 1980).

Achievement Orientation

Many of the more severe consequences of father absence are not surprisingly moderated by the behavior of the mother. Nonetheless, Hecksher's (1967) study of lower class Barbadian families found that mothers in nuclear families visited schools more often, gave more rewards for good school work, and held out higher specific aspirations for their children. Interestingly, little difference was found in the amount of control over the child in terms of punishment. Overall, the nuclear mother was higher in achievement orientation for her child than was the single mother. The question of achievement and the need to achieve has been discussed at length by McClelland (1967). In his research, McClelland found high need achievement was positively correlated with moderate risk taking, nongambling, ability to recognize one's own ability, refusal to enter a situation unless one can exercise control based on one's own ability, and intrinsic motivation. McClelland points out that these behaviors are rewarded in parent–child interactions from the onset of the socialization process. It has also been demonstrated that fathers of high need achieving boys favor and reward early independence in their sons. Rosen (1962), using a Brazilian population, points out that in homes where there is an authoritarian father-centered family, there is also lower need to achieve. It is hypothesized that these families tend to thwart self-reliant and autonomous behavior. Bradburn (1963) using a Turkish population concurs with the previously cited research. However, several studies, including Hunt and Hunt, 1975, have found that boys from father-absent homes in the United States do less well in achievement motivation. There does seem to be a real black–white difference in terms of this variable (Parker et al., 1975). In the Hunt study, even when controlling for social class, white father-absent boys were characterized by greater withdrawal from conventional paths of success and adult responsibility. They also experienced lower esteem as well as weakened sex-role identity. However, father-absent black males showed no important effect on conventional achievement such as school performance, educational aspirations, and marital aspirations. In fact, father-absent boys in the black population had more conventional aspiration than did father-present black males. These data give further confirmation of Liebow's (1967) notion of "shadow values." This term suggests that members of disadvantaged subcultures may actively aspire to the dominant values but do not internalize those values and, in fact, are more affected by the immediate social structure which makes the male presence a "marginal appendage." For further research on this subject see Boss, 1980, on family dysfunction.

This black–white difference was again studied by Worthy and Markle (1970). Internal motivation was measured by self-paced versus reactive sports. It was expected that a father-present boy would be more self-paced and thus a better pitcher than batter in baseball or a better scorer on free throws than in game action in basketball. Using statistics from professional baseball as well as from both college and professional basketball, they found whites significantly higher than blacks in self-paced activity, and in both cases the association is related to the variable of early father absence. In this study, the measure of father absence is rather weak as not all players were interviewed in depth and father presence and absence were inferred from general biographical data.

Another study of the long-range effects of father absence was carried out by Carlsmith (1973) using Harvard sophomores many of whom had experienced father absence during early childhood (World War II). Not only did father-absent boys score consistently higher on verbal rather than math scores for the SAT (Scholastic Aptitude Test), but they also showed greater delay in picking careers, expected to stay longer in college, and in general put off important life decisions.

Obviously, as compelling as much of this research seems to be, there are many problems involved. One of the major issues is the fallacy of attempting to hinge single factor explanations on complex phenomena. More importantly, there is the very real issue of the validity of the methodology used in cross-cultural research—for example, the selection of variables from widely divergent sources and the problem of coding once the selections of cultures are completed.

There are obvious areas of further research in terms of both more cross-cultural comparisons and investigations of what alternate family structures modify the effect of father absence. It is also important to further explore what appears to be a black–white difference in the data collected in the United States. Overall, however, it can be seen that the renewed interest in fathering may be more beneficial than we might have guessed.

References

Badaines, J. Identification, imitation, and sex-role preference in father-present and father-absent Black and Chicano boys. *Journal of Psychology,* 1976, *92*(1), 15–24.

Barry, H. S., Bacon, M. K., & Child, I. L. A cross-cultural survey of some differences in socialization. *Journal of Abnormal and Social Psychology,* 1957, *55,* 327–332.

Biller, H. B. The mother–child relationship and the father absent boy's personality development. *Merrill-Palmer Quarterly of Behavior and Development,* 1971, *17,* 227–241.

Blanchard, R. W., & Biller, H. B. Father availability and performance among third grade boys. *Developmental Psychology,* 1971, *4,* 301–305.

Boss, P. G. The relationship of psychological father presence, wife's personal qualities and wife/family dysfunction in families of missing fathers. *Journal of Marriage and the Family,* 1980, *42*(3), 541–549.

Bradburn, N. M. Achievement and father dominance in Turkey. *Journal of Abnormal and Social Psychology,* 1963, *67,* 464–468.

Brown, J. K. A cross-cultural study of female menstruation rites. *American Anthropologist,* 1963, *65,* 837–853.

Burton, R. V. Cross-sex identity in Barbados. *Developmental Psychology,* 1972, *6,* 365–374.

Carlsmith, L. Some personality characteristics of boys separated from their fathers during World War II. *Ethos,* 1973, *1*(4), 466–477.

Cohen, G. Absentee husbands in spiralist families. *Journal of Marriage and the Family,* 1977, *39*(3), 595–604.

D'Andrade, R. Anthropological studies of dreams. In F. Hsu, *Psychological Anthropology*, Homewood, Ill.: Dorsey Press, 1961.

Elrod, M. M., & Crase, S. J. Sex differences in self-esteem and parental behavior. Psychological Reports, 1980, *46*(3, Pt. 1), 719–727.

Erikson, E. H. *Childhood and society* (2nd ed.). New York: Norton, 1963.

Freud, S. [Totem and taboo] Translated by A. A. Brill. New York: Random, 1938.

Freund, K., Langevin, R., Zajac, Y., Steiner, B., & Zajac, A. Parent–child relationships in transsexual and non-transsexual homosexual males. *British Journal of Psychiatry*, 1974, *124*, 22–23.

Goldstein, H. Internal controls in aggressive children from father present and father absent families. *Journal of Consulting and Clinical Psychology*, 1972, *39*, 512–514.

Harris, M. *The rise of anthropological theory*. New York: Crowell, 1968.

Heckscher, B. T. Household structure and achievement orientation in lower class Barbadian families. *Journal of Marriage and the Family*, 1967, *29*(3), 521–526.

Hetherington, E. M. Effects of father absence on personality development in adolescent daughters. *Developmental Psychology*, 1972, *7*, 313–326.

Hoffman, L. W., & Hoffman, M. L. *Review of child development research*. New York: Russell Sage Foundation, 1966.

Hoffman, M. L. Father absence and conscience development. *Developmental Psychology*, 1971, *4*, 400–405.

Hunt, L. L., & Hunt, J. G. Race and the father–son connection: The conditional relevance of father absence for the orientations and identities of adolescent boys. *Social Problems*, 1975, *23*(1), 35–52.

Kardiner, A. *The individual and his society*. New York: Columbia University Press, 1939.

Lange, E., & Trubsbach, G. Details regarding courses of development, social surroundings and familial structure of 100 youthful habitual drinkers in Dresden who were arrested. *Psychiatrie, Neurologie und Medizinische Psychologie*, 1969, *21*(8), 311–317.

Lecorgne, L. L., & Laosa, L. M. Father absence in low-income Mexican-American families: Children's social adjustment and conceptual differentiation of sex role attributes. *Developmental Psychology*, 1976, *12*(5), 470–471.

Lefley, H. P. Model Personality in the Bahamas. *Journal of Cross-Cultural Psychology*, 1972, *3*(2), 135–147.

LeVine, R. A. Cross-cultural studies in child psychology. In P. H. Mussen (Ed.), *Carmichael's manual of child psychology* (Vol. 2). New York: Wiley, 1970.

LeVine, R. A. *Culture, behavior and personality*. Chicago: Aldine, 1973.

Liebow, E. *Talley's corner*. Boston: Little Brown, 1967.

Lifshitz, M. Long range effects of father's loss: The cognitive complexity of bereaved children and their school adjustment. *British Journal of Medical Psychology*, 1976, *49*(2), 189–197.

McClelland, D. C. *The achieving society*. New York: Free Press, 1967.

McCubbin, H. I., Dahl, B., Lester, G. G., Benson, D., & Robertson, M. L. Coping repertoires of families adapting to prolonged war-induced separations. *Journal of Marriage and the Family*, 1976, *38*(3), 461–471.

Marberg, H. M., & Susz, E. Development of a kibbutz girl who lost her father at the age of two years. *Acta Paedopsychiatrica*, 1972, *39*(3), 59–66.

Martindale, C. Father's absence, psychopathology and poetic eminence. *Psychological Reports*, 1972, *31*(3), 843–847.

Mead, M. *Sex and temperament in three societies*. New York: Marrow, 1935.

Mertz, R. E. The effect of father absence on the development of psychological differentiation among male black Carib students in Belize. *Dissertation Abstracts International*, 1977, *37*(12-A, Pt. 1), 7642–7643.

Moffitt, T. E. Vocabulary and arithmetic performance of father absent boys. *Child Study Journal,* 1981, *10*(4), 233–241.

Montare, A., & Boone, S. L. Aggression and paternal absence: Racial-ethic differences among inner-city boys. *Journal of Genetic Psychology,* 1980, *137*(2), 223–232.

Morval, M. Drawings of the family by children deprived of the father. *Enfance,* 1975, *1,* 37–46.

Munroe, R. L., & Munroe, R. H. Male pregnancy symptoms and cross-sex identity in three societies. *Journal of Social Psychology,* 1971, *84*(1), 11–25.

Munroe, R. L., & Munroe, R. H. Psychological interpretation of male initiation rites: The case of male pregnancy symptoms. *Ethos,* 1973, *1*(4), 490–498.

Nelson, E. A., & MacCoby, E. E. The relationship between social development and differential abilities on the Scholastic Aptitude Test. *Merrill-Palmer Quarterly,* 1966, *12*(4), 269–284.

Parikh, B. Development of moral judgment and its relation to family environmental factors in Indian and American families. *Child Development,* 1980, *51*(4), 1030–1039.

Parish, T. S., & Dostal, J. W. Relationships between evaluations of self and parents by children from intact and divorced families. *Journal of Psychology,* 1980, *104*(1), 35–38.

Parker, S., Smith, J., & Ginat, J. Father absence and cross-sex identity: The puberty rites controversy revisited. *American Ethnologist,* 1975, *2*(4), 687–706.

Rosen, B. C. The achievement syndrome and economic growth in Brazil. *Social Forces,* 1964, *42,* 341–354.

Santrock, J. W. Influence of onset and type of paternal absence on the first four Eriksonian developmental crises. *Developmental Psychology,* 1970, *3,* 273–274.

Santrock, J. W. Relation of type and onset of father absence to cognitive development. *Child Development,* 1972, *43,* 455–469.

Selzer, M. Psychohistorical approaches to the study of Nazism. *Journal of Psychohistory,* 1976, *4*(2), 215–224.

Shill, M. T.A.T. measures of gender identity (castration anxiety) in father absent males. *Journal of Personality Assessment,* 1981, *45*(2), 136–146.

Stolorow, R. D., & Lachmann, F. M. Early object loss and denial: Developmental considerations. *Psychoanalytic Quarterly,* 1975, *44*(4), 596–611.

Tseng, W. S. Psychopathologic study of obsessive-compulsive neurosis in Taiwan. *Comprehensive Psychiatry,* 1973, *14*(2), 139–150.

Uddenberg, N., & Englessen, I. Perception of mother in four-and-a-half-year-old children: A comparison with the mother's social and emotional history. *International Journal of Behavioral Development,* 1980, *3*(1), 27–45.

Waipuldanya, & Lockwood, D. *I, the Aboriginal.* New York and Cleveland: The World Publishing Company, 1970.

Whiting, J. W. M. Socialization process and personality. In F. Hsu (Ed.), *Psychological anthropology.* Homewood, Ill.: Dorsey Press, 1961.

Whiting, J. W. M., & Child, I. *Child training and personality.* New Haven: Yale University Press, 1953.

Whiting, J. W. M., Kluchhorn, C., & Anthony, A. The function of male initiation ceremonies at puberty. In E. Maccoby, T. M. Newcomb, & E. L. Hartley (Eds.), *Readings in social psychology.* New York: Holt, 1958.

Wohlford, P., & Liberman, D. Effect of father absence on personal time, field independence and anxiety. *Proceedings of the Annual Convention of the American Psychological Association,* 1970, *5*(Pt. 1), 263–264.

Worthy, M., & Markle, A. Racial differences in reactive versus self-paced sports activities. *Journal of Personality and Social Psychology,* 1970, *10*(3), 439–443.

Young, F., & Bacdayan, A. Menstrual taboos and social rigidity. In C. S. Ford (Ed.), *Cross cultural approaches: Readings in comparative research.* New Haven: H.R.A.F., 1967.

III

Issues in Applied
Psychological Research

This part of the book includes several chapters that report on the practical application of new techniques in learning styles for various age groups in education. In the first chapter, Alice Sterling Honig gives a cross-cultural overview of certain childrearing and educational practices. She concludes by emphasizing the need for innovative learning styles for children and adults to learn together, so that children may be prepared to face the future. The next chapter is contributed by Peter F. Merenda, who introduces the Rhode Island Pupil Identification Scale (RIPIS), the purpose of which is to identify schoolchildren with learning problems, particularly at the kindergarten level and in the first and second grades. The scale was successfully extended to include cross-cultural dimensions, and the chapter reports and discusses results obtained and problems encountered in Iran and in Italy. In the next chapter coauthors Ann M. Marmorale and Fred Brown advance some constructive suggestions regarding the interpretation of a series of intelligence test scores of public schoolchildren. These suggestions are based on research in which the Wechsler Intelligence Scale for Children was administered to black, white, and Puerto Rican children in the first grade and readministered to these same children in the third grade. Only the Puerto Rican children showed significant increments in all retest IQs. These results were explained in terms of culturally determined responses to cognitive tasks. Two different problems were encountered with African children by the authors of the following two chapters. Coauthors Sara Harkness and Charles M. Super explain problems that have been noted in test-related behavior of young children in Western Kenya, from the perspective of the larger cultural values *of obedience and respect. The behavior patterns were acquired with the early socialization practices that emphasize comprehension rather than verbal production. Daniel A. Wagner deals with issues of traditional and modern Quranic pedagogy. Today, the* msid *functions as a preschool for many Moroccan children, and Wagner explores the consequences that teaching/ learning styles employed in Quranic pedagogy may have for children's development of reading and writing skills. He points out the potential value of studies of Quranic schooling for future research on cognitive styles, learning, bilingualism, and literacy. The next author, Pierre R. Dasen, reviews the use of Flavell and Wohlwill's competence–performance model in cross-cultural Piagetian psychology. He proposes that training paradigms can help to differentiate competence from performance: Rapid learning indicates that training actualized an already existing competence. The results of eight training studies are summarized, in order to assess the occurrence of actualization in three populations (Baffin Island, Canada; Ivory Coast, West Africa; Kenya, East Africa), and with three concrete operational concepts. Hugh Mehan and Margaret M. Riel contributed the last chapter in Part III, which compares instructional strategies used by teachers and students in a classroom setting. Their observations call into question the usual distinction made between formal and informal teaching, as well as the association of the verbal modality of instructions with the former, and the nonverbal modality of instructions with the latter. The main conclusions were concerned with the direct consequences for the education of children of lower classes or of ethnic minorities. Furthermore, there may be functionally equivalent ways and procedures of communicating information by people from different cultural backgrounds.*

Caregivers and Children Learning Together: A Cross-Cultural View

ABSTRACT

The Year of the Child has sparked an inquiry into how communities can help parents rear their children in ways more suited to preparing them for lives in the future. New methods of rearing will involve a conceptualization of active learning on the part of parents in order to help the children become learners who can find their way in the technologically complex and humanly interrelated society of the future. The importance of understanding the relation of values, beliefs, and techniques as impediments to or facilitators of change toward new parenting styles is explored. Margaret Mead's expectation that a "prefigurative" society would be easy to build is analyzed. The ways in which some cultures carry out more sensitive rearing at certain stages, such as infancy, are documented. The importance of institutional support by educators and politicians in helping parents change to more interactive ways of rearing is stressed. Specific suggestions are made to encourage such support.

The Year of the Child has come and gone across the nations of the world. How much has happened at national or family policy levels to increase adult sensibilities to help children develop well and learn well? As long as adults think that a young child's learning and growing into adulthood are rooted exclusively or pre-eminently on adult modes and understandings and inputs handed down from the past, perhaps realistically there will be but a slim chance for the changes that are needed so that children can grow up prepared for, and equipped to cope with, the world of the future.

Margaret Mead, in her thoughtful essay "Culture and Commitment" (1970) looked at three views of the relation between adults and children.

CROSS-CULTURAL RESEARCH AT ISSUE

She characterized these cultural configurations as postfigurative, cofigurative, and prefigurative. In a postfigurative culture, a group of people consisting of at least three generations takes the culture for granted, so that as children grow they accept unquestioningly whatever is unquestioned by those around them. A cofigurative culture is one in which the prevailing model for members of the society is the behavior of their peers.

Mead did not advocate the abdication of parents and grandparents from the role of teachers and socializers of young people. Instead, she called for a new conceptualization of how adults and young people together could help formulate new ways of rearing:

> The children, the young, must ask the questions that we would never think to ask, but enough trust must be re-established so that the elders will be permitted to work with them on the answers. . . . We can change into a prefigurative culture, consciously, delightedly, and industriously, rearing unknown children for an unknown world. . . . [We need] to build a prefigurative culture in which the past is instrumental rather than coercive [pp. 74–75].

Mead's brave, categorical assertion that "we can change . . . delightedly and industriously" to rear children for the future is, I believe, somewhat simplistic and open to serious question.

This presentation will analyze some of the difficulties that may militate against putting into practice this conceptualization of caregivers and children learning together and from each other in ways that will ensure the child a chance at success in coping with the world of the future. Suggestions will be offered as to how this process might be facilitated.

Cultural Variables in Relation to Chances for Change

What are the tools for analysis that we need in order to understand the environments for living and learning at present offered to or imposed on young children in different cultures? In assessing impediments to or supports for change in childrearing, examination of current *values, beliefs,* and *techniques* can elucidate cultural differences in caregiver choices, sanctions, preferences, and taboos (Whiting, 1968).

Ultimately, the quality of education that young people around the world receive at home and in school may depend on a radically new human viewpoint. The viewpoint here espoused perceives the *caregiver as an active participant, within each distinctive cultural milieu, in learning about each child in order to become a prime facilitator of that child's optimal development.* Thus, it is important to analyze how values and beliefs currently shape childrearing and teaching practices and techniques in different cultures.

Otherwise, advocating a new world view of childbearing may leave caregivers either indifferent or threatened, depending upon how the advocacy is presented or implemented.

Values and Childrearing Practices

In any given culture, one or another socialization goal for children may be considered to be good or bad, more important or less so. A hierarchy of values will be implicated in the varieties of practices and programs available for young children or in the neglect of many rearing practices assumed important in another culture. Values held about young children permeate the social systems in which children are reared and profoundly influence practices used.

In some societies parents highly value independence. Erikson (1950) reports an episode where a Papago grandfather asked his 3-year-old granddaughter to shut the lodge door. Although the little one could at first barely budge the door, the adult waited patiently. Eventually the child succeeded in moving and closing the heavy door. The grandfather knew that children need time to accomplish difficult yet not insurmountable tasks. He encouraged autonomy and achievement through his patience and courtesy yet did not take away the pride in independent accomplishment by expecting too little of the child or doing the task for her.

Valuing a child as a source of subtle and not-so-subtle information about how best to meet that child's needs as a learner can enhance the efficacy of an adult in meeting those needs, whether in the home, the classroom, the community, or the nation. Sarason and Doris (1979) have noted, apropos of working with developmentally delayed persons, that the conditions for learning and growth must be for the server in order to affect the served. This precept can be applied to caregivers of children, and can serve as a caveat for change agents who work with parents and children.

Importance of Beliefs

Knowledge of adult beliefs about children can enhance our understanding of parent practices. Yet only in recent times have data become available to test a variety of beliefs about childrearing. Bell and Ainsworth (1972) have found that infants under 9 months whose crying was responded to promptly, whose needs were met promptly and perceptively, and who were given floor freedom to explore their living space, cried less during the last quarter of the first year of life. Such children were also more compliant and obedient to adult requirements in the second year of life. Mothers who use warmer voices in giving commands and who handle their babies more gently have infants who at 21 months are more compliant and cooperative, not only with their mothers but also with an infant tester and an adult play partner (Londerville & Main, 1981). Clearly, the old belief that picking up a baby will "spoil" the baby is not sustained by research.

Spare the rod and spoil the child is another age old belief. Yet research shows that children whose parents use physical punishment frequently, particularly in response to child aggressive behaviors, may be less competent (Carew, Chan, & Halfar, 1976; Matas, Arend, & Sroufe, 1978) and engage in more delinquent behaviors (Welsh, 1974).

Scientific studies thus may provide one way to help change ineffective beliefs. But adults have to believe that research is "good" or "useful." The opposite of such a belief is present quite often. In fact, among poverty and minority groups there may be great suspiciousness of researchers, regardless of their findings, and in some instances, because of their findings.

Sadly enough, the scientific community has not always elected to base its childrearing advice on research findings. Sometimes social scientists have given advice based mostly on their personal beliefs. One can only speculate with regret on the numbers of young children and their parents adversely affected by psychologist John Watson's professional advice, that the only sensible way to treat young children was as young adults. They should *never* be hugged, kissed, or held!

Parent Discipline Techniques and Early Learning

Discipline techniques that developmental theorists would characterize as inimical to the good emotional foundation for growth necessary for young children are widespread in many cultures. Strict and unquestioning obedience to adults is the highest valued goal for childrearing in many societies. Additionally, some societies may hold strong beliefs that the best ways to achieve such goals are to whip or frighten "bad habits" out of a child. Such pervasive beliefs may be accompanied by a lack of perceptivity to children's emotional needs. Nyansongo mothers, for example, believe that "if you want to teach a child anything you must cane him [LeVine & LeVine, 1963, p. 167]."

Among the Tarong in the Philippines, the most common threat invoked is the Wawak, a bogeyman who comes to take (kill, eat, etc.) bad children. The impression must be overpowering. "A painted wood Wawak mask is [put on] by one woman [who stalks] the barrio at dusk so that children will be good and kind and not selfish any more. . . . Children watch the apparition paralyzed, then run screaming to their mothers who hide and protect them, extracting promises of future good behavior in return [Nydegger & Nydegger, 1963, p. 830]."

Such techniques are not at all confined to nonwestern societies. In western countries, dire warnings about assorted professionals such as doctors, teachers, and social workers have been used to scare children into obedience. As overly fearful children have been found clinically to have less felicitous mental health histories, it might be more conducive to world mental health if childrearers less often resorted to invoking retaliatory evil ghosts, strangers, etc. in response to child behaviors not approved of. Adults in many cultures have learned that children may be terrified into obedience by such tactics. It does not seem surprising from a clinical point of view that children may later grow up to be reluctant to cooperate with "strangers"—from "foreign" places, from different tribal groups, or ethnic or religious minorities—in solving civic problems across and within nations.

It is extremely difficult to change widely held beliefs about the best ways to ensure child compliance. Research findings tend to confirm in home settings that frequent adult commands and prohibitions actually lead to greater noncompliance (Lytton & Zwirner, 1975). In a study (Honig, 1980a) of the interactions in day-care settings between caregivers and toddlers from low-income families, when teachers used control or negative techniques, compliance was slightly under 60%. When teachers used positive techniques, such as teaching, refocusing a child on an activity, or facilitating children, then compliance was about 77%. Ego-boosts got over 90% compliance. Praise works!

Obstacles to Change

Sex-Role Stereotypes

The valuing of male children above female children is a serious obstacle to global efforts to achieve more egalitarian ways of rearing children for the future. Throughout most of the developing world, male children are valued far more than female children. This value system may show itself in many ways: "There is a lack of equal opportunity for girls and women, particularly in developing countries. This second-class status begins early in life when girls—and their mothers—receive less of the family's limited food; men and boys eat first [Population Reference Bureau, 1979]."

One of the most prominent indices of this difference—the "valuing" of males' versus females' education—is reported in the UNESCO 1976 Year-book figures on school enrollment in different countries for boys and girls of 6–18 years. In developed countries, such as Japan, the Soviet Union, France, and the United States, over 85% of both sexes are in school at these ages. In Somalia 15% and in Afghanistan 5% of girls are schooled, although in both cases 30% of male children receive schooling. In India, almost 60% of male children are schooled, as opposed to only 36% of female children.

As a result of these conditions, of the world's 800 million illiterate adults, two-thirds are women. Another result is the perpetuation of high birth rates and poverty, as young girls who receive little or no schooling tend to have large families when they marry.

Inconsistencies of Beliefs

No guarantees exist that a cultural group with strong values and beliefs about the importance of infant gratification and attention to infant needs believes that such responsiveness need continue into further stages of early childhood. Indeed, in certain societies, initial indulgence may be followed by sharply severe maternal treatment in childhood years (Whiting & Child, 1953). Analysis of interviews of Korean mothers indicated a trend toward remarkable gratification in early infancy and markedly less indulgence for 3-year-olds (Honig, 1979a).

In Iloco barrios in the Philippines, toddlers are weaned suddenly, without warning, without regard for overwhelming child distress that often ensues. Mothers may apply bitter substances, dung, or pepper to the breast. Abruptly, cheerful, happy toddlers can turn into whining, inconsolable tots under these severe weaning conditions. That this is the way it is seems to be matter-of-factly accepted by the parents (Nydegger & Nydegger, 1963).

Conceptualization of the young child markedly affects rearing attitudes and techniques. Rajput mothers were puzzled by anthropologists' questions about the rearing of young children (Minturn & Hitchcock, 1963). There was nothing much to know about a young child. Early childhood was considered of little importance or interest. The Rajput mother insists that "all children are alike." Parental stimulation, creative play with a child, provision of interesting materials and toys do not occur in the life of a Rajput baby. "Until the child acquires the use of speech (s)he is not considered to be teachable [p. 319]." The child is viewed as a member of a group, an incarnation of a soul reborn many times, rather than a unique biological and psychological being.

Belief Changing

Help from Theory

Erikson's theoretical model of the life cycle may be useful in helping caregivers conceptualize what kinds of supports are most critical during which stages of a child's life. Erikson (1959) suggests that for optimal development, each person goes through a sequence of "phase-specific psychosocial crises." Mutually satisfying parent–infant interactions and nurturing in early infancy help to set up a firm emotional foundation for more cognitively oriented learning of school-age years.

Cross-cultural data suggest that many cultures, particularly in developing countries, give remarkable evidence of the positive outcomes of sensitive parent–infant tunings and mutually pleasurable interactions in the early months of life. Infants are frequently breast-fed on demand. Their needs for body comfort and adult attention are gratified easily as they are often carried on the mother's body for long periods of the day and sleep beside her at night.

In Uganda, Aisnworth (1967) found precocity in sensorimotor development in the first year of life associated with what she characterizes as "the Ganda mother's all-absorbing preoccupation with the infant [p. 329]."

In some polygynous cultures, infant needs are gratified in marvelously attuned ways by mothers who are freed from field or household labor by co-wives who assume many of the chores for which the new mother might otherwise have to take responsibility. Can western societies find other family support systems for nourishing the early development of mother–infant attachment so necessary to later mental health besides the institution of polygyny?

In many developing societies caregivers have learned that tuning in to babies to meet their needs promptly in the first year of life helps ensure survival and healthy development of babies. It is ironic that in "advanced" countries, where infant survival is not so problematic because of improved hygiene, babies may sometimes be more at risk for emotional deprivation and later child abuse.

Help from Research

Research findings emphasize the importance and advantages of early mutual learnings and adjustments between caregivers and infants. Middle-class mothers in the United States who often initiated affectionate contacts and were sensitive to infant signals tended to have babies who were emotionally well-balanced (Ainsworth, 1977).

One of the most systematic cross-cultural efforts to provide research evidence of the effects of infant stimulation was carried out by J. McVickers Hunt and colleagues in Iranian orphanages (1976). In a series of parametric variations on the enrichment theme over several years, Hunt taught caregivers to provide appropriate kinds of stimulation as well as responses to baby vocalizations. In previous decades, such institutional babies showed drastic drops in IQ. Many of these orphans could not sit up well after 1 or

2 years of age. Hunt's most advanced babies were those who received toy play and loving emotional experiences and verbal-responsive games. They tested in the normal range of IQ scores. They were interested and interesting babies—and therefore adoptable—unlike their predecessors.

Beliefs and Educational Practices

Beliefs can affect the quality of early educational experiences. If "almost anybody," especially a female, can care for young children, then society can accept the existence of custodial care services, staffed primarily by untrained and poorly paid female caregivers (Honig, 1977c). Such a belief could thus increase the probability that cycles of poverty and lack of educational preparedness will continue for poor families.

Several years ago, I had the opportunity to visit urban crèches for infants and toddlers in France. In one room, the caregiver was a neighborhood resident, with no training in child development. She had carefully placed all 10 of the babies in infant seats in a circle so that each infant faced outward to a blank wall. In response to a mild inquiry she explained that in this way the babies would stay quiet and tranquil. If they had been positioned facing each other they would have become animated, excited, and tried to move and wave their arms. Her belief that a passive, inert baby is a good baby cannot be easily overcome by simple provision of information about the pleasure and advantages of peer contacts among babies. Indeed, that caregiver had "learned" from observing her babies. She had learned that to achieve her valued goal of a quiet baby she had to find ways to decrease possible social as well as environmental stimulation.

How can social service professionals help caregivers learn new ways of caring for children if goals, values, and beliefs differ so radically? If such caregivers are taught to become better observers of children, they may simply become more ingenious in devising ways to thwart the kinds of developmental learnings that will promote optimal competence and mental health. Mead's championing of the need for new rearing styles takes insufficient account of potentially grim caregiver efforts to keep children from being a trouble to adults rather than to help children develop their full human potential.

Educational Settings and Reciprocity in Learnings

Because so many culture groups value education and many share a belief that schooling is important for children, change agents may find young teachers receptive to new ways of conceptualizing their jobs. Perhaps teacher-training institutions and school systems are one place where a society can begin to put into practice the theory that adults and children need to learn together.

Some innovative educational models of the past decades have reflected the theory that caregivers and children need to be equally implicated and active in a schooling environment (Honig, 1980b). Piagetian theory posits that interactional experiences with people, objects, and activities facilitate learning. A child then constructs his or her own knowledge about how the world works.

The Grugeons (1971) have described an "infant education" program in which these interactional ideas are carried out in certain British schools for children in early primary grades.

> Infinite flexibility and patience, listening to successes and sympathizing, approving, allowing for alternative procedures to encourage the child's enquiry to become fruitful; all these demand skills in relation to young human beings that one supposes are demanded of a scientist on the frontiers of research. Each child has to be adapted to [p. 15].

Learning Together in Chinese Kindergartens

In the People's Republic of China, the development of altruistic behaviors is an important curricular goal for teachers. Teachers elicit awareness of the importance of sharing, caring, and helping through moral lessons and the praising of real life examples. Teachers also value learning from children how best to help children become more altruistic. One teacher reported to the author during a trip to a Kwangchow kindergarten that a certain little boy had been very helpful in school but his parents complained of refusal to help at home. What did the teacher do? Her first response was to take the child aside and ask him about this. Before she could teach the child, she had to learn from the child how he viewed the situation. The preschooler explained that in kindergarten he received a little red star to paste on his chart whenever he was helpful and industrious. At home no stars were forthcoming. Why, then, should he help out? The teacher had a serious and comradely talk with the boy. She explained that "Chairman Mao wanted all citizens to be helpful and cooperate with each other so Chinese people could all do well."

Time and again our group of early childhood educators in visits to nurseries and kindergartens witnessed evidence of adults valuing learning from children as well as teaching children (Honig, 1978). Regularly we asked teachers how they handled problems of slow learning or misbehavior. Often teachers responded that first they would sit down and talk with the children and find out more about the problem. In many cases the teacher made visits to the home and tried to learn more about special circumstances in the child's life that might be contributing to the problem. Chinese society has always valued learning. What we saw that was new was a sense of valuing the mobilization of family and school and personal resources in order to help the child learn better.

Curiously, although Chinese teachers of the very young seemed to believe in the theme of caregivers and children learning together, adolescents were subjected to arbitrary, politically motivated and dictated decisions about their schooling and their careers. Service to the "middle and lower peasants" as well as political approval were required before a youth could get a higher education. Even after such education, job location was government decreed. This was another example of how a culture group may be sensitive to the needs of children at one age and arbitrary at other stages and ages.

Conclusion

New theories are needed to conceptualize the importance of the contributions of children as well as adults in childrearing. New techniques are needed to encourage the process of socializing the young into roles and learning more likely to ensure their fitness for tackling the unknown future in which they will live.

No one culture group has a monopoly on wisdom for implementing such processes. None has solved the problems of political and family change required to help inaugurate and support, on a society-wide level, interactive learning styles for adults and children together.

Research evidence needs to be more vigorously gathered in many cultures to discover what combinations of values, beliefs, and techniques of childrearing are resulting in children who seem to have a firm foundation for successfully growing into the future. One example of such research is the study carried out in the United States by Swan and Stavros (1973). They interviewed parents of black, low-income kindergarten-age children who were doing superbly in school as learners and getting along beautifully with peers and teachers. "The parents' philosophy included encouraging independence of the children and understanding and respecting the child's feelings and point of view. . . . They described their children in a very positive and competent light [Honig, 1979b, p. 12]."

Governments, anthropologists, and child development specialists need to seek out and support these cross-cultural efforts within their own and other nations that at one childhood stage or another do seem to offer aspects of perceptive, signal-sensitive care and teaching which are required to implement what Mead has termed "prefigurative" childrearing.

Research findings can be helpful. But scientific findings need to be wrenched loose from esoteric journals and implications of research lucidly conveyed in daily newspapers and on radio and television. Teachers as well as pediatricians need to have such materials included in their training. Child development specialists and parent workers need to become a part of community service teams to provide parents with new ideas and sensitive training in observing and responding to child cues in order to encourage competency for the future.

Change in techniques is not easy. But without an effort to explain that choices are available and that *caregivers can opt for new choices in child-rearing,* it is unlikely that adults will learn from and with children how to help them grow into the future. Adults will be too assiduously applying the ways of the past.

References

Ainsworth, M. D. S. *Infancy in Uganda: Infant care and the growth of love.* Baltimore: The Johns Hopkins University Press, 1967.

Ainsworth, M. D. D. Social development in the first year of life: Maternal influences on infant–mother attachment. In J. M. Tanner (Ed.), *Developments in psychiatric research: Essays based on the Sir Geoffrey Vickers Lectures of the Mental Health Foundation.* London: Hodder & Staughton, 1977.

Bell, S. M., & Ainsworth, M. D. S. Infant crying and maternal responsiveness. *Child Development,* 1972, *43,* 1171–1190.

Carew, J. V., Chan, I., & Halfar, C. *Observing intelligence in young children.* Englewood Cliffs, N.J.: Prentice-Hall, 1976.

Erikson, E. *Childhood and society.* New York: Norton, 1950.

Erikson, E. Identity and the life cycle: Selected papers. *Psychological issues* (Vol. 1, No. 1). New York: International Universities Press, 1959.

Grugeon, D., & Grugeon, E. *An infant school.* New York: Citation Press, 1971.

Honig, A. S. Comparison of childrearing practices in Japan and in the People's Republic of China: A personal view. *International Journal of Group Tensions,* 1978, *8*(1 & 2), 6–32.

Honig, A. S. *Cross-cultural study of maternal childrearing practices with infants and three-year-olds in five urban groups.* Paper presented at the biennial meeting of the Society for Research in Child Development, San Francisco, April 1979. (a)

Honig, A. S. *Parent involvement in early childhood education* (Rev. ed.). Washington, D.C.: National Association for the Education of Young Children, 1979. (b)

Honig, A. S. Staffing and training in day care: USA. *Journal of Pediatric Psychology,* 1979, *4,* 165–177. (c)

Honig, A. S. *Teacher technique and toddler compliance in five day care settings.* In *Proceedings of the Congres Internationale de Psychologie de l'enfant,* Paris: Presses Universitaires de France, 1980. (a)

Honig, A. S. The preschool child and you—learning together. *Young Children,* 1980, *35*(4), 2–12. (b)

Hunt, J. McV., Mohandessi, K., Ghodssi, M., & Akiyama, M. The psychological development of orphanage-reared infants: Interventions with outcomes (Tehran). *Genetic Psychology Monograph,* 1976, *94,* 177–226.

LeVine, B. A., & LeVine, B. B. Nyansongo: A Gusii community in Kenya. In B. B. Whiting (Ed.), *Six cultures: Studies of childrearing.* New York: Wiley, 1963.

Londerville, S., & Main, M. Security of attachment, compliance, and material training methods in the second year of life. *Developmental Psychology,* 1981, *17,* 289–299.

Lytton, H., & Zwirner, W. Compliance and its controlling stimuli observed in a natural setting. *Developmental Psychology,* 1975, *11,* 769–779.

Matas, L., Arend, R. A., & Sroufe, L. A. Continuity of adaptation in the second year: The relationship between quality of attachment and later competence. *Child Development,* 1978, *49*(3), 547–556.

Mead, M. *Culture and commitment: A study of the generation gap.* Garden City, N.Y.: Doubleday, 1970.

Minturn, L., & Hitchcock, J. T. The Rajputs of Khalapur, India. In B. B. Whiting (Ed.), *Six Cultures: Studies of childrearing.* New York: Wiley, 1963.

Nydegger, W. F., & Nydegger, C. Tarong: An Ilicos barrio in the Philippines. In B. B. Whiting (Ed.), *Six cultures: Studies of childrearing.* New York: Wiley, 1963.

Population Reference Bureau. *Children of the world: Rights and realities.* Washington, D.C., 1979.

Sarason, S., & Doris, J. *Educational handicaps, public policy and social history.* New York: Free Press, 1979.

Swan, R. W., & Stavros, H. Childrearing practices associated with the development of cognitive skills of children in low socio-economic areas. *Early Child Development and Care,* 1973, *2,* 23–38.

Welsh, R. S. *Severe parental punishment and delinquency: A developmental theory.* Paper presented at the meeting of the American Psychological Association, New Orleans, September 1974.

Whiting, J. Methods and problems in cross-cultural research. In G. Lindzey & E. Aronson (Eds.), *Handbook of social psychology* (Vol. 1). Reading, Mass.: Addison-Wesley, 1968, 693–728.

Whiting, J., & Child, I. *Child training and personality.* New Haven: Yale University Press, 1953.

The Rhode Island Pupil Identification Scale (RIPIS) in Cross-Cultural Perspective

ABSTRACT

The Rhode Island Pupil Identification Scale (RIPIS) is a teacher observational scale for classroom use, primarily at the levels of kindergarten and grades 1 and 2. The scale consists of 21 items in Part I which relate to observable classroom behavior of children, and 19 items in Part II which relate essentially to written work produced by pupils as part of their classroom work. The RIPIS was first released for operational use in the United States in 1972. Beginning in 1974, a number of cross-cultural studies were initiated in a variety of countries with the collaboration of an interested psychologist in each country. These countries include Brazil, Denmark, Great Britain, Haiti, Iran, Israel, Italy, Poland, and Taiwan.

Two common sets of objectives have been established in these cross-cultural studies. Accompanying each objective are sets of options to follow depending upon the degree to which the objectives would be met. One possibility is that the factorial structure revealed in the original form standardized in the United States will also reveal itself in the foreign language forms applied to the respective cultures. If this is the case, it is proposed to apply the RIPIS in the culture in which factorial invariance is demonstrated in much the same way it is used in the United States. Alternatively, it is possible that the original factorial structure will be approached, but not necessarily completely overlapped, by the structure revealed by the foreign language–culture version in question. In that event both a renorming of the subscales and a restructuring of the full RIPIS will become necessary.

The major portion of the chapter reports and discusses results obtained—and problems encountered—with the RIPIS in Italy and Iran, where the greatest progress has been made to date in this extensive cross-cultural research project. An attempt is also made to classify and discuss issues that have emerged in cross-cultural research involving the RIPIS as well as other instruments and techniques.

All rights of reproduction in any form reserved.
ISBN 0-12-044280-9

The Rhode Island Pupil Identification Scale

The Rhode Island Identification Scale (RIPIS) is a teacher observation scale for classroom use, primarily in kindergarten and grades 1 and 2. Its primary functions are (a) to help the classroom teacher identify children with learning problems; (b) to help the classroom teacher indicate more readily, using the scale language, the specific aspects of the school problem requiring attention; and (c) to permit the classroom teacher or the receiving specialist to address himself or herself more efficiently to the resolution of the specific school problem as observed in its natural surroundings (Novack, Bonaventura, & Merenda, 1972).

Characteristics of the Scale

ITEMS

The RIPIS comprises two parts, or clusters of items. The 21 items in Part I of the scale relate to observable classroom behavior; Part II consists of 19 items relating essentially to written work produced by pupils as part of their classroom work. The items reflect types of learning problems or behaviors that are typical of children who are referred for remedial help or for special placement.

Typical item statements for Part I are

Has difficulty cutting
Gives appearance of being tense
Tends to be discouraged

Typical item statements for Part II are

Mirrors and/or reverses letters, numbers, words, or other forms in copying
Runs words or parts of words together when visual stimulation is provided
Makes omissions, substitutions, or reversals of letters, numbers and/or words in reading

Each of forty items are evaluated according to a 5-point Likert-type scale ranging from 1 point (never) to 5 points (always).

FACTORIAL STRUCTURE

The factorial structure of the RIPIS is revealed through 16 principal component analyses with varimax rotation and 16 Rao Canonical Factor Analyses with direct oblimin transformation. The 16 separate analyses arise from one analysis per month over an 8-month period separately for Parts I and II.

A full report of these results can be found in Novack, Bonaventura, and Merenda (1976). As a result of these analyses, the following subscales have been standardized utilizing the original sample (N = 851) for norming the RIPIS on the basis of total scores and Part I and Part II scores.

Part I (67.8% of total variance accounted for)
  Body perception (K = 2)
  Sensory motor coordination (K = 6)
  Attention (K = 3)
  Self-concept (K = 6)
  Memory for events (K = 5)
Part II (69.0% of total variance accounted for)
  Memory for reproduction of symbols (K = 6)
  Directional or positional constancy (K = 3)
  Spatial and sequential arrangement of letters and symbols (K = 5)
  Memory for symbols for cognitive operations (K = 5)

INTERNAL CONSISTENCY

The internal consistency of the RIPIS subscales as well as of Part I and Part II scores has been established on relatively large samples (ranging from 603 to 782) drawn from the original standardization sample on 851 subjects. The statistic used to evaluate the internal consistency of the scales is the Cronbach coefficient alpha. The magnitude of this coefficient ranged from .78 to .95 for Part I subscales; from .79 to .88 for Part II subscales; from .79 to .80 for the Part I scale; and from .82 to .84 for the Part II scale. A full report on the internal consistency analysis of the RIPIS can be found in Merenda, Bonaventura, and Novack (1977).

RELIABILITY

The reliability of the RIPIS is demonstrated for total score by 28 test–retest correlation coefficients (N = 834) for intervals ranging from 1 to 8 months. These coefficients range from .532 (8 months) to .988 (1 month). The full matrix of test–retest reliability coefficients may be found in Novack, Bonaventura, and Merenda (1973). The test–retest reliabilities of the subscales, based on approximately 600 cases, with an interval of 5 months, range from r_{12} = .62 to r_{12} = .79 for the five subscales in Part I; and from r_{12} = .70 to r_{12} = .82 for the four subscales in Part II (Merenda, Bonaventura, & Novack, 1977). Canonical correlation analysis for Parts I and II scores, based on the same samples, with an interval of 5 months, revealed relationship patterns that were all statistically significant with redundancy values all hovering around .600. For Part I, the canonical correlation coefficients range from .448 (fifth) to .822 (first); for Part II, these coefficients range from .555 (fourth) to .851 (first). The complete results may also be found in Merenda, Bonaventura, and Novack (1977), and in Merenda, Novack, and Bonaventura (1981).

VALIDITIES

The validities reported for the RIPIS include concurrent, predictive, and cross-validity results. Criteria for validation include psychological test scores, academic performance measures, educational progress and outcome, and other teacher observation scale scores. All of the validity studies conducted to date have attested to the validity of the RIPIS in predicting or determining the existence of problems that impede the learning progress of young school-children. The design, development, and results of these studies are fully reported in the Manual for the RIPIS (Novack, Bonaventura, & Merenda, 1972) and in Bonaventura (1978).

Foreign Language Forms and the Design of Cross-Cultural Studies

CROSS-CULTURAL COLLABORATION

As information on the RIPIS became disseminated on an international scale through the publication of articles in professional journals and through symposia presented in international conferences,[1] a number of collaborative cross-cultural studies were initiated. It became evident shortly after the release of the RIPIS for operational use in 1973 that an instrument that is valid for the early detection of young schoolchildren with learning problems is of interest to psychologists and educators in foreign countries as well as in the United States. An overwhelming number of requests were received from professionals in a wide variety of countries for collaboration in research that might result in the development of foreign language forms.

In response to these requests, two common sets of objectives have been established along with selection of options to follow depending upon the degree to which the objectives would be met. These objectives and options are

1. The factorial structure revealed in the original and basic form standardized in the United States will also reveal itself in the foreign language forms applied to respective cultures. In setting this objective, it
   is assumed that the structure of the attributes being measured by the
   RIPIS is invariant across cultures. If this objective is met, it is proposed
   to apply the RIPIS in the culture in which factorial invariance is dem-

---

[1] A listing of these conferences at which symposia were presented as well as personal conferences is given in Appendix A.

onstrated in much the same way it is used in the United States. The only change being contemplated is the renorming of the nine scales.

2. The original factorial structure will be approached, but not necessarily completely overlapped, by the structure revealed by the foreign language–culture version in question. This will necessitate not only a renorming of the scales, but also a restructuring of the full RIPIS scale according to the factorial structure revealed in that particular culture.

CROSS-CULTURAL PROGRESS TO DATE

In chronological order, beginning in 1975, cross-cultural research studies on the RIPIS have been initiated in Italy, Israel, Denmark, Iran, Sicily, Great Britain, Poland, Taiwan, Haiti, Brazil, and Turkey. This has required the translation, with adoptive modifications, of the RIPIS (English version) into Italian, Hebrew, Danish, Persian (Farsi), Polish, Chinese, French, Portuguese, and Turkish.[2] The greatest progress to date in analyzing results in accordance with the two objectives elaborated in the preceding section has been with the Italian form based on data gathered in Milan, Italy and in Palermo, Sicily, and with the Persian version based on data from Shiraz, Iran. The French version is being prepared for analysis on the basis of data gathered in the late spring of 1979 and to be gathered in Fall of 1982. Substantial data were gathered on the Chinese form in Taipei in the spring of 1981, but final analysis awaits the inspection of nationwide application of the scale to 1500 schoolchildren in five widely scattered geographical locations in Taiwan in October 1981. Hence, the main discussion of issues encountered in cross-cultural research will be restricted to those experienced with the Italian and Persian forms of the RIPIS. However, generalizations to other foreign language forms not only of the RIPIS, but also of other instruments will be discussed later in this chapter.

PROBLEMS AND ISSUES ENCOUNTERED IN ITALY AND IRAN

Italy. The original Italian version of the RIPIS was developed by D'Amico and his associates in Milan. A sample of 259 pupils in grades 1 and 2 from the Polesine School District was used in investigating the factorial structure of the form. The overlap between the Italian and English versions was found to be quite good. The factor analysis of the Italian version produced nine factors, which is the number consistently revealed in factoring the 21×21 and 19×19 matrices for Parts I and II, respectively, of the English form. Most of the factors overlapped completely; for example, the sensory motor coordination factor. These comparative results are as follows:

---

[2] A listing of the translators of these forms who are the principal collaborators in cross-cultural research studies with the RIPIS is given in Appendix B.

Item	Loadings	
	USA	Italy
1. Has difficulty cutting	.538	.696
2. Has difficulty pasting	.532	.693
5. Has difficulty catching a ball	.753	.817
6. Has difficulty jumping rope	.754	.813
7. Has difficulty tying shoes	.710	.358
8. Has difficulty buttoning buttons	.588	.529

However, some of the factors overlapped only to a certain extent, and one factor, Attention, was surprisingly different, as shown here:

Item	Loadings	
	USA	Italy
9. Has difficulty standing still	.857	.458
10. Has difficulty sitting still	.868	.073
11. Has short attention span	.637	.296
15. Cries [a]	.029	.659
16. Fails to take reprimands well [a]	.478	.777

[a] These two items occur consistently in the self-concept factor in the English version. For the USA sample discussed earlier, the loadings in the self-concept factor for Items 15 and 16 are .732 and .613, respectively.

In addressing herself to the problem revealed by the data shown here for the attention factor, Rosalia R. Sparacino discovered a fault in the translation from English to Italian for Items 9, 10, and 15. For example, the sense of Items 9 and 10 is that the pupils have difficulty in remaining standing or sitting once they have assumed that position whereas the translated version directed the teachers' attention to the act of standing or sitting still. A thorough analysis was made for the Italian form on the basis of the discrepancies revealed by differences in the factorial structures toward the end of preparing a revised version that would correct the faults that had been detected.

A revised version was developed and was administered in the spring of 1978 to a sample of 988 schoolchildren in grades K–2 in four schools in Palermo. A Rao Canonical Factor Analysis with oblique rotation was performed on these data. Although a complete overlap between the United States and Italy factorial structures has still not been found, considerable improvements have resulted from the revisions made to the original Italian form. For example, Items 9 and 10 clustered together as they should, with high rotated factor loadings of .944 and .954, respectively. The research on this form continues, with a third large sample drawn during the 1979–1980 academic year in Palermo for the purpose of providing additional data upon which to base a decision regarding the two objectives discussed earlier.

Iran. The problems encountered so far in the application of the Persian form in Iran are of a different nature than those described for Italy, and they serve to expand upon issues that arise in cross-cultural research. Two major problems were encountered. Rezal Shapurian came to Rhode Island in the fall of 1978 as a visiting scholar on sabbatical leave from Shiraz, Iran with data from two samples drawn before he left and the intention of receiving additional data from colleagues in that country. Unfortunately, as history relates, the political turmoil that took place in that country in 1978–1979 caused both the national public school system and the university system to be shut down for the entire academic year. Hence, the samples which he brought with him were the only ones available for analysis during his stay in the United States. It was further discovered to the dismay of the researchers that the two Iranian samples were markedly discrepant, representing rather opposite extremes. One sample ($N = 33$) was drawn from a public school in an extremely deprived district whereas the other sample ($N = 98$) came from a private school in an upper-class district where the children were brought to school by their "nannies." Obviously, the total sample ($N = 131$) was hopelessly biased, and with the schools closed for the entire year it was impossible to draw additional samples as had been planned to render the total sample much more representative of the total Iranian population of young schoolchildren, as well as to increase its size. Analyses performed on the $N = 131$ and the $N = 98$ samples yielded the expected result: Much less overlap was found to exist among the United States, Italy, and Iran factor structures. It is interesting to note, however, that exactly nine significant factors were extracted—five for Part I and four for Part II, as were found to exist for the English and Italian versions of the RIPIS. No interpretations have been attempted on the basis of these factors, nor will they be attempted until more representative samples can become available to furnish more representative data.

In attempting to analyze the data based on the two restricted samples described here, another discovery was made. One of the items simply is inappropriate for young Iranian schoolchildren, namely, Item 25, "Turns in papers which show erasures." It was discovered that there was something wrong with that item when the factor analysis program failed to continue its computer run after the point of generating the correlation matrix. No correlation coefficients could be calculated between this item and all the remaining items because it possessed zero variance. Further inspection revealed that all of the ratings assigned to this item were "never" for which the scale value was one point. Hence, the ratings for the item yielded a mean of 1 and a standard deviation of 0. In analyzing the cause of this unusual result it was quickly determined that what should have been obvious to the experimenters had been overlooked. The Iranian schoolchildren at that low grade level do not use pencils with erasers. Rather they use ink brushes to write in Farsi, the official Persian language. Therefore, this item was eliminated from the scale and the rerun of the factor analysis computer program produced the output of factors described earlier.

In the preparation of the Persian form, other necessary modifications were recognized and the proper adjustments were made to render the affected items adoptable to the Iranian culture. For example, Item 28 reads "Starts writing in the middle of the paper rather than from the left margin." In writing in the Persian language one starts at the right margin and goes to the left.

Classification of Issues in Cross-Cultural Research

Classification Based on Research with the RIPIS

TRANSLATION

The 40 items appearing on the RIPIS are, in the main, simple declarative statements which for the most part require merely a literal translation from English to the appropriate language. Nonetheless, a serious translation error was committed in the Italian version of the RIPIS. The translations of two items, "Has difficulty standing still" and "Has difficulty sitting still," apparently misled the teachers to focus on the act of standing–sitting rather than on the ability to *remain* in standing–sitting position. When the items were rewritten and the revised form used, the expected results were achieved. A related problem arose with Item 15, "Cries." The straightforward translation to *piange* was correct. However, whereas teachers in the United States interpret this statement as intended, that is, as "cries excessively," Italian teachers evidently interpret it literally. Consequently, in the revised version an explanation of what is being called for was added to the item.

CURRICULUM DIFFERENCES

The RIPIS was designed for use primarily in kindergarten and grades 1 and 2. The reason for this is the belief that learning problems can be detected as early as kindergarten; in 4–5-year-olds problems that may seriously impede learning in later years become observable. However, in some cultures children do not begin their schooling until they are 7 years old. As a consequence, the Danish form has been standardized on older children primarily in grades 1 and 2, and the Iranian data thus far are based on samples that do not include kindergarten children.

CULTURAL FACTORS

The situation that arose relative to Item 25 in the Persian form of the RIPIS was due to a cultural factor. In the early grades, Persian schoolchildren write with a brushlike pen. Hence, statement of the item, "Papers show many erasures," is not appropriate for use in the Iranian culture. It is interesting to note, however, that when the same issue was raised with E. Miao regarding the Chinese form, her response was that no such problem exists. Children in Taiwan use pencils with erasers in learning to write the Chinese characters.

Classification Based on Instruments Other than the RIPIS

Although this chapter deals with cross-cultural issues involving the RIPIS, I feel it may be of interest to discuss issues I have encountered in cross-cultural research with other instruments. Two major cross-cultural research projects I have participated in are entitled "Identification of Talent in Developing Countries: A Project Talent for Sicily" and "Public Perceptions of International Leaders."

A PROJECT TALENT FOR SICILY

This research project was initiated in 1967 through the Laboratory of Applied Psychology, University of Palermo, Sicily. It is designed to identify the latent talents of Sicilian youth and to nurture these talents in fulfilling manpower needs on a national basis. Over the years, the project has been financed through the Council for the International Exchange of Scholars, the Fulbright Commission, the Commission for Cultural Exchange between Italy and the United States, and grants from the Italian National Research Council, as well as from the Scientific Affairs Division of NATO.

In the identification of talent phase of this project, the principal data on subjects have been gathered utilizing psychological test batteries and other psychometric devices including personal history inventories. Among these have been instruments standardized in the United States and translated into Italian. In the translation and adaptation process, certain specific problems arose that were relevant to issues in cross-cultural research.

One such problem illustrated the fact that the influences of cultural differences can never be totally predicted even with careful preplanning. One of the tests in a battery measuring cognitive skills is skill with vocabulary (WVCAI, 1960). In this test the testee is presented with a brief dictionary definition of a word plus the first letter of the word sought followed by a number of blank spaces equal to the number of letters required in completing the word. One of these items in the original form reads: "Money, especially ready money; currency or equivalent paid promptly after purchasing." The correct response is *cash*. In preparing the Italian form, the correct response was indicated by "C _ _ _ _ _ _ _," an eight-letter word beginning with C. The Italian equivalent to *cash* is *contanti,* and was expected to be as well known to students in Italy as it is to students in the USA. However, when the item analysis on that test was performed with Italian data, this particular item revealed a high difficulty level, that is, the *p* value of the item was low, contrasted to the high *p* value that was known to exist for American samples. Subsequent investigation revealed that as many students wrote *cambiale* as did the correct response. It was a mere coincidence that *cambiale* is also an eight-letter word beginning with C. Although the word does not fit the dictionary definition, it was recognized immediately after the disclosure was made that it, too, had to be considered a correct response. In the Italian culture, cambiale are a way of life, especially among the working class people. They are analogous to script money and are used as cash. If a person does not have the lira to pay for a purchase, that person may go to a bank and be issued the cambiale in the amount of the purchase just so long as that person is employed and has had no history of defaulting on repayment to the bank, including interest, on a monthly installment basis.

Another area of potential problems was the translation of the interest inventory used originally in the United States "Project Talent" (Flanagan, Davis, Dailey, Shaycroft, Orr, Goldberg, & Neyman, 1964). In the occupations–activities section of the inventory, several items had to be modified because of cultural and social differences (Merenda & Migliorino, 1973). These modifications were as follows:

Item	English	Italian
16	College President	Rector
23	Rancher	Farm Landlord
29	Office Clerk	State Worker
38	Credit Manager	Bank Clerk
64	Clergyman	Priest
65	Certified Public Accountant	Accountant
87	Sports Referee	Soccer Referee
88	Guidance Counselor	Professional Orientator
110	Religious Worker	Lay Brother
122	Public Administrator	Prefect

PUBLIC PERCEPTIONS OF INTERNATIONAL LEADERS

This long-standing cross-cultural study was begun in 1963 and is being conducted in a variety of countries, with foreign collaborators. The countries involved have been England, France, Germany, India, Iran, and Italy. The instrument used in these studies is the activity vector analysis (WVCAI, 1959), an adjective checklist designed to measure multiple-inferential selves of the self-concept. The studies involve obtaining public images of such international leaders as Krushchev, Kosygin, DeGaulle, Wilson, Heath, Shah Pahlavi, and Johnson, Nixon, Carter, and Reagan among others. When necessary, the appropriate foreign language forms are used. In the development of these forms it has sometimes been necessary to translate the adjective appearing on the original form standardized in the United States to some other grammatical form. The following are selected examples (some of these examples are from forms not yet used in the studies):

Adjective (English)	Translation	Foreign language
Good mixer	se mélange bien (aux autres)	French
Gregarious	aime vivre en groupe	French
Appealing	pieno di fascino	Italian
Composed	de modales tranquilos	Spanish
Dependent	abhängig Unselbständig	German
Accommodating	gefällig entgegenkommend	German
Self-conscious	consciente de mim mesmo	Portuguese

Appendix A: International Meetings of Professional Organizations and Personal Conferences held on RIPIS

Sept. 1974: International congress sponsored by Centro Problemi Educazione, Naples, Italy

Feb. 1975: Private conference held in Milan, Italy with D'Amico and the teachers of the Polesine School District

July 1976: Private conference held in Palermo, Sicily with Sparacino

July 1978: Private conference held at the University of Surrey, England with Heggarty

July 1978: 36th Annual Convention of the International Council of Psychologists held in Munich, West Germany

Aug. 1979: 37th Annual Convention of the International Council of Psychologists held in Princeton, New Jersey

July 1980: 38th Annual Convention of the International Council of Psychologists held in Bergen, Norway

Aug. 1981: First Asian Regional Conference held jointly by the International Council of Cross-Cultural Psychology and the International Council of Psychologists in Taipei, Taiwan

Appendix B: Principal Collaborators in Cross-Cultural Research on RIPIS, by Country

Brazil: Bettina Katzenstein Schoenfeldt, Head, Psychological Institutes, Julio de Mesquita Filho University, São Paulo.

Denmark: K. Spelling, Dansmarks Laererhojskole, Copenhagen.
Great Britain: Janice M. Fields and Seamus Heggarty, National Foundation for Educational
                  Research in England and Wales, Windsor, England.
Haiti: Madeleine Bourrelly Laroche, Consulting School Psychologist, Port-au-
                  Prince.
Iran: Reza Shapurian, Department of Psychology, Shiraz University, Shiraz.
Israel: Chanan Rapaport, Director, The Henrietta Szold Institute, The National
                  Institute for Research in the Behavioral Sciences, Jerusalem.
Italy: Guido D'Amico, Didactic Director, Polesine School District, Milan.

                  Rosalia Russello Sparacino, Palermo, Sicily.
Poland: Jozef Rembowski, Director, Institute of Psychology, University of Gdansk.

                  Boleslaw Hornowski, Director, Institute of Psychology, Adam Mickiewicz
                  University, Poznan.
Taiwan: Emily S. C. Miao, Dean of Students, Chinese Culture University, Taipei.
Turkey: Gündüz Vassaf, Bogazici University, Istanbul, Turkey.

Acknowledgments

This chapter was produced with the assistance of Harry S. Novack and Elisa Bonaventura, Rhode Island College.

References

Bonaventura, E. *A longitudinal study of differential prediction by the Rhode Island Pupil Identification Scale of upper grade achievement.* Unpublished doctoral dissertation, University of Connecticut, 1978.
Flanagan, J. C., Davis, F. B., Dailey, J. T., Shaycroft, M. F., Orr, D. B., Goldberg, I., & Neyman, C. A. *Project Talent: The American college student.* (Final report for Cooperative Research Project No. 635.) Washington, D.C.: U.S. Office of Education, 1964.
Merenda, P. F., Bonaventura, E., & Novack, H. S. An intensive study of the reliability of Rhode Island Pupil Identification Scale. *Psychology in the Schools,* 1977, *14,* 282–289.
Merenda, P. F., & Migliorino, G. Interests of Sicilian versus American male youth. *Annals of the College of Economics and Commerce,* University of Palermo, 1973, *27,* 1–27.
Merenda, P. F., Novack, H. S., & Bonaventura, E. Promoting early teacher identification of children with learning problems. *School Psychology International,* 1981, *1,* 26–30.
Novack, H. S., Bonaventura, E., & Merenda, P. F. Manual for the Rhode Island Pupil Identification Scale. Providence, R.I.: RIPIS, 1972.
Novack, H. S., Bonaventura, E., & Merenda, P. F. A scale for early detection of children with learning problems. *Exceptional Children,* 1973, *40,* 98–104.
Novack, H. S., Bonaventura, E., & Merenda, P. F. Factorial structure of the Rhode Island Pupil Identification Scale. *Perceptual and Motor Skills,* 1976, *43,* 75–82.
Walter V. Clarke Associates, Inc. *Manual for activity vector analysis.* Providence, R.I., 1959.
Walter V. Clarke Associates, Inc. *Manual for measurement of skill.* Providence, R.I., 1960.

ANN M. MARMORALE
FRED BROWN

11

Constancy of WISC IQs of Puerto Rican, White, and Black Children[1]

ABSTRACT

The constancy of IQs in Puerto Rican, white, and black children was compared. The Wechsler Intelligence Scale for Children (WISC) was administered in the first grade of a public school to 77 Puerto Rican, 44 white, and 48 black children. The WISC was readministered to these three groups at the end of the third grade. The Puerto Rican children showed significant increments ($p < .01$) in all retest IQs, whereas neither the white nor black groups showed any significant change. The increments shown by the Puerto Rican children were explained in terms of culturally determined responses to cognitive tasks. An English language handicap was found to be of no significance.

Decisions about a child's education made as early as kindergarten or first grade are based on test results. These test results may show variations depending on the child's ethnic background. Frequently, Puerto Rican children referred for psychological testing obtain poor scores on such tests as the Wechsler Intelligence Scale for Children (WISC). Although these low scores have generally been attributed to "bilingual factors" or "impoverished background," they have nonetheless been treated as valid indices of the Puerto Rican child's long-range academic potential. It generally has been assumed that the predictive value (generally considered good) of a WISC score is equal for children from different ethnic backgrounds, and few attempts have been made to test such an assumption.

[1] This research was conducted as part of the Mount Sinai School Project which was supported by the Edith and Percy Straus Fund.

CROSS-CULTURAL RESEARCH AT ISSUE

137

Several earlier studies suggested that intelligence levels of Puerto Rican children tended to increase with age (e.g., Morrison & Goodman, 1959; Talerico & Brown, 1963). Unfortunately, because these studies suffered from methodological problems (e.g., lack of control groups, sample sizes of less than 20, poorly matched cross-sectional groups, exclusive reliance on non-verbal performance tests, incomplete administration of the WISC, use of non-Spanish-speaking examiners, psychiatric patients as subjects), it has never been clearly established whether significant increments in IQ scores in fact occurred. The purpose of the present study was to eliminate these methodological flaws and investigate the changes, if any, that occur in the IQs of Puerto Rican children in comparison with those observed in white and black children when the groups were retested after an interval of several years.

Method

Subjects

The subjects were 77 Puerto Rican, 44 white, and 48 black children who were enrolled in the first grade of a public school in New York City. The Puerto Rican and black children came almost exclusively from working-class families whereas the white children came largely from middle-class Jewish homes. No attempt was made to match the subjects for social class differences as this study was not primarily concerned with the level of IQ scores in the three ethnic groups but rather with the relative degree of change manifested in these test scores with increased maturity.

Procedure

The entire WISC (including digit span and mazes) was administered to each child during the first 4 months of the first grade and readministered during the last 4 months of the third grade. The average time that elapsed from the first to the second test administration was 2½ years. Because almost all the Puerto Rican children had difficulty with English, the WISC was administered to them in Spanish by a bilingual examiner.

Results

The data were analyzed by *t* tests, first, for correlated means for comparisons of first and third grade and, second, for uncorrelated means for comparisons among three ethnic groups.

Table 11.1
Mean IQs and Standard Deviations of Puerto Rican, White, and Black Children
(N = 116)

		Verbal			Performance			Full scale		
		Grade 1	Grade 3	Dif-ference	Grade 1	Grade 3	Dif-ference	Grade 1	Grade 3	Dif-ference
Puerto Rican (n = 77)	M	77.77	87.76	+9.99*	90.89	94.44	+3.55*	82.69	90.10	+7.41**
	SD	11.96	11.66		11.48	11.91		11.44	12.20	
White (n = 44)	M	109.27	110.22	+.95	106.40	106.59	+.19	108.72	109.36	+.64
	SD	15.74	16.34		14.52	13.07		15.49	14.93	
Black (n = 48)	M	94.08	95.81	+1.73	95.60	94.85	−.75	94.37	94.79	+.42
	SD	14.45	11.66		11.74	11.09		12.88	11.70	

* $p < .01$.
** $p < .001$.

Table 11.1 shows the results of the WISC verbal, performance, and full scale IQ means obtained by the Puerto Rican, white, and black children in the first and third grades. In addition, a Scheffé test was performed to test for possible significances of the comparisons among means. The results are given in Table 11.2.

In the first grade, the Puerto Rican children's mean IQs (verbal, 77.77; performance, 90.89; full scale, 82.69) were all significantly below those of the white children (verbal, 109.27, $p < .001$; performance, 106.40, $p < .001$; full scale, 108.72, $p < .001$), as well as significantly below those of the black children (verbal, 94.08, $p < .01$; performance, 95.60, $p < .05$; full scale, 94.37, $p < .05$). The black children's mean scores in the first grade were all significantly below those of the white children ($p < .01$). All the IQ means of the black and white children fell within the range 90–109. The Puerto Rican children's mean IQs fell below this range, except for the performance mean (90.89).

Table 11.2
Scheffé Test for Comparing Differences between Ethnic Groups, Types of Tests, and Repetition of Tests[a]

	Verbal tests		Performance tests		Total tests	
	Grade 1	Grade 3	Grade 1	Grade 3	Grade 1	Grade 3
PR × W	sig.	sig.	sig.	sig.	sig.	sig.
PR × B	sig.	sig.	n.s.	n.s.	sig.	n.s.
W × B	sig.	sig.	sig.	sig.	sig.	sig.

[a] PR = Puerto Rican students, W = white students, B = black students; sig. = $p < .05$, n.s. = no significant difference.

By the end of the third grade, the Puerto Rican children showed significant increases in all their scores. Their verbal mean IQ showed a significant ($p < .001$) increment of 9.99 points, their performance mean IQ showed a significant ($p < .01$) rise of 3.55 points, and their full scale mean IQ showed a significant ($p < .001$) increase of 7.41 points. None of the mean IQs of either the white or black groups manifested any significant change at the end of the third grade.

The performance mean IQ of the Puerto Rican group in the first grade was found to be significantly higher ($p < .001$) by 13.22 points than the verbal mean IQ. By the end of the third grade, the performance mean IQ of the Puerto Rican group was still significantly ($p < .01$) higher than their verbal mean IQ, although the difference (6.68 points) between the two means was much smaller than in the first grade. No significant differences emerged between the mean verbal and mean performance IQs of the white and black children in either the first or third grade.

Table 11.3 shows the distribution of full scale IQs for the three ethnic groups in the first and third grades. In the first grade 72% of the Puerto Rican children had IQs below 90. By the end of the third grade this figure had decreased significantly ($p < .01$) so that 48% of the Puerto Rican children placed below 90. Neither the white group (12–12%) nor the Black group (39–39%) showed any change between the first and third grades in the percentage of full scale IQs classified below 90. The Puerto Rican group showed a significant ($p < .01$) increment in the percentage of IQs that fell in the 90–109 range—from 26% in the first grade to 47% in the third grade. In both the black group (48–50%) and the white group (31–34%), there was no significant change in the percentage of full scale IQs classified in the 90–109 range. The percentage of scores that fell above 109 for the Puerto Rican group showed no significant change from the first (1%) to the third grade (4%). Neither the white (57–54%) nor the black group (12–11%) showed any significant change from the first to the third grade in the percentage of scores falling above 109.

Table 11.3
Percentage Distribution of Full Scale IQs in the First and Third Grades

IQ	Puerto Rican		White		Black	
	1	3	1	3	1	3
Above 109	1	4	57	54	12	11
90–109	26	47	31	34	48	50
Below 90	72	48	12	12	39	39

Discussion

The major finding of this study is that IQ scores of public school Puerto Rican children did not remain constant but rather showed large significant increments over a period of several years, whereas the IQs of white and black children did remain constant during the same period. Gains for the Puerto Rican children were particularly dramatic in verbal areas although the performance areas also showed improvement.

One explanation for the Puerto Rican group's gains that was frequently given by the clinician in interpreting test scores was based on the language factor. It might have been assumed that as these children acquired competence in English, their test scores would rise accordingly. However, lack of English comprehension could not be used to explain the results obtained in the present study given that the Puerto Rican children were tested in Spanish in both the first and the third grades. It was significant that after 2½ years in school, the Puerto Rican children's English was still sufficiently inadequate for a valid administration of the WISC in English. This apparent tendency to cling to the native language was consistent with Brown's (1960) findings.

The test behavior of the Puerto Rican children suggested that the results obtained might be explained by attitudinal and motivational factors embedded in Puerto Rican cultural patterns. When tested in the first grade, most of this Puerto Rican population, unlike the white or the black children, were consistently described by the examiner as quiet, uncommunicative, and unresponsive. It was noted that quite frequently the Puerto Rican children would make no response at all when test questions were posed. These observations supported the findings of Hertzig, Birch, Thomas, and Mendez (1968) who reported that the Puerto Rican children in their study usually met demands for cognitive functioning with passive and silent unresponsiveness. The increments in the IQ scores of Puerto Rican children found in the present study could therefore be explained in terms of such response tendencies. As these ethnically determined behavioral patterns weakened with the Puerto Rican children's continued and prolonged exposure to different ethnic influences and behavioral styles, the children grew less passive and increasingly responsive to the test items and their intelligence test scores began to rise. Although Hertzig et al. (1968) hypothesized that the behavioral response to cognitive tasks observed in their Puerto Rican children would be resistant to change as would, by implication, any test scores affected by such response, the results of the present study did not support such a hypothesis. Rather, these results suggested that Puerto Rican children showed a considerable potential for intellectual growth and development as they became adjusted to their public school environment.

These ethnically determined patterns of responses were probably causing the differences in levels of the verbal and the performance tests obtained among the three ethnic groups. The consistent superiority of the performance scores over the verbal scores shown by the Puerto Rican children supported the finding of Hertzig *et al.* (1968) that Puerto Rican children were much more likely to make responses to performance than to verbal items.

The change from first to third grade in the Puerto Rican children's distribution of full scale IQs was significant only in the lower and middle IQ ranges. It may be that the Puerto Rican group's IQs will continue to increase until adolescence when their distribution might more closely approximate that of the standardization group. Evidence in support of this hypothesis comes from some of the earlier studies. Morrison and Goodman (1959) found the largest IQ increment in their adolescent groups. Talerico and Brown (1963), although observing much less growth in their younger groups than in the present study, reported that whereas no members of their two younger groups achieved scores above 109, 26% of their adolescent group did so.

A number of important implications emerged from this study. Obviously, an IQ score obtained by a young Puerto Rican child, even when a test has been administered in Spanish, should be interpreted with great caution. It is highly doubtful that all Puerto Rican children with low IQs should be placed routinely in the traditional "slow" classes. For the great majority of these children, intellectual deficits are only apparent and a reflection of ethnically acquired modes of responding to the highly verbal, cognitive demands of the typical school. Furthermore, repeated testing throughout childhood and adolescence appears to be required to determine which of these youngsters is genuinely lacking in ability. Finally, it may be necessary to innovate new teaching techniques for these children. Perhaps some of the effort devoted to increasing English language fluency might be directed toward the development of group techniques which might promote identificatory learning through role playing in order to expedite the adjustment process of Puerto Rican children. Other teaching innovations should take into account the relative superiority of the Puerto Rican child's achievement when presented with performance or action-oriented tasks.

References

Brown, F. Intelligence test patterns of Puerto Rican psychiatric patients. *Journal of Social Psychology*, 1960, *52*, 225–230.

Hertzig, M. E., Birch, H. G., Thomas, A., & Mendez, O. Class and ethnic differences in the responsiveness of preschool children to cognitive demands. *Monographs of the Society for Research in Child Development*, 1968, *33*(1, Whole No. 117).

Morrison, J. C., & Goodman, S. *Developing a program for testing Puerto Rican pupils in the New York City public schools.* New York: Board of Education, City of New York, 1959.

Talerico, M., & Brown, F. Intelligence test patterns of Puerto Rican children seen in child psychiatry. *The Journal of Social Psychology,* 1963, *61,* 57–66.

Wechsler, D. *Wechsler Intelligence Scale for Children.* New York: Psychological Corporation, 1949.

Why African Children Are So Hard to Test[1]

ABSTRACT

It is common in reports of cognitive testing of African children with relatively little exposure to western culture to note difficulties arising from the testing situation itself. Two aspects of socialization that are important in the ontogeny of test-related behavior are discussed using data from a Kipsigis community in western Kenya. First, the Kipsigis norms of interaction offer little practice in the kind of talking required in psychological tests. Second, the relationship between the Kipsigis child and important adult figures emerges during the second and third years of life as one with a particular type of social distance that discourages verbal expressiveness. Traditional emphasis on language comprehension rather than production is discussed from the perspective of larger cultural values of obedience and respect, and in relation to anthropological theories of culturally mediated patterns of early socialization. Support for this analysis is seen in a contrast between psychological tests that require verbal production and those that do not.

When child psychologists explore the generality of their theories in other cultures, they frequently turn to Africa. An examination of LeVine's bibliography (1970) in Mussen's *Manual of Child Psychology*, for example,

---

[1] An earlier version of this chapter appeared in L. L. Adler (Ed.), *Issues in Cross-Cultural Research,* Annals of the New York Academy of Sciences, 1977, *285,* 326–331. Field research was supported in part by a grant from the Carnegie Corporation of New York to the Child Development Research Unit (Bureau of Educational Research), University of Nairobi, where the authors held research appointments; and in part by a grant to the second author from the William T. Grant Foundation. All statements made and views expressed are the sole responsibility of the authors.

indicates that Africa has been the locus of nearly half the existing cross-cultural research on children, and this is especially true for reports of performance on psychological tests. Yet difficulty in testing the children often figures prominently in these reports—not only problems of adapting test content to the local culture, but also problems that seem to relate to the test situation itself (Gay & Cole, 1967; Greenfield, 1966).

Consider, for example, our experience in testing children in Kokwet, a rural farming community of Kipsigis people in Western Kenya. Several children—siblings or neighborhood peers—are brought to a traditional hut, where a familiar local woman administers several tests in a friendly and relaxed context. Children waiting to be tested play nearby, and because the house is used by our project staff, there is often someone making tea or doing other familiar chores. As part of the test battery the child is told a story, ten sentences long, about a boy who was given a special stick to help him herd the family's cows. He is then asked to tell the story back to the experimenter. The chances that the child will comply at all, no matter how short or garbled the repetition, are not great: Only 10% of the 3-year-olds say anything in this situation, and the proportion of children answering does not reach 50% until 6 or 7 years. Even by age 10, a full third of the children do not give a scorable reply.

These children are generally healthy and well nourished. In everyday circumstances they can be as active and vocal as children anywhere, swinging from the rafters of a maize storehouse, boisterously roughhousing, or gleefully teasing a goat. What needs to be explained, then, is why the children of Kokwet—and apparently much of the rest of sub-Saharan Africa—are so hard to test. Why does the testing situation, even the most friendly and familiarized version of it, produce such inhibition of thoughtful response?

Researchers commenting on this problem have suggested that the testing situation conflicts with behavior required of children in traditional settings. "Only when the authority figure withdraws," writes Greenfield (1966) of her work in rural Senegal, "does the child turn fully to the logically essential parts of the action [p. 250]." Similarly, Gay and Cole (1967) look to traditional life for an explanation of problems in eliciting responses from their Liberian subjects. "If [the Kpelle child] asks 'Why' or acts in a manner unsanctioned by tradition," they write, "he is likely to be beaten [p. 16]." Little attention, however, has been directed toward the ontogeny of test-related behavior in African children. Thus our purpose here is to present some observations on early childhood socialization that contribute to a fuller, more differentiated understanding of the problem.

Our observations are drawn from a study of child language socialization (Harkness, 1975) that included 20 children in the community of Kokwet, whose ages ranged from 2 to 3½ years. The children's speech and that directed to them were recorded at home in naturally occurring situations, and the mothers were interviewed about beliefs and values related to child language development. The study of child language socialization is pertinent to our present concerns for two reasons: First, the structure of verbal interactions between the young child and others should indicate how much practice the child receives in the type of talking that is necessary for responding to psychological tests; and, second, the acquisition of communicative competence reflects the child's learning of more general norms of social behavior with different classes of people.

Research has indicated that American middle-class mothers typically adapt their speech to infants in several ways (Broen, 1972; Snow, 1972). In addition to simplifying their speech, these mothers seem consciously oriented toward teaching their children to talk. Teaching techniques include, for example, eliciting practice through questions (Remick, 1975) and through conversation based on picture books (Moerk, 1974). Gleason (1973) has described verbal interaction between middle-class American mothers and older preschool children as an extension of this earlier teaching situation in which the focus is now on the acquisition of sociolinguistic rather than purely linguistic skills. A prime characteristic of these mothers' speech is that it is responsive to the interests and initiatives of the child (Engle, 1981). That this kind of speech behavior represents a strong cultural value has been interestingly demonstrated by a study in which the occurrence of "motherese" characteristics as well as the absolute frequency of talking were enhanced by the subjects' knowledge that they were being observed (Graves & Glick, 1978). LeVine (1980) has also noted that categories such as "dialogue" and "reciprocity" used by social scientists to characterize mother–infant interaction encode American middle-class ideologies and values.

These kinds of verbal interaction between American middle-class mothers and children lay a favorable groundwork for the child's subsequent reaction to testing situations. In addition to purely linguistic skills, the child has learned some important sociolinguistic norms for language use with adults. First, conversation with adults is apt to be framed as teaching and learning, and the child's role is to perform well as a pupil. Second, the attention of adults is available to be recruited, not only for the satisfaction of material needs, but also for the communication of the child's own thoughts.

The early sociolinguistic training of children in Kokwet presents several contrasts to the American middle-class picture. The Kokwet mothers, by their own report, do not consider language teaching as a major function of their verbal interactions with babies and young children. When interviewed about their language-training practices, all the mothers reported that it was important to talk to babies even before they understand or answer; but the reasons given were mainly affective or social: "You talk to the baby because

you're happy," or "You talk to the baby so he'll know you're his mother."
Only one-fourth of the mothers mentioned language teaching as a reason
for talking with babies. When asked about language training for young
children, 20% claimed they did none at all, and over half the mothers
thought that the children learned to talk more from other children than from
the mothers themselves. The teaching technique that mothers most frequently mentioned using (60%) was commands, such as "Bring me the
kettle," or "Watch out, it's hot!" Deictic speech, such as "There's Daddy"
or "Look at the cow," was mentioned somewhat less frequently (40%) as
a language-teaching technique.

Observed speech behavior in the Kokwet mothers and children corro-
borates the mothers' descriptions. By comparison with American studies, the
low frequency of the Kokwet mothers' speech to their young children is
remarkable. Vocalizations by and to each of the 20 children in the sample
were tape-recorded at home, using a radio transmitter which the child wore
in a small vest, for approximately 2 hours. Care was taken that the mother
be present for at least part of this time. Nevertheless, the mothers averaged
only 67 utterances per recording, and almost a third of the mothers hardly
spoke to their children at all. In recorded speech obtained from the remainder
of the mothers, imperatives were the most common form of utterance (47%).
An obvious feature of imperatives is that they generally demand a response
in action, not words. Questions, which do require a verbal response, were
a poor second in frequency (27%), and statements, which constitute the
bulk of dialogue, were third (19%). The normal mode of Kokwet mothers'
speech to their young children seemed to be sporadic utterances whose
purpose was to direct or control, to comfort, or to scold.

Relationships between the children's language environment and their age
and sibling status indicate clearly the thrust of child language socialization
in Kokwet. These trends reflect Kipsigis norms of communicative competence, regardless of their relationship to purely linguistic competence. As
mentioned previously, the children in the Kokwet study ranged in age from
2 to 3½ years, a period that spans the transition from late infancy to early
childhood. During this time, most children in Kokwet move from the favored
status of youngest member of the family to the peripheral position of second
to youngest—no longer the object of the playful attention characteristically
bestowed on babies but not yet old enough to contribute to the maintenance
of the household.

The social transition from late infancy to early childhood in Kokwet is
reflected by several measures, which are listed in Table 12.1. First, the
behavior observations show that the children who were older or who were
not the youngest member of the family spent less time interacting with adults
than the younger or last-borns, and correspondingly more time with other

Table 12.1

Correlations between Subjects' Age and Sibling Status, and Language Environment Variables[a]

	N	Subjects' age	Subjects' sibling status
Subjects' time with adults	19	−.45*	.56*
Subjects' time with children	19	.58**	−.53*
Others' talk to subjects	19	−.56*	.72**
Subjects' talk	19	−.38	.52*
Mothers' insults and reprimands	13	.60*	.28

[a] Youngest sibling is coded positive; nonyoungest as negative.
* $p < .05$ (two-tailed).
** $p < .01$ (two-tailed).

children. They were also talked to less, and did less talking themselves. At the same time, the social content of the mothers' verbal interactions with the children shifted, as shown in the greater proportion of reprimands and insults to the older subjects. Reprimands and insults included remarks such as "What's that you're doing?" (delivered in a threatening tone of voice), "Sit properly, damn you," and the inevitable "I'll beat you." Whereas the younger children were hardly ever reprimanded or insulted by their mothers, remarks of this type comprised up to 20% of the mothers' utterances to the older children. In short, the Kokwet mothers' verbal interactions with their toddlers tended to become more directive and more negative as the children grew older and acquired a younger sibling, and the total amount of attention the children received from adults decreased.

All these trends point to the socialization of an important aspect of communicative competence in Kipsigis society: silence when in the presence of older or higher status people. This behavior carries over to adulthood and is difficult to alter, as we have found, to our discomfort, with various research assistants. These trends are not generally supportive of rapid acquisition of competence in verbal production. At the same time, however, it is evident that young children in Kokwet learn a great deal about *not* talking.

Thus, we suggest two aspects of socialization that are important in the ontogeny of test-related behavior in the children of Kokwet. First, by comparison with mother–child verbal interaction in middle-class America the Kipsigis norms of verbal interaction offer little practice in the kind of talking required in psychological tests. Second, the relationship between the Kipsigis child and important adult figures undergoes a profound change during the second and third years of life, which has the effect of creating social distance between the child and adults and of discouraging verbal expressiveness.

Explaining the African child's test behavior in terms of early socialization, however, only begs an explanation at the next theoretical level; namely, why should the mothers of Kokwet differ from middle-class Americans in their modes of language socialization, and why should the social relations between the toddler and important adults undergo the developmental change we have described? The relatively low frequency of language teaching by the Kipsigis mothers is somewhat reminiscent of class differences in speech to young children in western societies (Kagan & Tulkin, 1972; Snow, Arlman-Rupp, Hassing, Jobse, & Joosten, 1976). It has been suggested that styles of verbal interaction between American working-class mothers and their infants reflect the mothers' fatalistic attitude toward the future (Kagan & Tulkin, 1972). Without reviewing the complexities of the literature on class differences, we may note that in comparison to American middle-class mothers, the Kokwet mothers give *more* training in some areas, specifically motor development (Super, 1976). Any theory of general cultural impoverishment or maternal fatalism, therefore, is clearly not applicable to the Kipsigis case. We suggest a more positive reason for the Kipsigis approach to child language socialization: Comprehension, not production, is the important linguistic skill by traditional criteria. The traditional attitude may well be that children will learn to talk on their own soon enough, but that they must be taught to understand requests and commands, and to respond appropriately to them.

The traditional emphasis on language comprehension rather than production fits within the larger cultural values of obedience and respect as they are realized in many African societies (LeVine, 1974; Munroe & Munroe, 1972). Obedience and respect are required in many relationships between people of differing status in sub-Saharan Africa: children and parents, women and men, younger people and older people, apprentices and masters, clients and patrons. The expression of obedience and respect characteristically entails a quiet, even impassive demeanor and may actually be encoded as an avoidance requirement between certain classes of people. LeVine (1973) has attributed the emphasis on obedience characteristic of traditional African societies to economic insecurity, whereas Whiting & Whiting (1974) look to the African extended family structure for an explanation. The Whitings suggest that the greater disciplinary harshness of mothers in societies similar to Kipsigis results from the necessity of raising children who will quickly take their place as responsible and contributing members of a large household, to be entrusted with child care and other chores essential to the well-being of the family. The Whitings demonstrate that such societies are characterized by greater social distance between the father and other members of the family than is the case in societies with nuclear family arrangements. The social distancing between mothers (as well as other adults) and their children that is evident in our observations of child language socialization seems to reflect a similar norm. The period corresponding to the early stages of child language learning is precisely that time when the child must learn to take his place as a contributing member of the family group. For the traditional Kipsigis mother, the most important aspect of her child's development at this stage is not self-expression but rather the acquisition of obedient and respectful responsibility.

Now let us return to the testing problem described at the beginning of this chapter: In a simple task of retelling a story, a substantial proportion of the Kokwet children aged 3–10 failed to respond at all. Clearly, the primary skill required in this task was verbal production. If the child could not produce anything verbally, no other skill such as memory or cognitive organization could be measured. What of the children's performance on tasks that did not require verbal production? In Kagan's Matching Familiar Figures Test (Kagan, 1965) the child is required to understand verbal instructions and to follow them by pointing to the figure that exactly matches a standard. Of the 185 children tested, only 2 failed to respond to this test. This pattern is repeated in other tests in the battery—frustrating reticence to tasks demanding verbal responses, a high rate of response to those that do not.

The use of psychological tests with nonwesternized African children is a difficult endeavor. First, as others have pointed out, the test materials and test situation are culturally strange. Second, the status differential between the adult tester and the child subject interferes with free responses through the norms of obedience and respect. One answer to this problem, we suggest only half in jest, is that the best psychological testers for traditional African children might be other children. Finally, better results with psychological tests will be obtained from African children if we consider the modes of response to which children are socialized at home. Only when all these problems are minimized will we be able to chart the children's cognitive development in the sense originally intended.

References

Broen, P. The verbal environment of the language-learning child. *Monograph of the American Speech and Hearing Association,* 1972, 17.

Engle, M. Language and play: A comparative analysis of parental initiatives. In H. Giles & P. Robinson (Eds.), *Social Psychology and Language.* London: Pergamon Press, 1981.

Gay, J., & Cole, M. *The new mathematics in an old culture.* New York: Holt, Rinehart & Winston, 1967.

Gleason, J. B. Code switching in children's language. In T. Moore (Ed.), *Cognitive development and the development of language.* New York: Academic Press, 1973.

Graves, Z. R., & Glick, J. The effect of context on mother–child interaction: A progress report.

The Quarterly Newsletter of the Institute for Comparative Human Development, 1978, *2,* 41–46.

Greenfield, P. On culture and conservation. In J. S. Bruner, R. R. Olver, & P. Greenfield (Eds.), *Studies in cognitive growth.* New York: Wiley, 1966.

Harkness, S. *Child language socialization in a Kipsigis community of Kenya.* Unpublished doctoral dissertation, Harvard University, 1975.

Kagan, J. Individual differences in the resolution of response uncertainty. *Journal of Personality and Social Psychology,* 1965, *2,* 154–160.

Kagan, J., & Tulkin, S. Mother–child interaction in the first year of life. *Child Development,* 1972, *43,* 31–41.

LeVine, R. A. Cross-cultural study in child development. In P. Mussen (Ed.), *Manual of child psychology* (Vol. 2). New York: Wiley, 1970.

LeVine, R. A. Patterns of personality in Africa. *Ethos,* 1973, *1,* 123–152.

LeVine, R. A. Parental goals: A cross-cultural view. *Teachers College Record,* 1974, *76,* 226–239.

LeVine, R. A. Anthropology and child development. In C. M. Super & S. Harkness (Eds.), Anthropological perspectives on child development. *New Trends for Child Development, 8,* 1980.

Moerk, E. Changes in verbal child–mother interactions with increasing language skills of the child. *Journal of Psycholinguistic Research,* 1974, *3,* 101–116.

Munroe, R. L., & Munroe, R. H. Obedience among children in an East African society. *Journal of Cross-Cultural Psychology,* 1972, *3,* 395–399.

Remick, H. Maternal speech to children during language acquisition. In W. von Raffler-Engel & Y. Lebrun (Eds.), Infant speech and baby talk. *Neurolinguistics,* 1975, *4.*

Snow, C. E. Mothers' speech to children learning language. *Child Development,* 1972, *43,* 549–565.

Snow, C. E., Arlman-Rupp, A., Hassing, Y., Jobse, J., Joosten, J., & Voorster, J. *Mothers' speech in three social classes. Journal of Psycholinguistic Research,* 1976, *5,* 1–20.

Super, C. M. Environmental effects on motor development: The case of African infant precocity. *Developmental Medicine and Child Neurology,* 1976, *18,* 561–567.

Whiting, B. B., & Whiting, J. W. M. *Children of six cultures.* Cambridge, Mass.: Harvard University Press, 1974.

Quranic Pedagogy in Modern Morocco[1]

ABSTRACT

Quranic schooling is the traditional and oldest type of formal schooling in North Africa. The pedagogy that forms the base of this schooling has remained virtually unchanged over the last millenium. In Morocco, Quranic pedagogy coexists with modern European-style schooling. The present chapter describes the nature of historical and present day Quranic pedagogy, and explores the development of children's learning in this traditional context. The question of learning style, and "rote" learning, is discussed in the light of data collected by the author and others. The concluding section provides a discussion of the various and interesting avenues of research in learning, literacy, bilingualism, and related issues that may be studied within the context of Quranic education.

Traditional pedagogies are those which were predominantly used in most formal schooling contexts prior to the eighteenth century advent of mass public education. Such pedagogies were often used for the transmission of religious knowledge and belief, and may be generally distinguished from more modern pedagogies by their emphasis on: literal (or "rote") recitation; a fixed body of written liturgy; individualized instruction (including long-term

---

[1] An earlier version of this chapter was presented in the symposium entitled "Traditional factors in modern Morocco," at the Annual Meetings of the Middle East Studies Association, Ann Arbor, Michigan, November 1978. Funding for this research was provided by the Social Science Research Council, the Council for the International Exchange of Scholars, and the University of Pennsylvania. Support for writing this paper was provided in part by grants from the National Institute of Education and the Spencer Foundation.

CROSS-CULTURAL RESEARCH AT ISSUE

apprenticeship); and lack of age-graded curricula. Judaism, Christianity, and Hinduism used traditional pedagogies for the training of religious elites and laypersons over many centuries, but contemporary use has declined rapidly in the nineteenth and twentieth centuries. However, Islamic or Quranic education has continued to thrive in such disparate societies as Indonesia in South Asia, Senegal in West Africa, and Yemen in the Arabian Penninsula (for a recent comparative study see Wagner, 1982; and Wagner & Lotfi, in press). This chapter deals with Quranic schooling and Quranic pedagogy in the North African country of Morocco. A brief overview of its historical roots and present-day trends is followed by a discussion of children's learning styles and the socialization of cognitive skills and literacy within the framework of traditional Quranic pedagogy.

Varieties of Quranic Schooling

In Morocco, variation in Quranic schooling depends more on the number of years of study than on individual and regional pedagogical differences in what is taught or how material is learned. In fact, there appears to be a fair amount of standardization in both material and pedagogical technique. This is not surprising, perhaps, as the material to be mastered is often limited to passages of the Quran itself, and the pedagogy appears to be rote memorization.

Until the advent of European influence, Quranic schooling was the only type of formal education available to children in Morocco and elsewhere in the Muslim world. Historically—although Muslim education was to begin in the home as soon as the child could speak, and various simple passages (*suras*) of the Quran were to be mastered subsequently—it was only at 7 years of age that the child was sent to a Quranic school where systematic study of the Quran was begun. Traditionally, Quranic schooling was limited to boys, as it was considered improper to teach girls to read and write (Goldziher, 1927, p. 205).[2] Nonetheless, many exceptions to this rule were apparently made, particularly in Morocco. (And, indeed, today many Quranic schools in Morocco, particularly those for younger children, have full participation of girls.) Subjects of study were generally reading, writing, recitation, arithmetic, and rituals associated with religious prayer. The traditional goal of Quranic education was and is the complete mastery or memorization of the Quran, which often takes 6–8 years (cf. Eickelman, 1978).

---

[2] The "impropriety" of Quranic training for girls varied greatly from region to region in the Muslim world. Although religious learning per se was universally accepted, the traditional argument against Quranic training for girls was related to literacy skills which were thought to lead women into nonreputable or immoral areas (see Goldziher, 1927, for a historical review).

In contemporary Morocco, Quranic schooling begins in the *msid,* which may be an annex to the local mosque, but in many cases may be a small or medium-sized room that is provided to the Quranic teacher (*fkih*). In contrast to historical description, the present-day *msid* enrolls primarily young boys and girls, beginning at about age 3–4. There appear to be no current statistics on the number of *msids* in Morocco, but an informal survey indicates that most communities, whether in large urban centers or in rural villages, have *msids.* In his description of childhood in Morocco, Radi (1969) assumes that all Moroccan children go to a *msid* for one or more years. However, I have found a number of small, primarily Berber-speaking communities in the Middle Atlas mountains where Quranic schooling did not exist. Other communities maintained by donation a *fkih* (usually from across the mountains to the south), who was engaged to teach only a handful of children of the wealthier village families.

Interestingly, the present-day *msid* appears to function primarily as a preschool setting for Moroccan children. A 1974 survey I made of two sectors of urban Marrakech and several rural Middle Atlas communities showed that the average number of years spent in the *msid* varied from a high of 1.92 years in Marrakech to a low of .33 years in rural mountain villages (*douars*). However, the *range* of years spent in the *msid* varied dramatically by age and region. Many children surveyed had never attended the *msid,* or had done so for only a few months. Some children, particularly in the rural nonschooled sample, attended an *msid* for as long as 6–7 years, probably as a substitute for modern formal schooling. It is interesting to note that few modern schoolchildren (whether urban or rural) attended more than 2 years of *msid,* and yet these children had the highest average years of attendance. These statistics confirm the observation that parents increasingly view the *msid* as a general preschool setting and believe that their children should obtain the rudiments of learning skills, as well as religious skills, before entering modern primary schools. (For further information, see Wagner & Lotfi, 1980.)

Thus, for most Moroccan children, these 1–3 years of Quranic education represent most of the formal religious education that they will obtain;[3] others, however, will decide not to attend modern public school immediately, and will seek further training. Quranic training beyond the age of 5–7 can take place under the instruction of an individual *fkih,* or the student may enroll in a more "advanced level" *msid*—often, though not always, associated with a mosque. Sometimes such schools are located near religious sites or *zawiyas* where a number of *fkihs* might reside. The earlier Quranic training

---

[3] This statement refers to full-time religious studies; many Moroccan schoolchildren do continue religious studies as a part of the national primary and secondary school curriculum.

in the *msid* is insufficient for mastery of the Quran; this is usually accomplished between the ages of 5 to 12 in the second Quranic setting. Little current statistical information is available on such "intermediate" schools, though they appear to be much fewer in number than the *msids* for young children. This level of schooling provides the basis for advanced learning in Islamic education, and a future career as a *fkih* or Quranic teacher.

The best known institutions of higher Islamic education are the two great mosque-universities: the Qarawiyin in Fes, and the Yusufia in Marrakech. In the excellent review by Eickelman (1978), these universities are described as being concerned with learning that goes well beyond memorization of the Quran, and includes poetry, history, literature, astronomy, logic, and grammar. Eickelman cites earlier sources which indicate the student population of these schools in 1931 was about 1200.[4] Less well-known institutions are the smaller schools that are mainly located near rural religious sites. Typical of these are Sidi Zouine near Marrakech, and Tamegroute in the Draa valley in southern Morocco. Although the school at Tamagroute appears to have ceased functioning some years ago, the school at Sidi Zouine in 1978 had over 50 enrolled students, ranging from 10 to about 35 years of age. Quranic students in this school spent an average of almost 11 years in Islamic study, with some students studying as many as 17 years. Students at Sidi Zouine live in hostel-like rooms near the mosque. Most have come from small villages from the Haouz plain or from the High Atlas mountains, although at least one student came from across the Sahara in Mauretania. Like students in urban mosque-universities, "graduates" of Sidi Zouine generally expect to become *fkihs* themselves, often, though not always, returning to their region of origin.

Context, Pedagogy, and Learning by "Rote"

Description of the traditional *msid* is available from a number of sources. In Meakin's (1902) classic work entitled *The Moors*, the *msid* is described as follows:

> [They] are held in the mosques, or in rooms about the town belonging to them, . . . in which all sit on the ground, the teacher facing his pupils, whose bare pates are all within reach of the switch in his hand. Instead of books or slates, each one is provided with a thin board, narrowed to the lower end, rubbed over with a sort of pipe-clay on which they write with reed pens, and ink prepared from charred horns, or wool and water. One of the bigger boys being set to teach them to write the alphabet which they have already been taught by ear, the letters are

---

[4] The present enrollment is reported to be about 200 students.

Figure 13.1. Traditional Quranic scholar studying text written on a wooden luh (in a rural town near Marrakech, Morocco).

written out on the board for them to copy. The lessons are then read aloud by all together, rocking to and fro to keep time, some delighting in a high key, others jogging in lower tones . . . [p. 304].

Present-day Quranic pedagogy depends on the stage of schooling. The "intermediate" schools for children about 7–14 years of age conform most closely to the historical description (see Fig. 13.1):

School hours commence in winter before daylight, but in summer after it, somewhere between three and five a.m.—earlier hours being kept in the country—and continue until a quarter after twelve, a break for food having been made about nine or ten. From half-past one again they last till an hour before sunset, and some come again before supper. Those who do not learn their lessons in class are kept in till they do so by good *fkihs* . . . [Meakin, 1902, p. 305].

This description is rather similar to the daily life of the students or *tolba* of Sidi Zouine, and of other *tolba* of the rural Middle Atlas.

Contemporary *msids* for young children—"preschool" Quranic education—are somewhat different from "intermediate" or "advanced" schools. Because children are quite young (3–5 years), they often attend schools for only a morning session. And, unlike the older *tolba,* these younger children have little knowledge of reading or writing, and so spend most of the school time in following the *fkih* in chanting verses of Quran. Occasionally, the *fkihs* have a blackboard available to begin teaching the Arabic alphabet and simple words. In some schools the script board (*luh*) is still used, although in more urban areas a small fiberboard slate written on with chalk seems to be gaining popularity. The children are expected to copy the written letters and words on their *luh,* and repeat the *fkih's* pronunciation until the symbol is memorized. In an interesting parallel with western education, some *fkihs* concentrate on the "whole-word" method whereas others appear to try to teach the alphabetic principle. No systematic data is yet available on these differences in pedagogy.

Pedagogical style is one of the best known, and most criticized, characteristics of Quranic schooling, past and present. According to Hodgson (1974), "Education was commonly conceived as the teaching of fixed and memorable statements and formulas which could be adequately learned without any process of thinking as such. A statement was either true or false, and the sum of all true statements was knowledge. . . . Education meant inculcating as many of these statements in as sound a form as possible [p. 438]." MacDonald (1911) describes higher Muslim education as follows: "It trains the memory and the power of reasoning—always in formal methods—and then gives to neither any adequate material on which to work. The memory is burdened with verbatim knowledge of the Quran and some outlines of Theology and law, and the reason is exhausted in elaborate argumentations therefrom deduced [pp. 288–289; cited in Dichter, 1976]." Meakin (1902) adds: "The whole of the first school course is the Koran, which has to be learned by heart before anything else can be done, though little of it may be understood [p. 306]." Hardy and Brunot, in their early study of Moroccan children, suggest that memory is the only "mental faculty" that is well developed in the Moroccan child. They claim that "the Moroccan child is capable of retaining, without excessive effort, sentences and even entire chapters [of the Quran], without understanding the meaning [1925, p. 8]."

Such historical description captures rather well several contextual features of present-day Quranic education. Moroccan children at the younger ages usually have little understanding of reading or writing, and appear to do most of their learning by rote imitation of the *fkih*. Children who speak Moroccan dialectal Arabic apparently have some, though incomplete, understanding of what they are saying. Berber-speaking children, in contrast, apparently have little or no way of making more than elemental sense of what is being said in the classroom. (It should be noted here that many of these Berber children will have a similar problem when they enter modern public schooling, where classes are taught in Arabic or French. It may be the case that this preschool experience facilitates school entry for these children.) One question that would be interesting to pursue is how and when Berber children learn to understand and read and write the Quran. In the early years, imitation is clear, but it is not known how these children compare to Arabic-speaking children in later Quranic education.

Much has been written, by Muslim and European observers alike, about the effects of Quranic schooling on memory abilities and learning styles of the *tolba*. Most suggest (cf. Hardy & Brunot, 1925, and studies reviewed by Eickelman, 1978) that the years spent in the *msid* have later consequences. Hardy and Brunot state that the Moroccan child who goes on to modern public school is so "exuberant with his memory that his imagination is smothered [1925, p. 8]." Zerdoumi (1970) has further suggested that "Quranic school imposes on [the child] a purely mechanical, monotonous form of study in which nothing is likely to arouse his interest. The school thus tends to curb his intellectual and moral activity at the precise moment when it should be developing rapidly [p. 196; cited in Miller, 1977]." Finally, Miller (1977) posits that many of the contemporary problems in modern Moroccan schooling arise out of the "reflexive" and unenlightened nature of traditional Quranic schools. In sum, most historical and contemporary observers focus on memory or rote learning which is held to inhibit modern school learning and "critical thinking."

Yet are we certain that memory displaces critical thinking? Psychologists and anthropologists have been trying to answer this question at least since the publication of *How Natives Think* by Levy-Bruhl in 1910. Moreover, it is interesting to note that none of the preceding observations were based on actual comparisons of the memory ability of Quranic and non-Quranic scholars. In a study of over 400 Moroccan children from modern-schooled and nonschooled backgrounds, and including a sample of Quranic *tolba,* I found that, on a variety of memory tasks, the *tolba* remembered no better than other nonschooled children, and considerably less well than modern schoolchildren (Wagner, 1978). Care was taken so that all children understood the memory tests, and this was evidenced by significant above chance-level performance. Results from the study of recall and recognition memory showed that schoolchildren learn a variety of memory skills that are apparently not readily available to the *tolba*.

Such experimental evidence does not, of course, preclude the possibility that the *tolba* have other, special memory skills that were not "tapped" in my earlier investigation. In fact, a later ethnographic and film study of the *tolba* in study situations found that they used a variety of mnemonic techniques that were not used by typical schoolchildren. Some of these were noted by Meakin (1902) in his description (cited earlier) of the chanting, rocking, and tonal variation in the verbal productions of the *tolba*. It seems clear that the *tolba* have developed mnemonic techniques that enable them to ingest large amounts of sometimes little-understood material. (One problem in the experimental study of Quranic memory is, of course, the difficulty of measurement of how much a given student knows and understands the Quran. This factor would affect measured memory ability greatly.) In a study of adult literacy in Liberia, Scribner and Cole (1978) found that Muslim literates who had studied in Quranic schools appear to learn more by "rote" (i.e., by stringing items together) than by categorizing or clustering the items to be remembered. The latter mnemonic techniques were used more by public school students and graduates.

One implication of such memory research is that we actually know very little about the real learning styles and memory faculties of Quranic students. The hypothesis that Quranic memorizers become "rote" learners in later modern schooling is difficult to support as other, noncognitive factors covary with Quranic education and have not yet been studied seriously. Some of these factors would include rigid and conservative discipline by *fkihs*, long hours of study under difficult conditions, disdain for "modern ways of thinking" and "new ideas," and so on. In other words, both social and cognitive factors in Quranic education may influence learning abilities in subsequent schooling. Also, it may be that the modern French pedagogical emphasis on designated material to be learned has reinforced the Quranic "rote" tradition more than many modern educators would like to believe. In any case, it is not yet clear in what ways, if at all, Quranic memorization styles may be responsible for poor learning habits in public schoolchildren, as suggested by Miller (1977) and other contemporary observers.

Conclusions and Implications for Further Research

In a review of European research on Quranic schooling, Dichter (1976) found that most observers were highly critical of *msid* education, with characterizations "of the student as a robot, of parents and teachers as willing collaborators in an endeavor to render education a completely mechanical process [p. 92]." Such criticism is echoed in modern Morocco, with public school teachers occasionally decrying the old-time methods still used in the *msid*. And yet there remain many supporters of Quranic education. Parents consider Quranic schooling and *fkihs*' rigid and disciplinary manner to be a way of training children to "respect" authority and "behave." Other observers (e.g., Eickelman, 1978) have discussed advanced Quranic training as providing (at least traditionally) the successful student with "cultural capital" that could be applied to obtaining a high status job as a learned gentleman (such as a religious judge or *cadi*). Thus, present-day Quranic schooling in urban Morocco is increasingly viewed by parents as an important preschool religious opportunity for their children. Furthermore, the Moroccan government currently supports the extension of such Quranic schooling, in part by subsidization, and in part by requiring that all children have at least 2 years of traditional education before entering the modern public school system.

The study of traditional Quranic schooling would be of considerable social significance if only for the fact that tens of millions of children in many nations of the world attend them. This statistic indicates that Quranic schooling is one of the largest relatively homogenous forms of preschooling in the world today, even though it is rarely under the complete control of government educational authorities. Within the domain of literacy, Quranic schooling may be viewed as one of the few remaining indigenous cultural institutions providing formal training in reading and writing.

From the perspective of developmental psychology and early childhood education, Quranic schools provide an excellent terrain in which to study a number of contemporary problems in cognition. First, there is the general issue of the transfer of learning styles from the *msid* to the public school setting—Do traditional learning habits carry over to the modern classroom? How are mnemonic skills acquired in Quranic study used in the acquisition of a more modern generalized curriculum? To what extent are reading and writing skills achieved in the *msid*? How is this achievement related to the material used (the Quran) and to the individual pedagogical methods and skills of the teacher? What are the effects of native language (e.g., Berber) of the child on the written and spoken language (Arabic) used in the *msid*? How does this latter problem parallel problems of literacy acquisition in other parts of the world (e.g., among Spanish-speaking Americans), where children learn to read in a second language?

These questions are only a subset of some of the major pedagogical questions we face today—questions concerning cognitive styles, basic literacy, child bilingualism, and schooling. The Quranic school provides a rather special window for seriously examining these issues. For example, the question of how literacy is acquired in school has often been confounded by the factor of the child's out-of-school reading activities. Such activities include parental tutoring or experience with books in the home, or such modern cultural artifacts as *Sesame Street* or similar educational television programs. In Morocco, however, out-of-*msid* reading activities are virtually nonexistent, as parents are often illiterate, books are unavailable, and there is no television. Also, Quranic schooling is markedly different from modern public schooling, and so would provide a good example for the transfer (or conflict) of learning styles from one school context to the next. This sort of contrast is not available in Western educational systems precisely because they were designed to avoid such conflicts. The question remains, of course, as to whether the contrast or conflict has actually been eliminated. Further studies are being undertaken by our research group to explore these issues and to illuminate the general processes by which children begin to learn in different cultural contexts.

Acknowledgments

The author would like to thank Abdelhamid Lotfi for his help in some of the fieldwork on which this chapter is based.

References

Dichter, T. W. *The problem of how to act on an undefined stage: An exploration of culture, change and individual consciousness in the Moroccan town of Sefrou—with a focus on three modern schools.* Unpublished doctoral dissertation, University of Chicago, 1976.

Eickelman, D. F. The art of memory: Islamic education and its social reproduction. *Comparative Studies in Society and History,* 1978, *20,* 485–516.

Goldziher, I. Muslim education. In *Encyclopaedia of religion and ethics* (Vol. 5). Edinburgh, Scotland: Clark, 1927.

Hardy, G., & Brunot, L. *L'enfant marocain.* Rabat, Morocco/Paris: Editions de Bulletin de l'Enseignement du Maroc, No. 63, 1925.

Hodgson, M. G. S. *The venture of Islam* (Vol. 2). Chicago: University of Chicago Press, 1974.

Levy-Bruhl, L. *How natives think.* New York: Washington Square Press, 1966. (Originally published, 1910.)

MacDonald, D. B. *Aspects of Islam.* New York: Macmillan, 1911.

Meakin, B. *The Moors.* New York: Macmillan, 1902.

Miller, G. D. Classroom 19: A study of behavior in a classroom of a Moroccan primary school. In L. C. Brown & N. Itzkowitz (Eds.), *Psychological dimensions of Near Eastern studies.* Princeton, N.J.: Darwin Press, 1977.

Radi, A. Processus de socialization de l'enfant marocain. *Annales de Sociologie* (Rabat), 1969, 33–47.

Scribner, S., & Cole, M. Unpackaging literacy. *Social Science Information,* 1978, *17,* 19–40.

Wagner, D. A. Memories of Morocco: The influence of age, schooling and environment on memory. *Cognitive Psychology,* 1978, *10,* 1–28.

Wagner, D. A. *Indigenous education and literacy in the Third World.* Paper presented at the Annual Meetings of the American Association for the Advancement of Science, Washington, D.C., January 1982.

Wagner, D. A., & Lotfi, A. Traditional Islamic education in Morocco: Sociohistorical and psychological perspectives. *Comparative Education Review,* 1980, *24,* 238–251.

Wagner, D. A., & Lotfi, A. Learning to read by "rote" in the Quranic schools of Yemen and Senegal. *International Journal of the Sociology of Language,* in press.

Zerdoumi, N. *Enfants d'hier: l'education de l'enfant en milieu traditionnel algerien.* Paris: Maspero, 1970.

PIERRE R. DASEN **14**

Cross-Cultural Aspects of Piaget's Theory: The Competence–Performance Model[1]

ABSTRACT

When Piaget's epistemology is used as a basis for a psychological theory of cognitive development, the structural properties have to be expanded to encompass more contextual aspects. This has led Flavell and Wohlwill (1969) to elaborate a model distinguishing competence from performance. Competence refers to the logical representation of what the organism could do in an ideal environment; performance refers to the overt behavior given the constraints of real life or experimental situations. This chapter reviews the use of this model in cross-cultural Piagetian psychology, taking into account the influence of cultural environment.

It is suggested that training paradigms can help to distinguish competence from performance: If the underlying operational structure is present (competence), but is not expressed in the initial task performance, the training "actualizes" the existing competence, resulting in rapid learning. To assess the occurrence of actualization in three populations and with three concrete operational concepts, the results of eight training studies are summarized. The competence–performance model seems to explain some, but possibly not all, cases of the performance of 12–14-year-old children in those samples where the development curves seem to reach an asymptote (i.e., when the last substage of concrete operations is seemingly not reached in some proportion of the population). The usefulness as well as the limits of the model are discussed in this context.

---

[1] This chapter combines in a revised and shortened form the following two papers: P. R. Dasen. Cross-cultural cognitive development: The cultural aspects of Piaget's theory. In L. L. Adler (Ed.), *Issues in Cross-Cultural Research*. Annals of the New York Academy of Sciences, 1977, *285*, 332–337; and P. R. Dasen, L. Ngini, & M. Lavallée. Cross-cultural training studies of concrete operations. In L. H. Eckensberger, W. J. Lonner, & Y. H. Poortinga (Eds.), *Cross-cultural contributions to psychology*. Amsterdam: Swets & Zeitlinger, 1979, pp. 94–104. With kind permission of the publishers and editors.

CROSS-CULTURAL RESEARCH AT ISSUE

When discussing Piaget's theory in the context of cross-cultural psychology, we first of all have to make a distinction between Piaget's own major goal and the way in which his theory has been used by developmental psychologists: Piaget is an epistemologist rather than a psychologist; his concern is the ontogenetic and phylogenetic development of scientific knowledge. Developmental psychologists (including those interested in cultural aspects) have used Piaget's epistemology as a theoretical framework to study cognitive development in individuals. Under their influence, Piaget's structural theory, and especially his concepts of "stage" and "structures d'ensemble," have gradually been expanded to encompass more contextual aspects.

Flavell and Wohlwill (1969), for example, have suggested a model that introduces a distinction between competence and performance, patterned on Chomsky's theory of psycholinguistics. In their view:

> A psychological theory that accounts for complex behavior will have two principal components: a *competence* model, which is a formal, logical representation of the structure of some domain . . .; an *automaton* model . . ., which represents the psychological processes by which the information embodied in competence actually gets accessed and utilized in real situations. The competence model gives an abstract, purely logical representation of what the organism knows or could do in a timeless, ideal environment, whereas the automaton model has the job of describing a real device that could plausibly instance that knowledge or skill, and instance it within the constraints (memory limitations, rapid performance, etc.) under which human beings actually operate [p. 71].

The probability that a given child will solve a given task can be formulated in the following equation:

$$P(+) = P_a \times P_b^{1-k} \qquad (14.1)$$

where P_a reflects the degree to which a given operation has become established in a particular child, in other words, the presence or absence of the operational structure (competence); P_b is an attribute of the task and represents the likelihood for any given task that the operation will in fact be called into play and its end product translated into the desired output. The parameter k has to be introduced because these task-related variables vary with age. The values of all three factors are expected to vary between 0 and 1, which gives rise to a four-phase process of cognitive development. In the initial phase, $P_a = 0$, that is, the child lacks the given operation. In a transitional phase, P_a changes from 0 to 1, whereas k is assumed to remain equal to 0. In a period of stabilization, the contribution of the task-related variables gradually decreases ($1 - k$ tends toward 0), and during the terminal phase the child "is able to bring the operation to bear on the problem successfully, regardless of the situational and task variables involved [p. 101]." The model is able to handle many empirical results on horizontal décalages and lack of intertask consistency.

But whereas P_b in Flavell and Wohlwill's model is an attribute of the task, what is needed to explain the competence–performance distinction in some cross-cultural situations is a variable that is an attribute of the culture. Thus I propose to introduce the variable P_c, representing the likelihood for any given task that the operation will in fact be called into play in a given cultural milieu. P_c is likely to increase with age; this is why it has to be raised to the power k. The complete equation now becomes:

$$P(+) = P_a \times P_b^{1-k} \times P_c^k \qquad (14.2)$$

One of the tasks of cross-cultural Piagetian psychology is to define more precisely how cultural factors influence the different components of the equation,[2] particularly whether they influence competence (P_a) or performance (P_b^{1-k} or P_c^k).

Flavell and Wohlwill's (1969) competence–performance distinction was first introduced to cross-cultural Piagetian psychology by Heron (1974) to explain the discrepancy in performance on tasks that ought to be characteristic of the same stage. Heron concludes: "I find myself increasingly inclined to the view that the apparent unity of [the concrete operational] stage ·has been generated by the cognitively-relevant cultural homogeneity in development of the children serving as subjects in most European and North American studies [p. 100]." Consistency in performance across tasks is only an ideal end product of the stage; this seems to be rarely attained in "non-western" or "nontechnological" milieux, where a sort of "stretching of Piaget's transitional period [p. 97]" seems to occur. Heron suggests that, over and above such factors as "schooling" or "European contact" or urban–rural residence or social class, which have often been shown to influence the rate of development of concrete operations, one should consider the cognitive "ambience" in which the children develop. By this term, he means the "values with cognitive relevance that are *implicit* in the total pattern of adult and older sibling behaviour within which (early) development takes place [Heron, 1974, p. 97]."

One should not assume that this cognitive ambience is generally favorable or unfavorable to the development of all concrete operational concepts. Dasen (1975a) has demonstrated that rates of development are not uniform across different areas of concrete operations, and that these rates may reflect the adaptive values of the concepts concerned. Extending Berry's (1976)

---

[2] I am using this formula as a heuristic device. It is not essential to this discussion, and I do not wish to suggest that we may be able to attach real probabilities to its components.

model of ecological functionalism to Piagetian developmental psychology, it was predicted that nomadic, hunting, subsistence economy populations would develop spatial concepts more rapidly than sedentary, agriculturalist groups, whereas the latter would attain concepts of conservation of quantity, weight, and volume more rapidly than the former. The model was supported by the results of a study involving 190 children aged 6–14 from three cultural groups: Canadian Eskimos, Australian Aborigines, and Ebrié Africans.

Such a quasi-experimental study is a modest step toward specifying the variable P_c, which is seen to vary according to the ecocultural demands placed on a population (or, in other words, according to the ecocultural relevance of the particular concrete operational concepts). If we hypothesize these ecocultural factors to determine P_c to a greater extent than P_a, this distinction is not trivial. It implies that the competence for concrete operational structures is likely to be universal, but that the way in which this competence is translated into spontaneous behavior is culturally determined.

According to the competence–performance model, an initial answer a child gives to a Piagetian task may not necessarily reflect his "true" cognitive level, that is, the underlying structure or competence. There are indications that, in some cases at least, only a little "help" is needed—in the form of further questioning, additional task situations, or exposure to other operational tasks and training procedures—in order to "actualize" the latent structure.

De Lemos (1969), for example, discussing the effects of familiarity with the testing situation in Australian Aborigines, states that "because the Aboriginal society does not appear to recognize or encourage the development of concepts of conservation, these may not be clearly formulated even when the operational capacity is present. In this case it is likely that a little experience with the test situation would be sufficient to develop the concepts [pp. 264–265]." Examples of such rapid "Aktualgenese" are provided by Bovet (1974) in Algerian illiterate adults, when testing for conservation of weight and, to some extent, for conservation of length. During the interview, some of Bovet's subjects went through the complete sequence from pseudoconservation to nonconservation to end up with operational conservation, and others changed from nonconservation to operational conservation after weighing the two pieces of clay once. On other concepts, such as speed and time, which were thought to be less culturally relevant, no such actualization occurred. In Bovet's study, illiterate children also gave more advanced answers after being exposed to some training situations.

Pinard, Morin, and Lefèbvre (1973) report on the average similar rates of learning conservation of quantity (liquids) in French Canadian, unschooled Rwandan, and schooled Rwandan children aged 7 years. One difference however was found among the three groups: In the unschooled Rwandan group 7 (of 16) subjects were successful on the training exercises after a single session, as opposed to only 3 in the schooled group and none in the French Canadian group.

We can assume that if very rapid learning is achieved through training, the "competence" or underlying operational structure must be present but is not expressed in the initial task performance; the training "actualizes" the existing competence. In other words, these children are probably at Flavell and Wohlwill's Phase 3, where P_a is equal or close to 1, but k still equals 0. The immediate effect of the training procedure is not to change P_a but to change the value of P_b^{1-k}. If the training is successful but improvement in performance occurs more slowly, it is more likely that the operational structure is not present but is built up during the training. If no learning occurs, little can be said, as the technique may simply be inadequate in the given situation (see also Flavell, 1977, pp. 226–227).

The problem is to define just how "rapid" the learning must be in order to reflect "actualization." Dasen, Lavallée, and Retschitzki (1979) have attempted the following definition:

1. The change in behavior has to be important; that is, the final substage has to be reached (and has to remain stable over time).
2. This change has to occur under the influence of a minimal amount of stimulation—for example, simple retesting (as in a control group) or only one or two training sessions when normally three or four are needed for successful training.

To assess the occurrence of actualization in different populations and with different concrete operational concepts, eight training studies were carried out; the details of the techniques, samples, and results appear elsewhere (Dasen, 1975b, 1977; Dasen et al., 1979; Lavallée & Dasen, 1980). Three Piagetian tasks were used: (a) conservation of quantity (liquids); (b) quantification of class inclusion; (c) horizontality (level of liquid in a round bottle). The three populations were (a) Central Eskimo, Baffin Island, Canada (cf. Dasen, 1975a, b); (b) Baoulé (Akan), Ivory Coast, West Africa (cf. Dasen, Inhelder, Lavallée, & Retschitzki, 1978); (c) Kikuyu (Bantu), Kenya, East Africa.

The training procedures for conservation followed the technique developed by Lefèbvre (1971; Lefèbvre & Pinard, 1972); for class inclusion they were adapted from Inhelder, Sinclair, and Bovet (1974). These procedures were designed to create a conflict, leading the child to integrate and coordinate existing schemes into new structures. The technique for horizontality training was based on a more empiricist model, the child simply being given

Table 14.1
Training Effects and Actualization in Eight Training Studies

Study Task	Population	Age	Experimental or control	Number of subjects	Is sample on asymptote?	Training effect[a]	N Stage 3	% Stage 3	N Actualization	% Actualization
1 Conservation	Eskimo	10–11	E	4	No	.05	0	0	0	0
2 Conservation	Eskimo	12–14	E	7	Yes	.01	7	100	7	100
3 Conservation	Baoulé	7–9	E	14	No	.02	8	57	0	0
4 Class inclusion	Baoulé	7–9	E	14	No	n.s. (.05)[b]	7	50	0	0
5 Class inclusion	Kikuyu	12–14	E	13	Yes	.01	12	94	11	85
			C	12	Yes	.02	5	42	5	42
6 Horizontality	Baoulé	7–9	E	14	No	.001	0	0	0	0
			C	14	No	n.s.	0	0	0	0
7 Horizontality	Baoulé	13–14	E	11	Yes	.001	9	82	4	36
8 Horizontality	Kikuyu	12–14	E	20	Yes	.001	13	65	1	5
			C	9	Yes	n.s.	0	0	0	0

[a] Significance level, Friedman analysis of variance by ranks.
[b] Log-likelihood ratio test between pretest and delayed posttest.

the repeated opportunity to copy the surface line of water in a round bottle tilted in various positions, and to establish the parallelism between this line and the reference frame.

The results of the eight training studies are summarized in Table 14.1. A significant training effect (Friedman analysis of variance by ranks) was obtained in all experimental groups except one, and in one of the control groups. (Control groups were not used in every study because of the small number of subjects available.) This analysis takes into account any move along the developmental sequence. If we look at the proportion of subjects achieving a stable Stage 3 (i.e., complete concrete operational) performance, which is maintained over at least 1 month, the results differ with age: Not surprisingly, the proportion is larger in older children. In other words, the training effect depends largely on the readiness of the children.

For the present discussion, the most interesting aspect of these results is the proportion of children who display "actualization," as defined earlier; the last two columns of Table 14.1 provide these figures. Studies 2, 5, and 7 show that the operational structure must have been present from the start in at least some and occasionally all of the subjects. These three studies deal with older children (12–14 years), at an age when the development curves in these samples have reached an asymptote. On the other hand, Study 8 also deals with older children and an asymptotic development curve, and yet only one of the children clearly showed "actualization."

Overall, these studies suggest that the asymptote in the development curves may, in some but possibly not all cases, be explained by the competence–performance distinction. On the other hand, there are also cultural differences in the development of competence for concrete operational concepts. From a functional ecological perspective, these differences are adaptive, together with predominant value systems; the training studies show that, if it were deemed desirable, these differences could be reduced or bridged by adequate training techniques. The competence–performance model has an important role to play in our understanding of cultural differences, but it cannot be a panacea.

References

Berry, J. W. *Human ecology and cognitive style: Comparative studies in cultural and psychological adaptation.* New York: Wiley, 1976.

Bovet, M. C. Cognitive processes among illiterate children and adults. In J. W. Berry & P. R. Dasen (Eds.), *Culture and cognition: Readings in cross-cultural psychology.* London: Methuen, 1974.

Dasen, P. R. Concrete operational development in three cultures. *Journal of Cross-Cultural Psychology,* 1975, *6,* 156–172. (a)

Dasen, P. R. Le développement des opérations concrètes chez les Esquimaux Canadiens. *Journal International de Psychologie*, 1975, *10*, 165–180. (b)

Dasen, P. R. Are cognitive processes universal? A contribution to cross-cultural Piagetian psychology. In N. Warren (Ed.), *Studies in cross-cultural psychology* (Vol. 1). London: Academic Press, 1977.

Dasen, P. R., Inhelder, B., Lavallée, M., & Retschitzki, J. *Naissance de l'intelligence chez l'enfant Baoulé de Côte d'Ivoire.* Bern: Hans Huber, 1978.

Dasen, P. R., Lavallée, M., & Retschitzki, J. Training conservation of quantity (liquids) in West African (Baoulé) children. *International Journal of Psychology*, 1979, *14*, 57–68.

de Lemos, M. M. The development of conservation in Aboriginal children. *International Journal of Psychology*, 1969, *4*, 255–269.

Flavell, J. H. *Cognitive development.* Englewood Cliffs, N.J.: Prentice-Hall, 1977.

Flavell, J. H., & Wohlwill, J. F. Formal and functional aspects of cognitive development. In D. Elkind & J. H. Flavell (Eds.), *Studies in cognitive development.* New York: Oxford University Press, 1969.

Heron, A. Cultural determinants of concrete operational behaviour. In J. L. M. Dawson & W. J. Lonner (Eds.), *Readings in cross-cultural psychology.* Hong Kong: University Press, 1974.

Inhelder, B., Sinclair, H., & Bovet, M. C. *Learning and the development of cognition.* Cambridge, Mass.: Harvard University Press, 1974.

Lavallée, M., & Dasen, P. R. L'apprentissage de la notion d'inclusion de classes chez de jeunes enfants Baoulés (Côte d'Ivoire). *Journal International de Psychologie*, 1980, *15*, 27–41.

Lefèbvre, M. *Apprentissage de la conservation des quantités par une méthode de conflit cognitif.* Unpublished Master's thesis, Université de Montréal, 1971.

Lefèbvre, M., & Pinard, A. Apprentissage de la conservation des quantités par une méthode de conflit cognitif. *Revue Canadienne des Sciences du Comportement*, 1972, *4*, 1–12.

Pinard, A., Morin, C., & Lefèbvre, M. Apprentissage de la conservation des quantités liquides chez des enfants rwandais et canadiens-français. *Journal International de Psychologie*, 1973, *8*, 15–24.

HUGH MEHAN
MARGARET M. RIEL

15

Teachers' and Students' Instructional Strategies[1]

ABSTRACT

The distinction between formal and informal learning, often a topic of cross-cultural research in foreign settings, was examined in a domestic setting by comparing teachers' and students' instructional strategies in a naturally occurring classroom context. Classroom teachers taught academic material to a member of a primary school group; that student then taught the same material to the rest of the work group.

The frequency and sequential organization of instructional moves in the teacher-led and student-led portions of these "instruction chains" were charted. Although there was little difference in the total number, the range, or the average number of the instructions used, there were differences in the distribution of moves in teacher- and student-led instruction. Student teachers used more directives than adult teachers. Adults used more general orienting instructions; they gave twice as much feedback to learners as did student teachers. These differences in frequency distributions speak to differences in teacher and student strategies for capturing attention and maintaining learner involvement.

The sequential organization of teacher-led instruction chains was similar to the questioning sequences representative of formal classroom lessons. They had a three part structure, and concluded with the teacher's evaluation of the student's immediately preceding reply. Student-led instruction was dominated by "directive and example" sequences rather than elicitation–reply–evaluation sequences. "Teaching by example" was the primary move in both teacher and student led instruction chains. However, adult teachers were much more likely to *elicit* examples, whereas student teachers were more likely to *give* examples.

A reciprocal difference existed in the characterization of the learner roles in the two situations. Whereas with adult teachers the learner's most frequent con-

[1] The materials for this study were gathered through Ford Foundation Grant 740-0420.

tribution was to provide responses to teacher elicitation, with student teachers the learners took a more active role in eliciting instructions from the teacher.

The stereotypic association of the verbal modality of instruction with formal learning and the nonverbal modality with informal learning was not ratified in this study. Adult and student teachers combined linguistic and extralinguistic channels to accomplish communicative functions. This finding challenges the claim that language is the primary mode of instruction in school-based learning and demonstration is the primary mode of informal instruction.

A distinction has often been made between formal and informal education, especially in cross-cultural studies of cognition and development. Formal and informal education are seen as two poles anchoring a continuum, and can be described by means of a set of contrasting statements: Whereas informal education is embedded in daily activities, formal education is set apart from the context of everyday life; whereas the learner is responsible for obtaining the knowledge and skill in informal learning, the teacher is responsible for imparting knowledge and skill in formal learning; whereas informal learning is personalistic or particularistic, with relatives or other intimates serving as teachers, formal learning is impersonalistic or universalistic, with strangers serving as teachers; informal learning has little or no explicit curriculum, whereas formal learning does; maintenance of continuity and tradition are valued in informal learning, whereas change, discontinuity, and innovation are valued in formal learning; informal learning is characterized by observation and imitation, whereas formal learning is characterized by verbal interchange, especially questioning; demonstration is the method of informal learning, verbal representation of general principles the method of formal learning (list distilled from Scribner & Cole, 1973; Greenfield & Lave, 1979).

Although the formal versus informal learning distinction has been the topic of much cross-cultural research in foreign settings, a unique opportunity enabled us to consider this distinction in a domestic setting. Courtney B. Cazden, a noted authority in child language and education, (e.g., Cazden, 1972; Cazden, John, & Hymes, 1972), took leave from the Harvard Graduate School of Education during the 1974–1975 academic year to return to an earlier career as an elementary school teacher. She taught with LaDonna Coles in a cross-age, ethnically mixed classroom in San Diego, in which there were 25 black and Chicano children in a combined first–second–third grade. This classroom has already been written about in Cazden's (1976) personal account of the teaching experience, and has served as the basis for analyses of peer teaching (Carrasco, Vera, & Cazden, 1979; Cazden, Cox, Dickinson, Steinberg, and Stone, 1979; Steinberg & Cazden, 1979) and of the structuring and acquisition of the structure of formal lessons (Mehan, 1979, 1980; cf. Cazden, 1979). This chapter offers another dimension to the analysis of teacher–student and student–student interaction.

Whereas the other studies mentioned here are microethnographic studies of a few "instruction chains," this study treats a larger number in more general terms.

Studying Formal and Informal Instruction in a Classroom Setting

The team teachers (Cazden and Coles) had set up learning centers in their classroom. This arrangement facilitated the introduction of a quasi-experimental procedure of intervention into the ongoing classroom routine. The intervention took the form of an "instruction chain." As the first link in the chain, one of the teachers instructed a child on an academic task. Next, this student was asked to formulate the instructions he or she would use to teach his or her work group, and the teacher and student completed the task. Then, the student teacher assembled his or her usual work group, and carried out instruction about the assigned task. Twelve instances of this instruction chain serve as the basis of our comparison of informal and formal learning.

Our expectation—based on the distinctions made between informal and formal learning in exotic cultures and on analyses of classroom discourse (Mehan, 1979b; Shuy & Griffin, 1978; Sinclair & Coulthard, 1975)—was that the adult teacher's instruction to the student teachers would have the characteristics associated with formal teaching (i.e., would be highly verbal in nature, replete with questions, replies, and elicitations of information, and with information presented primarily in the verbal channel). We wished to see whether the student teachers' instructions to their work groups would also have the characteristics of formal instruction, or whether they would more closely approximate the characteristics of informal learning (i.e., would utilize observations, demonstrations, imitations, with nonverbal channels predominating over the verbal channel as a means of presenting information).

Procedures

The instruction chains were videotaped in the classroom as they occurred during the everyday classroom routine. The tasks used in the instruction chains were similar to others used in this classroom. Most concerned some aspect of the reading process, and were designed with two considerations in mind (Steinberg & Cazden, 1979): (a) they were to have components that the students already understand but that were assembled in some new and nonobvious way; and (b) the student teacher was to have information that the learners lacked but needed in order to complete their work.

The audio portion of the videotape was transcribed with speakers and turns identified. The transcripts and videotapes served as the basis for analysis. The categories employed by Pratt, Scribner, and Cole (1977) were modified for the purpose of this analysis.[2] Pratt *et al.* classified the function of each utterance in their protocols into one of seven general categories. Because their experimental task was a board game, five of their seven categories were concerned with various types of game-related information: descriptions of materials, general characteristics of the game, starting rules, and specific rules for the play of a turn. A sixth category comprised all statements serving general orienting functions; all other statements were categorized as "miscellaneous."

Our modifications were related to the fact that our domain was educational projects and not board games. For example, we changed all references to "game related information" to "educational task information." Both adult and student teachers broke the educational tasks into components, used orienting moves to prepare the instructional scene, provided comments on work completed, and taught by example. Therefore, we added "subtask" codes, "directives," "feedback" (positive, neutral, and negative), and "examples" to the list of categories. We classified examples according to modality (purely verbal, purely gestural, and mixed), direction (taken or given), and initiator (teacher or learner).

Our unit of analysis is the "move" (Bellak, Kliehard, Hyman, & Smith, 1966; Goffman, 1976)—behavior, verbal or other, taken to accomplish an action. Moves were catalogued on transcript protocols while watching videotape. The raw number of moves and their frequencies were calculated. This calculation gives the frequency distribution of teacher and student moves. We also kept track of the sequential organization of the teaching–learning episodes—the order of moves from the beginning to the end of an episode—in order to examine teaching–learning as a process.

Discussion

FREQUENCY DISTRIBUTIONS

The distribution of instructional moves across the nine coding categories is given in Table 15.1. There is a preponderance of moves in certain categories (e.g., 5–6, "procedures"; 7, "examples"; and 9, "feedback"), with very few moves in other categories. Particularly notable is the almost complete absence of moves that "frame" the instructional task (2, "global instructions for the task," and 8, "general outcome"), by either the adult or student teachers. Teachers sometimes orient to the immediate, pragmatic

---

[2] See Appendix I for a sample coding sheet, code definitions, and some coding problems encountered in this study.

purpose of the task: "the object of this game is to get rid of all your cards" (protocol #21, teacher–student portion), but do not mention the overall, academic purpose of the task (in this case, sound–letter correspondence). The paucity of framing moves suggests that teaching often concentrates more on *how* tasks are performed, and less on *why* tasks are performed.

Although Pratt *et al.* (1977) reported considerable reference to materials in all conditions of their experimental task, we found very little discussion of the materials to be used in the instructional tasks. With both adult and student teachers, such discussion took place only when the materials were different from the usual classroom equipment.

The teacher- and student-led portions of the instruction chains displayed little difference in the total number, the range, or the means of instructions used; nonetheless, there were differences in the distribution of the instructional moves. Student teachers used more directives than adult teachers; adult teachers used more general orienting instructions (Category 3). Furthermore, adult teachers gave twice as much feedback to learners as did student teachers. These distributions speak to the different strategies for capturing attention and maintaining learner involvement used by adult and student teachers (Carrasco *et al.*, 1979; Cazden *et al.*, 1979).

SEQUENTIAL ORGANIZATION

The sequential organization of teacher- and student-led instruction chains gives further insight into the teaching–learning process. The typical adult-led instruction chain began with directives to organize the teaching situation: "Um, now, I want to explain something to you so that you can explain it to Everett. Let's see, come sit over here." Directives were followed by orienting statements: "Now, here are some words. And I'm going to cut them into separate word cards. Now, see if you can put those in a row so that they make a good sentence."

A series of examples was typically elicited after the procedural orientation statement:

T: . . . *for instance, let's see, number, the first one*
S: (reading): *Regina is a girl and Cynthia is—*
T: *One of these words will fit in these and make sense.* (reading): *Cynthia is a blank girl*
S: (pause) *another*
T: *"another"* right

These example elicitation sequences are similar in many respects to the questioning sequences found in whole group and small group formal lessons (Mehan, 1979; Shuy & Griffin, 1978; Sinclair & Coulthard, 1975). Both

Table 15.1
The Percentage of Student and Teacher Moves

Protocol #[a]	Teaching portion[b]	Instructional moves										N
		1 Directives	*2* Global	*3* General orientation	*4* Materials	*5–6* Procedures	*7* Examples	*8* Outcome	*9* Feedback	*10* Miscellaneous	
11	T→S	5	0	13	0	21	45	0	16	0	38
	S→Ss	18	0	0	0	9	64	0	0	9	33
15	T→S	0	0	3	3	17	40	0	37	0	30
	S→Ss	4	0	0	0	7	67	0	11	11	45
16	T→S	2.5	0	0	0	25	35	0	35	2.5	40
	S→Ss	16	0	6	0	12	18	4	27	21	49
17	T→S	1	0	9	0	30	26	4	9	13	23
	S→Ss	6	0	6	0	6	46	4	4	27	48
18	T→S	4	0	5	0	5	45	0	36	4	55
	S→Ss	8	0	4	0	12.5	33	0	21	21	24
19	T→S	4	1	8	3	27	19	0	32	6	73
	S→Ss	6.2	0	6.2	9	4.1	16	0	9	12.5	32

Protocol[a]	Type[b]										Total
21	T→ S	0	0	4	8	27	30	3	17	11	92
	T→ Ss	1	0	1	4	27	39	3	12	14	75
22	T→ S	10	2.5	2.5	2.5	20	37.5	0	.25	0	40
	S→ Ss	2	0	4	0	33	51	0	5	5	55
25	T→ S	4.5	0	4.5	7	13.5	27	0	30	13.5	44
	S→ Ss	15	3	0	0	6	3	3	10	66	71
27	T→ S	3	6	12.5	9.5	21	24	0	19	8	63
	S→ Ss	0	0	13	3	19	28	0	22	6	32
28	T→ S	0	0	2	5	8	55	0	28	2	164
	S→ Ss	0	0	2	0	20	60	0	13	5	55
29	T→ S	14	0	24	0	5	19	0	33	5	21
	S→ Ss	0	0	3	0	30	59	0	8	0	31
Teacher Total		5	0.5	7	3	18	34	0.5	27	5	683
Student total		6	0.5	4	1	16	40	1	12	17	553

Mean 57 47

Range T→ S 21–92
S→ Ss 22–75

[a] Protocol number refers to number on videotape.
[b] T→ S = adult teacher to student; S→ Ss = student to work group.

had a three part initiation–reply–evaluation structure, concluding with the teacher's evaluation of the student's immediately preceding reply.

After a number of example rounds, adult teachers closed with either a reminder of subtask procedures or a statement about the general outcome that was expected: "Now, after you finish, put the words into these sentences, then, here you write the number of syllables."

A "sentence" representing the typical teacher-led instruction chain would be written as:

directive; general orienting procedure; specific procedures; examples; general final outcome or restatement of procedures.

Whereas the sequential organization of the various adult-led teaching sessions remained fairly constant, the sequential organization of the student-led sessions was more variable. There was a variety of organization of moves for gathering and managing the group, conveying authority, and accomplishing the teaching–learning task. Nonetheless, even here a number of generalizations can be made.

For example, the student-led sessions were opened in one of two ways, which were employed with approximately equal frequency. The first way involved beginning with a general orientation to the task and/or a comment about procedures, and then either demonstrating the task or eliciting an example from the group. In such openings, the second or third utterance typically contained an example.

Greg: *You, you, you, you know how to do this? You know how to do it? The,*
        circle, the sentence that, that are good (pause) *cross the sentences that*
        are bad. "Mother is at home." Is that good or is that bad?
                                                        (from #29, Greg)

Children who opened the session in this way (15, 18, 21, 22, 28, 29) continued to teach by moving back and forth from comments about procedures and examples, with much less use of directives, orienting comments, or evaluations.

The other way involved beginning with either a directive or an orienting comment, and then describing the task through a combination of directives, orienting comments, descriptions of materials, and procedural statements before moving to examples. Throughout these sessions, student teachers used fewer procedural statements (9% versus 21% used by the other group), and fewer examples (29% versus 51% for the other group).

Both groups end the task in similar ways, with either a final example, a restatement of a procedure, and/or an evaluative comment about the completion of the task. Frequently, the session simply dissolved into the next classroom activity, with completion signaled by the putting away of materials.

A sentence for the sequential order of the student-led teaching sessions would look like this:

orientation, example, procedures, examples, task completion
directive, orientation, procedures, examples, task completion

TEACHING BY EXAMPLE

Teaching by example was the primary move in the instruction chains. It was the modal category in all but two of the adult-led protocols, and all but one of the student-led protocols. However, there are interesting differences in the ways examples are organized in the two portions of the instruction chains.

Adult teachers were much more likely to *elicit examples from* learners, whereas student-teachers were more likely to *give examples to* the members of their work groups. Table 15.2 shows that 81% of adult teachers' examples were elicited, compared to 19% of student teachers'; whereas 58% of student teachers' examples were given, compared to 9% of adult teachers'.

The following is an example of an adult teacher eliciting examples:

T: *Number two says . . .*
S: *No*
T: *"No." What's the opposite of no?*
S: *Yes*
T: *Ok. How do you spell "yes"?*
S: *Y–E–S*
T: *Alright. Now, what are you going . . .*
S: (crosses out letters y–e–s on chalkboard) *Told*
T: *What do you have left?*
S: *Told*
T: *Alright. So, what are you going to write here?*
S: *Told*

The next segment is from the same instruction chain; the student who was receiving instruction in the preceding dialogue is now in the teacher role and gives examples:

L: *See you gotta do the opposite of "no." No is yes on number two. No is yes.*
So you gotta write y–e–s. Then you have "told" left. So you write told.
(from #22, Leola)

Moreover, learners spontaneously supplied more examples in the case of

Table 15.2
The Percentage of Examples Elicited and Given by Adult Teachers, Student Teachers, and Learners

		Examples				
Protocol #[a]	Teaching portion[a]	Teacher-elicited examples	Teacher-given examples	Learner-elicited examples	Learner-given examples	N
11	T→ S	100	—	—	—	17
	S→ Ss	—	85	14	—	21
15	T→ S	92	—	—	—	12
	S→ Ss	—	93	3	3	30
16	T→ S	78	7	—	14	14
	S→ Ss	22	22	33	22	9
17	T→ S	16	—	83	—	6
	S→ Ss	—	37	9	51	22
18	T→ S	96	—	4	—	25
	S→ Ss	25	25	25	25	8
19	T→ S	79	7	—	14	14
	S→ Ss	40	60	—	—	5
21	T→ S	28	67	—	3	28
	S→ Ss	34	61	3	—	29
22	T→ S	93	7	0	—	15
	S→ Ss	—	71	7	21	28
25	T→ S	100	—	—	—	12
	S→ Ss	—	100	—	—	2
27	T→ S	93	7	—	—	15
	S→ Ss	11	67	11	11	9
28	T→ S	92	8	—	—	91
	S→ Ss	18	60	9	12	33
29	T→ S	100	—	—	—	4
	S→ Ss	80	10	10	—	20
	Teacher total	81	9	7	3	253
	Student total	19	58	10	12	486

[a] T→ S = adult teacher to student; S→ Ss = student to work group.

student-led instruction than in the case of teacher-led instruction. Table 15.2 shows a difference of 22%–10% in this respect.

This difference between examples given and examples taken seems to suggest that interaction is more under the control of the teacher when an adult rather than a student is in the teacher role. When learners were with adults, they waited for the teacher to teach; but when they were with a peer, the learners played a more active part in the teaching–learning process— sometimes questioning the ability of the student teacher to teach. Moreover, when learners were with an adult teacher, there was little initiation of interaction on the part of the learners. Learner behavior most often falls under a heading such as "response to teacher's question." But when a student is in the teacher role, the learners take a more active part in extracting information. This difference can be seen in Table 15.2. Note the increased number of entries under the "learner elicited" and "learner given" heading when students, not adults, are teachers. Thus, although both adult and student led instruction is socially accomplished, student-led instruction seems to be more open to negotiation.

VERBAL AND NONVERBAL INSTRUCTION

The verbal–nonverbal distinction is at the heart of the formal–informal education dichotomy. Informal education is said to use the nonverbal channels of communication to a greater extent, whereas verbal explicitness is seen as a sign of more advanced, context-free teaching. Childs and Greenfield (1979) cite Margaret Mead's example "you do it like this" as representative of context-dependent verbalization in informal education. Many observers point out that children who do not go to school use language in a more context-dependent manner than children who have some formal education (Greenfield, Reich, & Olver, 1966). A similar observation has been made about lower class and ethnic minority children in the United States and Great Britain.

The student teachers' formulation of instructions to their work groups often appeared at first to be like Mead's example, that is, less elaborate and explicit than the adult teacher's. For example, consider the following formulations of instructions:

Edward (to work group):   *Alberto, here . . . I help you. See there? You, yeah, you do that. There, you're supposed to trace it all over. Do, do these numbers down there.*   (from #16)

Alberto (to work group):   *Know how to do it? You have to, to, to put a line to put a line on what things go into the house. This, this, this, this, this, this. Out. This, this, this, this, this, this, this, this go out. That's all.*   (from #15)

Although these instructions seem to be less explicit, the reduction in information in the verbal channel was not critical for the communication of instructions by the student teachers to their work groups. At each step in these instruction chains, the student teachers encoded information extralinguistically in combination with linguistic signals to locate materials and to communicate the operations to be performed on the materials. Demonstration was clearly combined with what seemed to be context-dependent verbalization to achieve communicative ends (cf. Childs & Greenfield, 1979;

Greenfield & Lave, 1979), a finding that belies the claim that demonstration is an ineffective method of instruction.

The general conception of formal teaching is that the teacher uses the verbal modality to represent information. This stereotype did not hold up in these instruction chains. The adult teacher, like the student teacher, combined linguistic and extralinguistic channels to accomplish communicative functions. This finding is illustrated in Table 15.3, which shows the majority of examples were communicated via mixed modalities, not by verbalization alone. The use of demonstrated instructions, perhaps found as a result of the more careful analysis afforded by repeated viewings of videotape, challenges the claim that language is the primary means of exchanging information in the school situation.

MEDIATING STRATEGIES

There are two instances of the student teacher delegating authority to others in the work group. In one case (18), the student teacher asked another student to teach, so that the instruction chain became student-to-student-to-student, instead of student-to-work group. In another case, the student teacher enlisted the help of a friend who was not supposed to be involved in the task to mediate. This interaction is interesting, because it represents the use of a third person as a social resource to accomplish a task and to maintain the order of a social arrangement (Hood, McDermott, & Cole, 1980).

FEEDBACK

Another difference between adult- and student-led sessions had to do with the amount and type of feedback (see Table 15.4).

Adult teachers used more than twice as much feedback, consisting mostly of positive evaluations ("good," "right," etc.), and neutral comments (repetitions, "ok," etc.). Student teachers very rarely gave any positive evaluation that was easily coded. They often looked at the work of other students, and either said nothing (not coded), repeated an example (neutral feedback), or provided negative evaluation ("you did it wrong" or "no, you're supposed

Table 15.3

Frequency of Examples during Teaching Sessions by Modality (%)

Teaching portion	Modality			N
	Verbal	Gestures	Mixed	
T→ S	44	9	47	253
S→ Ss	46	3	50	486

Table 15.4
Types of Teacher and Student Feedback (%)

Protocol #	Teaching portion	Feedback			N
		Positive	Neuter	Negative	
11	T→ S	100	—	—	6
	S→ Ss	—	—	—	0
15	T→ S	46	54	—	11
	S→ Ss	—	20	80	5
16	T→ S	50	50	—	14
	S→ Ss	15	30	55	13
17	T→ S	100	—	—	2
	S→ Ss	—	50	50	2
18	T→ S	40	50	10	20
	S→ Ss	—	100	—	5
19	T→ S	17	74	9	23
	S→ Ss	—	—	100	3
21	T→ S	12	81	6	16
	S→ Ss	11	77	11	9
22	T→ S	10	70	20	10
	S→ Ss	—	66	33	3
25	T→ S	15	85	—	13
	S→ Ss	—	—	100	7
27	T→ S	58	42	—	12
	S→ Ss	—	43	57	7
28	T→ S	46	48	6	16
	S→ Ss	0	43	57	7
29	T→ S	14	85	—	7
	S→ Ss	—	66	33	3
	Teacher total	42	53	4	99
	Student total	2	38	48	98

to do it this way"). Most positive evaluation that did occur in these sessions occurred after an example was elicited by the student teacher, or after a student provided an example.

Conclusion

The main conclusions that emerge from this investigation of students' and teachers' instructional strategies have to do with the association of nonverbal instruction with informal education and verbal instruction with formal education.

First of all, we found it difficult to keep these two distinctions distinct. Informal education is supposed to involve demonstration by the skilled person, observation by the learner, followed by participation in the completion of tasks. Participation implies that the learner is cooperating with the teacher. Formal education, by contrast, is said to involve the presentation of general principles and the questioning of students' knowledge, both by verbal means. Formal education is also said to be more privatized. As learners gain more experience in school, cooperative work declines in favor of individualized effort.

In making comparisons across situations or groups, social scientists often compare a new situation or group with tacitly held assumptions about the well-known situation or group. For example, *studies* of informal education are contrasted with *assumptions* about formal education. Greenfield and Lave (1979) found a great variety of instructional techniques in informal educational settings. Trial and error, focused observation, and verbalization were all very common in the weaving and tailoring situations they studied. We found the same mixture in formal teaching situations. There were few purely verbal instructions; most instructions operated in mixed modalities. Teachers presented verbal instructions with demonstrations and actual performance, and cooperatively completed tasks with learners.

Thus, not only does the stereotyped association of nonverbal instructional strategies with informal education seem inappropriate (Greenfield & Lave, 1979), but the association of verbal instructional strategies with formal education also needs to be reexamined.

The formal–informal and verbal–nonverbal distinctions have direct consequences for the education of "minority" children. Lower class and ethnic minority children have often been characterized as having an impoverished or restricted version of adults' communicative codes (Bereiter & Engleman, 1972; Bernstein, 1971; Hess & Shipman, 1968). Before accepting such a characterization, however, it is necessary to determine the manner by which communicative functions are fulfilled.

The reduction of information in the verbal channel was not critical for the communication of instructions by the teachers to learners. If children do not duplicate adult forms of communication, it does not necessarily imply that they have limited competence. The transfer of information across modalities is part of the functional aspect of competence (Shuy & Griffin, 1978). Those who conclude that children who do not speak like adults have a limited competence overemphasize the verbal mode of expression and the grammatical aspects of language. They equate the use of well-formed sentences with intellectual achievement. Such views do not recognize that there are different means to express the same communicative end, and that people, especially those from different cultural backgrounds, may have different but functionally equivalent procedures for communicating information.

Appendix: Coding Information

TAPE #: CIS_____   TASK_____

Portion_____

Part 1: Coding Form

	N			Total	%
1. Directive					
2. Global description of the task					
3. General orienting procedures for overall task	Given		Taken		
4. Description of materials					
5. Specific procedures for subtask					
6. Specific outcome for subtask					
7. Examples for completing task or subtask					
7.1 Teacher elicits example from Ss	Words	Gest	Mixed		
7.2 Teacher gives example to Ss	Tell	Show	Mixed		
7.3 Ss elicit example from Teacher	Words	Gest	Mixed		
7.4 Ss give example to Teacher	Tell	Show	Mixed		
8. General final outcome					
9. Feedback					
a. positive					
b. negative					
c. neutral					
Total					

10. Misc. representative sequences_____

_____

_____

Comments_____

_____

_____

Part 2: Definitions
   1. *Directives*—Moves organizing learners to prepare for instruction, in-
      cluded are requests for attention, materials, and spatial rearrangement.
   2. *Global description of the task*—Moves describing or relating to the
      task as a whole; distinguished from descriptions of parts of the task.
   3. *General orienting procedures for the overall task*—Moves that gave
      learners an overall sense of the purpose of the task; framing moves.
   4. *Description of materials*—Specific references to the materials to be
      used in the completion of the task.
   5. *Specific procedures for subtask*—Moves that oriented learners to parts
      of the task, distinguished one component from another.
   6. *Specific outcome for subtask*—Moves that referred to the end point
      or product of a component or part of the task.
   7. *Examples*—This category was arranged using three pairs of binary
      opposites: (*a*) participants (student/teacher); (*b*) direction of examples
      (given by teacher or taken from learners); and (*c*) modality (verbal,
      "words," or "tell"; nonverbal, "gestures," or "show"; and mixed).
   8. *General final outcome*—Moves that referred to the end point or prod-
      uct of the task as a whole.
   9. *Feedback*—Three types of moves were identified: (*a*) positive (e.g.,
      "good, fine, nice"); (*b*) negative ("Oh, you did a bad job");
      (*c*) neutral ("Ok," repeats of previous replies).
  10. *Miscellaneous*—Side sequences, discussions or orientations to people
      outside of group; plays in a game which did not have obvious in-
      structional value (see coding problems in Part 3 of this appendix).

Part 3: Coding Difficulties
In addition to the difficulties generally associated with coding operations
(i.e., taking behavior out of context) (Cicourel, 1964), there were a number
of specific problems encountered in this study.

   1. Category 5 "specific procedures for subtask" was almost impossible
      to distinguish from Category 6 "specific outcome for the subtask," at
      least insofar as the participants referred to instructional materials. We
      resolved this problem by collapsing the categories during the course
      of the study.
   2. The verbal–nonverbal distinction was inadequate to capture any shifts
      in modality in the course of instruction. Virtually every instruction was
      "mixed."
   3. Many students "talked out loud" while working on tasks. It was not
      clear whether this talk was an intentional attempt to communicate to
      others present (e.g., by giving an example or indicating progress of
      work) or simply externalized monologue.

4. When the task involved gamelike situations, after initial instructions the group often "played the game." In such cases, each move in the game could be coded as an instance of Category 7 "an example." We chose not to do this however.

Acknowledgments

Sue Fisher and Nick Maroules helped gather the videotape data and transcribe audio portions. Irene Villanueva transcribed the Spanish. In addition to agreeing to have their teaching practices subject to daily scrutiny, Courtney B. Cazden and LaDonna Coles have made many valuable suggestions about ideas presented in this chapter.

References

Bellack, A. A., Kliebard, H. M., Hyman, R. T., & Smith, F. L., Jr. *The language of the classroom.* New York: Teachers College Press, 1966.

Bereiter, K., & Engleman, S. *Teaching the disadvantaged child in preschool.* Englewood Cliffs, N.J.: Prentice-Hall, 1972.

Bernstein, B. *Class, codes and control.* London: Routledge & Kegan Paul, 1971.

Carrasco, R. L., Vera, A., & Cazden, C. B. Aspects of bilingual students' communicative competence in the classroom. In R. Duran (Ed.), *Discourse processes 4: Latino language and communicative behavior.* Norwood, N.J.: Ablex, 1979.

Cazden, C. B. *Child language and education.* New York: Holt, Rinehart & Winston, 1972.

Cazden, C. B. How knowledge about language helps the classroom teacher—or does it? A personal account. *The Urban Review,* 1976, *9,* 74–90.

Cazden, C. B. Peekaboo as an instructional model: Discourse development at home and school. *Papers and Reports on Child Language Development,* No. 17, Stanford University, Department of Linguistics, 1979.

Cazden, C. B., Cox, M., Dickinson, D., Steinberg, Z. You all gonna hafta listen: Peer teaching in a primary classroom. In W. A. Collins (Ed.), *Children's language and communication.* Hillsboro, N.J.: Lawrence Erlbaum, 1979.

Cazden, C. B., John, V. P., & Hymes, D. (Eds.). *Functions of language in the classroom.* New York: Teachers College Press, 1972.

Childs, C. P., & Greenfield, P. M. Informal modes of learning and teaching. In N. Warren (Ed.), *Advances in cross-cultural psychology.* London: Academic Press, 1979.

Cicourel, A. V. *Method and measurement in sociology.* New York: Free Press, 1964.

Goffman, E. Replies and responses. *Language in Society,* 1976, *5,* 257–313.

Greenfield, P. M., & Lave, J. Cognitive aspects of informal education. Unpublished manuscript, 1979.

Greenfield, P. M., Reich, L., & Olver, R. R. On culture and equivalence, II. In J. S. Bruner, R. Olver, & P. Greenfield (Eds.), *Studies in cognitive growth.* New York: Wiley, 1966.

Hess, R. D., & Shipman, V. C. Maternal influences on early learning. In R. D. Hess & R. M. Bear (Eds.), *Early education.* Chicago: Aldine, 1968.

Hood, L., McDermott, R., & Cole, M. Let's *try* to make it a good day—Some not so simple ways. *Discourse Processes,* 1980, *3,* 155–168.

Mehan, H. *Learning lessons.* Cambridge, Mass.: Harvard University Press, 1979.

Mehan, H. The competent student. *Anthropology and Education Quarterly* XI, 1980, *3,* 131–152.

Pratt, M. W., Scribner, S., & Cole, M. Children as teachers: Developmental studies of instructional communication. *Child Development,* 1977, *48,* 1475–1481.

Scribner, S., & Cole, M. Cognitive consequences of formal and informal education. *Science,* 1973, *182,* 553–559.

Shuy, R., & Griffin, P. (Eds.). *The study of children's functional language and education in the early years.* (Final Report to the Carnegie Corporation.) Arlington, Va.: Center for Applied Linguistics, 1978.

Sinclair, J. M., & Coulthard, R. M. *Toward an analysis of discourse.* New York: Oxford University Press, 1975.

Steinberg, Z. D., & Cazden, C. B. Children as teachers—of peers and ourselves. *Theory into Practice, 18*(4): 258–267.

Modernization and Stereotypes

Part IV is launched very ably and effectively by coauthors Eleanor Leacock and June Nash, who question—using Arapaho and Aztec counterexamples—Levi-Strauss's universal dichotomization of nature and culture as (inferior) female and (superior) male. In their chapter, they draw on Aztec data to show the general trend from female-oriented, to androgynous, to bisexual, to all-powerful male gods. They point out that Aztec female-centered themes were distorted by the early Spaniards, and continue to be distorted by contemporary interpreters, to fit western ways of thinking. From the old to the new: The next chapter by Fairfid M. Caudle opens a new door in cross-cultural research with its discussion of advertising. This form of social communication is a rich source cross-culturally for investigations of value systems and for observations of trends in social changes. The author focuses on two specific aspects in advertising which have particular relevance to cross-cultural issues. The first concerns advertising's appeal to social motives, such as achievement, power, and affiliation; the second concerns the way in which advertising mirrors the cultural sex-role stereotypes. The next chapter investigates attitudes that accompany the modernization process. Robert C. Williamson's research included extensive testing of middle-aged adults and college students from various socioeconomic backgrounds in six countries, both developed and developing. The results disclosed that cultural and generational differences were as important in predicting attitudes as the stage of development. For example, with the rationalism–traditionalism scale samples from the United States responded far more traditionally than did their

German and Japanese counterparts. However the most traditionalistic scores were obtained from the Chilean, the Colombian, and the Spanish samples. The author of the next chapter, Pauline A. Jones investigated the determinants of individual family traditionalism–modernism and examines the effects of holding more traditional values. The research reported involved high school students and their mothers in both Canada and Australia. Two specific areas of investigation were the focus in this cross-national research: The first was concerned with family structure scales, and the second was centered on childrearing scales. The results showed great consistency. It was observed that students with higher traditionalism scores had mothers whose socialization practices hindered the development of independence. Such students were also more likely to live in small communities. The chapter concludes by evaluating predictors of modernism and traditionalism. In the next chapter, Florence L. Denmark, Nira Weinberg, and Joyce Block discuss the persistence of sexual inequality in the Soviet Union and Israel—two nations that had made sexual equality a fundamental tenet. In the USSR women carry double responsibility. At work, they perform the jobs just as do the men (though without complete equality); at home, they have primary responsibility for taking care of the household and doing "women's work." In contrast, with Israel's development into an industrialized nation, the participation by women in the productive economy was no longer needed. Women's responsibilities came to center upon childrearing, and in time there was a reemergence of the traditional sex roles. Yet in both the USSR and Israel the myth of equality persists. The authors conclude that a reevaluation of female and male roles—and an integration of "masculine" and "feminine" values within each culture—is essential if changes are to be effected. The next chapter is not truly cross-cultural as it utilizes subjects from only one country, India. However, by implication and comparison, the research discussed in this chapter presents an important topic for cross-cultural research. Usha Kumar and Urmil Arora observed the interactions of married couples working together on structured and unstructured tasks. All couples had been questioned intensively and selected for participation on the basis of their ego identity status, which, in Erik Erikson's terms, implies a subjective feeling of self-perception, and uses the Western, or specifically the American-European formulation of the psychosocial developmental stages. (Eighty percent of the marriages were arranged by the parents, whereas the remaining marriages had been arranged by the couples with or without parental consent.) As hypothesized, the psychosocial maturity of the couples determined the quality of their relationship and interaction when they performed their tasks together. The last chapter reports the results of a cross-national study by Uwe Gielen, who compared the ideal self-ratings (based on a 63 adjective

Q-sort) of university students from Germany and the United States. The responses of the samples from the two countries differ greatly. Both German and American students follow certain national stereotypic ego ideal qualities. Yet, there are some areas of expected characteristic behaviors that were not reflected in their ego ideals.

Ideologies of Sex: Archetypes and Stereotypes[1]

ABSTRACT

This chapter takes issue with Lévi-Strauss on his formulation of a universal dichotomization of nature and culture as (inferior) female and (superior) male. The authors argue that the nature–culture dichotomy as defined by Lévi-Strauss is characteristically western, and they use materials from the egalitarian Arapaho of the Great Plains to illustrate alternate symbolizations of natural and cultural, and female and male. They then draw on Aztec data to illustrate the trend from female-centered, to androgynous, to bisexual, to all-powerful male gods as an egalitarian society became transformed into a military state, and to show how the earlier female-centered or androgynous themes were distorted in the writings of the early Spanish as well as in present-day analyses, in both cases being revised to fit western categories of thought.

At present, research is documenting the practical importance of women in economic, social, and political decision making in egalitarian societies, and the historical sources of women's relegation to an inferior status are being examined (Brown, 1975; Etienne & Leacock, 1980; Hoffer, 1974; Leacock, 1978; Lebeuf, 1971; Nash, 1978; Rohrlich-Leavitt, 1976; Sacks, 1975; Schlegel, 1977; Sutton, 1976). Nonetheless, following a line of argument initiated by Lévi-Strauss, some scholars contend that women have been ideologically devalued in all societies and that their symbolic subordination has always led to social subordination. It is our intention here to

---

[1] A longer version of this chapter appeared in L.L. Adler (Ed.), *Issues in Cross-Cultural Research,* Annals of the New York Academy of Sciences, 1977, *285.*

CROSS-CULTURAL RESEARCH AT ISSUE

disclose the superficiality of cross-cultural generalizations that are filtered uncritically through European categories of thought, by (a) pointing out the western background for Lévi-Strauss's supposition that a dichotomy is universally drawn between women as inferior "nature" and men as superior "culture"; (b) illustrating nonwestern formulations, citing Arapaho philosophy and Aztec theology as examples; and (c) showing how alternate formulations have been distorted by western colonizers and western observers, using the Aztecs as a case study.

Statements of the Nature–Culture Thesis

Lévi-Strauss (1969, 1970a), to whom "human society is primarily a masculine society" built an assumed devaluation of women and nature into his thesis of culture origins, and de Beauvoir (1952) elaborated upon it in her exposition of the masculine ideology in which women are today entrapped. Drawing on these writers, Ortner (1974) has reasserted a female–male dichotomy as universally linked with a nature–culture polarity, in response to "the most generalized situation in which all human beings, in whatever culture, find themselves," and as underlying what she sees as the subordination of women to men "in every known society," past and present.

Lévi-Strauss does not address himself to female subordination as such; he simply takes it for granted. In fact, he could well argue that women are valued highly, for they are, he writes (1969, pp. 62, 65, 479, 496), "the group's most important asset," "the supreme gift." It is through the exchange of this "most precious possession" that men set up the network of intergroup ties that supersedes the family, in Lévi-Strauss's view, and "ensures the dominance of the social over the biological." Women are even central to the emergence of symbolic thought, Lévi-Strauss states, for this development "must have required that women, like words, should be things that were exchanged."

De Beauvoir's aim was to challenge the prevailing ideology of western culture with regard to sex, and to demonstrate the ramifications of men's definition of women as the "other," as deviants from a norm, as the inessential object by contrast with the essential subject. Her contribution to the understanding of women's position, particularly its psychological aspects, was considerable, and we do not wish to discount it. Our argument with de Beauvoir lies with her implicit acceptance of Hegel's (1952, p. 31) formulation that man is the active principle, in consequence of his differentiation, whereas woman is the passive principle, because in her unity she remains undeveloped, and with de Beauvoir's projection of the existential phrasing of woman as "immanent" and man as "transcendent" beyond patriarchal society onto the totality of human experience.

"This has always been a man's world," de Beauvoir (1952, pp. 57–67) states by way of introduction to early society, and she pictures women, in "the age of the club and the wild beast," as suffering under "the bondage of reproduction," "a terrible handicap in the struggle against a hostile world." Women produced more children than they could care for; their "extravagant fertility" prevented them from increasing group resources while they "created new needs to an indefinite extent." Hence men "had to assure equilibrium between reproduction and production." Women knew no pride of creating; engaged in "natural functions," not "activities," they were trapped in repetitious tasks that "produced nothing new," while men were the inventors, furnishing support through "acts that transcended . . . animal nature," "prevailed over the confused forces of life," and "subdued Nature and Woman." In woman "was to be summed up the whole of alien Nature."

In developing her recent formulation of "Is female to male as nature is to culture?" Ortner (1974, pp. 75–76) necessarily recognizes and pays respects to accumulating information on women's roles as substantial creators of culture. Ortner's position is that women's procreative functions and "domestic" activities overrule their other cultural contributions. Women are seen as *closer* to nature than men, she argues, as "something intermediate between culture and nature, lower on the scale of transcendence than men." Ortner parenthetically relegates the whole association of men with culture and women with nature to the realm of the unconscious, an area less subject to falsification by contradictory data.

To be sure, the processes whereby symbolic equations are made and concepts linked are largely unconscious. However, the linkages, if they exist, must reveal themselves in art, literature, religious belief, and/or social injunction. The propositions listed here should thus be reflected in symbolic clusterings associated with female and male terms in worldwide ideological materials. Yet artistic, mythological, and religious materials from different times and contrasting cultures negate the proposition that male as culture is universally conceived as superior to female as nature. Instead, crosscultural data indicate that:

1. The linked derogation of women and nature is not a characteristic of egalitarian societies.
2. Male assertiveness does not automatically flow from some archetypical source, but is related to a developing competition over social and economic prerogatives among men and between men and women in technologically elaborated horticultural societies.
3. Ideological trends foreshadowing the European ethos accompany the emergence of full-scale hierarchical organization in both eastern and western hemispheres.
4. The formulas regarding female nature as opposed to and inferior to

culture are suspiciously European, and in some respects of recent vintage.

As Lévi-Strauss's own work demonstrates, the earth, the sky, the heavenly bodies, the weather, and plants, animals, and minerals are individually symbolized as variously female and male; the situation is never one of nature as the sum total of existing things counterposed to human society and manufactures. Yet Lévi-Strauss does not ask what the general lack of terms for a dichotomized "nature" and "culture" might signify in societies structured differently from our own, nor does he inquire into the import of wholly different conceptions of nature.

The classical Ionian philosophers used the term *nature* to refer to the essential character or essence of a phenomenon. This remained the normal sense of the term in Greek writings, although its alternate sense as an aggregate appeared in the late fifth century (Collingwood, 1960, pp. 43–46). Yet it was a nature still endowed with purposive intelligence of a human order, like the once universal conception of the nonhuman world as alive with spirits that had to be variously honored, respected, or feared. The historian, Lynn White (1968), suggests that the idea of humanity as standing apart from nature and rightfully exercising intelligent authority over it accompanied heightened and conscious exploitation. By destroying "pagan animism," White writes, "Christianity made it possible to exploit nature in a mood of indifference to the feelings of natural objects [p. 86]."

The contemporary concept of mastering nature through science in the interest of social benefit received its full expression in the hands of Bacon in the seventeenth century, when commercial and technological expansion, linked with colonial exploitation, was laying the foundations for the industrial revolution. William Leiss (1972) writes that the seventeenth century was absolutely obsessed with the idea of dominating nature and achieving mastery over "her" secrets. Nature "was said to require the superintendence of man in order to function well," an idea that "was used to justify the conquest and resettlement of the so-called backward areas, such as the New World . . . where it was claimed the native populations were not improving sufficiently the regime of nature [p. 74]." Descartes wrote of the new practical knowledge that if we know the movements of natural forces "as we know the different crafts of our artisans," we can "render ourselves the masters and possessors of nature [cited in Leiss, 1972, p. 81]." Such mastery was expressed in male–female terms. Bacon's phrasing, Leiss notes, "displays strong overtones of aggression, . . . including the sexual aggression connected with . . . the use of 'her' as the pronoun . . . 'hounding,' 'vexing,' and 'subduing' nature [p. 60]."

This, then, is the European view. It stands in direct contradiction to the "primitive" view that human society should be at peace so as not to offend the gods of the animals and the weather and upset—in our terms—the "balance" of nature.

Dichotomy as Unity in the Sex Symbolism of the Arapaho

The Arapaho of the Great Plains were agricultural villagers who became mobile buffalo hunters when horses became available, trade in buffalo hides profitable, and settled life difficult. The principal Arapaho ceremony was the Sun Dance, recorded in detail by George Dorsey (1903) who also, with Alfred Kroeber (Dorsey & Kroeber, 1903), collected Arapaho myths. Suggestions of a European deity are the only foreign element in this material. Given the military and economic conditions of the nineteenth-century Plains, one might expect elaborations on themes concerning men as warriors and a corresponding devaluation of female attributes. The absence of such themes attests to the strength of Arapaho resistance and their commitment to contrasting goals and ethics based in an egalitarian society of the Eastern Woodlands type, where the full public participation of women in early times is documented ethnohistorically (Brown, 1975; Reid, 1970) and archaeologically (Winter, 1968). When Leacock (1946) systematically collated and examined all overtly stated symbolic linkages in the ritual and mythic materials collected by Dorsey and Kroeber, the following associations emerged:

1. Generative force and nurturance as central concerns link and subsume maleness and femaleness, which are ritually expressed as principles in beneficial union, not as opposite qualities. In symbolic objects, ritual acts, and certain deities, interpenetration and occasional interchangeability of male and female symbols recur. Moon, as brother of Sun, married a human woman. Their original intercourse caused the "first flow of blood, meaning the child," seen on the moon's face. The moon's marks are also Water Woman, Sun's wife, and in this form Moon, "our Mother," also represents the pregnancy of women and the growth of humanity. Moon may be spoken of as both male and female by the same informant in the same statement. Such usage is also true of Lone Star, or Morning Star, variously the son of the Sun and the Moon, or of the Moon and the human woman, whose rising tells of the first intercourse and the origin of humanity, and who is ceremonially called both the "father of humanity" and "our mother."

2. "Natural" physiological attributes, such as human blood and urine, buffalo feces, and the "spitting" of a skunk, are not treated as alien to intelligence of a human cultural order. For instance, the story of Skunk winning a dispute with Bear by spitting in Bear's eyes symbolizes the spitting of the healer (Skunk) when fighting sickness and evil (Bear), and the cleansing rite of spitting also symbolizes breath, life, and knowledge. Blood, far

from being polluting, is associated with the people, with ritual paint, life, fire, earth, the female form, old age as a valued goal, and meekness as a central virtue for both sexes.

3. Women emerge in the mythic materials as commonly associated with skills and technical knowledge of a practical order as well as with important ritual information. Women's skills are stressed in descriptions of material comforts, and women appear as mythic givers of knowledge. The common mythic occurrence of males giving birth appears in Arapaho mythology. [Because the pregnant man of mythology contradicts the nature–culture as female–male formulation, Lévi-Strauss (1970b, p. 127) disposes of him summarily as "human antinature."]

4. In place of a nature–culture dichotomy that expresses human feelings of separation from and superiority over nature, animals and other natural phenomena are assumed to have human motivations. No sharp line is drawn between animals and humans, who can on occasion enter each other's worlds. Yet Lévi-Strauss, who has himself documented these well-known ideological features of nonstratified societies, incorporates them into his system of binary oppositions through the selectivity of his analytic method. For example, a common Plains myth relates how a man (Blue Feather in the Arapaho case) married the daughter of Lone Bull, leader of the then man-eating buffalo, and defeated him, thereby making the buffalo useful to human beings. Lévi-Strauss reduces this conflict between humans and the buffalo to his formulation of nature's subjugation through male manipulation of women by making two assumptions that the unwary—if insensitive to their attachment to western "terministic screens" (Burke, 1966)—might not catch. By simply equating the buffalo with nature as a whole, and marriage with the exchange of women, Lévi-Strauss (1970b) can write, "the marriage exchange thus functions as a mechanism serving to mediate between nature and culture," thus, in his view, confirming his suggestion that "the 'system of women' is, as it were, a middle term between the system of (natural) living creatures and the system of (manufactured) objects [p. 128]."

However, Blue Feather's marriage was matrilocal, anathema to a theory of woman exchange, and consideration of the buffalo as a whole in Arapaho thought reveals a philosophy that does not dichotomize human experience into two levels, but that builds on all possibilities for symbolizing interconnections among its various aspects. The buffalo, in one story, "in a sense a murderer, because it starved the people" by its absence, figures as a monster in some myths; but the buffalo skull is also a central and revered symbol in the Sun Dance ritual, through which the fight against hunger is linked with the fight against disease, with warfare against human competitors for the buffalo, and with the goals of health, old age, and increase of the tribe. All this lacks the elegance of Lévi-Strauss's deep structures; nor can it be reduced to transformations that arise, in Lévi-Strauss's (1970a) terms, from the tendency "to exhaust all the possible codings of a single message [p. 332]." A richer dialectic emerges, however, from consideration of the ways symbolic associations are interlinked in response to actual social relations, and from a comparison of such linkages in different types of societies.

Ideological Transformations in the Central Plateau of Mexico

In the Central Plateau of Mexico, evidence from the archaeological record and from written codices shows the transformation from worship of natural forces through the intermediacy of females, to propitiation of those forces through androgynous representations. This was followed by paired bisexual deities who, in turn, began to be supplanted by male deities at the apex of a supernatural hierarchy. This emergent tendency, visible in the late Aztec period, was reinforced by the arrival of the Spanish conquerors, who projected their own image of the world on Aztec cosmology.

In the early farming villages of the plateau, there was no social differentiation beyond those of sex and age. The most frequently found figurines in the early sites were female. The usual designation of these figurines as "fertility representations" is far from adequate, especially in the case of figurines from El Arbolillo where interest is centered on the head, or on a variety of crafts and productive activities, and not on the procreative parts of the body. With the emergence of status differences (as indicated by grave goods in the early preclassic period) such figurines are found along with male representations, which Vaillant (1947) interprets as meaning that a "theology was becoming more complex." However, even then there is indication of a high valuation of women in the grave goods.

In the early fifteenth century, major changes occurred in the warring city-states of the Central Plateau giving rise to a new ideology. Netzahualcoyotl, the king of the Texcoco city-state, initiated a trend toward worship of a single god. The Aztecs at the same time elevated the tribal god, Huitzilopochtli, to a high status as a god of war. Huitzilopochtli was said to have chosen the Mexica for the great mission of bringing together all the nations in the service of the Sun. By rationalizing the conquests in the interest of feeding the sun with the hearts of slain captives, the Aztecs possessed an ideology for predatory conquest by a militaristic nobility (Fehrenbach, 1973, pp. 69, 94). There is some evidence of the resistance to this transformation on the part of the intellectuals who served as astronomers and engineers. Many of them continued to believe in the "Lord of Duality," Ometotl (sometimes called Tloque), Lord of the Near Vicinity, or Ipalnemouhuani, Lord of the Giver of Life. This godhead had two aspects, a masculine one, Ometecuhtli, and a feminine one, Omecihuatl (Leon-Portilla, 1962, p. xxiv).

The transformations in the Aztec cosmology that occurred before the arrival of the Spaniards were inspired by changes in the social relations in the developing Aztec state, and they in turn provided a rationalization for the concentration of power and consolidation of control. In the early archaeological record of the horticultural and hunting societies, there is no evidence for class distinctions, and it is more than likely that matrilineal descent characterized the Tula and possibly early Aztec society (Soustelle, 1962, pp. 88, 182–183). In the Florentine Codex, the ideal great-grandmother is said to be the "founder, the beginner of her lineage," although there is no such designation for great-grandfather (Dibble & Anderson, 1961, pp. 45, 51, 55). Judging from the legend of the battle waged by the "Guerrilla Princess" on the advice of the Priestess to save her kingdom in the year 1035 (Figure 16.1), it is likely that reigning powers were female as well as male.

The emphasis on egalitarian relations between the sexes in the early years of settlement in the Central Plateau seemed to be eroded in later days as concessions were made to the warriors, allowing them to take pleasure in the brothels provided by the army. The change in moral standards is shown in the god figures: In the Codex Borgia, Xochipilli-tlamacazqui, the god of love, is shown fighting with Xochiquetzal, representing conjugal love, as he fondles the breast of the *ahuiani*, or companion of the warriors (Figure 16.2).

European and North American scholars tend to ignore or play down the androgynous and/or female personifications of natural forces among Tula and Aztec divinities. Coatlicue, as represented in the monumental stone image found in the central plaza of Tenochtitlan, is a prime example of the simplification by the Spaniards, who called the image "Lady of the Snaky Skirt," and treated it as a mother-earth symbol. The art historian, Justino Fernandez, has done an extensive analysis (Fernandez, 1959) in which he convincingly demonstrates that Coatlicue is an amalgam of various deities,

Figure 16.1. The "Guerrilla Princess" advised by the Priestess to wage war to save her kingdom (Sten, 1972).

Figure 16.2. The god of love, Xochipilli-tlamacazqui between the goddess of conjugal love and the patroness of the brothels.

both male and female, which contains all of the basic components of the Aztec cosmology (Figure 16.3). Investigations of the Tepantitla murals in Teotihuacan reveal that the central figure of the mural, the deity Tlaloc, has neither male nor female characteristics. Pasztory (1976) describes the figure as bisexual and combining all the destructive and constructive potential of the universe. She adds that the interpretation of the diety as female or as ambisexual, rather than as male, is supported by the priests shown wearing female dress, which they wore when attending female deities. Furthermore, the symbols of a tree, cave, and spider appearing in the mural have feminine connotations. The significance of this interpretation is not so much that one of the principal gods of the Aztecs was either female or bisexual in its early representations, but that there was a transition in forms responding to ideological orientations that reflected the changing social outlook of the nation.

Dualistic notions of the earth as female and the sky as male made it difficult for European scholars of the sixteenth century to recognize the dual representations of the earth in Tlazolteotl, the female power, and Tlatecuhtli, the male power (Seler, 1963), or of the sky in Ilancueye and Iztec Mucatle. Similarly, the divine pair Ometecuhtli and Omecihuatl, to whom the creation of the world and the other gods is attributed (Soustelle, 1962, p. 91), were often reduced to Ometecuhtli or the "Lord of Duality" (Vaillant, 1947, p. 72; Fehrenbach, 1973). Similarly, Coyolxauhqui is the counterpart to Tezcatlipoca, the night sky, but it is the latter who rose in the Aztec hierarchy

Figure 16.3. *Coatlicue.*

of the gods and whom Sahagun favored as the most likely counterpart to the Christian god (Hellbom, 1967, p. 248; Seler, 1963, pp. 47–54). The written record of the preconquest cosmogeny was more subject to the distortions caused by filtering myth and history through the Spanish chroniclers than were the pictographs of the Aztec Codices. The 20 divine couples of the Codex Borgia bear witness to the equality of male and female representations, shown at an equal level (Figure 16.4).

Along with this upgrading of a single male deity by European scholars, there was an opposite tendency to downgrade female deities. One of the striking examples of this is the transmogrification of the goddess "Civacoatl," the goddess of Earth and birth (Figure 16.5). Sahagun calls her "the goddess who granted adverse things." She had indeed become "a presage of war and other disasters" as the goddess of the souls of women who died in

Figure 16.4. *Xochiquetzal, lunar deity and goddess of love, with Tlamacazqui.*

childbirth and of those who protested the loss of their children and husbands in the mounting death tolls of the late Aztec wars (Hellbom, 1967, pp. 23, 38), but not the cause of them. She was often called "our mother" as her name signifies, "she who plants root crops" (Hellbom, 1967, p. 38). In a late representation she is shown putting the sacrificial knife in the crib of a newborn baby. The simplistic equation of women = life-givers / men = life-takers (Rosaldo & Atkinson, 1975) is denied in the complexity of Aztec dialectics. To die in childbirth was the equivalent for women of men dying in battle; however, the man who took a captive in war was the equivalent of a woman who gives birth to a live child (Seler, 1963, p. 25). Men and women are both givers and takers of life, as the Aztec ideologues were asserting the claim the military held over the citizens and denying the life-giving principle of the deities. An even more subtle transmogrification occurs with the goddess Chantico, the goddess of fire and water, whose name means "inside the house" or "peace where the fire is." It also signifies the fiery chile plant which is eaten with every meal and immediately after a fast. As a synecdoche for food, since it accompanies every meal, the chile draws the faster back over the threshold to human existence when one is in a liminal state. However, Seler (1963, p. 25) interprets this as a sign of the eternal Eve, tempting man to depart from holy ways as she delivered him over to temptation.

What seems to be happening in the European interpretations of New World cosmology is an attempt to limit and codify a pantheon, the essence

Figure 16.5. *Civacoatl, goddess of birth and earth, shown with a dagger held over the cradle of a newborn baby.*

of which was diversity and transformation, the linked duality of male and female principles, and to exaggerate or acclaim those tendencies toward hierarchy and male dominance. In Aztec philosophy, it was the dialectical interaction of dark and light, sun and moon, fire and water that gave life and movement. For the Spaniards, who kept the world going through hierarchy and dominance, this was a difficult if not repugnant conception, and they treated it either by funneling the binary concept into a unitary deity or by forcing the constantly transforming deities into a static mold.

In the domestic mode of production characteristic of Aztec society, the division of labor by sex was well established in the late Aztec period. The Florentine codex shows men teaching boys to fish, cultivate, and work metal, while women show the girls how to weave, tend babies, and cook (Figure 16.6). But what is often left out of summary accounts, both in the modern period as well as in colonial times, is the fact that women were not only destined to domestic roles, but were also professional doctors, priestesses, and merchants in local trade. Among the *macehuali,* or commoners, women

Figure 16.6. *Division of labor by sex was well defined, but productive roles were carried out by both girls, under the supervision of women, and boys, under the supervision of men.*

were horticulturalists and they hunted small animals. Hellbom (1967, p. 130), who compared the text and pictures of the codices, points out that there is a consistent tendency for Sahagun to gloss over the sex distinctions in occupations or to refer only to men in his text, but Aztec pictures reveal women weaving, cooking, cloth-dyeing, and dressmaking; these were professional activities entering into exchange. The three dieties who supported, and in turn were worshiped by, the common people—Chalchihuitlicue, goddess of water; Chicumecoatl, goddess of food; and Vixtocivatel, goddess of salt—were all female (Hellbom, 1967, p. 28). The codices reveal the sense of pride in work, the love of material splendor created by both male and female craftspeople, who had both male and female deities in charge of the guilds.

Within a few decades after the Spanish conquest, the Christian ideology had become impressed upon the relations between the sexes, reinforcing those tendencies that were emerging in the theocratic state. The suffering Virgin Mary replaced the powerful fecund image of Coatlicue as the Indians were brought under the control and domination of the Spaniards.

Conclusion

Throughout the twentieth century, anthropologists of the western world have aimed at understanding the conscious representations of people from diverse cultures in their own terms and categories. Lévi-Strauss and others have tried to go beyond such relativistic constructs. However, in going underground, into the subconscious, they project their intuitive understanding, based on Judeo-Christian precepts, onto a presumed universal structural framework of human thought. Through this ahistorical method, cross-cultural comparisons are being made about universals and particulars of sex-role definition that serve to crystallize the ethnocentric categories already imposed on the ethnographic data in the process of fieldwork and subsequent interpretation. We have reviewed material that is available in the ethnographic and archaeological literature. This chapter is by no means a voyage of discovery, but a cruise through familiar territory. However, although the data are familiar, the interpretations are forced into Eurocentric categories that require reexamination. We hope we have demonstrated some of the selective biases and distortions of indigenous beliefs in the New World as they were cast into the stereotypes and archetypes of European iconography. This brief exercise points to the need for a thorough analysis of the processes by which aboriginal thought has been distorted in terms of European assumptions.

References

Brown, J. K. Iroquois women: An ethnohistoric note. In R. R. Reiter (Ed.), *Toward an anthropology of women.* New York: Monthly Review Press, 1975.

Burke, K. Terministic screens. In K. Burke, *Language as symbolic action.* Berkeley and Los Angeles: University of California Press, 1966.

Collingwood, R. G. *The idea of nature.* New York: Oxford University Press, 1960.

de Beauvoir, S. *The second sex.* New York: Alfred A. Knopf, 1952.

Dibble, C. E., & Anderson, A. J. O. (Trans.). *Florentine Codex, Book 10.* Santa Fe: School of American Research, 1961.

Dorsey, G. A. The Arapaho sun dance. *Field Columbian Museum Publication, 75,* Anthropological Series 4, 1903.

Dorsey, G. A., & Kroeber, A. L. Traditions of the Arapaho. *Field Columbian Museum Publication, 81,* Anthropological Series 5, 1903.

Etienne, M., & Leacock, E. (Eds.) *Women and colonization: Anthropological perspectives.* New York: Praeger, 1980.

Fehrenbach, T. R. *Fire and blood: A history of Mexico.* New York: Macmillan, 1973.

Fernandez, J. *Coatlicue.* Mexico City: Instituto de Investigaciones Esteticas, Universidad Nacional Autónoma de México, 1959. .

Hegel, G. W. F. *Philosophy of nature.* Atlantic City, N.J.: Humanities Press, 1952.

Hellbom, A. La participación cultural de las mujeres indias y mestizas en el México precortesiano y postrevoluciónario. *The Ethnographical Museum Monograph Series,* No. 10, Stockholm, 1967.

Hoffer, C. P. Madam Yoko: Ruler of the Kpa Mende confederacy. In M. Z. Rosaldo & L. Lamphere (Eds.), *Women, culture and society.* Stanford: Stanford University Press, 1974.

Leacock, E. *Some aspects of the philosophy of the Cheyenne and Arapaho Indians.* Unpublished Master's essay, Columbia University, 1946.

Leacock, E. Women's status in egalitarian society: Implications for social evolution. *Current Anthropology,* 1978, *19,* 247–275.

Lebeuf, A. M. D. The role of women in the political organization of African societies. In D. Paulme (Ed.), *Women of tropical Africa.* Berkeley and Los Angeles: University of California Press, 1971.

Leiss, W. *The domination of nature.* New York: George Braziller, 1972.

Leon-Portilla, M. *The broken spears: The Aztec account of the conquest of Mexico.* Boston: Beacon Press, 1962.

Lévi-Strauss, C. *The elementary structures of kinship.* Boston: Beacon Press, 1969.

Lévi-Strauss, C. *The raw and the cooked.* New York: Harper & Row, 1970. (a)

Lévi-Strauss, C. *The savage mind.* Chicago: University of Chicago Press, 1970. (b)

Nash, J. The Aztecs and the ideology of male dominance. *Signs: Journal of Women in Culture and Society,* 1978, *4,* 349–362.

Ortner, S. B. Is female to male as nature is to culture? In M. Z. Rosaldo & L. Lamphere (Eds.), *Women, culture and society.* Stanford: Stanford University Press, 1974.

Pasztory, E. *The murals of Tepantla, Teotihuacan.* New York: Garland, 1976.

Reid, J. P. *A law of blood: The primitive law of the Cherokee nation.* New York: New York University Press, 1970.

Rohrlich-Leavitt, R. Women in transition: Crete and Sumer. In R. Bridenthal & C. Koonz (Eds.), *Becoming visible: Women in European history.* Boston: Houghton Mifflin, 1976.

Rosaldo, M. Z., & Atkinson, J. M. Man the hunter and woman: Metaphors for the sexes in Ilongot magical spells. In R. Willis (Ed.), *The interpretation of symbolism.* New York: Wiley, 1975.

Sacks, K. Engels revisited. In R. R. Reiter (Ed.), *Toward an anthropology of women.* New York: Monthly Review Press, 1975.

Schlegel, A. (Ed.). Sexual stratification: A cross-cultural view. New York: Columbia University Press, 1977.

Seler, E. *Comentarios al Codice Borgia.* Mexico: Fondo de Cultura Economica, 1963.

Soustelle, J. *The daily life of the Aztecs on the eve of the Spanish conquest.* New York: Macmillan, 1962.

Sten, M. *Las extraordinarias historias de los codices mexicanas.* Mexico: Editorial Joaquin Mortiz, 1972.

Sutton, C. R. The power to define: Women, culture, and consciousness. In R. S. Bryce-Laporte & C. S. Thomas (Eds.), *Alienation in contemporary society.* New York: Praeger, 1976.

Vaillant, G. *The Aztecs of Mexico, origin, rise and fall of the Aztec empire.* Garden City, New York: Doubleday, 1947.

White, L., Jr. *Machine ex Deo: Essays in the dynamism of Western culture.* Cambridge, Mass.: MIT Press, 1968.

Winter, H. D. Value systems and trade cycles of the Late Archaic in the Midwest. In L. Binford & S. Binford (Eds.), *New perspectives in archaeology.* Chicago: Aldine, 1968.

FAIRFID M. CAUDLE **17**

Advertising as a Basis for Cross-Cultural Comparisons[1]

ABSTRACT

As a form of social communication, advertising reflects cultural values and meanings and thus provides an important, and as yet relatively unexplored, source of data for cross-cultural studies. This chapter surveys the major strategies employed in contemporary advertising and suggests how studies of diversification and patterns in advertising styles and frequencies of utilization can add an important tool to those already available to the cross-cultural researcher. Two aspects of advertising are considered to have particular relevance to cross-cultural issues. One is the relative frequency of appeals to various social motives, including the needs for achievement, affiliation, and personal power, as well as the use of techniques that rely primarily on creating anxiety or guilt for their effectiveness. The second is the manner in which advertising reflects cultural values concerning sex roles. The portrayal of women in advertising is discussed as a potentially fruitful area of cross-cultural research.

As a form of social communication, advertising reflects cultural values and meanings and thus provides an important, and as yet relatively unexplored, basis for cross-cultural comparisons. The purpose of this chapter is to suggest a tentative framework for cross-cultural studies of advertising through illustrating basic advertising strategies, raising questions, and suggesting some working hypotheses. It should be noted that the term *cross-cultural* is used in its broadest sense; the suggestions that follow can be applied to

---

[1] An earlier version of this chapter was presented at the meeting of the New York State Psychological Association, New York, N. Y., May 1980.

CROSS-CULTURAL RESEARCH AT ISSUE

many levels of comparison, including cross-national comparisons and comparisons of smaller subgroups within and across cultures.

Limitations on Research Using Advertising

The media of advertising—magazines, television, etc.—impose several important limitations on any research. First, the cultures that can be studied are limited to those in which advertising exists in some form. For printed advertising there is an additional assumption of literacy sufficient to understand the verbal component of advertising. Finally, there is the assumption that those to whom the advertising is directed have an economic status sufficient to purchase representative goods and services advertised. Thus, cross-cultural comparisons of advertising provide a means of comparing cultures and cultural subgroups that are relatively advanced in terms of educational and economic levels.

Concerning the relationship between advertising and economic level, one area that the cross-cultural comparison of advertising might address is that of delineating those cultural differences that persist and those that may become less pronounced once a particular educational and economic "threshold" is reached. One working hypothesis that might be explored is the following: *The higher the educational and economic levels of the segment of the population to which advertising is directed within particular cultures, the more similar will be the cultural characteristics reflected in the advertising, when cross-cultural comparisons are made.*

Cultural Characteristics Reflected in Advertising

Just what aspects of a culture, nation, subculture, or marketing segment are reflected in advertising? In general, advertising provides information that denotes the availability of goods and services, distinguishes them from others in the same category, and seeks to stimulate buying in a number of ways. Most advertising is, to a greater or lesser extent, based on the assumption that "members of a given culture, subculture, or marketing segment behave in uniform and predictable ways [Markin, 1974, p. 469]." Advertising is designed to appeal to those similar in one or more of such characteristics as age, sex, income, geographic location, occupation, lifestyle, education, beliefs, and attitudes. Although an individual advertisement may reveal little concerning the society in which it is found, the common trends revealed through analysis of many advertisements can provide a profile of cultural characteristics, particularly those relating to motivational issues.

Basic Advertising Strategies

Logical and Emotional Styles

Martineau (1971) has described two contrasting styles of advertising: (a) logical, rational approaches which rely on explanations and demonstrations concerning how particular products are superior and how they differ from their competitors; and (b) emotional approaches which seek, frequently through nonverbal (pictorial) communication, to arouse and appeal to wishes, needs, fantasies, and motives of which the buyer may not be consciously aware. Martineau points out that the use of such emotional appeals in advertising grew out of the discovery by advertisers of Freudian concepts and the realization that behavior is influenced at least as much by irrational and unconscious factors as by rational processes.

For example, Figure 17.1 conveys a logical and quantifiable reason for smoking one brand of cigarettes rather than another; the advertised brand contains less tar than other brands mentioned. In contrast, Figure 17.2 relies primarily on the illustration to convey its message and to evoke feelings and attitudes that need not be verbalized in order to affect behavior. The message is the same whether the picture appears in a United States, or, in this case, an Arabic publication: The Marlboro man is powerful, strong, tough, rugged. Thus a man buying Marlboros may unconsciously do so in order to assume such characteristics himself.

The benefits of comparing these broad advertising strategies across cultures result from their providing indications of *what* is valued within a culture. Advertisements, and, in particular, emotional appeals, provide indices of what constitute desired or valued behaviors, attitudes, characteristics, or qualities of life within a society. One question that cross-cultural research might address concerns, for a given product category, the relative emphasis on logical and emotional advertising styles across cultures. A second working hypothesis that might be explored is the following: *For a given product category, the basic types of appeals employed within logical styles of advertising will tend to remain fairly constant across cultures, whereas the bases of emotional styles of advertising will show greater variability and will tend to reflect values characteristic of specific cultures.*

The Association of Ideas in Advertising

Perhaps the single most important aspect of cognitive functioning that is utilized in advertising is the association of ideas, which occurs when one thought leads to, or is associated with, another. Aristotle recognized that when we remember past thoughts or events, we tend to associate, and thus

U.S. Government Report:

Box or menthol:

Ten packs of Carlton

have less tar than <u>one</u> pack of...

	Tar mg./cig.	Nicotine mg./cig.		Tar mg./cig.	Nicotine mg./cig.
Kent	11	0.9	Parliament Lights	9	0.7
Kool Milds	13	0.8	Salem Lights	11	0.8
Marlboro Lights	12	0.8	Vantage	11	0.8
Merit	8	0.6	Vantage Menthol	11	0.8
Merit Menthol	8	0.6	Winston Lights	14	1.1

Carlton is lowest.

Less than 1 mg. tar,
0.1 mg. nic.

Of all brands, lowest...Carlton Box: less than 0.5 mg. tar
and 0.05 mg. nicotine av. per cigarette, FTC Report Dec. '79.

Warning: The Surgeon General Has Determined
That Cigarette Smoking Is Dangerous to Your Health.

Box: Less than 0.5 mg. ''tar'', 0.05 mg. nicotine; Soft Pack and Menthol:
1 mg. ''tar'', 0.1 mg. nicotine av. per cigarette, FTC Report Dec. '79.

Figure 17.1. An example of the "logical" style of advertising.

Figure 17.2. An example of the "emotional" style of advertising (reprinted with permission of Philip Morris, Inc., New York, New York).

remember together, things that are either similar, or contrasting, or that have been experienced together at an earlier time. Thus when you think of the word *table* you are also very likely to think of the word *chair* because you have experienced them together so frequently.

Advertising utilizes this aspect of cognitive functioning by pairing a product or service with something (an object, situation, person, or symbol) that *already* has associated with it positive feelings, attitudes, and values. The intent is to insure that the product will itself come to elicit the same positive feelings as the object with which it is paired and thus become more attractive to the potential purchaser. Thus we might state a postulate that would underlie cross-cultural comparisons utilizing advertising: *The associations evoked by the objects, situations, persons, or symbols chosen for association with products indicate feelings, attitudes, characteristics, and circumstances positively valued within a society.*

The question then arises as to *what* is chosen for association with a product and whether there are consistent differences (or similarities) among cultures in the sorts of associations that advertising is designed to elicit. Figure 17.3 is a United States advertisement designed to utilize positive associations that readers of the advertisement *already* have with regard to President Lincoln: for example, honor, integrity, and morality. In addition, because Lincoln is shown as sculptured in Mount Rushmore there are further implications of strength, endurance, and solidity. Figure 17.4, an advertisement for a French cognac (advertised in a German magazine), cleverly establishes, through the bottle's "shadow," that the product is "the brandy of Napoleon." Thus, the advertiser evokes the associations of continuity with the past and of quality worthy of a great historic figure. Analysis of the types of objects selected to elicit such associations within and across cultures provides an intriguing avenue for future research.

Social Motivation in Advertising

Comparisons of levels of motivation among societies have for some time been part of the stock in trade for cross-cultural researchers. McClelland's landmark study of achievement motivation (1961) provided both a theoretical framework and a methodology for comparing levels of achievement motivation across many cultures through analyzing such things as the stories contained in children's readers. In view of the extensive motivational research upon which much advertising is based, it seems reasonable to propose that advertising, like children's readers, reflects motivational characteristics of a society, and that one can thus infer motivational characteristics of a culture from an analysis of advertising within that culture. A second postulate related to cross-cultural research in advertising can be stated as follows: *A motive*

NAME THE MAN ON THE RIGHT AND YOU'LL NAME ONE OF AMERICA'S LARGEST LIFE INSURANCE COMPANIES.

Lincoln. It's a name you remember.

We're Lincoln National Life. We have nearly 4,000 agents who make us easy to remember—by preparing life, disability income, group, and retirement programs just right for you, your family, your business and your future.

That, plus 74 years of insurance experience, is just another of the reasons why we're among the top 1% of more than 1700 life insurance companies in America.

Lincoln National Life. For millions of Americans who buy life insurance, we're the name that's easy to remember.

LINCOLN NATIONAL LIFE

WE'RE EASY TO REMEMBER.

The Lincoln National Life Insurance Company, Fort Wayne, Indiana

Figure 17.3. *An example illustrating the association of President Lincoln with a life insurance company (reprinted with permission of Lincoln National Life Insurance Company, Fort Wayne, Indiana).*

Figure 17.4. An example illustrating the association of Napoleon with a brand of cognac. [Reprinted with permission of Hiram Walker (International) S.A., Montreux, Switzerland.]

will be reflected in advertising to the extent that it leads to behaviors or events valued within a culture.

The forms of social motivation that might be assessed through the study of advertising include the need for achievement, the need for affiliation, and the need for power. In the sections that follow, definitions of these motives have been derived from scoring categories developed for the Thematic Apperception Test and summarized in McClelland and Steele (1972).

The Achievement Motive

In the simplest sense, the achievement motive centers on a concern for doing things well. This can be expressed in a number of ways, including outperforming someone else, meeting or surpassing some self-imposed standard of excellence, doing something unique, or being involved over a long term in doing something well (McClelland & Steele, 1972).

Appeals to the achievement motive can take many guises. For example, any advertisement whose message states that use of the product will enable performance to be improved in some specific way is appealing, at least in part, to the achievement motive—whether the particular claim is for a product that improves engine performance, a camera that enables more precise photography, or track shoes that provide better support and thus enable a runner to run faster. (Of course, advertising that claims more effective performance may also be appealing to other needs such as a desire for greater economy.) In addition, the achievement motive is appealed to when the product is associated with a recognized symbol of achievement, as in Figure 17.3. Figure 17.5 provides another example of advertising that appeals to the achievement motive. Proudly displaying a loaf of home-baked bread, the woman proclaims her achievement as she says "I did it." The message of this advertisement is that use of the brand of flour advertised will enable someone to achieve excellence in the preparation of bread.

There are numerous other ways in which achievement motivation can be incorporated into advertising. The questions that cross-cultural research needs to address concern the relative prevalence of achievement motivation in advertising: Is achievement motivation limited to certain categories of products or does it appear across many categories? Does it appear as much in advertising directed at females as opposed to males? Is advertising containing achievement-related appeals directed more often at individuals in one age group rather than another?

The Affiliation Motive

The affiliation motive centers on a desire to be with others. It concerns both family and social relationships and can be expressed through such

Figure 17.5. An advertisement appealing to the achievement motive (reprinted with permission of General Mills, Inc., Minneapolis, Minnesota).

behaviors as establishing, restoring, or maintaining a close, warm, friendly relationship, participating in social activities such as reunions or parties, or being emotionally concerned over separation from another person (Mc-Clelland & Steele, 1972).

Advertising that appeals to the need for affiliation tends to illustrate some way in which a product or service can contribute to aspects of relationships mentioned previously. Figures 17.6 and 17.7 illustrate the affiliation motive in advertising. In Figure 17.6, from an Italian publication, the brand of soap advertised is portrayed as one that the entire family can use, thus promoting family togetherness. The illustration portrays a smiling attractive family and elicits associations of happiness, health, and the closeness that results from caring. Figure 17.7 is a more direct appeal to the affiliation motive in which a child uses the telephone to talk to a young friend. The telephone is depicted as a means of maintaining a relationship through the suggestion to "reach out and touch someone," a theme appearing frequently in this company's advertising.

Cross-cultural examination of affiliation motivation in advertising can yield information concerning such questions as the relative importance within societies of social relationships and family relationships, the most desirable settings in which relationships are fostered, and attitudes toward relationships among different age groups.

The Power Motive

The power motive leads to behavior that results in having an impact, or making an impression, on others. It can be expressed through actions that attempt to control, influence, or persuade others, to affect one's reputation, or to increase one's prestige. Appeals to the power motive can also be made through portraying actions that directly affect others, such as aggressive actions or acts of winning over others (McClelland & Steele, 1972).

Advertisements that appeal to the need for personal power include those whose message is, in effect, "If you use this product, you will become more powerful or have greater prestige." The message can be stated verbally or communicated nonverbally through associating a product with powerful models and/or situations, or with symbols of power and status. Figures 17.8 and 17.9 are both based on appeals to the need for personal power. Figure 17.8 provides an example of an attempt to associate a product with the same feelings and responses as are associated with such luxury items as an expensive car and a sailboat. Figure 17.9 is a more direct appeal to the need for personal power; its message is, in effect, that a man with a full head of hair is a more powerful man. In addition to the attractive young model, the advertisement contains illustrations of powerful figures from his-

Figure 17.6. An advertisement appealing to the affiliation motive (reprinted with permission of STAR, S.p.A., Stabilimento Alimentare, Milan Italy).

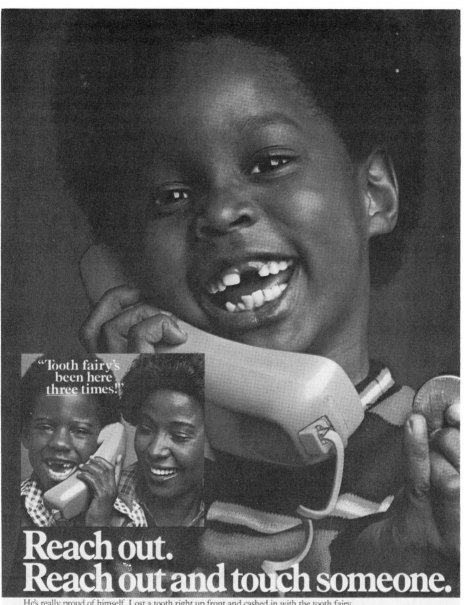

"Tooth fairy's
been here
three times!"

Reach out.
Reach out and touch someone.

He's really proud of himself. Lost a tooth right up front and cashed in with the tooth fairy.
Fifty cents' worth. Now to talk to his cross-country friend and fill him in on the news.
But it seems that his buddy is a veteran of the tooth fairy game himself!
Share your life with faraway family and friends. They'll be thrilled to hear from you.
Reach out and touch someone. Give 'em a call.

Ⓐ Bell System

Figure 17.7. An example of affiliation motivation (reprinted with permission of
AT&T–Long Lines, New York, New York).

Figure 17.8. An example illustrating the association of a brand of whisky with symbols of prestige and power.

THE POWER OF HAIR.

A man's hair has always been a symbol of personal power: political power, religious power, sexual power, a power that reflects what a man thinks of himself and how he wants people to think of him.

At Hair Again Ltd. we believe that every man wants a full head of good-looking, natural looking, even wild-looking hair. We can give you the excitement of regaining a power you might have reluctantly lost: the power of your hair.

Our booklet tells you why Hair Again Ltd. is the biggest and the best. Why our method is exclusive, uncomplicated, and virtually impossible to detect. It educates you to the potential embarrassments and costly liabilities of other hair replacement methods like hairpieces, hairweaves and transplants. For our free, fully-illustrated booklet, mail coupon or call (212) 832-1234.   © Hair Again Ltd., 1978

Three stages of replacing hair by the retainer implant method.

Send to: Hair Again Ltd.
14 East 60th St., New York City, N.Y. 10022

Name _____
                    (Please Print)
Address _____
City _____
State _____
Zip _____
Dept. G 1-79   **HAIR AGAIN LTD.**™

Line drawings courtesy of The New York Public Library Picture Collection

Figure 17.9. A more direct appeal to the need for personal power (reprinted with permission of Hair Again, Ltd., New York, New York).

223

tory, all with ample hair; the advertisement thus provides a strong stimulus to the man who has lost hair due to balding.

Both of these advertisements convey information about the sorts of qualities and characteristics that, in the United States at least, endow a person with power. Among the questions that could be explored through cross-cultural comparisons of power motivation are issues such as the categories of persons viewed as having power and status within a culture, the relative distribution of power to males and females and to different age groups within a culture, and the sorts of goals considered worthwhile enough to exercise power to attain. In addition, cross-cultural comparisons could be made of those objects that confer power and status on those who possess them.

The Arousal of Anxiety in Advertising

Another motive that can be aroused through advertising is anxiety, which can be stimulated through portraying the loss of achievement, affiliation, or status that might result unless one uses a particular product or service, or by portraying the loss of security or some valued commodity. For example, Figure 17.10 arouses anxiety by depicting the dangers of fire; purchase of the product, a smoke detector, provides a means to allay the anxiety. The arousal of guilt is another advertising strategy, used, at least in the United States, to elicit behaviors such as contributing to charities and preserving the environment.

One question that arises is that of the extent to which anxiety is an important motivator within a culture and the sorts of threats or losses that are deemed important to avoid. Other questions concern the particular attitudes and beliefs within societies that provide contexts for the arousal of guilt.

Sex and Sex Roles in Advertising

In a book that has stirred up considerable controversy, Key (1973) has laid claim to documenting numerous examples of covert or "subliminal" appeals to sexual wishes and fantasies in United States advertising. Without passing judgment on the specific claims made by Key, it is of interest to ask whether such hidden appeals are to be found primarily in United States advertising or whether they appear in the advertising of other nations and/ or cultures and, if so, the extent to which such practices are attempts to imitate or widen the audience influenced by advertising approaches developed in the United States. (Such imitations indicate, to some extent, the process of cultural diffusion, another topic suitable for exploration through cross-cultural comparisons of advertising.)

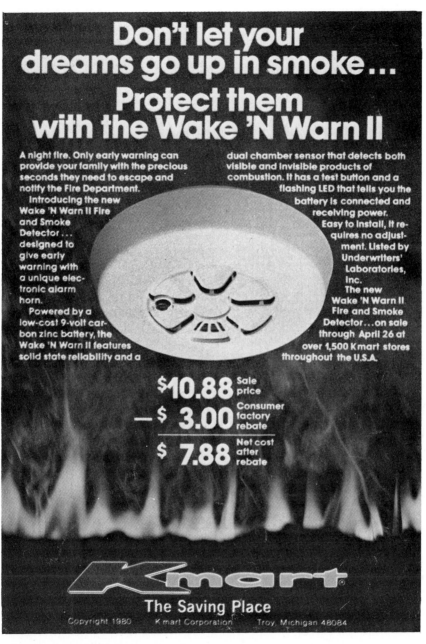

Figure 17.10. An example illustrating the arousal of anxiety (reprinted with permission of K Mart Corporation, Troy, Michigan).

Figure 17.11 (from a contest advertisement in a United States publication) and Figure 17.12 (from a German magazine) might be interpreted as containing covert sexual symbolism. In Figure 17.11, the product, a can of shaving cream, is nestled between the halves of a coconut. The configuration of the can and the two spherical forms, in addition to eliciting associations appropriate to the tropics, may also be construed as representing male genitalia, although the reader may not be consciously aware of this. Finally, the instruction to "scratch 'n sniff," placed at the tip of the can, may elicit associations to the acts of touching and smelling that go beyond the overt message in the advertisement. Figure 17.12 also illustrates a product in a manner that may suggest male genitalia. Note the configuration of the bottle and lemons (in the small inset picture), as well as the very name of the product, "Lift," and its typography, both of which may elicit associations

Figure 17.11. An example of sexual symbolism.

Figure 17.12. An example of sexual symbolism (reprinted with permission of McCann-Erikson, Hamburg, West Germany).

related to thoughts of penile erection. Insofar as cross-cultural comparisons are concerned, it would be of interest to determine both the frequency and the effectiveness of such sexual symbolism within different societies.

Although the study of sexual symbolism in advertising may provide a somewhat controversial basis for cross-cultural research, comparisons of sex roles, status, and stereotypes across cultures have long been of interest. In addition, the increasing attention paid to women's issues has stimulated considerable research pertaining to cross-cultural comparisons of sex roles. Some of the gender-related questions that might be explored through studies of advertising include access to rewards, prestige, and power; attitudes toward sex roles in childrearing; sexual mores and behavior; social mobility; and standards of beauty and attractiveness.

Some work has been done in the study of sex roles as they are portrayed in advertising. Millum (1975) has proposed an extensive system of classification of illustrations. The system evaluates advertisements in women's magazines according to such features as general form and style and characteristics of props and settings. Goffman (1979) has provided a study of how portrayals of males and females in advertising reveal cultural values when they are analyzed for such aspects as gesture, expression, and posture. Caudle (1979) has documented attitudes in the United States toward the older woman as reflected in advertising and has defined systematic relationships between the approximate age of the model and the type of product advertised.

Some Additional Questions

Although limitations of space preclude a full discussion of the many additional questions that might be addressed through cross-cultural comparisons of advertising, a few topics for future study can be mentioned briefly: attitudes toward children and motivational characteristics of advertising directed toward children; the portrayal of racial and ethnic groups; the basis of humor (e.g., sexual themes as compared with aggressive themes); the "rules" that are followed when products of one culture are advertised in publications of another culture. Finally, characteristics of "advertising" from noncapitalist societies could provide a basis for cross-cultural comparisons. For example, although consumer advertising is not permitted within the Soviet Union, Soviet attitudes and values are "advertised" to other cultures through publications such as *Soviet Life* and *The Soviet Woman*. Analysis of such publications might provide a basis for cross-cultural comparisons, especially with regard to motivational issues.

Because the preceding discussion has focused on examples taken from magazine advertising, it is important to mention the possibility of cross-cultural comparisons of television advertising as well. Television advertising may provide a fertile ground for cross-cultural comparison for the very reason that television advertising is so tightly controlled, and national attitudes presumably determine, at least in part, what is and is not permitted by the codes regulating commercials.

As should be apparent by now, the purpose of this chapter has been to raise questions rather than to answer them, and it is hoped that those who undertake cross-cultural research will view advertising as an innovative tool for the comparison of educationally and economically advanced societies.

References

Caudle, F. M. *Advertising's image of the older woman.* Paper presented at the meeting of the New York State Psychological Association, Saratoga, N.Y., May 1979.

Goffman, E. *Gender advertisements.* New York: Harper & Row, 1979.

Key, W. B. *Subliminal seduction.* Englewood Cliffs, N.J.: Prentice-Hall, 1973.

McClelland, D. C. *The achieving society.* New York: Van Nostrand, 1961.

McClelland, D. C., & Steele, R. S. *Motivation workshops.* New York: General Learning Press, 1972.

Markin, R. J. *Consumer behavior: A cognitive orientation.* New York: Macmillan, 1974.

Martineau, P. *Motivation in advertising: Motives that make people buy.* New York: McGraw-Hill, 1971.

Millum, T. *Images of woman: Advertising in women's magazines.* Totowa, N.J.: Rowman & Littlefield, 1975.

ROBERT C. WILLIAMSON **18**

Attitudes Accompanying Modernization in Advanced and Developing Societies

ABSTRACT

The chapter begins by examining the variables of modernization including the class system, urbanization, and on the negative side, alienation. The study focuses on several sociopsychological factors accompanying modernization as based on interviews with 988 adults and questionnaires administered to 611 university students in four advanced nations (West Germany, United States, Japan, and Spain), and two developing ones (Chile and Colombia). Orientation to change was hypothesized to correlate with (a) high levels of social participation; (b) perceived personal mobility and general optimism about the future; and (c) modernism as determined by scores on a modified rationalism–traditionalism scale. Findings according to the chi-square test gave some support to the first hypothesis, marginal support to the second, and strong support to the third. However, cultural differences were as important as the development continuum itself. For instance, the United States sample was nearly as conservative or traditionalistic as the samples of societies in development.

As modernization occurs in various regions throughout the world, questions arise as to its differential effects. In the context of the present study, two such questions seem fundamental: What attitudes and values accompany and follow industrialization and urbanization? How do these attitudes and values vary among nations for "subcultures," for example, those based on social class or age?

Although it is more a pilot study than an exhaustive analysis of variables associated with modernization, the present study illustrates several psychological correlates of social change. The study includes adult and student samples from Colombia, West Germany, Japan, and the United States, together with adult samples from Chile and Spain (a university strike and vacation schedules prevented the inclusion of Chilean and Spanish students respectively). Elsewhere I have reported in detail findings regarding class differences in Colombia and Chile as well as the results of a cross-national comparison among student samples (Williamson, 1968, 1970, 1972). I have also provided a more complete analysis of these cross-national data (Williamson, 1977). In this chapter, I shall review the data in the light of more recent approaches to the assessment of modernization.

Factors of Modernization

A number of studies of social change have focused on the question of how a society becomes modern (e.g., Inkeles, 1969; Inkeles & Smith, 1974). The debate as to what constitutes modernization has been in part a result of differing perspectives, not least because the causes are complex and the effects are no less baffling. Still, there is general agreement that modernization is both a technical and an economic process in which quantitative and qualitative changes are involved (Black, 1976; Garner, 1977). Insofar as it represents a movement from agricultural to industrial production, modernization is a multifaceted and yet a homogenizing process (Huntington, 1976).

At the basis of modernization is a shift to urbanization, which generally accompanies industrialization. Yet, in a study of Asia and Latin America, Firebaugh (1979) points to regressive land tenure and to high density in rural areas rather than industry as important factors. In any event, persons moving to the city display more rationalistic attitudes as compared to the traditionalism of a rural population (Williamson, 1963).

There is also the variable of social class. In a critique of the attempts to measure modernization, Armer and Schnaiberg (1972) note the similarity between the responses to a modernism scale and responses to scales associated with middle-class belongingness, a position supported by my own research in Latin America (Williamson, 1972). Other studies point to educational level as an index of modernism (Holsinger & Theisen, 1977).

Consequently, it is not easy to arrive at a definition of modernization. Even more difficult is its measurement. However, it is my contention that a study of attitudes—such as the extent of social interaction, sense of mobility, and secularism and related values—among samples from representative areas at given levels of socioeconomic development will reveal varying degrees of acceptance of modernism.

In this context, I accept a structuralist–functionalist approach, that is, (a) societies are "systems of interrelated parts," with cause and effect relationships that are "multiple and reciprocal"; (b) integration between old and new is often partial and imperfect; and (c) change is a slow, adaptive development, often reflecting forces outside as well as within the system (Van den Berghe, 1973).

In what follows, I shall analyze a constellation of attitudes that precede and follow social change. Modernization depends on a number of processes involved in urbanization—education, rise of the mass media, growth of a middle class. In the context of classical theory, one might define this shift as one from Gemeinschaft to Gesellschaft, from sacred to secular norms, and from primary to secondary group affiliations. Although the development varies with different cultures and with different types of economic developments, institutional shifts—notably in the family, church, and economic and political institutions—imply that universalistic norms assume dominance over particularistic norms. Each nation or region may have a different sequence of development, but the catalog of traits involved in modernization include flexibility, rationality, role segmentation, and a sense of mobility, both horizontal and vertical. The differentiation of the social system as it moves from primary to secondary and tertiary economic activities leads to cleavages within the society that are relatively absent in the colonial and feudalistic societies found in the third world. Also, there is tendency for "modernizing stimuli" to produce higher levels of aspiration among individuals moving into urban areas. Seldom can society satisfy the aspirations at the rate expected by persons undergoing this kind of social change (Kelman & Warwick, 1973).

There is conflicting evidence as to whether members of a society experience alienation when a fairly static social system undergoes modernization (Godwin, 1975; Kahl, 1968). For example, Lewis (1952) views movement to the city as enriching the urbanite's economic, social, and cultural life, whereas Redfield (1941) finds that urbanization leads to personal and social disorganization. Such differences probably reflect the use of different populations and settings. According to my own research, the migrant to the Latin American city—despite the initial shock and despite an uneasy path to employment—finds expanded economic, health, and educational opportunities (Williamson, 1962, 1968). The acceptance of rationalistic, secular, and universalistic values and is a much slower process.

The present investigation draws on a lengthy research tradition, including Lerner's (1958) classic study on the effects of mass media and other modernizing agencies in the Near East. Also of importance was Joseph Kahl's (1968) modernism scale, employed in Brazil, Mexico, and the United States.

The most complete study of modernization was undertaken by Alex Inkeles (1969; Inkeles & Smith, 1974) in six nations (Argentina, Chile, India, Israel, Nigeria, and East Pakistan), and stressed the factors of industrial employment, urbanization, the mass media, and, above all, education. These various research studies have led to more discriminating scales used to test populations of varying technical and educational levels (Armer & Isaac, 1978; Fliegel, Sofranko, Williams, & Sharma, 1979).

The Conceptual Framework of the Present Study:
National and Generational Comparisons

Any analysis of development and underdevelopment must be viewed in the context of national cultures. Three of the developed nations chosen for this study experienced a far-reaching dislocation in the middle of this century. Germany and Japan were defeated in war with enormous changes in the institutional fabric, notably the governmental structure, and with a consequent gulf developing between the younger and older generations. The case of Japan is especially complex because of its blend of eastern and western value systems, which presumably deepened insecurity feelings and the questioning of the present and past (Tsurumi, 1970). The third nation, Spain, was engulfed in a civil war, followed by a dictatorship at the same time it was evolving from a quasi-feudalistic order.

The United States differs as much from the other three industrialized nations as they differ from each other. It has had relative continuity in its social, economic, and political development. The drive for upward mobility as well as an ideological tradition has made for a stronger conformity than is found in nations that have had severe political and cultural disruptions and, until recently, a lower standard of living (Williams, 1970).

Among developing nations even more discontinuities are apparent than among advanced nations. Yet this third world has a number of common problems: a feudalistic land tenure system, a rapidly increasing population without commensurate increases in capital or technological skills, inadequate educational opportunities, and either an unstable democracy or an authoritarian regime superimposed on a monoproduct economy. In addition to the existence of vested interests within the national power structure that inhibit social change, most nations have inherited a semicolonial status vis-à-vis the developed world, which in the case of Latin America is the United States. Besides the impact of foreign imperialism, the individual feels victimized by local elites, whether landowners, a political–military oligarchy, or, in some cases, the Church authorities. Still, national differences are acute within this broad spectrum. For example, Colombia exhibits an archaic social order, but its industrialization has passed the incipient stage, and its political process has nervously remained in the democratic ledger. Furthermore, in Bogotá, its capital and major city, at least a fourth of the population could be labeled as middle class. Like Colombia, Chile was marked by polarization in its social class system and ideology along with a sharp contrast between urban and rural societies. However, the country was more advanced in its educational facilities, industrialization, and its attachment to European values.

One characteristic linking the Latin American and Japanese samples is the traditional militancy of the university student subculture. Student strikes have been institutionalized in Colombia, Japan, and in Chile until the 1970s.

Research Design

The investigation was based on clusters of working hypotheses oriented to several aspects of modernism: (a) social participation; (b) optimism about the future and orientation to mobility; and (c) rationalism as indicated by higher scores in selected items of a modernism–traditionalism scale.

The adult samples were selected from lower and middle-class residents on a representative but nonrandom basis from Allentown, Pennsylvania (95); Munich, West Germany (102); Tokyo, Japan (139); Bogotá, Colombia (229); Santiago, Chile (329); and Barcelona, Spain (98). Of the total 992 adults in the total sample, 473 were lower class and 519 middle class. Of the total student sample of 611, the Americans (321) were drawn from public and private institutions in eastern Pennsylvania; the Germans (96) from five Fakultäten (law, medicine, natural sciences, philosophy, and technology) of the University of Munich; three-fourths of the Japanese (112) from Tokyo Metropolitan University, the remainder from the International Christian University; and the Colombians (82) from five facultades (economics, education, engineering, medicine, and psychology) of the National University of Bogotá.

The adult samples were from representative neighborhoods with every fifth to seventh house selected. Interviews averaging 55 minutes in length were conducted both day and evening, with slightly over half of the interviewees being women. Except for a rate of almost 50% in Germany, the refusal rate averaged 33%. As for students, the questionnaire was administered in representative classes; however, in Germany the questionnaire was given in small groups of a randomized sample from the five Fakultäten.

Description of the Sample

The samples primarily represented manual workers in the lower class, and white-collar and a small number of skilled workers in the middle class. The average age was in the upper 40s in the advanced nations but dropped to 45 for Chile and 38 in Colombia, reflecting the younger age profile for developing countries. The mean educational level was nearly 15 years for the United States, 12 for Germany and Japan, 8 for Spain and Chile, and 7 for Colombia. The greatest income differential was in Colombia with a gap of nearly four to one between the two classes, and both Bogotá and Santiago had the highest percentages of immigrants to the city.

The student samples were disproportionately of middle-class origin, especially in the Colombian sample. The German sample was 78% male, the Japanese and Colombian 59%, and the American 46%. However, sex was less a determinant of responses than was nationality. The average age was 20.7 years, and the students had been at the university for 1.9 years.

Findings and Interpretation

The items were analyzed by a t test and the chi-square technique. The following discussion analyzes a limited number of responses to several clusters of hypotheses with reference to both national and generational differences. The effects of social class and the responses to items of purely national significance are reported in the articles cited earlier.

Patterns of Social Participation

In line with other studies, orientation to change was associated with a relatively high level of communication and social participation. For one thing, the samples in the advanced nations had greater exposure to the mass media, including newspapers, television, and motion pictures. One exception was radio listening, which is something of a window on the world for the submerged masses in developing countries.

In regard to the nature of primary group ties, preference for friends over relatives was shown for the advanced nations and for students as compared to the older generation. Again, national or broad cultural differences took precedence over the level of development. Even though the European and United States samples surpassed the Colombian respondents in the number of "intimate friendships," the lowest number was reported by the Japanese, who were the only instance of adults surpassing students. The middle class had wider social contacts than did the lower class. In Colombia, where affiliation to kinship is strong, the middle class was more kin-oriented than was the lower class, for whom finances and distance allowed little interaction with either relatives or friends. Moreover, a tendency to go to someone outside the family for resolving personal problems characterized the adults in advanced nations and the student sample in general. However, the Japanese adults were nearly as kinship-oriented as were the Colombians. In a previous study I found adult samples in El Salvador and Costa Rica to exhibit this preference for kin even more dramatically (Williamson, 1962). Although generally there was a tendency of developed nation samples to move away from kinship moorings, the cultural base was a factor in its own right—the Latin tradition of strong family ties as opposed to the individual autonomy found in northwestern Europe and the United States.

Mobility, Satisfaction, and Future Aspirations

As another measure of modernism, a number of items centered on the respondent's perception of the status quo and his or her sense of mobility for the future. It was hypothesized that optimism about the present and future would be correlated with orientation toward change.

The tendency of respondents to see a brighter economic future for themselves in 10 years followed no orderly relation either to the level of development or to the generational differential, even though the difference in response between the samples (both adult and student) was statistically significant. The optimism of Americans and Colombians stood in contrast to the pessimism of the Germans, with Japanese, Chileans, and Spanish occupying an intermediate position. Possibly the optimism of the Colombians was because they had the furthest to move, but it is questionable whether in a decade after this investigation one would find their economic situation markedly improved. Yet the pessimism of the Germans, especially the students, is hardly justified in view of their continued economic advance over the last 3 decades. Possibly projections toward the future are more a measure of the restrained outlook within the national culture than of the events the respondents are judging.

The assignment of success to life chances ("To what degree does success in life depend on your own accomplishments or on fate?") would seem to be more a product of given cultures, as in the case of Latin and Japanese cultures, than of the level of development of the society or the respondent's stage of the life cycle. At least, dependence on fate was rejected in the German and United States samples. Self-accomplishment was especially stressed by students in these two countries.

With regard to the "world of 20 or 30 years in the future" the developing countries (Colombia and Chile) were the least sanguine. Except for the Americans, no significant difference was found between the two generations. Possibly all the samples would see a more foreboding future if the question were asked today. In any event, the adults were markedly more nostalgic about the past, and the students were more cautious about making any judgment—only the Japanese students were willing to think of the people of 100 years ago as distinctly happier or unhappier than those of the present.

On the whole, the projections of mobility and satisfaction, for whatever implications they might have in regard to modernism and acceptance of social change, did not give clear support to the hypothesis. The Colombians showed some negative affect in regard to the question of self-initiative and projected satisfaction, yet along with the Americans they were optimistic about their personal economic future. Also, it would be difficult to assert that students in the four cultures were necessarily more positive than adults on these indices of satisfaction.

The Rationalism–Traditionalism Continuum

Members of a society in the process of modernization were predicted to prefer rationalistic over traditionalistic values. As a measure of modernism, rationality is expressed by low kinship orientation, preference for an urban rather than an agrarian life style, belief in the mutability of "human nature," low stratification of life chances, universalistic norms for mobility, and related aspects of the urban-industrial value structure (Kahl, 1968). Generally the hypotheses were supported; however, both United States samples proved to be far more traditionalistic than were the German and Japanese. The most traditionalistic scores were for Chile, followed by Colombia, then Spain, which was close to the United States profile. Response differences reflected national culture values as well as the differences between advanced and developing nations. For example, the tendency to perceive the family in a particularistic stance ("We can only have confidence in those we know well") was high for not only Chileans but also for Germans. On the whole, the difference between advanced and developing societies held (with some exceptions on the part of the Americans), notably in the integrity of the family, subservience of children, and deference to authority.

Generational differences were more striking than national ones. The explanation lies in the educational level, differential receptivity to change, peer reinforcement of skepticism toward the status quo, and a socialized awareness of the need for transforming the society. These factors had minimal impact on the American student sample.

In summary, the findings supported the hypothesized relationship between rationality and socioeconomic development. Only the Chilean and Colombian adults failed to show a skeptical attitude toward political processes as, for instance, in the item "The best way of understanding what is going on in the world today is to listen to our national leaders." With the exception of Germans, no sample registered more than 30% agreement with, for example, "Most politicians are primarily devoted to the public good." With respect to stratification of life chances, there was a steep variation between developing and developed nations; for instance, only 7% of the Americans, but approximately two-thirds of the Colombian, Chilean, and Spanish adults, agreed with the statement, "The son of a worker has little likelihood of entering the professions." In other words, as compared to Germans and Japanese, Americans were more accepting of the mobility implied by rationalism than with its institutional aspects.

Conclusion

This chapter has focused on three aspects of orientation to change (social participation, indices of mobility and satisfaction, and given items in the rationality–traditionalism scale) as indicated in three developed countries (Japan, United States, and Western Germany) and three countries in various stages of development (Colombia, Chile, and as the most developed, Spain). In fact, because the Spanish sample was from Barcelona, that country was placed, if only marginally, in the developed ledger. Besides offering cross-national comparisons, the data also reflect generational differences (except for Chile and Spain for which only adult samples were surveyed).

In regard to the central hypotheses the following conclusions can be drawn:

1. Respondents in the advanced societies tend to prefer friends to kin and have wider social involvements. Various items also show a more interpersonal communication and greater exposure to mass media.
2. The hypothesis regarding mobility aspirations and satisfaction with the status quo is only minimally supported. Even though there are statistically significant differences between the national samples, there is no consistent relation between socioeconomic development of the nation and the respondent's tendency to feel optimistic about the present or future.
3. The clearest differentiation between advanced and developing societies is shown in the responses to the modernism or rationality items, but there is some discrepancy between cultural needs and the degree of social development. As an illustration of this, Americans stand close to the Latin samples in their traditionalism scores.

Students displayed considerably more social participation than adults, but they did not exhibit a clear difference in the measures of mobility. However, with very few exceptions the students were more rationalistic than the adults on modernism scale. Again, the German and Japanese students assumed less traditionalism than did the Americans, not surprising in view of the more militant outlook of students in Europe and Asia. Moreover, the American students were partly from private institutions with fairly conservative student bodies. The traditionalism of the Colombian students, although less than that of their adult counterparts, still seems surprising, but it must be recalled that only a minority of students are directly involved in the sociopolitical movements at most Latin American universities.

The factor of social class has largely been ignored in the discussion as it has been analyzed elsewhere (Williamson, 1962, 1968, 1972). However, in all six nations differences or lack of differences between classes generally supported the hypotheses concerning friendship, mobility aspirations, and items in the rationality–traditionalism scale. For example, only a minority of the items proved to be statistically significant between the middle and lower class for Americans and Germans, whereas in only 3 of the 11 items of the modernism scale did the difference fail to reach the .05 level of statistical significance in the Colombian sample. Despite skepticism about the significance of social status in respect to modernity scales (Godwin, 1975), I would contend that modernism is first visible in the middle and upper classes and slowly diffuses to the lower classes.

A few qualifications are in order. First, the samples should be considered as representative of given urban areas. For example, the Germans were from a city of over a million population, the third largest city in Germany; the American sample from an urban area of 600,000 on the edge of Megapolis; the Japanese from one of the three largest urban complexes in the world. Second, the rejection rate, especially high in the German sample, affected findings; possibly the willingness to be interviewed can be best interpreted as a predisposition to critically assess social problems. Finally, among other sampling problems was the varied sex ratio among the students, which may partly explain the relative conservatism of the American sample.

What can we take to be the implications of these findings? For one thing, although increasingly doubts have been expressed as to relevancy of industrialization for the underdeveloped world (Chodok, 1973, pp. 259ff.), the data do not indicate that modernization is necessarily good or bad. Nor does the study pinpoint the medium of communicating or socializing the values of modernism—conflicting data have been both positive and negative in regard to the specific contribution of education, class position, or the level of technological employment.

At the very minimum, the present findings imply some usefulness of the rationalism–traditionalism scale: Over four-fifths of the items proved to be statistically significant at the .05 level between two of the highly developed societies (Chile and Colombia). Or, more broadly, we can conclude that kinds of social interactions, attitudes toward present and future satisfactions and dissatisfactions, and some degree of secularization appear to accompany economic development—but always with the caveat that the national culture must be considered, as has been confirmed by a number of studies (e.g., Fliegel *et al.,* 1979). In other words, along with other inquiries into the psychological correlates associated with modernism, the present research can serve as a point of departure for more intensive analysis.

Acknowledgments

I am indebted to the Research Institute of Lehigh University, the Fulbright Commission, and the staffs of the sociology institutes of the Catholic University of Chile, the National University of Columbia, the University of Barcelona, the University of Munich, and the University of Tokyo for their assistance and collaboration in the project.

References

Armer, M., & Isaac, L. Determinants and behavioral consequences of psychological modernity: Empirical evidence from Costa Rica. *American Sociological Review,* 1978, *43,* 316–343.

Armer, M., & Schnaiberg, A. Measuring individual modernity: A near myth. *American Sociological Review,* 1972, *37,* 301–316.

Black, C. E. (Ed.), *Comparative modernization: A reader.* New York: Free Press, 1976.

Chocok, S. *Social development.* New York: Oxford University Press, 1973.

Firebaugh, G. Structural determinants of urbanization in Asia and Latin America, 1950–1970. *American Sociological Review,* 1979, *44,* 199–215.

Fliegel, F., Sofranko, A. J., Williams, J. D., & Sharma, N. C. Technology and cultural convergence: A limited empirical test. *Journal of Cross-Cultural Psychology,* 1979, *10,* 3–22.

Garner, R. A. *Social change.* Chicago: Rand McNally, 1977.

Godwin, R. K. The relationship between scores on individual modernity scales and societal modernization. *Journal of Developing Areas,* 1975, *9,* 415–432.

Holsinger, D. B., & Theisen, G. L. Education, individual modernity, and national development: A critical appraisal. *Journal of Developing Areas,* 1977, *11,* 315–334.

Huntington, S. P. The change to change: Modernization, development and position. In C. E. Black, *Comparative modernization: A reader.* New York: Free Press, 1976.

Inkeles, A. Making men modern: On the causes and consequences of individual change in six developing countries. *American Journal of Sociology,* 1969, *75,* 208–225.

Inkeles, A., & Smith, D. H. *Becoming modern: Individual change in six developing countries.* Cambridge, Mass.: Harvard University Press, 1974.

Kahl, J. A. *The measurement of modernism.* Austin: University of Texas Press, 1968.

Kelman, H. D., & Warwick, D. P. Bridging micro and macro approaches to social change: A social-psychological perspective. In G. Zaltman (Ed.), *Processes and phenomena of social change.* New York: Wiley, 1973.

Lerner, D. *The passing of traditional society.* New York: Free Press, 1958.

Lewis, O. Urbanization without breakdown: A case study. *Scientific Monthly,* 1952, *75,* 31–41.

Redfield, R. *The folk culture of Yucatan.* Chicago: University of Chicago Press, 1941.

Tsurumi, K. *Social change and the individual: Japan before and after defeat in World War II.* Princeton: Princeton University Press, 1970.

Van den Berghe, P. A structural-functional approach to modernization. In R. H. Lauer (Ed.), *Perspectives on social change.* Boston: Allyn and Bacon, 1973.

Williams, R. M. *American society: A sociological interpretation* (3d. ed.). New York: Knopf, 1970.

Williamson, R. C. Some variables of middle and lower class in two Central American cities. *Social Forces,* 1962, *41,* 195–207.

Williamson, R. C. Some factors in urbanism in a quasi-rural setting: San Salvador and San Jose, *Sociology and Social Research,* 1963, *47,* 187–200.

Williamson, R. C. Social class and orientation to change: Some relevant variables in a Bogotá sample. *Social Forces,* 1968, *46,* 317–328.

Williamson, R. C. Modernism and related attitudes: An international comparison among university students. *International Journal of Comparative Sociology,* 1970, *11,* 130–145.

Williamson, R. C. Social class, mobility and modernism: Chileans and social change. *Sociology and Social Research,* 1972, *56,* 149–163.

Williamson, R. C. Orientation to change in advanced and developing societies: A cross-national sample. In L. L. Adler (Ed.), *Issues in cross-cultural research.* Annals of the New York Academy of Sciences, 1977, *285,* 565–581.

PAULINE A. JONES **19**

Sociopsychological Correlates of Traditionalism in Values: Cross-National Findings[1]

ABSTRACT

The aim of this chapter will be to discuss the determinants of individual family traditionalism–modernism and to examine the effects of holding more traditional values. The larger project of which the present study formed a part was begun in the Canadian Province of Newfoundland and Labrador in the fall of 1974. During the first phase of this research 997 11th-grade students (482 males and 515 females) were tested. During 1977–1978, traditionalism–modernism and a variety of background measures were administered to a sample of approximately 264 Australian adolescents (138 males and 126 females) from towns and cities of varying size in the states of Queensland, New South Wales, and Victoria. For the present study, subscales in both traditionalism and modernism were formed in two areas: family structure scales and childrearing scales. Under the first group were three scales: meeting kinship obligations, family planning, and women's rights. Under the childrearing scales were five scales relating to the values one would favor fostering in children. The mother of each adolescent was given a questionnaire designed to classify mother–child interactions as fostering or interfering with the development of field independence. In order to examine the relationships between a number of background variables and traditionalism in values, a multiple regression analysis was performed for both the Newfoundland and Australian data sets. For both samples the three variables, socialization, sex, and community size, each contribute significantly to the prediction of the students' traditionalism in values, after the effects of the other background variables are taken into account. Results of the present research also give very convincing evidence of the importance of traditionalism in values for the prediction of a number of achievement aspiration variables. More traditional students in both

[1] This research was supported by Canada Council Research Grants S74–1101, S76–0156, and 410–77–0406.

Newfoundland and Australia desire not only less education, but also a lower occupational level, and they less frequently choose to attend a university. Of added interest is the finding that more traditional students in both countries give a lower rating of their own academic ability.

In this chapter I will present certain findings from a research project conducted in Newfoundland and subsequently replicated in parts of Australia. I will focus on one component of the traditional–modern syndrome, namely, one's role as a participant in family and kinship networks. My aim will be to discuss the determinants of individual family traditionalism–modernism, and to examine the effects of holding more traditional values.

The larger research project from which these findings are taken aimed at one level to test the validity of Dawson's (1973) model for potential attitude change by assessing the traditional and modern values of high school students who have been exposed to contrasting socialization practices. A second phase of the larger project was designed to examine modern attitude change and traditional–modern attitude conflict encountered by students from rural communities when they move to larger, more urban centers to attend vocational school, trade college, or university.

The analysis of "economic development" or modernization has become an important concern for social and behavioral scientists. Most researchers investigating the effects of psychological variables involved in modernization have been primarily concerned with the role of attitudes and values. Inkeles and Smith (1974) endeavored to examine whether transition in developing countries from village to city or from farm to factory and the subsequent modernizing experiences are harmful to mental health. They concluded that failure to become integrated in an urban industrial setting may generate "psychic strain." Kahl (1968), in studies in Brazil and Mexico and limited studies in the United States, found that education and socioeconomic status were the best predictors of modernism, and that modernism in values can be used as a predictor of educational aspirations and accomplishments.

There is an enormous literature on the impact of industrialization on the family. Although the classic statement by Parsons (1943) relates industrialization to the nucleation of the family, numerous researchers have found that the relationship is actually quite complex, with nucleation not at all consistently manifested, with ideals frequently not congruent with actual behavior, and with attitudes toward different areas of family life not necessarily in accord with each other. However, a general trend away from the authority of the elders and of the extended family, and toward egalitarianism in sex roles, has been noted repeatedly (Inkeles & Miller, 1974).

This trend is obviously a movement away from family traditionalism and toward family modernism, and may be expressed in individual as well as in structural terms. However, attempts to construct scales of family traditionalism–modernism measuring the orientation of individuals have not been numerous. Indeed, cross-national comparisons of the consistency of family modernism are very rare. Kahl (1968) constructed a three-item scale measuring low integration with relatives in both Mexico and Brazil. Guthrie's (1970) research in the Philippines included items relating to family control. The traditionalism–modernism scales constructed by Dawson and his colleagues for use in Australia (1969a) and elsewhere also included a small number of items relating to topics which may be subsumed under family modernism. However, these researchers had as their larger objective to test a theory concerning psychological modernity. Individual modernity has been conceived of as a complex set of interrelated attitudes, values, and behaviors fitting a theoretically derived model of the modern person. Whether this syndrome actually exists in nature, and is the same from country to country, has been one of the prime questions to which the larger projects by Inkeles and Smith (1974) and by others, including Jones (1977), have been addressed.

Research Design

Subjects

The larger project of which the present study formed a part was begun in the Canadian Province of Newfoundland and Labrador in the fall of 1974. During the first phase of this research 997 11th-grade students (482 males and 515 females) were tested. The students attended 11th grade in one of 45 communities or cities. Of these communities 20 were extremely small, with population less than 500. An additional 13 communities were isolated either by having no road links with other communities, as in coastal Labrador or parts of southern Newfoundland, or by being separated from the nearest community by a number of miles of gravel road. Other students lived in small towns ranging in size from 1000 to 10,000 or in the university cities of Corner Brook or St. John's (with populations of 25,000 and 120,000, respectively).

During the latter half of 1977 and of 1978, traditionalism–modernism and a variety of background measures were administered to a sample of approximately 264 adolescents (138 males and 126 females) from rural and urban areas of Australia. This sample included Australian white subjects from towns and cities of varying size in the states of Queensland, New South Wales, and Victoria.

In this chapter I will present findings from the samples of adolescent–mother pairs from both Newfoundland and Australia.

Instrumentation

The traditionalism–modernism test battery given to the full sample of Canadian adolescents in 1975 included five measures of traditional–modern attitudes, totaling 188 items. These scales have been fully described elsewhere (Jones, 1977), as have the results of factor analyses upon the items of the various scales. From these preliminary analyses a refined T–M attitudinal scale consisting of 86 items was developed for use in a second phase of the Newfoundland research and for use with the Australian sample. The traditional–modern item pairs included were shown to have a bipolar pattern of factor loadings.

For the present study subscales in both traditionalism and modernism were formed in the following areas: family structure scales, and childrearing scales. Under the first group were three scales: (a) meeting kinship obligations (which included items from Dawson, 1969a, b; Dawson, Law, Leung, & Whitney, 1971; Guthrie, 1970; and Kahl, 1968); (b) family planning (which included items from Smith & Inkeles, 1966, and Guthrie, 1970); and (c) women's rights (which included items on dominance of the male from Dawson, 1969a, b, and on authority of husband from Guthrie, 1970, and Dawson, 1969a, b). Under the childrearing scales were five scales relating to the values one would favor fostering in children. It has been argued by theoreticians in the modernism field that family modernism should reflect an aspiration to raise children who are disciplined (Dawson, 1969a, b), who value education (Guthrie, 1970; Smith & Inkeles, 1966), who are activists who feel that control and change are desirable and possible (Kahl, 1968), and who are trustful (Kahl, 1968). Low religiosity has been theoretically linked with increased modernism, but research has not produced clear, positive findings (Kahl, 1968). Following the research of those just cited, the present study included a number of questions about the values one attempts to inculcate in a young child. These were items in the five value areas just listed. The eight scales of family traditionalism–modernism comprised a total of 56 items (these forming a subset of the revised 86-item scale earlier described). Subjects responded to scale items using one of the following: agree strongly, agree, not sure, disagree, and disagree strongly. The T–M questionnaire was scored across the traditional items, and across the modern items for each of the eight family concepts. The traditionalism score referred to in the results presently being discussed is the sum across the traditionalism items of the eight concepts just described.

Adolescents in both the Newfoundland sample and the Australian sample were also given a background questionnaire to supply the relevant socioeconomic indices and measures of educational and occupational aspirations. Additionally, the mother of each student was given items from a question-

naire developed by Witkin and colleagues to classify mother–child interactions as fostering or interfering with the development of field independence.

Results and Discussion

The determinants of modernism have often been hypothesized to be
community background and various socioeconomic attainment measures,
principally education of the wife and her husband, along with family income
(see, e.g., Schnaiberg, 1970). Guthrie and his colleagues were concerned
with traditional–modern attitudinal differences in relation to proximity to
urban modern influences, sex of respondent, and social class. Their results
showed that there were few differences associated with proximity to urban
influences; there were virtually no differences in attitudes between men and
women. There were, however, consistent differences between educated and
financially secure people and those who were poor and less educated (Guthrie, 1970, p. 121). Similarly, in all six countries researched by Inkeles and
Smith (1964), "education emerged as unmistakably the most powerful force
in shaping a man's modernity score [p. 304]," whereas the city failed to
substantiate its claim to standing as an important school for making people
modern.

In order to examine the relationships between a number of such background variables and traditionalism in values, a multiple regression analysis
was performed for both the Newfoundland and Australian data sets. Table
19.2 contains the essential results of these analyses; Table 19.1 presents the
intercorrelations among all the variables of interest in this report and shows
the mean and standard deviation of the variables for both Newfoundland
and Australian data.

By examining the simple rs of Table 19.1, it may be seen that each
background variable (with the exception of number of siblings for the Australian sample) is significantly related to student's traditionalism in values for
both countries. To examine the contribution of any one predictor variable
in the presence of the other background variables, attention is drawn to
Table 19.2. The figures within the body of Table 19.2 are standard partial
regression coefficients. "Standard" means they are used when all the variables are in standard score form. "Partial" means that the effects of variables
other than the one to which the weight applies are held constant.

It is particularly important to note the consistency of findings across the
two countries sampled. For both the Canadian and the Australian sample,
three variables, socialization, sex, and community size, each contribute significantly to the prediction of the students' traditionalism in values, after the
effects of the other background variables are taken into account. Thus,

Table 19.1
Correlation Matrix, Means, and Standard Deviations for the Variables Entering into Regression Analyses[a]

		X_1	X_2	X_3	X_4	X_5	X_6	X_7	X_8	X_9	X_{10}	X_{11}	X_{12}	X_{13}	X_{14}	$\overline{X}$	S.D.
X_1	Community size		.06	.04	.27	.18	.21	.13	.42	-.34	.21	.23	.23	.20	.04	2.45	.69
X_2	Number of siblings	-.26		.01	-.07	-.08	-.03	-.08	.12	-.06	-.02	.01	-.04	.06	-.03	2.79	1.70
X_3	Sex	-.03	-.02		.09	.08	-.01	.08	-.02	-.22	-.00	.09	-.03	.05	-.06	1.52	.50
X_4	Father's education	.43	-.28	.01		.54	.45	.29	.06	-.30	.18	.39	.35	.31	.27	5.66	2.25
X_5	Mother's education	.36	-.26	-.02	.50		.26	.44	-.04	-.23	.15	.30	.27	.16	.24	5.74	1.79
X_6	Father's occupation	.39	-.26	-.05	.60	.43		.30	-.01	-.18	.01	.33	.25	.32	.31	544.37	123.0
X_7	Mother's occupation	.24	-.20	-.03	.35	.63	.39		.07	-.17	.15	.28	.23	.17	.22	459.26	92.87
X_8	Age	-.05	.16	-.07	-.21	-.19	-.10	-.11		-.20	.20	.09	.06	.06	-.02	196.0	7.77
X_9	Traditionalism in values	-.13	.12	-.15	-.10	-.08	-.11	-.08	.14		-.29	-.46	-.34	-.36	-.27	72.56	10.26
X_{10}	Socialization	.02	.00	.09	.08	.05	.04	.05	-.00	-.17		.26	.25	.25	.17	100.93	13.26
X_{11}	Desired educational level	.10	-.05	-.03	.18	.17	.14	.16	-.18	-.23	.05		.68	.70	.54	3.55	2.03
X_{12}	Desired occupational level	.14	-.12	-.01	.24	.17	.15	.15	-.10	-.19	.09	.48		.53	.45	615.98	138.06
X_{13}	University education	.16	-.18	-.02	.23	.16	.20	.19	-.18	-.22	.03	.57	.38		.45	1.38	.49
X_{14}	Self-rated academic ability	.03	-.12	-.04	.16	.12	.12	.15	-.19	-.20	.08	.42	.37	.43		11.9	2.95
$\overline{X}$		2.89	6.02	1.51	4.18	4.78	35.8	29.7	207.3	71.7	99.6	4.33	51.0	1.21	12.0		
S.D.		1.73	3.13	.50	2.76	2.48	14.7	12.2	9.07	9.49	13.7	1.57	13.1	.41	2.91		

[a] The correlations, means, and standard deviations are above the diagonal for the Australian students, and below the diagonal for the Newfoundland students.

Table 19.2
Regression Coefficients for Prediction of Traditionalism in Values

	Standardized regressions (betas)	
Independent variables	Newfoundland	Australia
Community size	−.10*	−.19*
Number of siblings	.07	−.06
Sex	−.14**	−.20**
Father's education	.03	−.13
Mother's education	.03	−.07
Father's occupation	−.06	−.06
Mother's occupation	−.03	−.01
Age	.12**	−.07
Socialization	−.16**	−.20**
R^2	.09	.25

  * $p < .05$.
 ** $p < .01$.

students having higher traditionalism scores have mothers whose socialization of their children hindered the development of independence. Additionally, for both the Canadian and Australian samples, male adolescents reported more traditional values in the family-related concepts under consideration in this chapter. And, as predicted, for both samples, adolescents who resided in small communities held a set of attitudes that represents a "traditional" view of the family.

Modernism in values is theoretically considered to be predictive of achievement within modern institutional settings. From studies in Brazil and Mexico, Kahl found, as was previously noted, that "modernism in values can be used as a predictor of educational aspirations and accomplishments . . . in a way that goes beyond predictions based solely on position in the social structure [1968, p. 21]." The results of the present research, as summarized through the regression coefficients of Table 19.3, give very convincing evidence of the importance of traditionalism in values for the prediction of a number of achievement aspiration variables.

By looking at Column 1 of Table 19.3 we see that the student's traditionalism in values is the most significant predictor of the student's desired level of education. This finding is held up across the two countries. More traditional students desire less education. In the presence of the traditionalism variable, the father's education was also found to significantly predict student's desired level of education. This finding was consistent across the Canadian and Australian samples. By examining the simple *r*s of Table 19.1 it can be seen that the variables, mother's education, father's occupation,

Table 19.3

Regression Coefficients for Prediction of Achievement Aspiration Variables[a]

	Dependent variables			
Independent variables	Desired level of education	Desired occupational level	Choice of university education	Self-rated academic ability
Community size	.01	.02	.04	−.08*
	.01	.09	.04	−.12
Number of siblings	.05	−.03	−.07*	−.05
	.02	−.03	.06	−.01
Sex	−.07*	−.03	−.05	−.08*
	−.01	−.12	−.02	−.13
Father's education	.10*	.18**	.11*	.11*
	.16*	.19*	.15	.08
Mother's education	.04	.02	−.05	−.04
	.05	.04	−.05	.08
Father's occupation	.00	−.03	.04	.01
	.15*	.06	.20**	.21**
Mother's occupation	.08	.06	.11*	.12**
	.11	.09	.04	.08
Age	−.13**	−.03	−.12**	−.14**
	−.00	−.05	−.03	−.03
Traditionalism in values	−.21**	−.16**	−.18**	−.18**
	−.36**	−.25**	−.28**	−.25**
R^2	.11	.09	.13	.10
	.32	.22	.22	.19

[a] Coefficients for the Newfoundland students are uppermost in each pair.

  * $p < .05$.

 ** $p < .01$.

and mother's occupation, each are significantly related to the student's desired level of education; and, again, this is true for both countries. However, these variables in general lose their significance as predictors in the presence of the student's traditionalism in values.

The findings as summarized for the dependent variable, desired level of education, are held up quite consistently as we consider each of the other three dependent variables. As seen by examining the bottom two rows of the body of Table 19.3, the student's traditionalism in values is the most significant predictor for all four dependent variables, and it holds this position for both Canadian and Australian students. More traditional students in both countries desire not only less education, but also a lower occupational level, and they less frequently choose to attend a university. Of added interest is the finding that more traditional students in both countries give a lower rating of their own academic ability. I might indicate here that this rating was performed across a five-point scale for each of four statements: ability compared with that of close friends; ability compared with other members of his class; ability to complete a university degree; and ability to complete a postgraduate degree. A composite score across these four statements was used in the regression analysis reported in Table 19.3. As with the desired level of education, either the father's educational or his occupational level was found to be a significant predictor of the three remaining dependent achievement aspiration variables, when the effect of traditionalism in values was statistically controlled.

The statistics of Tables 19.1 and 19.3 are firm evidence that traditionalism in values relates to educational aspirations. This observation might be compared with the findings of Inkeles and Smith (1974) to the effect that "education emerged as the most powerful force in shaping a man's modernity score [p. 304]." If this statement seems valid for the positive rs between modernism and educational achievement variables, what may be said of the negative rs between traditionalism and educational desires and achievement? Would we say that the lack of education is important in shaping a person's traditionalism score? One should be careful indeed when inferring causality from the correlations observed. Nevertheless, it appears that if one views modernism as a construct of importance for economic development and advancement, as many undoubtedly do, the traditional or modern values are important as predictors of performance, educational if the arena is the school, or occupational advancement if the arena is the industrial or professional world. At a higher level of elaboration, it may be suggested that the variables community size, parental education, and mother's childrearing practices (e.g., her stress upon independence), are background variables which may be viewed as influential socialization agents in shaping modernism or traditionalism in values. Then it would be reasonable to suggest that these values in turn play a significant part in the young person's achievement, both in terms of level of aspiration and actual performance.

References

Dawson, J. L. M. Attitude change and conflict among Australian Aborigines. *Australian Journal of Psychology*, 1969, *21,* 101–116. (a)

Dawson, J. L. M. Attitudinal consistency and conflict in West Africa. *International Journal of Psychology*, 1969, *4,* 39–53. (b)

Dawson, J. L. M. *Adjustment problems encountered by individuals in the process of modernization in the resolution of traditional–modern attitudinal conflict.* Paper presented at the East–West Culture Learning Institute, University of Hawaii, February 1973.

Dawson, J. L. M., Law, H., Leung, A., & Whitney, R E. Scaling Chinese traditional–modern attitudes and the GSR measurement of "important" versus "unimportant" Chinese concepts. *Journal of Cross-Cultural Psychology*, 1971, *2*, 1–27.

Guthrie, G. M. *The psychology of modernization in the rural Philippines.* Quezon City, the Philippines: Manila University Press, 1970.

Inkeles, A., & Miller, K. A. Construction and validation of a cross-national scale of family modernism. *International Journal of Sociology of the Family*, 1974, *4*, 127–147.

Inkeles, A., & Smith, D. H. *Becoming modern.* Cambridge, Mass.: Harvard University Press, 1974.

Jones, P. A. The validity of traditional–modern attitude measures. *Journal of Cross-Cultural Psychology*, 1977, *8*, 207–239.

Kahl, J. A. *The measurement of modernism: A study of values in Brazil and Mexico.* Austin: University of Texas Press, 1968.

Parsons, T. The kinship system of the contemporary United States. *American Anthroplogist*, 1943, *45*, 22–38.

Schnaiberg, A. Measuring modernism: Theoretical and empirical explorations. *American Journal of Sociology*, 1970, *76*, 399–425.

Smith, D. H., & Inkeles, A. The OM scale: A comparative socio-psychological measure of individual modernity. *Sociometry*, 1966, *29*, 353–377.

FLORENCE L. DENMARK
NIRA WEINBERG
JOYCE BLOCK

20

A Comparison of Women in the Soviet Union and Israel

ABSTRACT

In both early Israeli and Soviet societies, sexual equality was a fundamental tenet. Yet, when examined today, both societies—for different reasons, having to do with their different socioeconomic dictums and cultural heritages—fall far short of actualizing the early blueprints. Myths die hard, and the myth of sexual equality persists in both the Soviet and the Israeli cultures.

This chapter is a comparison of the different patterns of sexual inequality in the two cultures and of their genesis, in the light of initial stated egalitarianism.

A comparison of women in the Soviet Union and Israel is of particular interest given that both of these nations emerged from a revolution and a social movement that explicitly articulated adherence to the ideals of freedom and equality for both men and women. With modern communication technology, each successive revolution inevitably is influenced by the ones which precede it. Thus, the Zionist movement borrowed heavily from the specific experience of the Russian revolution, not to mention the writings of Marx and Engels, and the treatises of the founding fathers of the American Revolution. Each movement did take place, however, under unique historical circumstances, and these were perhaps more powerful determinants than were the ideological principles. As a newly founded nation, Israel encountered economic, political, and military pressures different from those faced by the Soviet Union.

Yet, the egalitarian impulse, to which both of these societies paid at least verbal homage, justifies a comparison of outcomes. The primary purpose of such a comparison is not to evaluate which culture permits more equality or freedom for women, but rather to help us understand the differences as they exist and the processes by which they developed.

For all intents and purposes, the role of women in Soviet society was to be undifferentiated from the role of men; an egalitarian vision was promulgated. The Zionist ideology was similar, if not indistinguishable. Consider the rhetoric of the First Communist International: "Social equality of man and woman before the law and in practical life. Radical transformation in conjugal rights and the family code. Recognition of maternity as a social function. Making a social charge of the care and education of children and adolescents. The organization of a civilizing struggle against the ideology and the traditions that make a woman a slave [in de Beauvoir, 1974, p. 142]." And now compare what the Zionists proclaimed:

"Complete and absolute equality of women will be upheld—equality in rights and duties, in the life of the country, society and economy throughout the entire legal system . . . assurance of maternity leave with pay with the right to return to the place of employment. . . . Equal wages will be ensured to both men and women workers for equal work . . . a man and a woman shall have equal status with regard to any legal proceeding; any provision of law which discriminates with regard to any legal proceedings, against women as women, shall be of no effect [in Aloni, 1973, p. 250]."

Today, the *myth* of equality for women persists in both cultures, but the similarity stops there. In the Soviet Union, for reasons to be explored in what follows, women's status as members of the general and professional work force more nearly approximates the ideal. However, women are required to carry a double burden, functioning as both workers and primary homemakers, and thus their status remains different from, and unequal to, that of men. In Israel, despite pockets of feminist rhetoric and consciousness, the attitudes toward women, as well as the actual roles women play in society, appear to have reverted to the inequalities associated with conventional sex-role differentiation. It is our intention to explore the conditions responsible for the divergent paths taken.

Feminist consciousness began to emerge in Russia among female student intellectuals at the turn of the century. Women were active participants in the political and military maneuvers that led to the 1917 uprising and the eventual establishment of the Communist nation (de Beauvoir, 1974). Yet, it was not until after the revolution that women's position in this society was altered radically. With the Bolshevik revolution, there was the promise of emancipation and sexual equality. Women and men were expected to work under similar conditions and to be paid equally for their labor. Sexual freedom and economic independence for men and women were socially sanctioned, in an attempt to create a climate wherein men and women could interact on an equal footing. Maternity was to be voluntary, thus implying the easy availability of contraception and abortion. Finally, married and unmarried mothers and their children had equal claim to the services of the State, for example, the financing of child care and paid pregnancy leaves. These Marxist-Leninist formulations did not, however, take into account the conflicting interests between working men and women which were to surface with the development of the nation's economy, nor did they provide for equality within the private domestic sphere.

The contemporary status of women in the USSR can be better comprehended as the result of the imperatives of industrialization, rather than as the fulfillment of the original socialist ideal of humanitarian equality between the sexes. Soviet government policy reflected pragmatic concerns with increased productivity and efficiency, and women's emancipation was subordinated to the quest for economic growth. Specifically, the Stalinist era, which was marked by labor shortage, low wages, collectivation, purges, and massive mobilization of men for military service during World War II, mandated an influx of women into industry. In 1930, there were 3 million women employees; and by 1932, the figure reached 6 million (Lapidus, 1975, p. 157). Although the Soviet women were rapidly joining the labor force, there remained for women a second, wageless working place: the home. The homemaking requirements of the Soviet women were particularly arduous. Soviet planning was centralized, and heavy investments were made in capital goods, with neglect in the development of service facilities and consumer products. In 1953, two-thirds of all urban families still obtained their water from a communal tap or pump (Lapidus, 1975). The Soviet women were the segment of the population most hampered by these conditions. The family laundry alone could consume the equivalent of 2 working days a week, and this and other domestic activities continued to be women's responsibilities. Perhaps as a consequence of the pressures placed on the individual household, and on women in particular, the birth rate declined. Official Soviet reaction was critical. Disregarding the espoused ideal of voluntary maternity, the government instituted corrective measures: In 1936, legal abortions were abolished, birth control was prohibited, and divorce became a complicated procedure. A potent press campaign was waged glorifying motherhood and women's role as sexual partner and reproducer as well as worker (de Beauvoir, 1974; Lapidus, 1978).

World War II further promoted the retrogressive trends that characterized the Stalinist era. In spite of the heroic performance of Soviet women during wartime, the norms differentiating masculinity and femininity were solidified. The ultimate expression of these sexist prescriptions came in 1943 with the abolition of coeducation.

In the Soviet Union today, women comprise over half of the labor force and 60% of the professionals. They represent 72% of the medical doctors, 63% of all economists, and 68% of the cultural workers and teachers. These are impressive achievements. However, as one moves up the hierarchy of status and authority, one finds fewer and fewer women. Chief physicians are disproportionately male. Women are noticeably underrepresented in positions of political sensitivity such as those in the Writer's Union, Soviet radio, and the press. Sexual stratification within the various specializations is unequivocal: Mechanical engineering is overwhelmingly male, whereas workers in the garment and textile industries are generally female. Women make up over 90% of trade and public catering employees, 98% of the nurses, 75% of the teachers, 98% of the nursery school personnel, and 99% of the typists and stenographers (Lennon, 1971). Although in comparison with western societies, women hold a respectable proportion of responsible positions in Soviet economic life, they do not hold positions commensurate to their training or work experience, and their absence in managerial roles is striking.

Whereas Soviet society has clearly encouraged women to function as full participants in production, the division of labor within the family remains largely traditional with respect to domestic activity. The commitment to female independence and equality has entailed the formulation of special rights for mothers, and women's legal rights are no longer affected by their marital status. Marriage as an institution is devoid of the obligation to support women as economic dependents, and women are not *obliged* by law to perform domestic services. However, in practice, women's family roles are apt to be reminiscent of earlier times (de Beauvoir, 1974; Lapidus, 1978; Lennon, 1971).

Although the state provides childrearing facilities, official dictum opposes the complete socialization of both child care and household functions. The option to hire domestic help was profoundly limited with the ideological devaluation of domestic labor. The social denigration of "personal service" work coupled with the availability of alternate opportunities for women in the labor force militates against women's emancipation from the double burden. These factors, when combined with the lack of any investment in sex-roles redefinition, yield the following outcome: Women spend over twice the amount of time that men do on housework, and consequently claim but a quarter of the amount of free time.

This sexual division of labor within the home has repercussions for the Soviet family as well as for the larger social system. The double burden placed on women by the combination of full-time employment and heavy family responsibilities functions to free men to pursue educational and oc-cupational advancements, while simultaneously restricting the mobility of women. Mothering the first child virtually terminates a woman's educational aspirations, whereas men can continue their education. Thus, economic independence did bring about a change for women, yet traditional marital patterns prevail.

Whereas the successful mobilization of Soviet women appears to have neglected their liberation from household responsibilities, Israel at the moment of its independence in 1948 seemed to be in a position to mobilize and liberate women simultaneously. For years Israelis prided themselves on the social equality they awarded to their women. Kibbutz women donned in shorts decorated Zionists' fund-raising ads; female soldiers with machine guns starred in official public relations productions. In its declaration of independence, Israel wrote that it will maintain "one rule of law for all inhabitants—the state will not discriminate between one person and another on the grounds of race, religion, language or sex [Aloni, 1973, pp. 248–256]." A list of social and economic principles were given legal status, placing Israel in its formative years among the most "advanced" Western nations. When women in various countries began to demand improved status, they repeatedly pointed to the Israeli women as a model they wished to emulate. All of the recent debates in the United States concerning equal wages for equal work, paid maternity leaves, the right to serve in the army and to maintain one's name upon marriage—these were battles long won by Israeli women, relics of past struggles. At least on paper, such rights were firmly established in Israel. What happened?

In the society envisioned by the social idealists who came to Palestine between 1904 and 1913, both ideology and necessity ensured a large measure of equality between the sexes. Socialist idealism—bred in revolutionary Russia—required such equality, and frontier conditions reinforced it. Both sexes were equally amateurish when it came to paving roads and clearing swamps. They were equally contemptuous of the bourgeois lifestyle in which they were raised. Nonetheless, 3 decades later, it was clear that the dream of sexual egalitarianism had been left behind.

One major blow to the code prevailing in the beginning days occurred in 1951, when the socialist government turned around and institutionalized Orthodox Judaism, granting exclusive jurisdiction over matters of marriage, divorce, and personal status to the official Rabbinate. This undemocratic concession to religious groups stemmed from political needs which were perhaps augmented by more emotional ones. There was a yearning for an Israeli state that would be the fountainhead of the Jewish people, and not merely a Levantine nation. Thus, the Zionist aim of egalitarianism and normalization was undermined and replaced by clericalistic overtones.

The traditions of Orthodoxy sharply differentiate the roles of men and women, and contribute to an acceptance of sexual inequality. It is unlikely that there is another modern state in which courts do not accept a woman as witness, yet the Rabbinical courts—which even today have jurisdiction over matters involving marriage, the family, and divorce—do not. Legally a married woman does not exist, as it is only when she is divorced that a woman can appear before the court. Israeli family law has been regarded by legal scholars as among the world's most archaic. It goes without saying there are no female judges, and in the eyes of the Orthodox establishment a woman's place is in the home, nurturing the young. (See Weinburg & Denmark, 1978, for a detailed account of Orthodox Jewish tradition.)

These religious attitudes have been reinforced by the demographic priority of increasing the birth rate. Until 1977, Israeli women were subject to prosecution for abortion and could receive sentences of up to 5 years of imprisonment. The only legitimate reason recognized by the state for the termination of a pregnancy was if the pregnancy endangered the physical health of the woman. The law currently in operation still does not grant women abortions on demand, but has extended the acceptable categories of women eligible for legal abortions to those women over the age of 40. This pronatalist national policy has its major impact on the female population as it is the women who function as the primary caregivers. Only a scant number of women in Israel—mostly intellectuals and of affluent classes— have adopted the new feminist consciousness typical of western countries in the 1970s. Recent research reveals that 68 out of 100 young women in Israel place their success as mothers and housewives above any other achievements (Segev, 1979). There is little reentry into the labor force after pregnancy, and motherhood is officially rewarded. Being single is stigmatized.

Women's roles as homemakers and mothers reduce their chances for steady employment and limit their career prospectives. Slightly over one-third of all women work outside the home in Israel, and the proportion of women in high-status professional and managerial occupations has remained markedly low (Rosenberg, 1977). Working women who are married tend to work outside the home only on a part-time basis. They are apt to choose employment that does not demand strong commitments or require great investments of time and energy. Although women constitute about 50% of the full-time university students, only 13% of all Ph.D.'s and 2% of all full professors are women (Hazelton, 1977).

Since 1948, Israeli women have yet to reach 10% membership in parliament. There are no women ministers, no women have responsibility for chairing legislative committees, and there are no women mayors. Only about 51% of the women in Israel serve in the army. Those who do generally are kept far from the fighting (Aloni, 1973; Hazelton, 1977; Rosenberg, 1977), and tend to be placed in clerical, medical, housekeeping, and teaching positions (Sanders, 1965). As recently as 1975, most people surveyed responded negatively to the question: "Should Israeli women fight alongside men?" (Aloni, 1976). Respondents felt that women were too fragile or too weak to fight in the army, and that their place was in the home. Mothers, married women, and pregnant women are exempt from military service, as well as women claiming poor health or those "insufficiently educated." Interestingly enough, men who are "insufficiently educated" are required to serve their country, and in the process are given further education.

Sex-role differentiation in the kibbutzim, which were originally designed to free women from the yoke of domestic services, is pervasive (Kahan, 1973). Although sexual equality was practiced to a considerable extent during the early 1920s when the kibbutzim were entirely agrarian, increasing industrialization within the communities has been associated with a reversion to traditional feminine and masculine roles. The kibbutz women themselves in large numbers have rejected the communal eating and sleeping arrangements, and have returned to the familial ones. Women generally work in low status positions: in the kitchen, the nurseries, and the communal laundry. Kibbutz women do more cleaning, cooking, laundering, nurturing, and babysitting than do nonkibbutz women (Rosenberg, 1977). These female-dominated spheres of work, which do not accrue revenue for the kibbutz, are looked down upon by men and women alike. The devaluation of these work activities by the community at large is concomitant with their association with women, and thus men are discouraged from entering and integrating these occupations.

Today, Israel's concern for its very survival reinforces the status quo. Within the context of Middle East hostility, dissension among women is regarded as unpatriotic, and the critics who point to women's deteriorating status in Israeli society are denounced as feeding anti-Israeli propaganda. Wars are followed by baby booms, and the energy that would be required for a major reshuffling of sex roles is deflected elsewhere—for women, into caring for children, for men into military mobilization—and is thus unavailable. Nevertheless, despite the realities, the myth of equality persists.

The original goals of sexual equality in the Soviet Union and in the state of Israel have yet to be achieved. In both instances, economic, political, and ideological factors have intervened and subordinated the ideal of egalitarianism to the practical considerations of survival. Women's status has not been perceived as a high priority issue by the men who have had the power to make relevant policy decisions.

In the Soviet Union, the overriding concern with national development was consistent with the mobilization of women for the labor force. However, there was an absence of sex-role redefinition within the private sphere, and women have been forced to bear the double burden. Their mobilization has not brought about their liberation, and women's power, status, and privileges remain unequal to those of men. In Israel, on the other hand, a complex combination of factors have pressured women to reembrace their traditional roles while simultaneously carrying on the rhetoric of liberation. The actual sex-role divisions observable in Israel today reflect the inconsistency between ideology and reality; between the culture's explicit and implicit beliefs about men and women. Israel's birth as a new and vulnerable nation, the memories of the holocaust, the composition of its diverse immigrant heritage, the ever-present threats to its survival, and the conglomeration of its religious and secular identities are all elements that contribute to the final configuration.

What emerges from this cursory examination of women's positions in the Soviet Union and Israel is the realization that the situation of women cannot be understood outside of the social, economic, and cultural environment in which they live. Ideals of sexual equality are frequently sacrificed to political and economic expediencies, and cultural redefinition of male and female roles fails to materialize. Initially, in both the Soviet and Israeli societies, women were encouraged to enter into traditionally male arenas, and thus being "more equal" became identified with being more "masculine." However, there was no simultaneous effort to transform the male role either within the public or the private arena. Tasks traditionally relegated to females remained low status and thus undesirable. There was no influx of men into these activities to parallel the mobilization of women and their movement into traditionally male-dominated domains. The outcome was different in the two cases. Soviet women were required to bear double responsibilities, and their "freedom" to do both men's and women's work limits their status and power. Israeli women took a different path. With the development of Israel into a modern industrialized nation, women's participation in the productive economy was no longer essential, whereas their reproductive functions were. Without a commitment on the part of Israeli men to share equally the childrearing responsibilities, the reemergence of traditional sex-role divisions was practically inevitable. For sexual equality to be established in these or any other nations, there must be a reevaluation of the female as well as of the male roles, and an integration within the culture of "masculine" and "feminine" values. Permitting women to be more "masculine" is not revolutionary if simultaneously men are not permitted to be more "feminine" without loss of status, power, or respect. These fundamental changes have not been effected in the Soviet Union or in the state of Israel, and so the liberation of women remains at this point a myth.

References

Aloni, S. The status of women in Israel. *Judaism*, Spring 1973, 248–256.
Aloni, S. *Women as human beings*. Jerusalem: Keter Publishing, 1976.

de Beauvoir, S. *The second sex.* New York: Vintage Books, 1974.

Hazelton, L. *Israeli women.* New York: Simon and Schuster, 1977.

Kahan, H. Women's liberation—An Israeli perspective. *New Outlook,* June 1973, 21–26.

Lapidus, G. W. *Women in Soviet society.* Berkeley: University of California Press, 1978.

Lennon, L. Women in the USSR. *Problems of Communism,* 1971, *20,* 47–58.

Rosenberg, B. Women's place in Israel. *Dissent,* Fall 1977, *24,* 408–417.

Sanders, R. The changing kibbutz. *Midstream,* June 1965, *11,* 51–59.

Segev, T. I am a woman, so what? *Ha-Aretz,* Dec. 1979.

Stites, R. Women's liberation movement in Russia, 1900–1930. *Canadian American Slavic Studies,* 1973, *7*(4), 460–474.

Weinberg, N., & Denmark, F. L. Israeli women, the myth of sexual equality. *International Journal of Group Tensions,* 1978, *8,* 112–119.

USHA KUMAR
URMIL ARORA **21**

Ego Identity Status
of Married Couples and
Their Interactions on Structured
and Unstructured Tasks

ABSTRACT

This study served to observe the behavioral indices of interactions between married couples of different levels of psychological maturity. It was assumed that in attempting to tackle unstructured and structured tasks, these couples would manifest their feelings of intimacy, ability to tolerate differences, and the perceptual perspectives of their relationships. The results of this study revealed that it was indeed the factor of the spouses' level of psychosocial maturity that dynamically determined the quality of their relationships in the joint performance of tasks.

The research reported on in this chapter was designed to follow up subjects of an earlier study (Kumar & Arora, 1980), in order to better understand the nature of their marital relationships (Kumar, 1978). In the earlier study, the young couples provided self-reports of their experience of intimacy and perceptions of specific issues relevant to their relationship. These spouses were identified on their levels of psychosocial maturity. Their identity status was found to correlate with experiences of intimacy, as well as with the quality of cognitions obtained through the matching and the mismatching of perceptions. In the present study, effort was directed to the observation of behavioral indices of interaction in the joint performance of tasks. The major assumption made was that these couples would bring their past history of affective and cognitive experiences into the performance of these tasks. The attempt in this study was not so much to correlate spouses' earlier self-reports about their relationship to the observed interactions, as it was to give a meaningful interpretation to the observed behaviors of the psychosocially assessed couples in an experimentally defined setting.

CROSS-CULTURAL RESEARCH AT ISSUE

Ego identity (Erikson, 1959) implies a subjective feeling arising from the self-perceptions of continuity running through one's past, present, and future. Ego identity status, however, is an empirically derived concept (Marcia, 1966) used to identify adolescents and young adults on their levels of psychosocial maturity. Four styles of coping used by individuals to resolve the dilemmas of identity were identified on the basis of the presence or absence of a decision-making period (crisis) and the degree of investment (commitment) in their decisions involving critical issues.

These four statuses, stated in order of the highest to the lowest level of psychosocial maturity, were identity achieved, foreclosed, moratorium, and identity diffused. The identity achieved (IA) persons appeared to have undergone a period of indecision about a number of competing alternatives from which they finally made a choice. The foreclosed (FC) persons seemed to have experienced few doubts and made few choices. They were, however, committed individuals who had preempted the active decision-making process. The moratoriums (M) were characterized by a state of current indecision and struggle among alternatives, and thus as withholding their commitment. The identity diffused (ID) remained uncommitted whether they experienced the crises or not.

Based upon the Eriksonian formulation of psychosocial stages and the sequential progression of psychosocial development, it was assumed that the levels of ego identity attained during adolescence influenced the pattern of interactions established by individuals in the subsequent stage, where establishment of closeness and distance with the spouse became the major issue for resolution of the developmental dilemma.

This study set out to observe the behavioral indices of interactions between married couples of certain psychosocial maturity. It was assumed that in attempting to tackle the unstructured and structured tasks, these couples would manifest their feelings of intimacy, ability to tolerate differences, and the perceptual perspectives of their relationships. As the tasks presented were complex and without the biasing effects of spouses' area preferences in decision making, it was assumed that observed patterns would be representative samples of their day-to-day interactions. The general expectation was that the couples higher on ego identity behaviors would display more sharing of responsibility in their performance than those lower on it.

Method

Subjects

The 45 couples in this study were selected from a group of 93 couples who initially agreed to participate. For quick identification of identity status, the Ego Identity Incomplete Sentence Blank was administered to everyone. Seventy-five couples forming the majority of the pairings, namely, 17 identity achieved wives–identity achieved husbands (I–I), 27 foreclosed wives–identity achieved husbands (F–I), 25 foreclosed wives–foreclosed husbands (F–F), and 8 foreclosed wives–moratorium husbands (F–M) were intensively interviewed on Marcia's (1966) Semi-Structured Interview Schedule before the final selection of 45 couples was completed. Three groups, comprising 10 I–I, 19 F–I, and 16 F–F spouse combinations, were further assessed on the dependent variables. Group characteristics of the sample are displayed in Table 21.1. No significant differences were observed among the three groups on age, education, or urban–rural affiliation. Of these marriages, 80% had been arranged by the parents, the remainder having been arranged by the spouses themselves with or without parental consent.

Measures

EGO IDENTITY STATUS

Ego Identity Incomplete Sentence Blank (EI-ISB). Used for preliminary screening, this test was adapted from Marcia's (1966) and Baker's (1971) tests of ego identity. The schedule for males consisted of 25 incomplete sentences adapted for the Indian setting and related to occupation, ideology, future orientation, and continuity from past to present. For females, the issues centered around religion, interpersonal relationships (especially views about sex), female role, future orientation, and continuity from past to present.

Semi-Structured Interview Schedule (SSIS). With some adaptations to fit the Indian context and with the inclusion of items from Morse's (1973)

Table 21.1
Characteristics of Spouses in the Sample

	Wife		Husband	
		Age		
	M	S.D.	M	S.D.
	24.04	± 1.84	28.88	± 2.48
	Years married 3.5 ± 2.32			
	Highest educational achievement[a]			
High school	24		0	
B.A./B.S.	20		2	
M.A./M.S.	44		22	
Professional degree (Ph.D., M. Tech., M.Ed., B.Ed.)	12		76	

[a] In percentage

schedule, Marcia's (1966) questionnaire was followed, in both content and scoring. Generally, the criteria used for determining the level of identity status consisted of two variables of crisis and commitment applied to the critical issues.

PSYCHOSOCIAL MATURITY QUESTIONNAIRE (PMQ)

This measure was based on the scales devised by Dignan (1965), Constantinople (1969), and Rasmussen (1964). It consisted of 50 items, 10 items for each of Erikson's first five psychosocial stages. Items were of the forced choice type with four alternatives—strong agreement, agreement, disagreement, and strong disagreement. This questionnaire yielded an overall score of identity development and subscale scores of maturity for each of the five stages (trust versus mistrust, autonomy versus doubt, initiative versus guilt, industry versus inferiority, and identity versus identity diffusion).

RORSCHACH INKBLOT TESTS

The Rorschach cards numbered IV, VII, and X were selected as standard stimuli to provide interactional information on couples assigned to complete a relatively unstructured task. Any of the ten cards could have served the purpose given their equal value in eliciting responses. The selection of these three cards was based on the rationale of providing both achromatic and chromatic as well as complex stimuli which could potentially elicit rich interactions between the spouses. In addition, Cards IV and VII, usually identified as father and mother cards, were considered appropriate for the study of cross-gender interactions.

PICTURE ARRANGEMENT TEST

Four series of picture arrangement tests ("children," "flirt," "fish," and "taxi") in the performance Wechsler Adult Intelligence Scale (WAIS) adapted for the Indian subjects, were selected to provide standard stimuli for observing interactions of couples on a relatively structured task. These four series with five or six cards in each were among the more complex ones in the subtest. The picture arrangement test, by providing a clear accuracy index, fulfilled the requirements of a structured task. And, because the test was devised to assess the social perceptiveness of subjects taking the WAIS, its inclusion fulfilled the intended purpose of judging the quality of interaction between the husband and the wife.

Procedure

In a counterbalanced order, a set of three Rorschach cards and a set of four series of picture arrangement tests were presented to the wife and the husband individually and, immediately afterwards, jointly. The standard instructions were given in all three sessions, with an additional request in the joint session that subjects give a mutually agreed upon response for each card. Both tasks were scored as defined by Walli (1969) on verbal productivity, based on the number of responses a subject(s) provided individually or jointly, the span of time taken to complete the task, the quality or accuracy of responses, and the introduction of new responses, if any, in the joint session. Additional observation of persistence and implementing ability (origin of accepted proposal), formal leading (making the decision), and practical leading (holding the card) were quantitatively scored for further analysis of the couple's interaction. Although only quantitative data obtained from these criteria are reported, the data were given meaning through the qualitative understanding of the interaction.

Results

The main focus in the analysis of results was to obtain validation of classification of couples along levels of identity status before proceeding to assess their performance on two tasks, structured and unstructured, and on the specified criteria. The assessment of performance of the husband and wife individually served mainly to obtain the baseline data for the subsequent joint performance.

Reliability

A comparison of ratings by two judges of EI-ISB and SSIS showed 82% agreement. The PMQ scores further confirmed the identity status of couples, yielding significantly different scores for the IA and the FC husbands [t (43) = 3.04, $p < .01$] as well as the IA and the FC wives [t (43) = 5.02, $p < .01$]. Using 2 × 5 design with repeated measures (2 identity levels × 5 stages of psychosocial maturity), significant differences were obtained between the IA wives and the FC wives [F (1, 43) = 9.59, $p < .005$] as well as among their scores of psychosocial maturity [F (4, 172) = 9.54, $p < .001$]. Similarly, the IA husbands also scored significantly higher than the FC husbands [F (1, 43) = 9.54, $p < .001$]. Significant variability in scores of the substages [F (4, 172) = 8.93, $p < .001$] was also revealed between the FC and the IA spouses. The performance scores on the structured and the unstructured task were analyzed in two ways: separate comparisons among husbands and wives and comparisons between spouses in a dyad. These results are presented in Tables 21.2 and 21.3, given in what follows.

Table 21.2

t *Values and Level of Significance of the Mean Differences between I-I, F-I, and F-F Dyads on Variables of the Unstructured and Structured Tasks*

Variables	Unstructured tasks			Structured tasks		
	I-I–F-F[a]	I-I–F-I[b]	F-I–F-F[c]	I-I–F-F[a]	I-I–F-I[b]	F-I–F-F[c]
Verbal productivity						
Number of responses	n.s.	n.s.	n.s.	—	—	—
Time span						
Total time spent						
jointly	3.46**	3.46**	n.s.	n.s.	n.s.	n.s.
Individual–Joint H	n.s.	n.s.	n.s.	n.s.	n.s.	n.s.
time spent W	3.05**	4.56**	n.s.	n.s.	n.s.	n.s.
New responses/ H	2.82**	2.08*	2.36*	n.s.	n.s.	n.s.
stories W	n.s.	n.s.	n.s.	2.39*	2.08*	n.s.
Errors in joint						
session	—	—	—			
Total errors by						
couple				2.22*	2.43*	n.s.
Joint–Individual				n.s.	n.s.	n.s.
Persistence and						
implementing H	n.s.	n.s.	n.s.	2.44*	4.05**	n.s.
ability W	n.s.	n.s.	n.s.	4.50**	3.56**	n.s.
Formal leading						
Decision making H	n.s.	2.35*	n.s.	2.88**	2.37*	n.s.
W	2.07*	2.35*	n.s.	2.92**	2.42*	n.s.
Communication of H	n.s.	n.s.	n.s.	n.s.	n.s.	n.s.
decision W	n.s.	n.s.	n.s.	n.s.	n.s.	n.s.
Practical activity H	2.89**	3.80**	n.s.	n.s.	n.s.	n.s.
W	3.86**	5.06**	n.s.	n.s.	n.s.	n.s.

   [a] df = 24.
   [b] df = 27.
   [c] df = 33.
   * $p < .05$.
  ** $p < .01$.

Unstructured Task

VERBAL PRODUCTIVITY

Number of responses. No differences were observed in the scores of husbands and wives, individually or jointly or as partners in groups.

Time span. In a one-way ANOVA, significant differences appeared in the total mean time spent on the cards jointly by spouses. The I–I dyads took longer than the other two dyads (Table 21.2). Husbands were alike in the time spent individually or jointly, but wives were different. The IA wives took shorter time when compared with the wives of the F–I and the F–F dyads in the joint session (Table 21.2).

Table 21.3

t *Values and Level of Significance of the Mean Differences between Spouses in Each Dyad on Variables of the Unstructured and Structured Tasks (W–H)*

Variables	Unstructured tasks			Structured tasks		
	I–I[a]	F–I[b]	F–F[c]	I–I[a]	F–I[b]	F–F[c]
Verbal productivity						
Time span	n.s.	n.s.	n.s.	n.s.	n.s.	n.s.
New responses stories	2.35*	n.s.	n.s.	n.s.	2.46*	2.04*
Errors						
Joint–individual	—	—	—	n.s.	n.s.	3.57**
Persistence and						
implementing ability	n.s.	3.45**	4.0**	n.s.	7.41**	3.78**
Formal leading						
Decision making	n.s.	6.94**	2.97**	n.s.	3.72**	6.38**
Communication of	n.s.	9.81**	8.24**	2.82**	5.55**	4.04**
decision						
Practical activity	n.s.	7.91**	9.29**	n.s.	5.50**	4.93**

[a] df = 18.
[b] df = 36.
[c] df = 30.
* p < .05.
** p < .01.

New responses. Wives' scores did not manifest any difference in the number of new responses given. Husbands' scores varied significantly in this respect, with the IA husbands of the I–I dyad giving more new responses than those of the other two groups and the IA husbands of the F–I dyads doing better than those of the F–F dyads (Table 21.2).

PERSISTENCE IN IMPLEMENTING ABILITY

These scores represented observations of which partner was able to implement his or her proposal as the joint response. Husbands' and wives' scores did not differ when scores were compared among husbands and wives independently (Table 21.2). In comparisons of spouses in the dyads, husband–wife differences appeared in the F–I and the F–F groups. In both cases, husbands' scores were higher than those of their wives. However, the I–I spouses did not differ in this regard (Table 21.3).

FORMAL LEADING

Scores in this category indicated who terminated the discussion by deciding which proposal was to count as the joint response, as well as who made the decision by guiding a goal-directed discussion to its conclusion. The *t* values indicated significantly higher scores on decision making for the IA wives as compared with the FC wives of the other two dyads. The IA husbands of the I–I dyads were significantly lower than the IA husbands of the F–I dyads (Table 21.2). Husbands of both the F–I and F–F dyads made and communicated more decisions than did their spouses. No such differences were observed for the IA spouses of the I–I dyads (Table 21.3).

PRACTICAL ACTIVITY

Scores on practical activity were obtained from the number of times a particular spouse picked up, held, or kept back the card. The *t* values revealed significantly higher scores for the husbands of the F–F and the F–I dyads when compared with the husbands of the I–I dyads. The IA wives, on the other hand, revealed more practical activity than the FC wives of the F–I or the F–F dyads (Table 21.2). Husbands of the FC wives were more dominant in practical activity than their wives whereas the IA spouses shared this activity more or less equally (Table 21.3).

Structured Task

VERBAL PRODUCTIVITY

Time span. No significant differences appeared in the time spans of either husbands or wives of the various groups (Table 21.2) or spouses in a dyad (Table 21.3). In addition, no differences were noted in the length of time spent on the cards individually and jointly by either of the two spouses.

New stories. Significant differences appeared on the number of new responses IA wives of the I–I dyads introduced in their stories when compared with the FC wives of the F–I and the F–F dyads (Table 21.2). Significant differences were also observed between spouses of the F–I and the F–F dyads, where again husbands scored higher than their wives in producing new stories. No such differences were observed in the I–I couples (Table 21.3).

Errors in joint sessions. The I–I couples had the least number of errors (Table 21.2). A significant number of errors appeared in the responses of the FC wives of the F–F dyads when compared with their husbands (Table 21.3).

PERSISTENCE AND IMPLEMENTATION

Significant differences were observed between the IA husbands of the I–I dyads and the husbands of the F–I and the F–F dyads. In each case, the IA husbands of the I–I dyads showed less persistence and implementing ability. In the case of wives, differences were reversed. The IA wives' scores indicated a persistence and implementation greater than that of the FC wives (Table 21.2).

When spouses were compared with each other, husbands of the F–I and F–F dyads had higher scores than their wives. The I–I spouses did not reveal any such difference (Table 21.3).

FORMAL LEADING

In decision making and implementation the IA husbands of the I–I dyads were lower than the husbands of the F–I and the F–F dyads. The IA wives, on the contrary, were higher than the FC wives of the other two dyads (Table 21.2).

No differences were observed in the decision-making activity of either wives or husbands (Table 21.3).

Although differences between wives and husbands in decision making were significant in the F–I and F–F dyads, with higher scores in both cases characterizing the husbands, it was not so for the I–I spouses. However, in communicating the decision, husbands of all three dyads were significantly more dominant than their wives (Table 21.3).

PRACTICAL ACTIVITY

No differences appeared on the practical activity either among husbands or wives (Table 21.2).

Significantly more practical activity appeared among husbands of the F–I and F–F dyads when compared with their wives. The IA couples did not differ in any significant way in this regard (Table 21.3).

Discussion

Barring a few specific differences across the two tasks, couples interacted more or less in the same way on both, with differences emerging along the identity status factor. The I–I dyads were distinctly different from the F–I and F–F dyads. Curiously enough, the absence of difference among husbands or among wives when compared separately as two groups, did not prevent differences from emerging in the dyads. For instance, as a group, husbands were no different from each other in the number of times they communicated the decision to the experimenter on the unstructured task. Nor were wives of the three dyads different. But as dyads, spouses of the I–I dyads were alike whereas the spouses of the other two groups were not. This trend was noted on several criteria.

The distinctiveness of the I–I dyads was seen on all criteria. For example, I–I dyads spent longer time in joint sessions. Their protocols revealed a qualitative difference, which accounted for the time factor. They talked more, sought clarifications, achieved consensus, with considerable cheerfulness and laughter in their interactions. They seemed to enjoy the task. (See Appendix for examples of two typical interactions.)

The speed with which the F–F dyads completed the task appears to be conditioned by the fact that little attempt was made to pool all their resources. Thus the time span differed little whether the spouses worked alone or together. The F–I dyads were sometimes in between in this respect, but more often tended toward the F–F dyads.

All three groups of husbands were different in the number of new responses they produced on the unstructured task, with the IA husbands of the I–I dyads producing the most and the FC husbands the least. Wives did not differ, which made the IA husbands and the IA wives look very different. However, the introduction of new responses by the IA wives on the structured task was higher than that of the other two sets of wives. In this, the IA wives did not differ from their IA husbands whereas the other wives did. However, because the structured task had an accuracy index, introduction of new responses increased the probability of the error score. The error scores of husbands of the F–I and the F–F dyads were significantly higher than the IA husbands of the I–I dyads. This was not true of the IA wives in the joint session. The I–I dyads had the lowest error score. This is where the I–I dyads' differences in interaction appear significant. They could play with new ideas before monitoring each other to select the correct response. This is still another indication that, rather than foreclose their choices prematurely, they were able to pool their options and thus select the correct response.

The I–I dyads showed no spouse difference in the frequency of whose proposal was accepted. According to Walli (1969), this category is more important than others because these scores are indicators of the quality of discussion leading to the proposal. Partners who are not in a constant competitive relationship with one another usually endeavor to reach the best possible solutions. In the formal leading as well, the spouses of the I–I dyads did not differ in the number of times each terminated the discussion by deciding which proposal was to count as a joint solution. Whereas husbands took the formal lead in the F–I and the F–F dyads, IA husbands of the I–I dyads did not differ from their IA wives. Similar observations were true for the spouses of the I–I dyads for practical activity as well.

The consistency with which the I–I dyads displayed differences in their interactions in handling these tasks leads one to assume with confidence that these differences were a function of their psychosocial maturity. Display of low sex-typed behavior as displayed in the husbands' egalitarian and wives' assertive behaviors suggested an androgynous quality to their development.

Development of a sense of identity provides a sense of anchor within individuals which frees them from the need of adhering to the socially approved sex-role behaviors. In the earlier study (Kumar & Arora, 1980) spouses of the I–I dyads scored higher on intimacy and lower on isolation, indicating ability to express closeness and at the same time able to tolerate differences without feeling threatened. The interactions observed in the present study provided behavioral confirmation of these attitudes. Effective pooling of resources was possible because spouses did not find differences of opinion threatening. Nor did these spouses foreclose options prematurely. Their initial congruent perceptual perspective (Kumar & Arora, 1980) enabled them to share and communicate while performing the task.

In the present study, the dilemma of the IA husbands of the FC wives again becomes salient. The interactions of the IA husbands of the F–I dyads, it seems, were determined by the FC wives' psychosocial maturity, just as one could state that the interactions of the IA husbands of the I–I dyads were regulated by their IA wives. In terms of interaction, the IA husbands of the F–I dyads were similar to the FC husbands of the F–F dyads. It appears that the foreclosed personality of their spouses pulled the IA husbands of the F–I dyads into playing the traditional sex role of the male, which the foreclosed husbands expressed to an even greater extent in their interactions with their foreclosed wives.

The results of this study reveal that it was the factor of spouses' level of psychosocial maturity which dynamically determined the quality of their relationships in the course of their joint performance of the tasks. The psychological attributes of different identity status dyads influenced the quality of the interactions observed.

Appendix

The following two segments illustrate the qualitative differences between the interactions of spouses in the I–I versus the F–F dyads.

I–I couple on picture arrangement ("taxi").
Wife arranges the cards in a certain order.
Husband looks and changes the position of a couple of them.
  Wife: *It is quite different.*
Husband: *All right, I'll do it your way.*
  Wife: *You are compromising.*
Husband: *He brought it from the art gallery.*
  Wife: *From the exhibition* (laughs). *That is why he has become an exhibitionist.*
Husband: *This man bought it from the exhibition, carries it under his left arm, hails a taxi cab, holds it and looks back.*
  Wife: *Did you change it?*

Husband: *Let it be.*
  Wife: *Then let my story be.*
Husband: *OK.*
Wife proceeds to narrate the story to E.

F–F couple examines a Rorschach inkblot card.
Husband: *It seems like the inside of the human body.*
  Wife: *It is right, but I said pelvic bone earlier.*
Husband: *But this is inside of the body.*
  Wife: *Let it go. It is OK.*

References

Baker, F. Measures of ego identity: A multitrait multimethod validation. *Educational and Psychological Measurement*, 1971, *31*, 165–174.

Constantinople, A. An Eriksonian measure of personality development in college students. *Developmental Psychology*, 1969, *1*, 357–372.

Dignan, M. H. Ego identity and maternal identification. *Journal of Personality and Social Psychology*, 1965, *1*, 476–483.

Erikson, E. Identity and the life cycle. *Psychological Issues*, Vol. 1. New York: International Universities Press, 1959. (Monograph)

Kumar, U. Functional and dysfunctional role of communication in joint family system in India. *International Journal of Group Tensions*, 1978, *8*, 120–129.

Kumar, U., & Arora, U. Ego-identity status of married couples and their perceptions of relationships and intimacy. *Abstract Guide*, XXIInd International Congress of Psychology, Leipzig, GDR, July 6–12, 1980, *2*(448).

Marcia, J. E. Development and validation of the ego identity status. *Journal of Personality and Social Psychology*, 1966, *3*, 551–558.

Morse, B. *The relationship of identity status and perceived parent child relationship in college women.* Unpublished Master's thesis, Ohio State University, 1973.

Rasmussen, J. E. Relationship of ego to psychosocial effectiveness, *Psychological Reports*, 1964, *15*, 815–825.

Walli, J. Joint Rorschach testing of partner relationships. *Family Process*, 1969, *8*(1), 64–78.

UWE P. GIELEN **22**

A Comparison of Ideal Self-Ratings between American and German University Students

ABSTRACT

In the present study, 131 German and 71 American students rated their ideal selves based on a 63 adjective Q-sort and the ratings were compared. Of the 63 cross-national comparisons, 54% were significantly different at the $p < .05$ level. The ego ideals of German students reflect a relative emphasis upon wanting to be critical, stubborn, dominating, informed, logical, and foresightful. American students stressed a desire to be loving, sensitive, perceptive, genuine, and empathic. A factor analysis of the ratings found two similar, but weak factors in the two samples.

In the 1940s and 1950s, studies of national character occupied an important place in the fields of social psychology and cultural anthropology. For practical reasons, these studies frequently focused on America's competitors, Japan (Benedict, 1946), the Soviet Union (Inkeles, Hanfmann, & Beier, 1958), and Germany (Erikson, 1950/1964). Not surprisingly, the portrait drawn by these authors is often unsympathetic and sometimes approaches political propaganda (e.g., Schaffner, 1948). A second type of study attempts to compare two cultures, such as the American and Chinese (Hsu, 1972), or the American and German (McClelland, Sturr, Knapp, & Wendt, 1958; McGranahan & Wayne, 1948). It is in this tradition of cross-cultural comparisons that the following study may be located.

Surveying studies on American national character, one may discover five themes that run through descriptions of an American culture and modal personality.

1. Americans are success and achievement oriented (McClelland, 1961). Foreign visitors since Tocqueville (1830/1954) have been struck by this theme, and there can be no doubt that it remains a central one.
2. Success and achievement have to be based upon *personal effort* and prove the worth of a person. This theme was emphasized by Max Weber (1930) in his masterful essay "The Protestant Ethic and the Spirit of Capitalism."
3. At any given moment, the person must be allowed to choose freely whatever he wants to do. Modern American psychological theories, such as those of Rogers and Maslow, proclaim that people function optimally when they are allowed to choose freely and thus to actualize themselves.
4. The person should be sensitive to others, and self-realization is possible only in the society of others. In a study comparing German and American high school boys, the students were asked to list activities they engaged in (McClelland *et al.,* 1958). American boys listed group activities five times as often as German boys. When compared to Germans, Americans seem to be more preoccupied with social approval and are more sensitive to the opinions of others. Perhaps, it is not accidental that the public opinion poll was invented in the United States.
5. The conscience of Americans is often "feminine." Gorer (1948) has pointed out that the average American child, whether boy or girl, grows up under the leadership of women. The position of the father in American families, compared to that in Germany and most other countries, is weak. He lacks authority and is often psychologically and physically absent. During the crucial years of early childhood, American children spend much of their time under the authority of teachers who typically are women.

Among the themes that have been emphasized as underlying the German national character, we will select four:

1. Germans follow an idealistic code of philosophy. In German schools, the classical and early romantic period of German literature and philosophy is often portrayed as a high point in the development of German culture. Kant, Hegel, Goethe, and Schiller still have a profound influence on German minds.
2. The idealistic code has to be justified and "rationally" explained. Debates in Germany are frequently debates between adherents of comprehensive systems of philosophy which purport to explain and order

all existence. The universe, society, and one's personal life all have to follow some orderly system.

3. The person is expected to live up to a publicly recognized philosophy or code, displaying willpower, self-control, efficiency, foresight, and planning. It is interesting to note that German psychologists have paid much attention to the human will, whereas in American psychology the will has been completely neglected.

4. Compared to the American, the German is much more likely to be asked to submit to some authority—be it parents, society, fate, destiny, or a philosophy. The structures of German society and of German thinking patterns are more likely to be authoritarian (Erikson, 1964). Authoritarianism leads to rebellion when society becomes weak and one's personal life threatens to become meaningless. Psychoanalytically oriented scholars have connected these authoritarian tendencies to rigid toilet training and the development of "anal" character traits. These traits include mental rigidity, preoccupation with self-control, stubbornness, orderliness, emphasis on precision and detail, etc. (Abraham, 1927).

The following study investigates the German and American national characters by comparing ideal self-ratings of German and American university students. Specifically, it is hypothesized that the ideal self-ratings of German students will reflect a greater emphasis on self-control and the rational will, whereas the American students are expected to stress more other-oriented values such as sensitivity, love, and empathy. The data presented are part of a larger study that compares radical and nonradical German and American students with respect to factors such as motivation, moral judgment, and political attitudes (Gielen, 1976).

Method

Subjects

Two samples were selected for this study. The German sample consisted of 131 students from the University of Cologne, West Germany. There were 103 male and 28 female students. The sample was about equally divided between radical students (as defined by various radical protest activities and opinions) and a random sample of the student population. The radical students were contacted through a snowball system; the random sample was established by contacting students in cafeterias, at home, and in classrooms. As is usual at German universities, the majority of the students were professional students in their early-to-mid twenties who lived either at home or in their own apartments. The American sample consisted of 71 Harvard students, including 50 males and 21 females. Fourteen of the 71 students were graduate students. About 45% of the American sample were selected because they were known to have participated in radical political activities; the other 55% were randomly selected from a list of students. Both the German and American students were interviewed by other students from the universities. The interviews lasted about 1½–3 hours each and were conducted in the spring (Harvard) and summer (Cologne) of 1969.

Materials

The German and American questionnaires are reprinted in Gielen, 1976. They are concerned with various background items, political attitudes and behaviors, a TAT test, the Kohlberg Moral Judgment Scale, a Q-sort for real self (Cologne University only), and ideal self-ratings. In this chapter, only findings pertaining to the ideal self-ratings will be reported.

Procedure for Ideal Self-Ratings

The interviewer asked the subjects to order a pile of 63 cards, each with a different adjective printed on it. Students were asked to order the cards on a "continuum so as to describe the person *you would like to be*. Please sort the cards into 7 piles of 9 cards each so that they range from most like your ideal self to most unlike your ideal self." This Q-sort is based upon the methodology of Stephenson (1953), and was taken from a study by Haan, Smith, and Block (1968). It was translated into German using the backward translation method.

Results

A comparison between mean ideal self-ratings of Harvard and Cologne students is presented in Table 22.1. In order to be included in Table 22.1, the mean ratings of a given adjective had to differ significantly (two-tailed t test; $p \leq .05$) between the two samples. A first glance at the table shows that German and American ratings differ dramatically, with 54% of the comparisons between the 63 ideal self-ratings reaching statistical significance levels.

Many of the differences between German and American ratings fall into two clusters. The ego ideals of German students reflect a *relative* emphasis upon wanting to be critical, stubborn, dominating, informed, logical, fore-sightful, rebellious, argumentative, self-controlled, ambitious, competitive,

Table 22.1

Comparison between Ideal Self-Ratings of Harvard and Cologne Students[a]

Adjectives[b]	Harvard $\overline{X}$[c]	Cologne $\overline{X}$	t test (two tailed)	df	Significance level
Critical	2.44	5.23	13.46	200	.000
Loving, tender	4.73	1.83	−12.14	153	.000
Sensitive	4.52	2.09	−10.67	139	.000
Curious, questioning	4.38	2.17	−10.17	171	.000
Perceptive, aware	5.38	4.14	−7.34	200	.000
Assertive	2.25	3.82	7.12	148	.000
Authentic	4.90	3.12	−7.30	200	.000
Adventurous	4.41	2.97	−6.31	146	.000
Stubborn	1.14	2.58	6.08	200	.000
Dominating	.87	2.20	5.84	200	.000
Empathic—feels	4.70	3.64	−5.13	148	.000
Informed	4.03	5.01	4.92	130	.000
Foresightful— plans ahead	2.82	3.87	4.75	152	.000
Self-denying	1.66	2.61	4.28	160	.000
Logical, rational	3.86	4.73	3.84	160	.000
Rebellious	1.75	2.73	3.79	169	.000
Idealistic	4.03	3.11	−3.63	200	.000
Energetic, vital	4.83	3.97	−3.55	200	.000
Argumentative	.97	1.73	3.33	200	.001
Sociable, gregarious	3.07	3.80	3.32	157	.001
Self-centered	.69	1.37	3.27	200	.001
Needs approval	.83	1.41	3.20	200	.002
Courageous	4.24	3.47	−3.18	147	.002
Tolerant, accepting	3.87	4.64	3.15	153	.002
Self-controlled	3.32	3.92	2.64	147	.009
Talkative	1.93	1.46	−2.48	200	.014
Feels guilty	.52	.92	2.46	169	,015
Ambitious	2.04	2.68	2.39	146	.018
Competitive	1.72	2.31	2.38	134	.019
Considerate	4.52	4.13	−2.19	166	.030
Feminine, masculine	3.35	2.82	−2.04	200	.043
Practical, shrewd	2.59	3.08	2.04	150	.043
Effective	3.62	3.13	−2.02	200	.045
Uncompromising	1.32	1.80	2.02	152	.045

[a] N = 131 Cologne; 71 Harvard.

[b] For adjectives to be included, significance level had to be $p \le .05$ for two-tailed t test.

[c] Mean values $\overline{X}$ can range from 0 (complete rejection of trait) to 6 (complete acceptance of trait).

and shrewd. There is a certain hard, tight, analytical, "anal" quality to this ego ideal. This relative stress upon critical rationality is only weakly counteracted by the greater emphasis of German students on wanting to be sociable and tolerant. The Harvard students stress as their ego ideal the desire to be loving, sensitive, perceptive, genuine, empathic, and idealistic. This indicates a warmer, softer, more "feminine" ideal self which appears to reflect humanistic values.

In order to gain further insight into the ideal self-ratings of German and American students, the ratings were factor analyzed using the principal components method. Table 22.2 presents the results of the factor analysis for Harvard students, and Table 22.3 shows factor loadings for the Cologne ideal self-ratings. Five factors have been extracted accounting for 23.4% (Harvard ratings) and 20.5% (Cologne ratings) of the variance.

Although these factors account only for a relatively modest proportion of the variance, it is nevertheless useful to look at the two most powerful factors.

Table 22.2
Principal Components Factor Analysis of Harvard Ideal Self-Ratings (N = 71)

	Principal components factor loadings					
Adjectives	1	2	3	4	5	Commu-nality
Conventional	+.264	−.156	−.052	+.007	+.228	.149
Energetic, vital	+.116	+.081	+.305	+.006	+.069	.118
Adventurous	−.216	+.146	+.319	+.528	−.002	.448
Loving tender	+.202	−.480	+.066	−.274	−.029	.351
Assertive	−.040	+.543	+.000	+.073	+.298	.390
Ambitious	+.390	+.328	+.110	+.051	+.100	.285
Artistic	−.547	−.038	+.094	+.265	+.147	.401
Calm, relaxed	+.319	+.198	−.044	−.159	−.538	.457
Playful	−.168	+.093	+.482	+.317	−.197	.458
Competitive	+.492	+.449	+.125	+.123	+.146	.495
Courageous	+.220	+.074	+.108	+.235	−.220	.169
Considerate	+.553	−.447	−.122	+.017	+.011	.522
Critical	−.301	+.066	−.199	−.368	−.376	.412
Optimistic	−.214	+.193	−.119	+.323	−.236	.257
Dominating	+.036	+.757	−.085	+.151	+.110	.617
Curious, questioning	−.392	−.159	+.434	−.167	−.131	.412
Needs approval	−.180	−.062	−.375	+.199	+.099	.226
Self-centered	−.256	+.570	+.059	−.147	−.249	.478
Fair, just	+.365	−.536	+.090	+.192	+.239	.523
Self-controlled	+.457	−.006	−.328	−.321	−.377	.562
Aloof, uninvolved	−.164	.241	−.015	−.261	−.399	.312

(continued)

Table 22.2 (Continued)

Adjectives	Principal components factor loadings					Commu-nality
	1	2	3	4	5	
Generous	+.126	−.503	−.201	+.317	−.396	.566
Feels guilty	+.107	−.280	−.262	−.115	+.112	.184
Helpful	−.030	−.224	−.468	+.406	−.121	.450
Proud	−.143	+.481	+.217	+.024	+.006	.281
Idealistic	−.357	−.030	−.182	−.122	−.026	.177
Creative, imaginative	−.364	−.020	+.296	+.021	−.231	.274
Impulsive	−.608	−.021	+.200	+.283	+.110	.490
Doubting, uncertain	−.587	−.304	−.142	−.125	+.120	.487
Independent	−.112	−.054	+.386	−.232	−.057	.221
Informed	+.341	+.118	+.437	−.260	−.270	.462
Tolerant, accepting	+.133	−.514	+.144	−.163	−.020	.330
Practical, shrewd	+.390	+.437	+.047	−.257	+.049	.414
Moody	−.638	−.123	−.132	−.195	+.076	.483
Foresightful, plans ahead	+.650	+.144	−.103	−.251	+.114	.529
Open, frank	−.228	−.266	−.074	−.177	+.011	.160
Orderly	+.349	+.274	−.456	+.169	+.217	.480
Sociable, gregarious	+.456	−.046	+.051	+.149	+.122	.250
Perceptive, aware	−.139	−.324	+.222	−.459	−.111	.397
Logical, rational	+.337	+.327	−.064	−.229	+.233	.331
Rebellious	−.576	+.073	+.113	−.055	+.259	.420
Reserved, shy	−.150	−.166	−.018	−.071	−.177	.087
Responsible	+.561	−.095	−.076	+.050	−.066	.337
Restless, discontented	−.564	−.069	−.167	−.372	−.088	.498
Free, unfettered	−.077	+.154	−.000	+.004	−.389	.181
Self-confident	+.365	+.002	+.225	−.410	−.134	.370
Self-denying	−.056	−.231	−.591	−.043	+.220	.456
Amusing	+.061	−.119	+.176	+.268	+.107	.132
Sensitive	−.375	−.511	−.176	−.080	+.179	.471
Show off	−.169	+.496	−.513	+.273	−.083	.618
Stubborn	−.175	+.445	−.128	+.100	−.479	.485
Sympathetic	−.035	−.487	−.128	+.048	+.305	.350
Empathic, feels for others	+.036	−.727	+.044	+.178	−.006	.564
Talkative	−.252	+.248	+.099	+.356	+.393	.417
Responsive	−.076	−.478	+.087	−.182	+.119	.289
Worryful, fearful	−.382	+.092	−.472	−.093	−.069	.390
Genuine, authentic	+.008	−.454	+.074	−.026	+.317	.313
Feminine, masculine	+.415	+.068	+.308	+.133	+.078	.295
Effective	+.620	+.094	−.056	−.200	+.047	.438
Individualistic	−.369	+.150	+.328	−.041	+.046	.270
Uncompromising	−.341	+.317	−.190	+.108	+.052	.267
Argumentative	−.316	+.393	−.389	−.201	+.099	.456
Altruistic	+.256	−.452	−.213	+.080	−.106	.333
Latent roots	7.300	6.620	3.714	3.040	2.770	23.444

Table 22.3

Principal Components Factor Analysis of Cologne Ideal Self-Ratings (N = 131)

Adjectives	Principal components factor loadings					Commu-nality
	1	2	3	4	5	
Conventional	−.141	+.151	+.419	+.061	+.294	.308
Energetic, vital	+.371	+.396	+.012	+.231	−.071	.352
Adventurous	+.169	+.011	+.250	−.202	−.194	.169
Loving, tender	−.535	−.218	−.042	−.036	+.098	.347
Assertive	+.369	+.373	−.211	+.257	+.130	.403
Ambitious	+.087	+.356	+.288	+.272	+.092	.300
Artistic	−.154	−.052	+.112	−.582	−.024	.378
Calm, relaxed	+.148	+.067	+.177	−.173	+.108	.098
Playful	−.531	+.010	+.128	−.413	−.152	.492
Competitive	+.120	+.449	+.060	+.320	+.249	.384
Courageous	+.490	+.223	−.065	−.007	+.197	.342
Considerate	+.053	−.516	+.086	+.100	+.121	.301
Critical	+.220	−.251	−.581	+.021	+.000	.449
Optimistic	+.301	−.261	+.320	+.030	−.244	.321
Dominating	+.348	+.476	+.117	+.126	+.140	.397
Curious, questioning	−.443	+.079	+.075	−.085	+.080	.222
Needs approval	−.352	+.146	+.305	+.108	−.172	.280
Self-centered	−.440	+.407	+.089	−.111	+.320	.482
Fair, just	+.385	−.375	−.037	+.023	+.361	.421
Self-controlled	+.348	+.165	+.107	−.003	+.072	.165
Aloof, uninvolved	−.345	+.123	+.067	−.160	+.170	.193
Generous	+.110	−.334	+.048	−.268	+.272	.307
Feels guilty	−.405	−.009	+.050	+.252	−.173	.260
Helpful	+.093	−.418	+.291	+.175	−.093	.307
Proud	−.165	+.263	+.131	−.079	+.525	.396
Idealistic	+.047	−.145	+.185	+.363	−.017	.193
Creative, imaginative	+.055	−.283	−.058	−.547	+.015	.386
Impulsive	−.415	+.036	−.064	−.205	−.067	.224
Doubting, uncertain	−.606	−.106	−.151	+.002	+.036	.402
Independent	+.258	+.060	−.103	−.356	+.094	.216
Informed	+.211	−.131	−.489	−.050	−.006	.304
Tolerant, accepting	+.309	−.355	+.110	−.298	+.351	.445
Practical, shrewd	+.452	+.157	+.054	+.060	−.141	.255
Moody	−.571	+.245	+.111	−.242	+.053	.460
Foresightful, plans ahead	+.311	+.087	−.199	+.025	−.153	.168
Open, frank	+.157	−.527	−.070	+.178	+.210	.383
Orderly	+.344	+.214	+.242	+.210	+.114	.279
Sociable, gregarious	+.327	−.003	+.330	−.157	−.447	.440
Perceptive, aware	−.116	−.481	+.021	+.104	+.279	.333
Logical, rational	+.326	−.020	−.454	−.225	+.080	.370
Rebellious	−.266	−.098	−.547	+.085	−.167	.415
Reserved, shy	−.481	−.233	+.293	+.299	−.003	.461

(continued)

Table 22.3 (Continued)

| Adjectives | Principal components factor loadings | | | | | Commu-nality |
	1	2	3	4	5	
Responsible	+.444	−.176	+.005	+.204	+.266	.340
Restless, discontented	−.467	−.013	−.410	+.104	−.178	.429
Free, unfettered	+.238	−.040	−.403	−.233	−.337	.388
Self-confident	+.561	+.138	−.103	−.127	−.258	.427
Self-denying	+.118	−.417	−.078	+.253	−.196	.296
Amusing	+.129	+.060	+.267	−.270	−.382	.311
Sensitive	−.535	−.211	−.054	+.150	−.012	.356
Show off	−.621	+.180	+.223	+.016	−.040	.482
Stubborn	−.029	+.272	−.448	+.207	+.186	.353
Sympathetic	+.382	+.013	+.343	−.013	−.439	.456
Empathic, feels for others	−.088	−.508	+.028	−.004	+.014	.267
Talkative	−.377	+.111	−.110	+.130	−.162	.210
Responsive	−.069	−.417	−.025	+.142	+.059	.203
Worrying, fearful	−.535	−.051	−.055	+.281	−.112	.383
Genuine, authentic	+.063	−.134	+.194	+.131	−.117	.090
Feminine, masculine	+.173	+.088	+.089	−.237	+.194	.139
Effective	+.075	+.340	−.022	−.134	−.285	.221
Individualistic	+.016	+.041	+.085	−.316	+.199	.148
Uncompromising	−.029	+.561	−.276	+.200	+.005	.431
Argumentative	−.427	+.373	−.329	−.132	−.080	.454
Altruistic	−.046	−.291	+.020	+.434	−.205	.318
Latent Roots	6.947	4.624	3.317	3.030	2.596	20.515

Table 22.4 compares the two main factors underlying the German and American ratings. All those adjectives that load at least .400 on Factors 1 or 2 in either one of the two samples are included in the table. Thus, when an adjective in Sample 1 loads at least .400 on one of the two factors, it is included in Table 22.4, together with its loading on the corresponding factor in Sample 2. A comparison of the 51 pairs of loadings shows that in 48 cases the loadings are in the same direction, though the size of the loadings may differ considerably. This suggests that the first two factors in the German data agree relatively closely with the first two factors of the American data. Both German and American students seem to inhabit a similar "meaning universe" when making their ideal self-ratings.

Factor 1 appears to reflect an emphasis upon "confident self-control versus restless uncertainty." Among the German students, this factor is perhaps related to the tradition of German idealist thinking. This tradition goes back to Kant, Schiller, and Goethe, and stresses the "rational will." Among American students, Factor 1, "confident self-control," with its emphasis upon

Table 22.4

Factor Loadings ≥ .400 for Cologne and Harvard Ideal Self-Ratings[a]

Positive loadings

	Factor 1: Confident self-control			Factor 2: Self-centered domination	
Adjective	Cologne	Harvard	Adjective	Cologne	Harvard
Foresightful	.311	.650	Dominating	.476	.757
Effective	.075	.620	Self-centered	.407	.570
Responsible	.444	.561	Assertive	.373	.543
Self-confident	.561	.365	Show off	.180	.496
Considerate	.053	.553	Proud	.263	.481
Competitive	.120	.492	Competitive	.449	.449
Courageous	.490	.220	Stubborn	.272	.445
Self-controlled	.348	.457	Practical, shrewd	.157	.437
Sociable, gregarious	.327	.456	Uncompromising	.561	.317
Practical, shrewd	.452	.390			
Feminine, masculine	.173	.415			

Negative loadings

	Factor 1: Restless uncertainty			Factor 2: Responsive empathy	
Adjective	Cologne	Harvard	Adjective	Cologne	Harvard
Moody	− .571	− .638	Empathic	− .508	− .727
Show off	− .631	− .169	Fair, just	− .375	− .536
Impulsive	− .415	− .608	Open, frank	− .527	− .266
Doubting, uncertain	− .606	− .587	Considerate	− .516	− .447
Rebellious	− .266	− .576	Tolerant, accepting	− .355	− .514
Restless, discontented	− .467	− .564	Sensitive	− .211	− .511
Artistic	− .154	− .547	Generous	− .384	− .503
Sensitive	− .535	− .375	Sympathetic	+ .013	− .487
Worrying, fearful	− .535	− .382	Perceptive, aware	− .481	− .324
Loving, tender	− .535	+ .202	Loving, tender	− .218	− .480
Playful	− .531	− .168	Responsive	− .417	− .478
Reserved, shy	− .481	− .150	Genuine, authentic	− .134	− .454
Curious	− .443	− .392	Altruistic	− .291	− .452
Self-centered	− .440	− .256	Helpful	− .418	− .224
Argumentative	− .427	− .316	Self-denying	− .417	− .231
Feels guilty	− .405	+ .107			

[a] N = 131 Cologne; 71 Harvard.

responsible, effective, foresightful, practical action, probably is an expression of the "Puritan ethic." Factor 2, "self-centered domination versus responsive empathy," appears to reflect an interest in assertive, self-centered competitiveness and domination. Such behavior is perhaps deemed necessary by the students for survival in these two highly developed capitalist countries.

However, although the appearance of highly similar factors among German and American student raters is interesting, it would be wrong to overestimate their importance. Together, they only account for 11.6% of the variance in the German data and 13.9% of the variance in the American data. They are, in other words, rather weak factors.

The samples of students in this study are atypical and contain radical as well as nonradical students. Thus, it may be argued that differences between radical and nonradical students outweigh national differences. Table 22.5 attempts to address this issue. It compares ideal self-ratings of radical Cologne students with ratings of nonradical Cologne students. It can clearly be seen that differences between Germans and Americans (Table 22.1) far outweigh differences between German radicals and nonradicals (Table 22.5). Whereas 54% of the 63 ideal self adjectives are rated significantly different in the cross-cultural comparison, only 16% of the ratings by Cologne radicals differ from those done by Cologne nonradicals. Of the 63 comparisons between

Table 22.5

Comparison of Ideal Self-Ratings between Cologne Nonradicals and Radicals[a]

Adjective[b]	Nonradicals	Radicals	t test	Significance level
Rebellious	2.02	3.70	4.536	.000
Restless, discontented	.96	2.24	3.987	.000
Informed	4.57	5.33	3.182	.002
Adventurous	3.37	2.62	−2.421	.017
Critical	4.87	5.44	2.407	.018
Stubborn	2.22	3.07	2.395	.019
Dominating	2.66	1.89	−2.340	.021
Doubting, uncertain	1.13	1.80	2.153	.034
Orderly	2.87	2.18	−2.080	.040
Talkative	1.15	1.72	2.070	.041

[a] $N = 47$ Nonradicals; 54 radicals. Thirty students were excluded from the comparison because their political activities and opinions placed them in a category intermediate between "radical" and "nonradical."

[b] For adjective to be included, significance level had to be $p \leq .05$ for two-tailed t test.

[c] Mean values $\overline{X}$ can range from 0 (complete rejection of trait) to 6 (complete acceptance of trait).

Americans and Germans, 33% differ at the $p \leq .001$ level, whereas only 3% of 63 comparisons between German radicals and nonradicals reach the $p \leq .001$ level.

Discussion and Conclusions

Let us now recapitulate our findings. Our main hypothesis is well supported: German students, when compared to their American counterparts, are much more likely to incorporate in their ego-ideal qualities like wanting to be more foresightful, self-controlled, logical, dominating, argumentative, and so on. The German ratings may be seen as reflecting authoritarianism, rebelliousness, critical judgment, and the rational will. Americans are more interested in being loving, sensitive, genuine, and perceptive. They appear to be more other-directed and to have a softer, more "feminine" ego ideal. What is especially interesting about these findings is the size of the differences. However, not all of the national character differences emphasized in the introduction receive support by the data. For example, Americans appear *not* to be more success oriented in this study; their ideal self-ratings de-emphasize ambitiousness and competitiveness (Table 22.1, adjectives #29 and #30). Similarly, Germans are *less* likely than the Americans to stress an idealistic ego ideal (Table 22.1, adjective #17).

When interpreting the data some pointers may be useful. Generally, it is better to look at patterns among adjectives and not to be overconcerned with any specific adjective. It was often difficult to translate the Q-sort and it may well be that some of the adjectives have somewhat different connotations in the two languages. It is much less likely that these translation difficulties would have affected a whole pattern of adjective ratings. When looking at the mean ratings (Table 22.1) it is useful to remember that the cross-cultural differences are relative differences. Both groups may rank a given adjective negatively (or positively) and yet there may be a highly significant difference in the *degree* of negative (or positive) ranking. For instance, adjective #9 (stubborn) is ranked negatively by both groups (Harvard $\bar{X} = 1.14$; Cologne $\bar{X} = 2.58$), and yet the means differ at the $p < .001$ level. The idea that the patterns among Q-sort ratings are of importance derives further support from the results of the factor analyses. Factor 1 (confident self-control versus restless uncertainty) and Factor 2 (self-centered domination versus responsive empathy) are found both among American and German ratings. It is interesting to note that the positive pole of Factor 1 (confident self-control) seems to incorporate many of the adjectives that distinguish German from American students. The negative pole of Factor 2 (responsive empathy) includes many of the adjectives that were rated higher by the Harvard students.

It is of considerable importance that the differences between radical and nonradical students are much less often significant than the cross-cultural differences. The same appears to be true about sex differences. Preliminary comparisons between male and female ratings among both the Cologne and Harvard students showed fewer significant differences than the cross-cultural comparisons. This is in part a statistical artifact: The number of subjects in the political and cross-sex comparisons is smaller than in the cross-cultural comparisons and therefore mean differences between the sexes and the political groups have to be larger than mean differences between Germans and Americans in order to reach significance. However, a comparison of *mean differences* (not *t*-test differences) still shows larger differences between cultures than between political groups.

The data reported here concern only ideal self-ratings. The Harvard students were not asked about real self-ratings. The Cologne students, on the other hand, were also interviewed about real self-perceptions ranging from "6 = most like me" to "0 = most unlike me." These real self-ratings of Cologne students can be compared to real self-ratings of Berkeley students in the Haan *et al.* study (1968) which used the same Q-sort. In general, differences between Berkeley and Cologne students with respect to real self-ratings are similar to the cross-cultural differences in ideal self-ratings found between Harvard and Cologne students, lending further support to the significance of the findings reported in this study. National character differences appear to be alive and well.

References

Abraham, K. *Selected papers*. London: Institute for Psychoanalysis and Hogarth Press, 1927.

Aronson, E. *The handbook of social psychology*, Vol. IV (2nd ed.). Reading, Mass.: Addison-Wesley, 1965.

Benedict, R. *The chrysanthemum and the sword*. Boston: Houghton Mifflin, 1946.

Erikson, E. *Childhood and society* (2nd ed.). New York: Norton, 1964.

Gielen, U. P. *A social-psychological study of German radical and non-radical students*. Unpublished doctoral dissertation, Harvard University, 1976.

Gorer, G. *The American people*. New York: Norton, 1948.

Haan, N., Smith, M. B., & Block, J. Moral reasoning of young adults: Political-social behavior, family background and personality correlates. *Journal of Personality and Social Psychology*, 1968, *10*, 183–201.

Hsu, F. *Americans and Chinese* (2nd ed.). Garden City, N.Y.: Natural History Press, 1972.

Inkeles, A., Hanfmann, E., & Beier, H. Modal personality and adjustment to the Soviet socio-political system. *Human Relations*, 1958, *11*, 3–22.

McClelland, D. C. *The achieving society.* Princeton, N.J.: D. Van Nostrand Company, 1961.

McClelland, D. C., Sturr, J. F., Knapp, R. N., & Wendt, H. W. Obligations to self and society in the United States and Germany. *Journal of Abnormal Social Psychology,* 1958, *56,* 245–255.

McGranahan, D. V., & Wayne, F. German and American traits reflected in popular drama. *Human Relations,* 1948, *1,* 429–455.

Schaffner, B. *Fatherland: A study of authoritarianism in the German family.* New York: Columbia University Press, 1948.

Stephenson, W. *The study of behavior: Q-technique and its methodology.* Chicago: University of Chicago Press, 1953.

Tocqueville, A. de. *Democracy in America* (2 vols.). New York: Vintage, 1954. (Originally published, 1830.)

Weber, M. *The Protestant ethic and the spirit of capitalism.* New York: Scribner's, 1930.

V

Assessment and Evaluation

In the first chapter in Part V, Gordon F. Derner reviews the history of the Peace Corps and the selection, training, and duties of Peace Corps volunteers. There is much that is of great relevance to cross-cultural scientists in this discussion of the advance training and orientation about local conditions given to Peace Corps volunteers entering new countries and unfamiliar cultures where different languages and dialects are spoken. The next chapter by John Cawte is an account of the conflicts that arose among interdisciplinary fieldworkers during a crisis which created a state of ideological shock. The interaction of several disciplines becomes useful in tackling problems in cross-cultural mental health. An important point in this cross-cultural report is the impact created by an influenza epidemic on the local community; and greater than this, the discovery that members of the research team have also contracted the illness. Other problems occur, for instance in filming the local ceremonies and rituals. The forceful effect of an unfamiliar situation created by the film crew and the presence of scientists seem difficult to accept under ordinary circumstances in the western world, but in the "bush" in Australia it becomes a stressful condition and can create reverse culture shock. In the chapter that follows, John Beatty and Junichi Takahashi discuss another problem of particular relevance to cross-cultural research, namely, that of linguistic expressions. Words that carry several meanings in one language present difficulties to any translator. The authors give numerous examples by pointing out the inconsistencies in analyzing the meaning and the expression of such words as homosexual/heterosexual and American Indian, before they devote a major part of the chapter to the evaluation and assessment of such emotional expressions as "love/hate." The translator will be aware of the difficulties, not only in assessing such complex issues as emotions in cross-cultural research, but in evaluating which of the verbal expressions of such nonverbal behavior are appropriate. In the next chapter an ongoing cross-national research project is reported by Barry J. Gurland and Joseph Zubin. The U.S.–U.K. project initially focused on obtaining reliable cross-national assessment of the mental status and psychiatric diagnosis of patients under 60 years. The current phase extended the minimum age to 65 years in order to compare the elderly people from a general population with the residents of psychiatric hospitals who are provided with long-term care. The U.S.–U.K. series of studies provides a yardstick for psychopathology which assesses the variations in mental disorder that may occur because of cultural influence on such aspects as professional reporting, etc. Although the authors offer some qualifications, they suggest that brain changes could be assessed by the recently developed noninvasive computer-assisted radiological techniques which offers promise to the evaluation and assessment of cross-cultural validity of the diagnosis. Next Jean G. Graubert and Leonore Loeb Adler discuss the results of a cross-national research that served to assess the attitudes of college students from eight countries toward "mental patient"/"mental hospital" (stigma-related) and "volunteer"/"peer" (stigma-free) stimuli. A figure-placement task served to measure (in millimeters) projected social distances. All the college students spoke English, though some students were bilingual with English as their second language. They all had similar academic backgrounds, and even used English/American textbooks in college. Results were similar across nations and for both sexes: Students chose near- or close-projected distances where stigma-free stimulus items were concerned. Far-projected distances occurred between the students' "self" and the stigma-ladden stimulus items, suggesting an expression of avoidance behavior. The authors propose that the similarity of the students' responses may have been due to the stigma-ladden stimuli's universal aversiveness that transcends differences in language and culture. The last chapter authored by Victor D. Sanua deals with the study of war-related bereavement. It is based on interviews with family members of American servicemen who were killed in Vietnam and Israeli servicemen who died in the Yom Kippur War. The socioeconomic variables, as well as cultural, educational, and religious effects, were judged important in helping the family to adjust to their bereavement. Comparisons presented show that both official procedures and personal ways of coping differed greatly between the two countries.

Selection for Intercultural Living: The Peace Corps Experiment

ABSTRACT

The establishment of the American Peace Corps in 1961 represented a break in the international tradition of disregard for the culture of the host country and cultural proselytizing by those from other countries. The purpose of the Peace Corps was to have American volunteers meet trained manpower needs in countries overseas to which they were invited, and in so doing promote better understanding among peoples. To insure that Peace Corps volunteers met the stated goals a comprehensive selection and training program was established. Psychologists developed and played key roles in the selection process and in the evaluation of the selection process and training. In-country training, strong emphasis on understanding the culture and learning the language of the host, and concentrated experience in the technical skills, along with person-to-person selection for training and for eventual assignment, produced a noteworthy experience in intercultural international effort. Success seems to have been greatest in countries with cross-cultural exposure where the volunteer was seen as more unusual. A review of research and reports of personal experiences support the value of psychologists in selection, training, and evaluation. The vitality of the early Peace Corps days is a worthy goal for the continuing Peace Corps.

For innumerable centuries groups of people or countries have been sending members of their group to other countries to carry a particular message that has priority of meaning to the dispatching group. Crusaders tried to save the world from the "infidels," missionaries have tried to convert "heathens" to their religion. Political groups have tried by subversion and direct force to change the political system of other countries. Others, whose purpose was not to convey a particular message, sought nonetheless to impose their system of values. Immigrants to the Hawaiian Islands considered the nakedness of the Hawaiian women sinful and insisted they wear loose-fitting clothing so that the shape of their bodies would be concealed. Multinational companies in their quest for profit have altered the work habits of peoples throughout the world. Some of these interventions have been devoted to what would appear to be worthwhile, even altruistic, purposes. Thus their stated goals have included an opportunity for the hosts to participate in decisions related to their lives, the acceptance of the equality of fellow human beings regardless of sex, color, or any other difference, the encouragement of health maintenance procedures to eliminate unwanted childbirth, illness, disease, crippling, and early death. However, most of these interventions were not in the context of the culture of the host nation, but rather often in direct contradiction to that culture, and they were frequently intended primarily for the welfare of the visitors.

Ironically, it has been said that the Hawaiian immigrants came to do good and did well. The discrepancy between host and visitor can be sharply brought to mind by stopping in London on the way to India. A visit to Westminster Abbey is a striking reminder of "the sun never sets on the British Empire" and the "romance" of colonization. Then a visit to the Red Fort in Old Delhi during a sound and light show will force awareness of the audacity of the British in taking over the vast subcontinent as if it had been mislaid and open for the taking. The recreated sounds of the "marching band and the soldiers of the Empire" invading that ancient country remind one that the Bengal Lancers were less the hero and more the villain in putting down uprisings of the nationals of India who wished to have their independence with their culture.

The history of the settlement of the United States gives us little solace from cultural arrogance, especially when one recognizes that our outstanding hero and first president, George Washington, had decreed a bounty for the head of Indians. The disregard for human rights and particularly cultural rights is more typical than atypical. At best there has been indifference on the part of visitors: Often ambassadors and other emissaries from foreign countries had little respect for the culture of their hosts, and frequently they were unable to speak the language.

In the context of such intercultural disregard a marvelous development occurred in 1961 with the establishment of the American Peace Corps. The stated purpose of the Peace Corps was to promote world peace and friendship by making available to interested countries, Americans willing to serve overseas who would (a) help people of these countries meet their needs for trained manpower; (b) help promote a better understanding of the American people on the part of the peoples served; and (c) promote better understanding of other people on the part of American people. With that proclamation began one of the most exciting cross-cultural developments in American history. The Peace Corps functioned through the use of volunteers who went to countries to which they had been invited. The volunteers served the host country under host country's supervisors and worked hand-in-hand with host country co-workers. They lived in a fashion similar to their co-workers. For example, in India they often lived in small villages in dwellings similar to those of their counterparts rather than in the cities. Curiously the India Peace Corps volunteers often were supplied with a servant because the tasks of daily living would have taken them away from any additional activity: The collecting of the wood for the fire, the preparation of the fire for cooking meals, the purchase and gathering of the food, and other household duties which are so time consuming. The volunteers would not have been able to devote their time to some of the tasks for which they were qualified and for which they had been trained. Nonetheless, the volunteers—in India and throughout the world—lived in a modest manner, in circumstances comparable to those of their co-workers. They received no hardship or cost of living allowances. They held no diplomatic privileges or immunities. They had no commissary rights. They had no vehicles unless vehicles were needed for the job. They learned to speak the language of the host country, learned to appreciate its customs, and were able to discuss adequately and intelligently matters relating to the United States. They were specifically required to refrain from political or religious proselytizing, and the measure of their success would be that the requested job would be well done. The allowance for living was modest and was supplemented only by a monthly allocation accumulated for the volunteers so that they might start anew when they returned to the United States. Peace Corps volunteers were not required to hold higher academic degrees; in fact, a special effort was made to attract farmers and craftsmen who had the specific skills and experience that would be useful to host countries. Emphasis was placed upon a period of training, which included instruction in the particular technical skills needed, as well as in the language and cultural values of the host country. It is interesting that advertisements for recruitment frequently made the hardships of Peace Corps life a positive factor. Sometimes such hardship was denied the Peace Corps volunteer, as life was often not as rugged as had been implied in the literature. Life was modest but not necessarily primitive. It is important to note that not only were trainees allowed to resign during the training program, but even as established volunteers they were free to resign before the termination of their tour of duty. The Peace Corps wanted only those who would serve of free choice.

The selection procedure for Peace Corps volunteers changed from time to time, but in the beginning it was primarily focused on an extensive input

of information from a variety of sources. The details of this selection procedure have been presented in a number of places (e.g., Derner, 1971).
In essence, the trainee arrived at a training site and went through a course
of training to prepare him for the position he would take for the next 2
years. On the training site a psychologist worked as an advisor as well as
an evaluator. This complex task required a special skill on the part of the
psychologist. Each training program had a number of people from the host
country to participate in the training in language, cultural knowledge, and
specialized skills. These teachers were able to evaluate the trainees on a
daily basis. Approximately midway through the training program the information on the trainees was shared with the field selection officer, another
psychologist who monitored the training program and made the final decision
on whether the person would be appointed as a volunteer at the end of
training. The selection officer prepared summations on the progress of each
trainee in a mid-program review and shared it with the trainee. The trainee
therefore had feedback to assist him or her in deciding whether to continue
in the training program, and the training board had the basis for its decision
as to whether the person would eventually become a Peace Corps volunteer.
At the end of the training period, the trainees were again evaluated, on the
basis of the information available at mid-program plus an update of their
success in the later period of the training program. For those who did not
seem likely to be successful as volunteers, termination from the Peace Corps
was discussed and future plans were made with the trainee. This system of
evaluation and information sharing has been changed over the years to a
greater emphasis on self-selection. Although the data are somewhat unclear
because of changing conditions, the number of early terminations seems to
have increased, but it is difficult to demonstrate whether this is solely because
of the change in the selection system.

During the early days psychologists associated with the Peace Corps did
extensive research to study selection procedures that would make possible
more appropriate placement of volunteers. Harris (1972, 1973) did extensive
work on the prediction of success of South Pacific volunteers. He found that
procedures based on a single pretraining interview or self-assessment were
not valid measures of future success. The method that was most effective
was an elaborate procedure involving a joint decision by a board which
made a democratically arrived at group judgment. In the report of his analysis
of volunteers to Tonga, Harris divided the volunteers into three groups—a
high overall success group, a moderate to marginal success group, and an
early termination group. The criterion that correlated highest with success
was basic character traits of the individual. The next highest correlation was
general technical competence, and then cultural interaction and interpersonal
relationships. Smith's (1966) research on Ghana volunteers in the first Peace

Corps program found measures of authoritarianism on paper and pencil tests and psychiatric ratings derived from two 50-minute interviews unrelated to the adequacy with which the person performed his Peace Corps task. Interestingly, the "mental health ratings" showed a positive correlation with assignment to cities and a highly negative correlation with assignment to the bush. It is interesting to note, however, that the items that were basic to the psychiatrists' judgments were not related to psychopathology but were those which are judged by clinical psychologists as characterizing "optimally adjusted personality." The ratings of the psychiatrists were more related to the eventual situation in which the volunteer was placed than to general competence. Smith also notes that in the initial Peace Corps group there were special morale problems among those who were assigned to the city. Their assignment diverged greatly from their expectations of their possible place of functioning in the Peace Corps.

Mischel (1965) found that there was lack of predictive validity in the 1-hour staging interviews, which were held to determine whether the person should be invited into a training program, and their selection as volunteers for Nigeria. His findings parallel the lack of predictive validity that Harris found for the 50-minute interviews for assignment to the South Pacific.

Most studies done on the effectiveness of Peace Corps volunteers related their overseas behavior to trainee attributes, performance per se, satisfaction in the position, adjustment to the new culture, and, particularly, completion of service. Although it should be self-evident that the overseas environment itself must be an important factor, the major emphasis was on the trainee as an individual rather than on the trainee in interaction with the environment. Proshansky, Ittleson, & Rivlin (1970) present the rationale underlying environmental psychology. Human actions are influenced by various characteristics of the individual and of the environment. It was this theoretical consideration that led Jones and Popper (1972) to investigate a variety of factors in the environment of the Peace Corps volunteers. In their study, they examined the environment for volunteers in 44 Peace Corps host countries. Six socioeconomic measures were included in the analysis: (a) population density, including miles of improved roads; (b) the per capita acres of agricultural land and the percentage of arable land; (c) the amount of assistance from the United States Agency for International Development; (d) the number of pupils per teacher in primary schools; (e) the population growth rate; and (f) the general development, including literacy, people per physician, percentage of labor force in agriculture, percentage of school population in primary grades, gross national income divided by the number of people in the country, the per capita electric power, and the ratio of motor vehicles to the size of the population. As a second set of measures, Jones and Popper looked at linguistic indices. In 52 Peace Corps countries there were a total of 191 different languages. By factor analyzing characteristics of these languages, Jones and Popper arrived at a factor called standardization which represents the universality of the particular language. For example, Spanish—which is widely used throughout Central and South America, the Caribbean, and, of course, Spain—has a high level of standardization, as does English.

Using the socioeconomic and linguistic variables as the environmental indices, Jones and Popper found two that were predictive of the completion rate for Peace Corps volunteers: the general development of the country and its language standardization. However, these two variables themselves were correlated. That is, those countries that had high universality of language also had high levels of socioeconomic development. Such countries were also the ones with the highest early termination rate. In contrast, Peace Corps volunteer satisfaction tended to be high in countries with low population density and growth and in relatively agrarian countries. Countries with these characteristics were the small non-French-speaking African countries and countries in the South Pacific area. To account for this pattern, Jones and Popper point out "In countries with high levels of cultural exposure, Volunteers will not be seen by host country nationals as particularly unusual, since foreign nationals have played a continuing role in the cultural exchange process for such a country [1972, p. 243]." In contrast, volunteers will be seen as more unusual in countries with lower levels of cultural exposure. Most volunteers wanted to be outsiders who would help bring about change desired by the host country. When the volunteers in countries with high social and economic development discovered that their role was not especially innovative, their attitude, performance, and level of satisfaction were consistently lower. As noted by Korman (1971) job satisfaction relates to the extent to which the environment contributes to the individual's sense of self-worth. If the volunteer were seen as just another foreigner doing what was already being done by the host country nationals, the job was less satisfying.

Outside the United States embassy in New Delhi one day I met a volunteer who had participated in a training program in which I had been the field selection officer. He was dressed in a kurta and dhouti typical of the Indian national. His placement was in a small village with a team of tube-well drillers. He was a young man who had come from a rural area where only limited intercultural activity had been available to him. He was extremely delighted in the opportunity to live in close proximity to people who saw him as unusual but helpful. He was enthusiastic about the way in which the environment in which he lived and the group with whom he worked were so different from that to which he had been accustomed in the United States. He relished the intercultural activity in which he was engaged.

Another field selection officer, who visited trainees in Thailand, shared his observations about the differences in the level of satisfaction of the volunteers that he met in various parts of the country. He reported that those volunteers who had been placed in Bangkok, the capital, were less satisfied with their Peace Corps activities than those who were placed upcountry where they lived under modest, even primitive, conditions with great satisfaction. In working with trainees assigned to teach English as a second language in Tunisia, I found that those who were assigned to Tunis or its suburbs were less happy or more apt to terminate early than those assigned to more remote locations. For service in Tunisia, volunteers were first taught French; when they had acquired sufficient skill in French, they were then taught Arabic. Those trainees who had studied Arabic and had been placed in areas where Arabic was more useful than French, expressed greater satisfaction with their assignments and with the opportunity to work more closely with the host country people. Such satisfaction occurred despite the volunteers' considerable resistance to the Tunisian attitudes toward women and the treatment of women in Tunisia.

Along with the positive value the volunteer placed on cultural variety, there was also an overwhelming need for volunteers to be culturally sensitive. In the very early days of the Peace Corps there was a front page "scandal" because a young woman had written on a postcard that roads were muddy and flies were numerous in the country to which she was assigned. The people of that country were offended by her report feeling their country had been dirogated and she had to return home. In another instance a well-qualified American auto mechanic was appalled that Indian auto mechanics were willing to take the motor out of an automobile and place it on the dusty ground to make the necessary repairs. He was equally offended to discover that Indian auto mechanics often used pliers or a crescent wrench as if they were a hammer. The niceties of the American garage were at some cultural remove from the Indian auto mechanics' purview, and the volunteer had to learn to respect this cultural difference. A nurse assigned to help teach operating room procedures had a dilemma which she presented to the overseas Peace Corps staff. What should she do about a surgeon who dropped a scalpel on the floor, picked it up, rinsed it off without sterilizing it, and went back to using it in an operation? Should she accept the hierarchial relationship of nurse and physician? Was the failure to sterilize the instrument negligence on the part of the physician or was the notion of the germ theory less pervasive in the host country? The issue of cultural sensitivity also arose in conjunction with a returned Vietnam veteran who wished to take a Peace Corps assignment in India but objected to cross-cultural studies on the grounds that he knew the Asian culture as he had served in Vietnam. The differences in the variety of cultures seemed to elude him and it was not possible to assign him to a Peace Corps placement. While it might appear self-evident that the Vietnam and Indian cultures might be different, even the subtle differences within the Indian cultures themselves were needed of those who wished to fulfill the Peace Corps mission.

Training in the host country culture developed awareness of subtle as well as gross differences between not only the host and American culture but also within the culture. Thus much staff attention was devoted to developing the most culturally appropriate program possible. In the earliest days training was done primarily in the United States. Some of the training was done in a fashion intended to replicate conditions in the host country to which the volunteers would be assigned. For example, in the Waipao Valley of Hawaii a typical Thai village was built. At the time that I went there to speak to the trainees about their Peace Corps activities and plans for the mid-training-period evaluation, they were engaged in total language immersion—only Thai was permitted except in an isolated "refuge" center on the training site. It was therefore necessary that my talk, which was delivered in English, be translated into Thai for the benefit of the trainees who of course were quite able to understand the English. In a way it was a bit like the scene in a Woody Allen movie in which an "interpreter" repeats in English with an Hispanic accent what Allen is saying in English in order to "interpret" for an American government official that he is meeting.

As Peace Corps developed, training programs were planned so that more time was spent in the host country itself and less in the American training sites. Early emphasis on physical training to toughen up the trainees was gradually diminished. The requirement of a 3-day period of wilderness living was eliminated, as was the test of the ability to untie oneself in the water when hands and feet were bound together. The long walks and hikes were no longer required. It had become clear that such physical training was not necessary for Peace Corps service. In like manner, it had become clear that if the trainees were to have some sensitive awareness of the country to which they were going it was preferable to have the training in the host country itself. Such a change was also desirable from a practical point of view. If one were to learn rice planting it was better to be in a rice growing area in the host country. If one were to learn dairy cattle breeding, it was better to work in the barns and fields of the host country. Artificial impregnation of cows by hand was somewhat different from fertilization with the gadgetry of the American farm. If one were to help the host country people learn to grow healthier and larger chickens through appropriate confinement, feeding, and watering, it was useful to see the contrast between those chickens raised by farmers who let them run loose to feed on grass and those raised under more controlled procedures. And the contrast between the anemic-looking chickens and the robust chickens of scientific breeding—both developed from the same type of chicks—was even more startling when seen in the host country.

The method and location of training became the subject of much research. Jones and Burns (1973) studied the satisfaction of 248 Peace Corps volunteers. Their finding was that the length of training time should not be too extended because the trainees began to be dissatisfied that they were not offering service to the host country. Further in-country training was preferred over training in sites in the United States. Extensive periods of training or training with limited or no in-country training was more apt to lead to dissatisfaction in the trainees. The Jones and Burns research also suggested that there was a need for standardizing training across programs and across study areas and probably across countries. They had found low satisfaction on the part of volunteers often could be attributed to the training project itself.

A study by Spradley and Phillips (1972), in which they used a cultural readjustment rating questionnaire with 83 returned Peace Corps volunteers along with other subjects, suggested that there are universal stresses encountered by those who experience cultural shock as well as direct culture-related differences in the definition of stress. Many other studies were of a more psychological than cultural nature. An example is a study by Masling, Johnson, & Saturansky (1974) relating oral imagery and perception of others with performance as evidenced in Peace Corps training. Fitness for Peace Corps work was positively related to oral imagery and accurate interpersonal perception in the case of males but not females. Exner (1973) used Peace Corps trainees for the validation of the self-focus sentence completion test which required the completion of sentences that had stems of self-reference, for example, *I*, *me*, and *my*. The research however, focused on the test rather than its direct usefulness in selection of Peace Corps trainees.

In addition to controlled research, there is available much anecdotal information about the important learning that occurred for those who spent time serving humanity by offering a helping hand in countries far from their home. Smith (1966) noted that those first volunteers who were assigned to Ghana developed an appreciation of the tragedy of racism particularly with respect to black Americans.

No one could spend a period of time living close to people with a remarkably different background and attitudes and come away without being enriched in his or her feeling toward others. The frustrations, demands, and rewards of the Peace Corps assignment have enriched many, old as well as young. The Peace Corps volunteers, on an interpersonal basis, must in turn have enriched the host country nationals with whom they were so closely associated. It is also probable that the host country nationals learned new methods of adaptation for health and happiness for their culture from their American counterparts. The Peace Corps has been a rich intercultural opportunity. Peace Corps volunteers went about their business without proselytizing. They extended an open hand to help others and they themselves learned in turn. It is true that the Peace Corps has not been without its politics. During the unhappy times of the Nixon administration, it was absorbed into an overall organization so the "Kennedy-oriented" Peace Corps would lose some of its identity. That incorporation established a structure that later forced Carolyn R. Payton, a distinguished Howard University professor who had served with the Peace Corps from 1964 until 1970 and then returned as the director of the Peace Corps under Carter, to resign. The resignation occurred because of political pressure as she tried to develop independence of the Peace Corps as an ongoing viable intercultural organization. Even evaluation research has been a political problem, as shown by Meyers (1975). Nonetheless, through the Peace Corps tens of thousands of Americans have shared in a rich experience with host country nationals across the face of the earth. The Peace Corps does live on, and we can only hope that it will regain the vitality it had in its early days.

References

Bibliography of research. Washington, D.C.: Peace Corps, Division of Research, November 1968.

Cotton, J. W. *Par for the Corps: A review of the literature on selection, training and performances of Peace Corps Volunteers.* Unpublished manuscript, University of California, Santa Barbara, 1973.

Derner, G. F. American idealism and the Peace Corps: Psychology's contribution. In D. S. Milman & G. D. Goldman (Eds.), *Psychoanalytic contributions to community psychology.* Springfield, Ill.: Charles C Thomas, 1971.

Exner, J. E. The self focus sentence completion: A study of egocentricity. *Journal of Personality Assessment,* 1973, *37,* 437–455.

Harris, J. G., Jr. Prediction of success on a distant Pacific Island: Peace Corps style. *Journal of Consulting and Clinical Psychology,* 1972, *38,* 181–190.

Harris, J. G., Jr. A science of the South Pacific: Analysis of the character structure of the Peace Corps Volunteer. *American Psychologist,* 1973, *28,* 232–247.

Jones, R. R., & Burns, W. J. Volunteer satisfaction with in-country training for Peace Corps: Reanalysis and extended findings. *Journal of Applied Psychology,* 1973, *57,* 92–94.

Jones, R. R., & Popper, R. Characteristics of Peace Corps host countries and the behavior of volunteers. *Journal of Cross-Cultural Psychology,* 1972, *3,* 233–245.

Korman, A. K. Environmental ambiguity and locus of control as interactive influences on satisfaction. *Journal of Applied Psychology,* 1971, *55,* 339–342.

Masling, J., Johnson, C., & Saturansky, C. Oral imagery, accuracy of perceiving others and performance in Peace Corps training. *Journal of Personality and Social Psychology,* 1974, *30,* 414–419.

Meyers, W. R. The politics of evaluation research: The Peace Corps. *Journal of Applied Behavioral Science*, 1975, *11*, 261–280.

Mischel, W. Predicting the success of Peace Corps Volunteers in Nigeria. *Journal of Personality and Social Psychology*, 1965, *1*, 510–517.

Proshansky, H. M., Ittleson, W. H., & Rivlin, L. G. The influence of the physical environment on behavior: Some basic assumptions. In H. M. Proshansky, W. H. Ittleson, & L. G. Rivlin (Eds.), *Environmental psychology*. New York: Holt, Rinehart & Winston, 1970.

Smith, M. B. Explorations in competence: A study of Peace Corps teachers in Ghana. *American Psychologist*, 1966, *21*, 555–566.

Spradley, J. P., & Phillips, M. Culture and stress: A quantitative analysis. *American Anthropologist*. 1972, *74*, 518–529.

JOHN CAWTE **24**

Interdisciplinary Conflict in Fieldwork: A Case of Ideological Shock

ABSTRACT

In this chapter, a case history is given of the way in which ideological conflict—value disagreements among workers from different social science disciplines—intruded into academic fieldwork. An interdisciplinary team of fieldworkers found itself in a state of ideological shock during a crisis created by an epidemic of illness. A brief account is given of how this conflict arose and of how it was worked out. It is concluded that lone fieldworkers have succeeded in avoiding interdisciplinary conflict, and thus tend to ignore it or to stereotype it. A team of interdisciplinary workers, on the other hand, is forced to confront value conflicts, especially if a crisis challenges their usual professional identity.

One outcome of open ideological conflict during fieldwork is the need and effort to resolve it. Another outcome is the recognition that a more serious conflict relates to lack of communication between researchers (ideologues), on the one hand, and people being studied, on the other. Social scientists have in the past felt free to ask questions and to publish results without much reference back to the citizens being studied. The ethics of this practice is questionable.

Nothing succeeds like a painful attack of ideological shock in reminding social scientists of the need to communicate better—with each other and with their subjects.

The various scientific disciplines that engage in cross-cultural research are themselves separate cultures, and find difficulty in communicating. This is particularly distressing to us because, while elegant studies may be coming from every disciplinary domain, the developing peoples who are being studied are not benefiting noticeably. Among other things, they suffer from the babel of tongues from the different disciplines describing them. Each discipline freely offers them prescriptions from its own culture. The consumers hear confusion, or nothing at all.

I am not convinced that this problem has been tackled genuinely anywhere in the world. There are some places where it has not even been defined as a problem. This is likely to occur in the scholarly halls, where departmentalization segregates scientific disciplines and even opposes them to one another. This is a form of parochialism and is sometimes responsible for the tunnel vision of academics, and for the stereotypes we develop about other disciplines. We academics live in narcissistic and incestuous clans and are not above feuding.

It is something to guard against. One of the principles guiding our research in Australia is that we are more likely to make an advance through a multidisciplinary approach. This is no shibboleth. We have on record many situations in intercultural psychiatry where the contribution of another discipline is a key to success or failure.

When we make a contribution to cross-cultural mental health—once some commitment is accepted to this world of cross-cultural suffering—information relevant to the science becomes vastly expanded. It expands in each of these dimensions: biological, psychological, societal, and cultural.

In fieldwork designed to focus adaptational problems of tribal societies, we have engaged specialists to help us study the "etics" of these dimensions. From the medical and paramedical disciplines, we have been helped by experts in medicine, pediatrics, social medicine, psychology, sociology, social work, dentistry, and genetics. From the less closely medicine-related disciplines, we have used experts in anthropology, law, education, theology, town planning, architecture, and photography.[1]

We learned something from all of them. In return we taught them a little about cross-cultural suffering, or at least, our patients taught them. We found that other scientific disciplines have stereotypes about psychiatry that, if left unchallenged, might preclude any collaboration at all.

An unexpected bonus of the multidisciplinary approach deserves greater attention. It concerns the contributions arising from the multiple method, which owes as much to the modal personality of people working in the particular discipline as to the discipline itself. (One has a strong impression that disciplines have modal personalities.)

---

[1] Accounts of these attempts at multidisciplinary collaboration in the field may be found in the literature. The book *Cruel, Poor and Brutal Nations* (Cawte, 1972) summarizes the *modus operandi* and findings of a short-stay multidisciplinary team. Another book, *Medicine is the Law* (Cawte, 1974), is written from the multidisciplinary viewpoint of physician, anthropologist, and psychiatrist. An account of the stumbling blocks against which we banged our shins in the attempt to achieve multidisciplinary rapport is given in a paper in *Excerpta Medica Congress* (Cawte, 1971).

Let me give an illustration of a spontaneously occurring research opportunity, in order to invite reflection upon how different disciplines may clash. During our team's expedition to Arnhem Land in early 1974, an epidemic caused by Influenza A virus swept through the population, with some fatal cases. It was accompanied by heightened ceremonial activity.[2]

Aboriginal cermonial (the *corroboree*) has recently been better appreciated by the white man's culture, as theater, involving music, song, poetry, acting, dancing, and painting. Seen by discerning eyes, these art forms become primal grand opera. Although appreciation of the etics of the ceremonial is commendable, it neglects the emics—the purpose to the performers.

Ceremonials reenact myths of the ancestral creators, with the object of releasing their power once more for the benefit of their earthly descendants. The ceremonial is carried out to reduce threats to security. Invoking the power of the ancestors is intended to restore harmony, resolve tensions, and relieve suffering. Thus the ceremonial may be viewed as contributing to mental health. These anxious people, some depressed and with influenza, whose relatives were dead or dying, enacted it continuously for days and nights in the midst of torrential monsoonal rain and bleak wind. They neglected their rest, their hygiene, and their nutrition. Those of us who were working with the sick in the little aid post were aware of ways in which this ceremonial actually added to the risks of disease.

It was an excruciating situation. If the Aborigines were suffering, they could take some comfort from the academics on that research team. They too were down with influenza, with all its malaises, and distempers. Beyond this, the team was moved by an awareness that the white man's viruses desolated this Aboriginal culture. Now, before their eyes, that primal pang unfolded, in that encounter with virus contagion invisible and inexplicable. It would be difficult to fabricate such a research design, but here it was spontaneously offering. Which part of this archetypal situation would the different academic disciplines use, and which ignore? It was as if each discipline was in some way on trial, needing to justify its utility and existence. That may seem an overheated reaction to the challenge, but The Wet of North Australia is an overheated season in every way.

The conflicting and contrasting viewpoints of these suffering professional persons can be sketched, abbreviated but only a little caricatured here as clan feuding.

Our physician seemed happy, listening to chests and putting up intravenous infusions. He was in demand. But being a good preventive doctor

---

[2] We were invited by the elders to make a documentary film of these mortuary rites. It is entitled *Aboriginal Mourning* and is available in a 16-mm print, color with sound, from the Australian Institute of Aboriginal Studies, P.O. Box 550, Canberra, A.C.T. Australia. 2600. A companion film, *Aboriginal Healing*, is also available.

he was also becoming concerned about the dead bodies lying about day after day in that festering heat. He would have liked them under the ground. The people refused to bury the dead until relatives arrived from the bush, and the song cycles were completed. As bodies decomposed, they stank. Were they perhaps a culture medium for pathogenic organisms? he wondered. One woman had died covered with pustules.

When he expressed his worry to an Aboriginal elder in authority, he received this resourceful instruction: Signal for the large refrigerator to be sent from the morgue in the nearest town! It was only 100 miles away by air. Later, the same elder, relenting a little, showed the doctor a can of deodorant spray which he was using on those bodies. He had found it in the store, where he happened to come across the label MUM-21: BODY FRESHENER. He could read large print.

The psychiatrist, myself, also a physician, was busy helping with those sick and dying. This may seem a clear role, but it is anything but that. Old Nyambi was dying with pneumonia. His sons angrily demanded that I treat the old man. Nyambi himself so greatly feared white men that he had always managed to avoid them. I had known of his presence for years, but I never spoke to him. Even as I listened to his chest sounds, he summoned his last strength to turn away from me. I knew that a penicillin injection would not save him. His sons demanded I give it. So I gave it, fearing I would then be blamed. He died that night.

An aspect of the ceremonial activity which struck me forcibly was that the rites were being inordinately strung out by two or three zealous elders who were using them as a means of reinstating their authority. Their power of command had been seriously threatened; some young men were questioning polygyny and rights to child brides. So these old men fanatically insisted on the full ritual for the funerals, which they supervised. It seemed to me important to pay these elders due respect in other ways if they were to relax this power play, but many others thought me misguided about this.

The medical anthropologist was in his element during the influenza wave, because the Aboriginal people were bringing out herbal remedies in profusion, and he was enlarging his collection of plants thought to have medicinal properties. He was also interested in psychosocial dwarfism (there is a scattering of tiny people in this population) and was able to observe the rather severe nutritional breaks that can be experienced by luckless infants during such ceremonies. So he was in some conflict, too.

There was no cultural anthropologist on the team at this time, or ideological shock would have intensified. We had worked with two in this population, and each had represented a contrasting viewpoint. The first was a cultural relativist who took the view that what the people did was in order for them, and that there was no place to intervene. This anthropologist espoused Illich's views on the heartlessness of modern medicine, and idealized traditional ways of doing things. The other anthropolgist was anything but a cultural relativist; he had a keen eye for psychopathology whenever it occurred, in societies as well as in individuals. He would have probably thought that this society had taken leave of its senses during the influenza. It was as well that both were not present now; knives would have flashed and one would have fallen. Intradisciplinary conflict is sometimes the bloodiest of all.

A Christian missionary at the height of the crisis delivered a big important sermon. He was a Methodist preacher from Fiji. He took the Prophet Jonah for his text. He explained how Jonah had got into the whale trouble because he declined to carry the news of the Israelite's Universal God to the Assyrians. Jonah was charged by his God to warn the Assyrians that they must mend their ways and accept the One God, or face doom. Jonah tried to escape God's command by going to sea, but fell out of the canoe during a storm, and spent three days inside a sea monster. Finally spewed up, he carried out God's instructions. He converted the Assyrians to God, and God forgave them.

Not many of the mourners and ritualists accepted Jonah's message at the time. However, I know that they were no fools, that often they listened, and were hungry for doctrine, especially if it had whales and boats in it. They would probably think about it later, and might soon be ripe for a Christian religious movement. (In fact, this later happened.)

Meanwhile, our cameraman seemed to be the least conflicted of our crew. He had received permission from the elders to film some of the funeral ceremonies and he was making the most of this valuable opportunity, filming between breaks in the dismal rain. Cameramen learn to be single-minded and not overly sensitive to the reflections of the people whom they have to shoot. One or two of our team, however, were worried that he was making free with sacred ritual, and they questioned whether he possessed the informed consent of everybody he was shooting. Of couse, he did not, and he was the last person to worry about that.

Not a day passed without some member of the team coming into a state of conflict with a colleague in another discipline, or even into conflict with himself. The crisis seemed to bring it all out. Good friends and colleagues became potentially resentful, suspicious, and obstructive. Happily, the influenza crisis was over in 2 weeks, leaving a rabble of spent and depressed people, including a couple of academics.

Much has been made of Oberg's insight into *culture shock* as it affects professional people studying abroad. Here is a variant: discipline shock or ideological shock, expressing conflict between the cherished goals and values of the scientific disciplines.

The obvious moral to draw from this brief example from fieldwork is that an interdisciplinary team should not go away together unless ties of friendship, respect, and mutual understanding are reasonably firm. To go into the field otherwise would be about as smart as going into an ocean yacht race with a crew that has not drunk together. When a storm comes up, everybody might want something different. Unfortunately, the departmentalization of universities gives little opportunity for such interdisciplinary practice. One encounters, in cross-cultural research, physicians who are quite unclear as to what anthropologists think, and anthropologists who have equally garbled stereotypes about physicians.

A less obvious, though possibly more important, moral is that while the different disciplines tend not to understand each other, the consumers understand them even less. After the team had ironed out its ideological differences, this was the stunning insight it was reduced to. The messages that tribal people receive from academics are at the best scrambled, because these people do not have the ability to unscramble them. They are not used to playing with new ideas.

Crossing that intercultural communication gap is even harder than crossing the interdisciplinary gap. We felt it was important to make an effort to supply one's findings in an intelligible form, for the consideration of the people who have been studied. This endeavor has come to seem more important than writing books and scientific articles for the academic elite. Increasingly, it seems unethical for social and behavioral scientists to collect data and publish findings without making a better attempt to find out what is wanted by the people studied. How will it help them? is the responsible question. This is a critical issue for the social and behavioral sciences, and it is capably reviewed in a book by J. A. Barnes (1979).

In an early effort to make amends we developed lay criteria to assist the citizens in identifying symptoms of mental disturbances (Cawte, 1972). In another effort, we produced a lay manual, summarizing the training of Aboriginal mental health workers (Kahn, Henry, & Cawte, 1976). In a further effort, we used a vernacular language KAP test to find the knowledge, attitudes, and practice regarding contraception (Forster & Cawte, 1975).

Finally, it seemed to us a good idea to bring out a modest quarterly journal, *The Aboriginal Health Worker*. This is published at a 12-year-old reading level, allowing tribal people to both read it and contribute to it. (Of course, we do not ask contributors to write at a 12-year-old reading level. We ask them to envisage their piece being read aloud in a group of indigenous health workers around a kitchen table.) This gives people practice at the game of new ideas. We hope that it paves the way for better communication between them and the academics who come to study them.

References

Barnes, J. A. *Who should know what? Social science, privacy and ethics.* New York: Penguin Books, 1979.

Cawte, J. Multidisciplinary teamwork in ethnopsychiatry research. *Excerpta Medica Congress*, 1971, *274*, 936–940.

Cawte, J. *Cruel, poor and brutal nations. The assessment of mental health in an Australian Aboriginal community by short-stay psychiatric field team methods.* Honolulu: The University Press of Hawaii, 1972.

Cawte, J. *Medicine is the law. Studies in the psychiatric anthropology of Australian tribal society.* Honolulu: The University Press of Hawaii, 1974.

Forster, L., & Cawte, J. Family health in tribal Aborigines. The use of the vernacular "KAP" test. *Medical Journal of Australia*, 1975, *2*, 27–32.

Kahn, M. W., Henry, J., & Cawte, J. Mental health services by and for Australian Aborigines. *Australian and New Zealand Journal of Psychiatry*, 1976, *10*, 221–228.

JOHN BEATTY
JUNICHI TAKAHASHI

25

Who Are We?
Who Are They?
And What Is Going on Here?

ABSTRACT

Problems involved in translating both language and concepts from one language to another can be seen in basically three areas. The first deals with the problems of a morpheme-to-morpheme or word-to-word relationship. The Japanese term *aoi* frequently translates into English as *blue* whereas at other times it translates as *green*. The lack of isomorphic congruence between the lexical semantics of two or more languages is well known.

The second problem area is at the level of grammatical construction. English can produce such sentences as *There is a book, There isn't a book,* and *There is no book*. Japanese, on the other hand, can produce the first two (*Hon ga aru, Hon ga nai*) but can not produce the third. There is no provision in Japanese for the existence of a nonthing.

A final problem, the one discussed in most detail in this chapter, is the question of the underlying presuppositions in semantics. This chapter examines the Japanese terms for *emotion* and investigates the implications of both English and Japanese terms. English, for example, often opposes "emotionality" to "rationality," whereas such an opposition is not made in Japanese.

One of the most significant problems faced by all scientists working in comparative fields is the question of equating various groups for the purpose of analysis. The (in)famous dictum: "Don't compare apples and oranges" is probably nowhere more complicated than in anthropology (which deals largely in the comparative method, comparing various cultures) and in comparative psychology (which compares animals at very different levels of organization).

CROSS-CULTURAL RESEARCH AT ISSUE

A quick look at the "apples and oranges" problem reveals some of the basic issues involved in trying to decide when two things are the same and when they are different. Apples and oranges are clearly different—unless of course you are comparing fruits and vegetables, in which case apples and oranges are both the same (fruits) as opposed to beans which are different (vegetables).

Even so, within the category "apples" there are Macintosh, Delicious, and Greenings (which are all kinds of apples—each of which is distinct from, but shares some similarity with, the others). In fact, every apple is different. When objects are grouped together, their differences are overridden and their similarities are emphasized. Each tree, each blade of grass, each grain of sand, each snowflake is different, yet those differences are ignored and the individual items are lumped together. In the early days of physical anthropology, almost every new skeleton found was given its own separate name. Later many were lumped together. *Sinanthropus pekinensis, Pithecanthropus erectus, Homo modjokertensis,* and a host of other finds have all become *Homo erectus.* The similarities were finally believed to outweigh the differences. The separate species *Homo neanderthal* was merged with *Homo sapiens* in a similar way. The next decade or two may see even more mergers of skeletal materials.

Such shifts in category are not restricted to highly technical material such as the skeletons of million-year-old creatures. Consider, for example, *Moby Dick.* There are several editions of the book: a Penguin edition, a Modern Library edition, and so on. Are each of these the same? Certainly the answer to that question requires some knowledge of the level at which the question is asked. From the point of view of a general understanding of the story, probably all editions can be equated. On the other hand, two people who have read the first 100 pages of the story in two different editions are likely to be at different places in the story as the size and spacing of the type is different. In that regard, the two editions are different. Even if two people have exactly the same edition, the two books are not the same. The theft of one upsets only the owner of that volume and not the owners of all the other copies of that edition. Consider also the problem of a copy titled *Moby Dick: Der weisse Wal.* Is this German translation the same as the English edition? Obviously at one extreme all things are the same, while at the other extreme they are all different.

Reclassifications are sufficiently common that the groupings established by a set of scientists at one time are rather different from those established by scientists at later dates. In the early days of anthropology, religion, magic, and science were all examined. Religion was defined as "belief in spiritual beings," whereas magic was seen as pseudoscience, which differed from science in that is dealt with mistaken cause and effect relationships, whereas science dealt with true cause and effect relationships (Tyler, 1874). Thus the earliest anthropologists established a division between religion on the one hand and magic and science on the other. Later, Malinowski (1948) argued that magic and religion shared a component of sacredness which science lacked; hence magic and religion should be lumped together and science kept separate. Tabulated by components, the three appear as follows:

	Manipulative cause and effect	*Sacred*
Magic	yes	yes
Religion	no	yes
Science	yes	no

Thus because magic and science both deal with a cause and effect relationship, it was possible to use that criteria to group them as Tylor, Frazer, and other evolutionists did. Similarly, by focusing on the "sacred" component (as Malinowski did), magic and religion are grouped together and science is kept apart. The only question that remains is why "sacred" should have primacy as a category over "manipulative cause and effect."

The "apples and oranges" problem appears in many areas of cross-cultural research. Two of these are discussed in this chapter: (*a*) the nature of the group; and (*b*) the nature of the action, attitudes, or behavior of the group.

The answer to "who" is being studied is not easily answered much of the time. In some cases, there is a general conflict between the people studying the group and the group's identification of itself (Beatty, 1979, p. 731). This problem can be seen in the study of deviants. In courses in abnormal psychology in many colleges, homosexuality is/was included in the curriculum. There has been great resentment on the part of many homosexuals that they are being classed as "deviants" or "abnormal," and until recently, when the American Psychiatric Association voted that homosexuals were not deviant, they had only their own opinions to back up their position.

But aside from the question of whether homosexuals are deviant or not, one can question what defines homosexuality (as well as deviance). Is it the homosexual act itself? Or is it just the thought of the act or a homosexual fantasy? Perhaps a particular lifestyle is the defining characteristic (i.e., homosexual—sex preferred—as opposed to "gay" going to bars, etc.).

For many people the actual sex act is the defining criteria. If a person has been brought to orgasm by another member of the same sex, the person is classified as homosexual (no one seems to have gone so far as to maintain that self-stimulation is homosexual). The problem, of course, is that many people who have experienced orgasm as a result of contact with a member of the same sex have also experienced it with members of the opposite sex.

Therefore they might also be classed as heterosexuals. In interviews, some people have paraphrased the old cliche that "if you have one drop of black blood (?), you are black" by saying "if you have had one homosexual experience you are homosexual." Aside from those who want to use homosexual and heterosexual for people who are 100% one or the other, and bisexual for those who have some sexual experience with both sexes, there are those who want to deal in rough percentages. Can a person with only one homosexual experience and hundreds of heterosexual experiences be classified as bisexual along with a person who has had hundreds of homosexual experiences and one heterosexual experience? Statistics are always fun. One person interviewed claimed that one homosexual act was sufficient to label a person homosexual. Later he admitted to a single homosexual act in his teens. When asked if he considered himself homosexual (as he had had a homosexual experience) he said he did not, because he had been the "active" member of the relationship. The problems of defining homosexuals by "active" and "passive" roles are not new (see, e.g., Beatty, 1979; Ford & Beach, 1951; Kinsey, 1948).

Another possibility for classifying homosexuals has to do with thought or fantasy. A man who has sex with another man and does not know it is a man, or who is fantasizing sex with a woman, may be said to be having a heterosexual experience. After all, in most masturbatory situations this is precisely what is happening. It is the fantasy, not the reality, that is involved. It is possible to work out a classification system in which people are grouped together by their fantasies, rather than their acts, although in actuality this is a difficult system to demonstrate.

In recent years, terms like "gay community" have begun to appear in magazines, newspapers, and scholarly publications. One might conceivably see the "gay community" as a group of people who are open about their homosexuality and who make both economic and political statements about their homosexuality. People who have "come out of the closet" are "gay"; those in the closet are, perhaps, "homosexual." In this sense, one can be classified as gay by one's integration with other gays and businesses catering to gays such as gay pornographic magazines. One wonders, given such a classification system, whether or not people who are not homosexual in act or fantasy, but who wish to support a gay political movement (and hence are integrated into the system) ought to be classified as "gays." Barbara Joans (1977) has in fact suggested that women involved in the women's movement should take the position that they are lesbians in order to neutralize the stigmatization.

Homosexuals are, of course, not the only group of people for which the problem of definition is complex. In the case of the people known generally as "American Indians," the complexity is even greater. The term *American*

Indian not only is a misnomer (in that Columbus was not in India), but also groups together various peoples who are related in virtually no other way than that they are human. No American Indian language seems to have had a word that meant all "Indians" as opposed to Europeans or non-Indians. The idea of a single category of "American Indians" is European and not an idea found in any one of the indigenous populations. A definition of American Indians is hard to come by. When one is found it is often circular: A person who is one-quarter American Indian is to be classified as an Indian (how do you decide if the person is one-quarter of the thing you are trying to define?). Aside from definitions such as "all those who lived in the Americas prior to A.D. 1200 and their descendents are American Indians" no definition is likely to work (and even that one has some problems with it). Traditionally, "Indians" defined themselves by political, linguistic, or kinship criteria, and named themselves accordingly. The development of a group of people known as "American Indians" and the acceptance of that label is a topic that merits study in and of itself, but need not concern us here. It is, however, interesting to note that while many "American Indians" are trying to be accepted as members of a category, many homosexuals are struggling to get out of a category (deviant).

Scientists as a group need to classify both people and events in order to see regularity in the universe. The classification of those acts is itself a cultural act and, as a result, tends to reflect the culture of the scientist doing the classifying. This is part of what has elsewhere (Beatty, 1974) been called the anthropology of science. It implies that science is very much a part of a specific culture and cannot be seen apart from the rest of the culture (see especially Hsu, 1973, and Owusu, 1978). In organizing the world around us, scientists try to establish meaningful categories with which they can work. These categories are constantly being defined and redefined on many grounds, which themselves are often in a state of flux, as a result of other cultural phenomena. The example of the definition of homosexuals indicates some of the problems of defining and redefining. (Kinsey, who was opposed to classifying people as homosexuals or heterosexuals, utilized a continuum approach rather than a dichotomous one as the basis for his conceptual framework.) The attempt at a definition is frequently very difficult even within a single culture. Cross-cultural definitions verge on impossible.

Linguists often hold that no two words in a language mean exactly the same thing. Cognitive anthropologists (Tylor, 1979, for example) have indicated the lack of exact mappings of the semantics of one language on another. For example, traditionally, the English word *blue* is translated into Japanese as *aoi,* and *green* as *midori.* Unfortunately, some things that are "green" in English are "aoi" in Japanese. Japanese claim that American red and green traffic lights are red and blue. The mapping of English *blue* and *green* onto Japanese *aoi* and *midori* is clearly not an exact one. (For other examples, see Conklin, 1964, and Frake, 1964.)

A further complication arises when one considers the way in which concepts are integrated into a system. It has been shown that both Japanese and English have concepts of masculinity and virility, but the two concepts integrate quite differently in the two cultures (masculinity is defined in part in terms of virility in the United States, but not in Japan) (Beatty, 1979). A number of American movies depict men commiting suicide or murder after being homosexually raped. In *Deliverance*, for example, a man who is homosexually raped convinces his friends that they must find the man who did it and kill him off so that no one will know that this had happened to him. Several American television shows that dealt with homosexual rape in prison showed the victim ultimately committing suicide. The Japanese find this somewhat incomprehensible. Why should a man commit suicide over a homosexual rape? From the Japanse point of view it is more understandable that a man who had prostituted himself homosexually might kill himself. Committing a homosexual act for money is, to the Japanese, an act worthy of suicide. Rape is not.

Taking as our starting point these two areas—definition of terms and the integration of those terms into the cultural system—let us examine some of the problems that arise in looking at the area of "emotion" in United States culture and in Japanese culture. This is not to be taken as a study of emotion in the two cultures, but, rather, as a way of exemplifying the problem of looking at anything in a cross-cultural perspective. Since defining groups and group membership has already been discussed (i.e., Who are we? and Who are they?), we can now turn our attention to the concept of activity (What is going on here?). In the discussion that follows, we will first look at the problems of trying to define the terms associated with "emotion" within the language and culture found in the United States, and then we will examine the problems of translating those terms into Japanese. Finally we will look at the ways in which emotions are integrated into the rest of the cultural system.

One of the first problems that one encounters in trying to establish a definition of a term like *emotion* is that in America one must contend with two levels of definition: a common everyday one and a technical one. In many other cultures, such a distinction may not occur (although Japanese is a culture that does distinguish a technical vocabulary from an everyday one). Specialized "scientific" or "technical" vocabularies need to be considered as well as the everyday usage of the terms.

Unfortunately, technical definitions of *emotion* vary somewhat depending on the theoretical position of the definer. *Psychology today*, an introductory textbook, defines *emotion* as "a feeling state of consciousness accompanied by internal body changes (e.g., rapid heartbeat, muscular tightening) [p. 725]." Alas, in looking up *feeling* we find "a physical sensation from the skin underlying tissues. A vague awareness, an emotional state [p. 726]." In addition to the circularity of the definitions, it is not clear what would constitute an emotion (for example, is "bravery" an emotion?) Nor is it clear how one distinguishes one emotion from another (for example, are "love" and "liking" the same emotional state differing only in intensity, or are they different emotions altogether?).

One can look at certain kinds of linguistic constructions in English to see how we use emotional terms and then substitute other "possible emotions" into the phrase to see whether they are acceptable. For example, "love" and "hate" are generally considered emotions. One can make a "linguistic frame":

He did it out of ————

In that blank both *love* and *hate* make sense. One might want to include "joy" as an emotion, because it can be substituted in the linguistic frame with a similar meaning. *He did it out of bravery* might also be acceptable. *He did it out of inspiration* seems somewhat unusual. One might conclude that "inspiration" is something of a different animal than "love," "hate," and "joy." Similarly, we might want to consider other possible linguistic frames such as

He ———— *her*

In this sentence *loves, hates,* and *inspires* are all linguistically correct, although the variation in meaning between *He loves her* and *He inspires her* is rather jolting.

This discussion should certainly not be taken to mean that we should in fact define emotions relative to some particular linguistic frame, but rather we should note how a linguistic frame can be used to establish some sort of insight into the semantics of the words with which we are dealing. For a particularly good example of this method, the reader should consult Bendix's *Componential Analysis of a General Vocabulary* (1966).

Assuming that an operational definition of *emotion* has been made by a scientist, one might then try to understand the semantic area in general. We would want to define not only *emotion* but also related words like *feelings* and possibly a large number of words that are subsumed into those categories (e.g., *love, hate, joy, sorrow*). Having established such a semantic area and identified the meanings of the terms contained in it, we would then have the task of seeing the ways in which the emotional system integrates with other aspects of the culture—with what it contrasts and how it is evaluated.

In general, in English, one finds that *emotional* is frequently used in contrast with *rational*. *Don't be so emotional, try to be more rational* is a common enough phrase in English to demonstrate the idea. *Star Trek's* Vulcans are supposed to be totally logical, as they got rid of all their emotions. *Emotional* also contrasts with *logical* on occasion (which may itself be interestingly contrasted with *rational*). Furthermore, emotions are generally (but not always) negatively evaluated. "Love" is one of the positive emotions, whereas "hate," "anger," and "rage" are negative. Even "love" however, is often called "blind" and there is a certain amount of negative charge to it in that sense.

In order to understand attitudes in the United States toward emotion, one needs to realize the place emotions have in the general cultural patterns. Such an analysis must also be undertaken for the other culture(s) one studies. The analyses would then have to be juxtaposed, and one would have to note the similarities and differences between them. The basic questions would be: Are emotions the same in different cultures? and Does the emotional system integrate itself into the rest of the cultural pattern differently in different cultures?

The brief analysis of Japanese emotional system that follows indicates some immediately obvious similarities and differences. These are only the beginning though. When one is required to deal with such topics as motivation as well as emotion and feelings, the task becomes truly formidable and well beyond the scope of this chapter. Yet the role of emotion in motivation cannot be overlooked, and many studies carried out by western observers (that deal with both emotion and motivation) have consistently used a western framework in attempting their analysis.

In Japanese culture, "emotion" is treated differently and is integrated into the rest of the culture differently. *Emotion* is commonly designated by three different words in Japanese: *kanjoo, ninjoo,* and *joocho,* all of which contain the morpheme *joo*. There is no single term in Japanese that can be used whenever English uses the term *emotion*. This indicates right from the start that the Japanese perception of emotions is rather different from the American perception.

Kanjoo, ninjoo, and *joocho* should not be regarded as referring to different classes of emotions which contrast with each other at the same taxonomic level the way *love* and *hate* do in English. Rather, each compliments the other in some way. For example, it can be said that *kanjoo* has a psychological (or phenomenological) aspect, *ninjoo* has an ethical aspect, and *joocho* an aesthetic one. Thus *Ano hito wa **ninjoo** ga aru* ('That person has *ninjoo*') and "*Ano hito wa **joocho** ga aru*" ('That person has *joocho*') are both common and reasonable statements, whereas *Ano hito wa* **kanjoo** *ga aru* ('That person has *kanjoo*') is not normally said, unless perhaps, one is talking about the Frankenstein monster. That is, *kanjoo* exist for every person normally, the way people have arms and legs. A person without *kanjoo* (*Kanjoo no nai hito*) is abnormal; a person without *ninjoo* (*Ninjoo no nai hito*) is not abnormal, but disgusting (as *ninjoo* is necessary for social relationships); and a person without *joocho* (*Joocho no nai hito*) is neither abnormal nor disgusting, but is likely to be boring.

As is the case with English *emotion*, Japanese *Kanjoo, ninjoo,* and *joocho* can be interpreted as a cause for action. However, the English statement *He did it out of emotion* will have drastically different implications in Japanese depending on which term is used for *emotion*. A person who acted out of *kanjoo* may be criticized for his thoughtlessness; but a person who acted out of *ninjoo* may be praised for his considerateness. A person who acted out of *joocho* may be praised for his taste. It is interesting to note at this point that many Americans indicate that they believe the Japanese repress their emotions. This is believed without any regard for the Japanese conception of emotion. If anything is true along those lines, it is that the Japanese may suppress *kanjoo* to some degree, but never *ninjoo* or *joocho*.

As the Japanese view emotion differently than Americans, so do they also view "rationality" differently. For example, "emotional" in Japanese does not oppose "rational." Just as "emotional" in Japanese culture is seen in three different ways which are complementary, so "rational" is also seen in a variety of ways. "Rational" in a particularistic interpersonal relationship is called *giri* (for an excellent definition of *giri* see Befu, 1971). *Giri* may sometimes contrast with *ninjoo,* but normally not with *kanjoo* or *joocho.* "Rational" in generalistic impersonal relationships is *doori.* It may contrast with both *ninjoo* and *kanjoo,* but not with *joocho. Risee,* which is "rational" in the most general philosophical sense may contrast with all of them, but the implication is different, depending on the contrast.

When *risee* is contrasted with *kanjoo* as in *risee-teki na hito* (a "rational" person) as opposed to *kanjoo-teki na hito* (an "emotional" person), the implication is a positive one, in that the former has what the latter lacks. If one is said to be *risee-teki na hito* (a rational person) rather than *ninjoo-teki na hito* (an emotional person), the implication may be negative in that the former lacks *ninjoo* which the latter has. Finally, when *risee-teki na hito* is contrasted with *joocho-teki na hito,* neither a negative nor positive implication occurs.

Two major problems can be raised on the basis of the preceding discussion. The first has to do with the dangers inherent in cross-cultural research that stem from the biases brought about by the cultural and linguistic background of the scientist conducting the research. Obviously, any attempt at cross-cultural studies of topics such as emotion must be undertaken with the utmost sensitivity toward the various cultural perceptions of the topics both in the culture of the scientist and in the cultures of the people being studied.

The second problem has to do with a more subtle issue, and that is the direction that science takes in other cultures as a result of contact with the West. Japanese psychologists for example, are basically trained in psychology from the standpoint of the West. The Western biases in concept and method are very obvious in the research carried out by scientists from other countries. It is clear that a great deal of work needs to be done to refine the definition of terms like *science* to come to an understanding of what science is in a cross-cultural context (see Beatty, 1977, p. 735).

In Japanese, the main tendency has been to adopt western concepts and theories to try to explain Japanese phenomenon. Technically, Japanese scientists have used *joocho* as the term for the English word *emotion*. In doing this, the complex network of terms and concepts dealing with emotions is lost, and the result has been the ignoring of *kanjoo* and *ninjoo* (as well as *joocho* in its original meaning) by Japanese psychologists. This result has been apparent not only in the study of emotion, but also in the study of virtually all other mental states.

The question of apples and oranges with which this chapter began cannot be resolved here. We mean only to make the reader aware of the problems of dealing with such complex issues as emotions in cross-cultural research. Is it, in fact, a case of comparing American apples with Japanese oranges when we try to deal cross-culturally with "emotions" and "kanjoo," "nin-joo," and "joocho"? Or are we in fact dealing with American "Macintosh" and Japanese "Delicious"?

References

Beatty, J. *On defining language and culture.* Lecture presented at the New York Academy of Sciences, New York, 1974.

Beatty, J. Oh would some power the giftie gie us, to see ourselves as others see us. In L. L. Adler (Ed.), *Issues in cross-cultural research.* Annals of the New York Academy of Sciences, 1977, *285*, 731–736.

Beatty, J. Sex, role and sex role. In M. Slater, J. Orasano, L. L. Adler (Eds.), *Language, sex and gender.* Annals of the New York Academy of Sciences, 1979, *327*, 43–49.

Befu, H. *Japan: An anthropological introduction.* New York: Chandler Publishing Co., 1971.

Bendix, E. *Componential analysis of general vocabulary: The semantic structure of a set of verbs in English, Hindi, and Japanese.* Bloomington, Indiana: Indiana University Research Center in Anthropology, Folklore and Linguistics, 1966.

Conklin, H. C. Hanunoo color categories. In D. Hymes (Ed.), *Language in culture and society: A reader.* New York: Harper & Row, 1964.

Ford, C., & Beach, F. *Patterns of sexual behavior.* New York: Harper, 1951.

Frake, C. The diagnosis of disease among the Subanum of Mindanao. In D. Hymes (Ed.), *Language in culture and society: A reader.* New York: Harper & Row, 1964.

Hsu, F. H. K. Prejudice and its intellectual effect on American anthropology. *American Anthropologist,* 1973, 75(1), 1–19.

Joans, B. *Lesbianism and women's studies.* Paper presented at the meeting of the Western Social Science Association, Denver, 1977.

Kinsey, A. C., Pomeroy, W., & Martin, C. *Sexual behavior in the human male.* Philadelphia: Saunders, 1948.

Malinowski, B. *Magic, science and religion.* Garden City, N.Y.: Doubleday (Anchor), 1948.

Owusu, M. Ethnography of Africa: The usefulness of the useless. *American Anthropologist,* 1978, 80(2), 310–334.

Tyler, E. B. *Primitive Culture.* Boston: Estes & Lauriat, 1874.

Tylor, S. A. *Cognitive anthropology.* New York: Holt, Rinehart & Winston, 1969.

The United States–United Kingdom Cross-National Project: Issues in Cross-Cultural Psychogeriatric Research

ABSTRACT

The United States–United Kingdom Cross-National Project has, since 1965, conducted a series of studies on the epidemiology of mental disorders. In a previous and companion paper (Zubin & Gurland, 1977), we presented the project's studies on *adult* patients below age 60. Here we discuss the project's *geriatric* studies with reference to the interaction between culture and psychopathology, and we outline methodological and administrative principles in the conduct of cross-national geriatric research. We also review evidence that New York psychiatrists tend incorrectly to diagnose dementia in cases that would be diagnosed as functional disorders and so treated by their colleagues in London.

Introduction

In a previous paper (Zubin & Gurland, 1977) we discussed the cross-cultural issues encountered by the U.S.–U.K. project in studying reported differences in the prevalence rates of mental disorder between the adult populations of the United States and the United Kingdom. The upper age limit for the subjects in that series of studies was 60 years. The major result was the documenting of an essential clinical similarity between London and New York patient populations in large mental hospitals, despite wide discrepancies suggested by hospital diagnoses. In the course of this study, the groundwork was laid for the development of basic methods and instruments for comparing psychiatric symptoms between different populations both intranationally and internationally. These have since been applied to a series of studies dealing with the adult population, as shown in Table 26.1.

Table 26.1
Principal Aims, Methods, and Key Results of the U.S.–U.K. Adult Studies

Study	Aims	Methods	Results
Adult inpatient study	To determine whether the large cross-national differences in the officially reported adult admission rates to public mental hospitals for schizophrenia and for affective disorders reflect real differences in the patients or differences in the use of diagnostic terms by the British and American hospital psychiatrists.	Independent examination of large numbers of hospital patients by project members using systematic face-to-face assessment techniques; collection of the routine hospital diagnoses made on these patients by the local hospital staff.	The reported large cross-national diagnostic differences were not reproduced when consistent methods of classification were used on the New York and London samples. New York hospital psychiatrists had a much wider concept of schizophrenia and narrower concept of affective disorder than did their London colleagues.
Videotape study	To generalize the results of the inpatient study to other regions of the U.S. and the U.K. To determine whether cross-national differences in the way psychiatrists make diagnoses reflect differences in the way they perceive patients' symptoms.	Examination of the diagnoses and ratings of videotapes of patients by audiences of psychiatrists in many parts of the U.K. and the U.S.	The tendency of American psychiatrists to diagnose schizophrenia more readily and affective disorder less readily than their British colleagues was shown to a greater or less extent throughout the U.K. and the U.S. (with notable exceptions). American psychiatrists record higher levels of psychopathology than do U.K. psychiatrists on the same patient. The higher ratings of U.S. psychiatrists are evenly spread over all forms of psychopathology when ratings are of carefully defined terms; but are exaggerated for schizophrenic symptoms when undefined technical terms are used.
Case record study	To determine whether the reported increase of schizophrenic admissions to the N.Y.S. Psychiatric Institute between the period 1932–1941 and the period 1947–1956 was due to differences in the patients or to changes in the concept of schizophrenia.	Submission of case records from the period 1932–1956 to contemporary psychiatrists for rediagnosis.	The reported large increase in schizophrenia between the two decades was not reproduced on rediagnosis of the cases. The concept of schizophrenia at the N.Y.S.P.I. broadened between the two decades. There was, however, a change also in the kind of schizophrenic admitted.

The methods developed by the U.S.–U.K. project initially focused on obtaining reliable cross-national assessment of the mental status and psychiatric diagnosis of patients already in contact with a public mental hospital. As methodological difficulties were overcome the scope of the work was gradually broadened. This broadening occurred in the following directions: (a) progression up the age scale to include the elderly; (b) a movement into the community to include nonpatients as well as patients; and (c) the assessment of psychiatric problems not only in their own right but also in the context of the person's other health problems and the physical and social environment. In this chapter, we will highlight some of the cross-cultural issues emerging from the project's geriatric studies.

The cross-national work was extended into the geriatric age range in order to investigate cross-national differences reported for this age group in admission rates and the outcome of hospitalization. The official national statistics for first admissions over the age of 65 years to public mental hospitals in the U.S. and the U.K. indicated that chronic organic brain syndromes (senile dementia and psychoses with cerebro-arteriosclerosis) were almost twice as common in the U.S. as in the U.K. However, this project's previous work warranted a skeptical view of cross-national differences as reflected in official statistics, and it was suspected that U.S. hospital psychiatrists were more inclined to make the diagnosis of organic brain syndrome than were their colleagues in the U.K. A challenging question was posed by Morton Kramer (1961) as to whether functional (mainly depressive) disorders in the elderly were being misdiagnosed as organic brain syndrome in the U.S., with the consequence that the patients were regarded as untreatable and thus denied valuable treatment opportunities.

Culture and Mental Disorder among the Elderly

The elderly are often separated from younger cohorts by differences in beliefs and customs that in effect lead to a cultural gap between generations even within the same family. The origins of this gap may derive from intergenerational differences in the exposure to geographic locale and socio-political climate that surround the impressionable years of life as well as from the intragenerational changes due to experiences that accrue with the passage of time that accompanies longevity, or from the physical effects of aging on body and mental processes.

These often divisive sociocultural forces can be mitigated by sympathetic interpersonal relationships between the generations, by general societal mediators of culture, and specifically by the educative efforts of the elderly directed toward the young. However, the role of the elderly in promoting continuity of culture between the generations is severely undermined by the low status of the elderly in a work- and youth-oriented society and by the priority given the nuclear family over more extended ties in western society.

To the extent that the expression of psychopathology is culture bound we can expect that a given mental disorder will show a pattern in the elderly that is distinct from that in younger persons in situations where a cultural gap has developed. This complicates the recognition of mental disorder in the elderly because psychiatrists are generally trained to diagnose conditions in younger persons. To make matters worse, the attitudes of the elderly patient and the psychiatrist (most often a member of the younger generation) toward each other, and their differing modes of communication, may impede the clear reporting of significant symptoms. Furthermore, both the aging process and the process of dementia are presumed to be so closely identified with inevitable deterioration in the biased view of some psychiatrists that the latter tend to regard all mental disorders associated with age as a form of irretrievable dementia.

Reported rates of mental disorder among the elderly of New York and London could thus be influenced by several cultural contexts: (a) the prevailing culture of the two cities and of the elderly cohorts; (b) the formal health care system; and (c) the informal support network. These contexts could act as modifying variables, altering the incidence or duration of the disorder, determining the selection of cases for admission into various institutions versus residing in the community, or determining the external expression and the labeling of the disorder. The U.S.–U.K. geriatric studies were designed to narrow down the impact of some of these variables and to indicate which were most likely to occur. The studies were not designed to assess culture directly nor to establish definitively a causal relation between culture and mental disorder in the elderly nor to rule out other etiological models of mental disorder. Their purpose was to chart the interaction of these cultural factors with psychopathology.

U.S.–U.K. Geriatric Studies

The planned sequence of U.S.–U.K. geriatric studies was as follows: (a) a hospital study to examine cross-national differences in the expression and labeling of mental disorder; (b) a community study to examine cross-national differences in the prevalence of mental disorder and in the formal and informal systems of care provided; (c) an institutional study to examine cross-national differences in the sequestration of cases from the community; and (d) a study of alternatives to institutional care for the elderly. The sequence of geriatric studies is shown in Table 26.2.

Table 26.2
Sequence of U.S.–U.K. Cross-National Geriatric Studies

Study 1.	Geriatric Hospital Study: Examination of 50 consecutive geropsychiatric admissions in New York and a like number in London. Three month follow-up.
Study 2.	Geriatric Community Study: Examination of a representative sample of 445 elderly subjects living in the community in New York and 396 in London. One year follow-up. Services received and family support also studied.
Study 3.	Geriatric Institutional Study: Examination of geriatric residents randomly selected from all long term care facilities in New York and in London. Organization and costs of institutions also studied.
Study 4.	Geriatric Alternatives to Institutions Study: Examination of quality, costs, and outcome of care given to matched groups of frail elderly in institutional and community based settings in New York and London (study ongoing).

Representative samples of subjects over the age of 65 were drawn for each study. In the hospital study 50 consecutive admissions were examined in each of two psychiatric hospitals, one in New York and the other in London. In the community study, 445 randomly selected elderly subjects from the general population were interviewed in New York and 396 in London. In the institutional study, 162 and 159 residents were randomly selected from the universe of long-term care facilities in New York and London respectively. By including the universe of all long-term care facilities in each city regardless of type it was possible to obtain comparable populations of individuals without encountering the difficulties of identifying cross-nationally equivalent types of institutions. The community and institutional samples when combined constituted a sample of almost all the elderly in the two cities.

In all the U.S.–U.K. geriatric studies a structured interview technique is used to establish the presence of psychopathology, and diagnoses are made in a uniform manner in both cities based upon the interview data. This technique was specially adapted for the elderly by incorporation of these features: (a) tests of intellectual functioning to detect and distinguish the memory impairments of normal aging and of disease states such as senile dementia; (b) questions on the subjective complaints of memory impairment which tend to occur in depression; (c) consideration of chronic physical illnesses which very often accompany mental disorder in old age and which may mimic psychopathology; (d) a tactful administration of the interview to avoid undue stressing of the elderly subject which may lead to a poor performance on mental tests or to failure to cooperate with the interviewer; (e) inclusion of items to distinguish between clinical levels of depression and the more usual demoralization (Dohrenwend, Oksenberg, Shrout, Dohren-wend, & Cook, 1979) that may accompany the inroads of old age; (f) assessment of levels of functional ability–disability and role performance commensurate with norms for retired persons; and (g) descriptions of the social environment of the elderly person. An effort is made to reduce cultural misunderstanding by keeping the questions as nontechnical and straight-forward as possible, by allowing the interviewer to paraphrase questions where they are not understood, by providing a definition of a positive response for each item of psychopathology rather than recording simple affirmative and negative responses to questions, by introducing redundancy into items on each type of psychopathology to enhance reliability, and by utilizing translated versions of the interview where a language barrier exists. In particular, the use of illness labels as indicators of the presence of psy-chopathology is minimized with major reliance being placed on the presence of characteristic symptom clusters or syndromes.

The structured interviews developed during the U.S.–U.K. series of geri-atric studies have been described more fully elsewhere; they include the Geriatric Mental Status (GMS) schedule covering psychopathology in great detail (Gurland, Copeland, Sharpe, & Kelleher, 1976); the Comprehensive Assessment and Referral Evaluation (CARE) which involves consideration of medical and social problems as well as psychopathology, and which is suitable for examining a cross-section of the elderly population (it has been provided with screening and institutional versions), (Gurland, Kuriansky, Sharpe, Simon, Stiller, & Birkett, 1977–1978); and the Performance Ac-tivities of Daily Living (PADL) test which objectifies functional ability (Ku-riansky & Gurland, 1976).

In some elderly subjects, especially those in institutions, intellectual im-pairment has progressed so far that though lengthy and complex questioning cannot be attempted, performance testing, observation, and simple questions yield valuable information on mental function. A screening instrument was devised to identify subjects who could comply only with a basic interview. In addition, structured interviews with suitable informants were utilized for such subjects.

In characterizing elderly subjects for the purpose of cross-national com-parison, emphasis is placed, where possible, on direct interview, testing, and observation of the subjects rather than on the reports of informants, as the latter may introduce further cultural bias. Even within the information gath-ered directly, certain items of psychopathology appear to have a more culture-fair diagnostic import than other items. Rather surprisingly, the rel-atively language-free "face–hand test," which involves recognition of double simultaneous tactile stimulation, was found to be more culture bound than questions on memory and orientation as an indicator of organic brain syndrome. The face–hand test was much more closely related to diagnosis in London than in New York, whereas memory and orientation were equally related to diagnosis in the two cities.

Results of the Geriatric Hospital Study

The hospital study (Copeland *et al.*, 1975; Gurland *et al.*, 1976) demonstrated that the patients' symptoms obtained on systematic interviews could provide in both cities valid discriminations between the research diagnoses of chronic organic brain syndrome (dementia) and functional psychiatric disorder (affective, schizophrenic, and paraphrenic disorders), but that routine hospital diagnoses were less well related to distinctive symptom profiles. There was a tendency for patients with certain symptom patterns to be classified as having functional disorders by the research teams in New York and London and by the London hospital psychiatrists but to be called demented by the hospital psychiatrists in New York. Furthermore, although there were discrepancies between the research diagnoses and hospital diagnoses in both cities, these discrepancies were random, having no characteristic pattern in London, but were systematic and patterned in New York (i.e., the research team diagnosed functional disorder whereas the hospital diagnosed dementia). These cross-national differences in diagnostic practice accounted in large part for the contrasting rates of dementia as reported by the hospitals; when the diagnostic distributions based on research diagnoses are examined there is no statistically significant difference in the cross-national rates of dementia.

One can go further than merely pointing out that there were cross-national differences in diagnostic practice. Evidence to show that the New York hospital psychiatrists were incorrectly overdiagnosing dementia comes from the analysis of cases in which disagreement took place between hospital diagnoses and project diagnoses. Patients on whom there was disagreement—those given a diagnosis of functional disorder by the project, but of dementia by the hospital staff—resembled the patients on whom there was agreement by both staffs on the diagnosis of functional disorder—in outcome and other characteristics—but did not resemble the patients on whom there was agreement on the diagnosis of dementia. This resemblance extended to similarity in symptom profiles, duration of hospitalization, psychological test scores, and functional ability.

A practical and potentially serious consequence of the overdiagnosis of dementia in the New York hospital was that patients with affective disorder who were mistakenly diagnosed as demented were less often given specific and appropriate pharmacological treatment in New York than in London.

Nevertheless, these misdiagnosed patients enjoyed just as quick a discharge from hospital and just as speedy a recovery from symptoms in New York as in London. Perhaps the administrative culture, which was heavily weighted in favor of early discharge in New York and toward prolonged observation in London, was a critical factor in mobilizing the patients' powers of recovery in those cases (i.e., of functional disorder) where remission is a possibility. Nevertheless, the danger inherent in the tendency toward misdiagnosis of dementia first hinted at by Kramer (1961) persists.

Discussion

The U.S.–U.K. series of studies have demonstrated that cross-national research is feasible and fruitful despite the difficulties arising from distance and differences in culture, language, and professional training. In fact, these issues have been more than problems to be overcome by methodological innovations. They served to uncover aspects of the diagnostic process which would not have been noted in an intranational study. For example, the cross-national similarity in outcome of subjects with a research diagnosis of functional disorder and of organic brain syndrome among the sample of elderly hospitalized psychiatric patients studied suggests that (a) the indicators of these disorders can be recognized by appropriate techniques with equal validity in the two cities; (b) the observed cross-national differences in pharmacological treatment and duration of hospitalization were not in themselves sufficient to provide a more favorable outcome in one or the other city; and (c) the local professional culture of the hospital psychiatrists led them to giving cross-nationally dissimilar labels to essentially similar psychiatric disorders.

Perhaps the single factor that facilitated these studies most was an enduring administrative relationship between the two research teams, one in each city. This relationship has now lasted uninterruptedly for nearly 15 years. Without this background, a great distance between research sites such as exists between New York and London undoubtedly could complicate the conduct of such studies at all stages of the work. At the earlier stages of research, constructing a design that is suitable for each city calls not only for a meeting of minds as to what issues have priority for study but also for local knowledge on such matters as where and how to find the subjects for study. In the institutional study it was discovered that the kind of elderly patients who reside in nursing homes in New York are found in geriatric hospitals, among other locations, in London. Geriatric hospitals are not found as such in New York while a negligible proportion of elderly patients reside in nursing homes in London and these nursing homes are not comparable to the New York institutions bearing the same title. In the community study, the sampling design in London was based on the information that virtually all elderly persons are registered with general practitioners whereas in New York a sampling frame was available as a legacy from a recent survey conducted by a state agency.

As a research project proceeds the collaborative spirit is put to the test by the necessity of meeting deadlines for closure on the methods for assessing psychopathology and associated issues. It may or may not come as a surprise to others that in our experience the most difficult matters for the two teams to resolve was with respect to the details of the content and style of the assessment instruments; agreement is reached much more readily on the aims of the research than on its exact method. The collaborative teams need a tradition and joint experience of past compromises to fall back on when faced with the need to agree on all aspects of the proposed assessment technique. It does not do for one team to dominate these decisions as the implementation of the assessment in a consistent manner in both research sites requires that both teams be convinced of the soundness of the method and be equally invested in its success.

Obtaining and maintaining consistency in assessment techniques between two teams working at a distance from each other is helped by frequent exchanges of personnel for the purpose of reliability trials and repeated discussion of the relevance to the research goals of the interview content. These discussions serve as reminders to team members of the specific importance of the interview content and are thus a strong stimulant to meticulous adherence to the procedural rules of the interview. In addition, a formal audiovisual training program has been developed by the U.S.–U.K. project to indoctrinate new interviewers in the standard technique of administering the interview. Willingness to follow the procedural rules of interviewing is a stronger determinant of interrater reliability than is a common membership in a professional discipline, as has been shown in a study of the reliability of the CARE interview with elderly subjects (Gurland et al., 1977–1978).

The research methods employed in the U.S.–U.K. series of studies have provided a consistent yardstick for psychopathology against which to assess the variation in mental disorder that might arise from cultural influences on professional reporting systems, on the expression of psychopathology, and on the frequency of mental disorder. However, the yardstick is still an imperfect one: It relies on behavioral information, it is not closely related to etiology, and there is no guarantee that it is culture free or even culture fair. It is true that evidence of the cross-cultural validity of these assessment techniques can be found by comparison in different settings with diagnosis and outcome data, but unquestionably this validity would be more stringently tested by comparison with more culture free and etiologically related indicators of mental disorder.

Although, the etiology of the disorders of the senium is still a mystery, scientific models can be provided for testing out the various etiological theories. Such a group of etiological models has been discussed by Zubin (1972) and consists of a framework ranging from the molecular biological sphere to the social-psychological and environmental spheres. The first sphere contains the genetic internal environment, and neurophysiological models; the latter contains the ecological, developmental, and learning theory models. These models do not operate independently and their interaction has been assumed to give rise to a vulnerable individual, who when subjected to sufficient stress will develop an episode of mental disorder (Zubin, 1976; Zubin & Spring, 1977). One of the most likely triggers for eliciting an episode in the vulnerable individual is a stress-producing life event of either external or internal origin. Each of the etiological models underlying the vulnerability model can supply indicators for identifying vulnerable individuals. Here we have room for considering only the extreme ends of the etiological spectrums—the ecological, from the environmental group, and the genetic and neurophysiological, from the molecular biological group.

Thus, assuming a genetic etiology, consanguinity with a recognized case of dementia can serve as an indicator. The diagnosis of dementia could be validated by the demonstration of a hereditary predisposition. Where it can be shown that the risk of morbidity in relatives of cases diagnosed dementia is the same in two different cultures then that diagnosis is by the same token likely to be culture fair or free.

Assuming an ecological etiology, the parameters of the niche occupied by the person might also help establish the diagnosis. Although the specificity of ecological indicators such as isolation, deviant social networks, etc., has not been established as firmly as the specificity of consanguinity (even the specificity here is also not very highly determined), there is nevertheless sufficient information to warrant their study.

At the present time it is clear that the ecological niche the elderly occupy in society is a potent factor in their adjustment. One of the more important parameters of the ecological model is the social network in which the individual is embedded (Hammer, 1972). The structure of this social network is so important that life itself seems to depend upon it. Thus, Berkman and Syme (1979) report that social network ties are an important determinant of survival even when the other important determinants of mortality are kept constant: (a) self-estimate of physical health; (b) socioeconomic status; (c) smoking; (d) consumption of alcohol; (e) obesity; (f) physical activity; and (g) health practices and utilization of preventive health services. That the social network plays an important role in disorders of the senium has been amply attested to by the impact of isolation (Bennett, 1980).

However, in this case, we are not so certain that this indicator is culture free or even culture fair, and much more basic work is necessary to establish its etiological relevance as well as its value in validating a diagnosis. Nevertheless, if the association between dementia and specific disturbances in social connectedness is found to be equal in the cultures under comparison, the data on social networks can be of help in confirming the cross-cultural validity of diagnoses.

Furthermore, the social network may operate not as an etiological factor but as a moderating factor, cushioning the impact of life-event stressors in the vulnerable where the social network is supportive or permitting the vulnerability to express itself when it is not supportive.

With regard to the neurophysiological model, the role of specific brain changes, assessed by the recently developed noninvasive computer-assisted radiological techniques, offers a promising approach to determining the cross-cultural validity of the diagnosis of dementia.

Gurland (1980) has pointed out that there are four main indicators for assessing the presence of dementia and in three of these (impaired adaptation, psychological test performance, and diagnosis) the cultural influence on assessment is not certain though they may be culture fair, whereas the assessment of the fourth, specific brain changes, is culture free, though its causes may be culturally determined. Operational definitions are available for each of these indicators including brain changes, as mentioned previously. The use of all four indicators in cross-cultural studies would be a powerful strategy for identifying the extent to which culture can affect the biological substrate of dementia, its psychopathology, its maladaptive sequelae, and the diagnostic labels applied to it. This paradigm would in the future be applicable to sociocultural studies of other mental disorders as the relevant indicators become available. But the complete strategy for assessing vulnerability to disorders of the seniuma involves all the etiological models, and efforts at uncovering indicators derived from each of them are essential in the understanding and conquest of the disorders of the aged.

References

Bennett, R. (Ed.). *Aging, isolation and resocialization*, New York: Van Nostrand & Reinhold Co., 1980.

Berkman, L. F., & Syme, S. L. Social networks, host resistance, and mortality: A nine-year follow-up study of Alameda County residents. *American Journal of Epidemiology*, 1979, *109*, 186–204.

Copeland, J. R. M., Kelleher, M. J., Kellett, J. M., Fountain-Gourlay, A. J., Cowan, D. W., Barron, G., DeGruchy, J., Gurland, B. J., Sharpe, L., Simon, R. J., Kuriansky, J. B., & Stiller, P. Cross-national study of diagnosis of the mental disorders: A comparison of the diagnoses of elderly psychiatric patients admitted to mental hospitals serving Queens County, New York and the former Borough of Camberwell, London. *British Journal of Psychiatry*, 1975, *126*, 11–20.

Dohrenwend, B. P., Oksenberg, L., Shrout, P. E., Dohrenwend, B. S., & Cook, D. *What psychiatric screening scales measure in the general population, Part I: Jerome Frank's concept of demoralization.* Unpublished manuscript, 1979.

Gurland, B. The borderlands of dementia: The influence of socio-cultural characteristics on rates of dementia occurring in the senium. In N. Miller & G. Cohen (Eds.), *Clinical aspects of Alzheimer's disease and senile dementia.* New York: Raven Press, 1980.

Gurland, B., Copeland, J., Sharpe, L., & Kelleher, M. The geriatric mental status interview (GMS). *International Journal of Aging and Human Development*, 1976, *7*, 303–311.

Gurland, B., Kuriansky, J., Sharpe, L., Simon, R., Stiller, P., & Birkett, P. The comprehensive assessment and referral evaluation (CARE)—Rationale, development and reliability. *International Journal of Aging and Human Development*, 1977–1978, *8*(1), 9–42.

Gurland, B., Kuriansky, J. B., Sharpe, L., Simon, R. J., Stiller, P., Fleiss, J. J., Copeland, J. R. M., Kelleher, M. J., Gourlay, A. J., Cowan, D. W., & Barron, G. A comparison of the outcome of hospitalization of geriatric patients in public psychiatric wards in New York and London. *Canadian Psychiatric Association Journal*, 1976, 421–431.

Hammer, M. Psychopathology and the structure of social networks. In M. Hammer, K. Salzinger, & S. Sutton (Eds.), *Psychopathology.* New York: Wiley, 1972.

Kramer, M. Some problems for international research suggested by differences in first admission rates to the mental hospitals of England and Wales and of the United States. *Proceedings of the Third World Congress of Psychiatry*, Montreal, 1961.

Kuriansky, J., & Gurland, B. The performance test of activities of daily living. *International Journal of Aging and Human Development*, 1976, *7*(4), 343–352.

Zubin, J. Scientific models for psychopathology in the '70s. *Seminars in Psychiatry*, 1972, *4*, 283–296.

Zubin, J. Role of vulnerability in the etiology of schizophrenic episodes. In L. J. West & D. E. Flinn (Eds.), *Treatment of schizophrenia: Progress and Prospects.* New York: Grune & Stratton, 1976.

Zubin, J., & Gurland, B. The United States–United Kingdom Project on diagnosis of the mental disorders. In L. L. Adler (Ed.), *Issues in cross-cultural research.* Annals of the New York Academy of Sciences, 1977, *285*, 676–686.

Zubin, J., & Spring, B. Vulnerability—A new view of schizophrenia. *Journal of Abnormal Psychology*, 1977, *86*, 103–126.

JEAN G. GRAUBERT
LEONORE LOEB ADLER

27

Attitudes toward Stigma-Related and Stigma-Free Stimuli: A Cross-National Perspective

ABSTRACT

Attitudes toward mental patients, related stimuli (attendants, psychologists), and stigma-free stimuli (volunteers, peers) were measured by a projective spatial technique, the figure-placement task. The participants were 714 English-speaking college students of both genders from eight countries: Australia, Canada, Great Britain, Israel, Hong Kong, the Philippines, South Africa, and the United States. Although gender of subject and ascribed sex of stimulus item yielded some significant differences, there was no significant difference for country. All subjects placed shortest projected distances between themselves and stigma-free items and the greatest projected distances between themselves and the most stigmatized items (mental patient and mental hospital). The similarity of results from geographically distant and culturally different countries was most likely a reflection of the powerful and universal stigmatizing effect of mental illness. Because all subjects were college students it was also possible that there was an effect of shared educational background and training that extended across national differences.

Proxemics may be conceptualized in two quite different ways. One conceptualization, following Hall (1966), is that of *personal space,* which has been variously expressed as a "bubble" each person carries around as a buffer in the interpersonal world (Horowitz, 1968), a space in which to maintain identity (Lyman & Scott, 1967), or a territory owned by the individual and defended against invasion (Ardrey, 1966). The size and shape of personal space have been shown to vary as a function of intrapersonal variables such as gender, age, personality, and culture membership (e.g.,

CROSS-CULTURAL RESEARCH AT ISSUE

Duke & Nowicki, 1972; Hayduk, 1978; Pedersen, 1973). The other conceptualization is that of *interpersonal distance,* in which stimulus characteristics of both persons interact with the social context of the situation to
determine the space between them although that space may have been
decided by only one of them. Studies of personal space emphasize territory,
protection, defense against invasion, crowding, etc. Studies of interpersonal
distance emphasize social expectancies in situations involving interpersonal
relationship, for example, degree of interaction and presence of stigma (Adler
& Graubert, 1976; Graubert & Adler, 1972; Kleck, Buck, Goller, London,
Pfeiffer, & Vukcevic, 1968; Worthington, 1974). Although there has now
been discussion of the difference between personal space and interpersonal
distance (Lecuyer, 1976; Patterson, 1975), historically this distinction was
not always made, and one was likely to find the term *personal space* used
in what was in fact a study of interpersonal distance (e.g., Little, 1965,
1968). To the extent that the stimulus object was differentiated (e.g.,
"friend," "mental patient") the terms for interpersonal distance were met,
leaving only the undifferentiated stimulus object as other in personal space
(e.g., Rodgers, 1972). As interpersonal distance was the result of an interaction between subject and object properties, it was necessary to specify
those properties for both object and subject. Kuethe (1964) described reg-
ularities in subject–object spatial relations as expressions of social schemata
which have been learned through social experience and were shared to the
extent that the experiences they represented were shared. The more fundamental the schemata the more widely they were shared and the more
independent of idiosyncratic or transitory differences among subjects. Thus
all interpersonal distance may have been seen as having had two components; the fundamental schemata were representative of large social entities
and an overlay of the individual subjects' idiosyncratic responses. The objective of all interpersonal distance research was to locate significant schemata
and to determine the degree of their generality in the social world.

Goffman (1963) suggested that the presence of a stigmatizing characteristic
resulted in avoidance of the stigmatized person by nonstigmatized others.
Interaction distance became the medium of expression of an attitude of
avoidance toward another person. In the Netherlands, Swarte (1967) reported that mental patients were almost as stigmatized as criminals and very
much more stigmatized than the physically ill. He described an attempt in
the Netherlands to reduce the stigma of mental illness by organized excur-
sions of schoolchildren to psychiatric hospitals. Barrios, Corbitt, Estes, and
Topping (1976) reported that subjects sat closer to a nonstigmatized than
to a stigmatized confederate in an interview situation. Worthington (1974)
reported a field study in which passers-by at an airport were approached

for directions by a visibly multihandicapped wheelchair occupant and an apparently nondisabled control. The interpersonal distance established by the subjects was almost twice as great from the wheelchair occupant as from the control. Kleck et al. (1968) showed that more stigma was attached to former mental patients than to persons with a variety of other disabilities. They found correspondence in their comparison between the *physical* interpersonal distance and the *projected* interpersonal distance which subjects established from stigmatized stimulus objects (ascribed epileptics). Using a similar procedure, Adler and Iverson (1974, 1975) also showed agreement between physical and projected interpersonal spacing. In several studies using the Kleck technique, Graubert and Adler (1972, 1973, 1976, 1977; Graubert, Adler, & Riva, 1974) found that stimulus items "mental patient" and "retardate" were placed at the greatest distances by high school and college students. Only those participants who did volunteer work with retardates and mental patients did not attach stigma to these two categories (Adler & Graubert, 1975).

Dosey and Meisels (1969) suggested that the increased distances subjects placed between themselves and stimulus objects reflected the use of space as a protection against threat, either to the subjects' physical integrity or to self-esteem. They reported increased distance as a response to stress in two of three experimental situations.

If the threat effect of stigma increases distance, does attraction reduce it? The evidence suggests that the relationship between attraction and spatial proximity is sufficiently well established so that interaction distance can be used as a measure of personal attraction between individuals. Little (1965) and Mehrabian (1968) found distance to be a significant index of a subject's liking for a stimulus object. A significant relationship between affect and distance was shown by Aiello and Cooper (1972). Tolor and Salafia (1971) reported less distance from stimulus objects perceived by subjects as having favorable characteristics than from those that were seen as having unfavorable characteristics.

Sex as an attraction–avoidance variable has been less stable than stigma. Kuethe and Stricker (1963) found that both women and men subjects grouped female and male stimulus objects together. Although there is some evidence for cross-sex attraction (Tolor & Salafia, 1971), most reports indicate shortest distance for female–female dyads (Adler & Iverson, 1974, 1975; Barrios et al., 1976; Dosey & Meisels, 1969; Horowitz, Duff, & Stratton, 1970; Lott & Sommer, 1967). This relates to the widely reported reduced distance from female stimulus objects regardless of the sex of the subject, which results in the most distance in male–male pairs. The complexity of gender variables with its overtones of competition and sexuality suggests that no statement of attraction–avoidance can be made without consideration of the circumstances defining the interaction.

The present study examines schemata relating to a stigmatized population: mental patients. Both gender of subject and sex of object and culture variables were included in the design in order to establish the robustness of the stigma avoidance schema.

The method used to measure projected interpersonal distance followed much of the literature on interpersonal spacing, in that a projective measure of distance was obtained by the use of symbols manipulated by the subjects. This technique measured attitudes in a way that did not need to be articulated or even recognized by the subjects and could therefore tap attitudes at variance with the subjects' verbally stated beliefs.

The subjects in the present study, both men and women, were English-speaking college students from eight countries: Australia, Canada, Great Britain (Scotland), Hong Kong, Israel, the Philippines, South Africa, and the United States. As had been pointed out by Sechrest, Fay, Zaïdi, and Flores (1973), college students, although not directly representative of a population, are highly influential members of a society and likely to have a disproportionate influence on developing social policy. The eight countries in which the study was conducted differed significantly in terms of history, culture, location, and languages. Among the eight countries, four had populations that were primarily monolingual and Western in culture; a fifth country, also Western in tradition and location, was partially bilingual. The three remaining countries were also bilingual: Two of these had a primarily Far Eastern population with a strong history of Western influence, and the third was primarily Western in major social policy although its population was a mix of Near Eastern and Western people. Social policy related to mental illness was varied even within countries that shared cultural heritages or geographic proximity. One could speculate that such differences in mental health services would contribute to differences in degree of stigma.

The following hypotheses were advanced:

1. Subjects, both men and women, from all eight countries, will place greater projected distances between themselves and stigmatized stimulus items than between themselves and neutral items.
2. Women subjects will have smaller overall distances than men subjects.
3. Subjects, men and women alike, will have greater distances from projected stimulus items of ascribed same sex than from projected stimulus items of ascribed opposite sex.
4. There will be greater similarity among monolingual subjects who share a common cultural ancestry than among bilingual subjects who do not.

Method

Subjects

A total of 714 undergraduate students participated in this research. Most of these college men and women attended introductory psychology classes at their respective colleges. Table 27.1, given in what follows, shows the geographical locations as well as the distribution of male and female participants. Most of these students were between 18 and 23 years, although a few students were some years older, and a few students were 17 years old. All the students received test booklets written in English. (Students from Hong Kong, Israel, and the Philippines, and, to some degree, French Canadian, used English language textbooks in their classes, although their primary language was not English.)

Figure-Placement Task

Projected interpersonal distances were measured (in millimeters) by means of a figure-placement task, similar to that employed by Graubert and Adler (1972, 1977), Adler and Iverson (1975), and Adler (1978). All participants were given a test booklet of 25 pages with one item per page and an instruction face sheet. The result of 11 items are reported here. In the center of each page (21.6 × 28 cm = 8½ × 11 in.) of white paper, was attached a round dot (sticker) (19 cm = ¾ in.). Across the top of each page was a sentence identifying the dot (sticker), for example, "The dot below represents a female person, who is a complete stranger, whom you have never met before." (See the Appendix for a list of all items discussed in this chapter.) The (sample) practice item "your bed" was always the first item, but all the other items were presented in randomized order. Each test booklet had a card attached with an equal number (i.e., 25) and the same type (i.e., round) and identical color dots (stickers of red or blue or any other color), identified to the subject as "your self." The instructions advised each participant to place the "self" dot "anywhere on the page." Usually data were collected during class time. All students were instructed together. They were told not to change their responses and not to leaf back through the test booklet. Some subjects received the task individually. Completion of the entire test booklet took about 10–15 minutes.

Results

Table 27.1 presents the means of the items by gender and by country. Because an analysis of variance indicated significant effects of country and

Table 27.1
Means of Items by Monolingual and Bilingual College Students: Projected Social Distance in mm

Country	N	Sex	Peer	Volun-teer ♀	Volun-teer ♂	Psychol-ogist ♀	Psychol-ogist ♂	Stranger ♀	Stranger ♂	Atten-dant ♀	Atten-dant ♂	Mental patient ♀	Mental patient ♂	Mental hospital
Australia	37	♂	29.84	7.87	32.74	39.15	64.14	28.60	54.60	32.19	62.85	58.53	67.95	75.30
Australia	40	♀	17.14	30.95	23.21	48.16	37.68	48.33	41.00	48.90	50.31	70.55	76.90	79.54
Great Britain	26	♂	22.92	16.10	26.96	31.35	44.96	16.71	51.42	39.13	53.96	53.10	61.85	64.23
Great Britain	68	♀	15.08	18.95	16.82	26.92	24.20	43.49	40.55	42.44	36.12	43.90	51.72	55.27
South Africa	18	♂	18.25	22.75	27.14	16.86	24.31	26.69	38.97	40.83	46.81	47.53	47.03	64.53
South Africa	78	♀	16.61	20.42	16.81	28.15	28.39	38.49	35.06	47.81	53.76	51.56	62.31	65.60
U.S.A.	33	♂	25.55	16.94	31.17	29.65	44.49	24.35	53.97	46.11	55.39	56.80	66.56	78.42
U.S.A.	80	♀	14.69	16.81	11.84	37.60	40.13	44.53	39.39	55.41	57.33	69.46	77.20	90.55
Canada	39	♂	28.63	21.05	32.62	27.28	35.69	26.91	45.21	40.42	47.47	54.08	68.65	66.68
Canada	39	♀	15.95	14.91	13.95	37.54	33.35	38.99	39.15	44.04	46.92	52.56	57.90	78.41
Hong Kong	41	♂	18.09	11.02	13.89	32.60	40.17	33.24	41.23	52.87	59.79	65.15	73.23	61.73
Hong Kong	58	♀	8.72	8.90	14.95	28.54	29.64	33.01	58.02	49.90	57.59	63.39	77.60	65.27
Israel	28	♂	30.02	21.20	25.43	27.20	36.77	37.45	53.61	50.18	50.50	42.14	44.04	60.68
Israel	38	♀	22.46	15.68	20.96	37.71	31.63	59.43	51.43	41.30	53.04	53.47	60.58	69.38
Philippines	36	♂	14.71	7.89	16.39	19.83	26.38	30.13	40.94	22.10	31.17	46.51	47.11	43.25
Philippines	55	♀	10.17	16.41	21.37	16.11	19.25	50.93	53.24	35.83	42.10	43.12	50.74	55.68

items, and a significant interaction between them, further analysis of the data employed the Duncan Multiple Range Test.

Hypothesis 1 was clearly confirmed. Stimulus items "male mental patient," "female mental patient," and "mental hospital" were the most distant and were always significantly ($p < .05$) different from "male volunteer," "female volunteer," or "peer," which were the closest.

Hypothesis 2 can only be partially accepted. The expectation that women will respond with smaller overall projected distances than men was the case with the stigma-free item "peer" (see Table 27.1). However, with the stigmatized item "mental hospital" the hypothesis was not confirmed. In fact, the greatest projected social distances in the present study were those by United States women subjects for the item "mental hospital."

Hypothesis 3 was also only partially accepted. A trend was apparent, especially by men subjects, for projected interpersonal distances to be greater for stimulus items with an ascription of same sex than for those with an ascription of opposite sex.

Hypothesis 4 was rejected in view of the considerable similarity of responses by both men and women of all eight countries. The remarkably parallel responses across countries for both stigma-free and stigma-laden stimulus items may be attributed to the robustness of the interpersonal variables. The similarity of the educational background of the subjects may have also contributed to this finding.

An analysis of the variance was performed to examine gender of subjects, ascribed sex of stimulus items, degree of stigma attached to stimulus items, and the eight countries. Results showed significant differences and significant interactions except for the variable countries. Further analysis (Duncan Multiple Range Test) indicated scattered significances without overall pattern for gender-related variables. For the stigma variable results were unambiguous: All subjects placed the shortest projected distances between themselves and the stigma-free items and the greatest projected distances between themselves and the stigma-laden items (see Table 27.2 for the ranking of the closest and farthest stimulus items). In the stigma-free items men subjects across countries responded similarly with less projected distance from ascribed opposite sex stimuli than from same sex stimuli. The greatest similarity across countries was that shown by women subjects for the item "mental hospital."

The clearest finding of the current research was the impressive similarity of responses across countries. Although the means varied somewhat the overall trends were the same in each country.

Figure 27.1 shows stigma-laden items (male and female "mental patient") and stigma-free items (male and female "volunteer"). Three categories of distance were found: *near*, which included the stigma-free items "peer" and

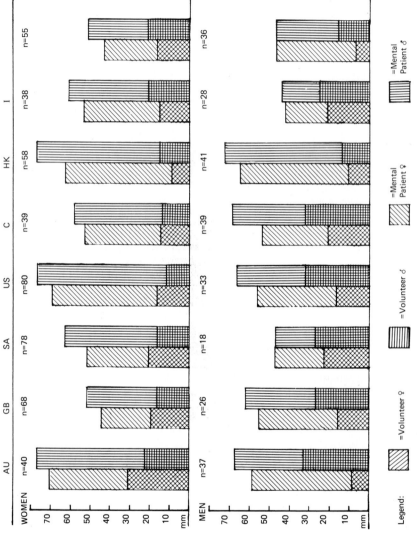

Figure 27.1. Women and men college students' mean projected interpersonal distance responses.

Table 27.2

Ranking of Closest and Farthest Projected Social Distance for Stigma-Free and Stigma-Related Items

Country	Closest	Farthest
	Women	
Australia	Peer	Mental hospital
Great Britain	Peer	Mental hospital
South Africa	Peer	Mental hospital
U.S.A.	Volunteer ♂	Mental hospital
Canada	Volunteer ♂	Mental hospital
Hong Kong	Peer	Mental patient ♂
Israel	Volunteer ♀	Mental hospital
Philippines	Peer	Mental hospital
	Men	
Australia	Volunteer ♀	Mental hospital
Great Britain	Volunteer ♀	Mental hospital
South Africa	Psychologist ♀	Mental hospital
U.S.A.	Volunteer ♀	Mental hospital
Canada	Volunteer ♀	Mental patient ♂
Hong Kong	Volunteer ♀	Mental patient ♂
Israel	Volunteer ♀	Mental hospital
Philippines	Volunteer ♀	Mental patient ♂

"volunteers;" *far,* which included "mental patients" and "mental hospital"; and *intermediary,* which included "psychologists" and "attendants" and same-sex "strangers." Although the size of the means varied, there was considerable agreement among subjects in the ordering of distances.

Discussion

Cross-cultural research recognizes that while the discovery of differences may be significant, the findings of similarities may provide even more meaningful information
                                   —ADLER (1977, p. 1)

The present study found no significant differences among the eight countries in the response to stigma-free and stigma-laden stimulus items. All groups responded with close projected distances from stigma-free items and large projected distances from stigma-laden items. In a previous study (Adler & Graubert, 1976) the similarity of the responses by college student subjects from four countries was attributed to the fact that the countries shared both a common language and Western culture. The present study added four countries with more than one language and different historical and cultural roots. Despite this diversity, the projected social schemata were similar in all groups studied. Adler (1978), reporting in a twin study with the same subjects, suggested that the common basis for the similar responses across countries may have been—in part—the use of the English language for the administration of the tasks. All subjects were university students who were familiar with English language textbooks and scientific journals. On the other hand, stigma-laden stimuli may have been universally aversive, transcending differences of language and culture.

The conclusions that may be drawn from the present research are as follows:

1. College students of both genders and from diverse cultures responded to stigma-laden stimulus objects with a large projected social spacing that appeared to express avoidance behavior.
2. Monolingual and bilingual English-reading subjects responded similarly.
3. Even with a subject-pool drawn from university psychology classes, the psychiatric patient labeling resulted in significant stigmatization.

In 1966, Jones warned of the danger of population stigma to the future of the mental health movement:

> The general public will readily assent to the proposition that the mental health services should be improved or that psychiatric patients should be treated with kindness, but lip service does not lead to action. Intellect pulls one way; emotion the other. This is where the stigma of mental disorder begins. . . . Fear may be projected in the form of aggression against those who provoke it: the patient, the therapist, and the institution [p. 15].

The current findings do not indicate a change in attitude since these words were written. In the United States the present social policy of decentralization of psychiatric treatment centers and briefer institutionalizations of mental patients increases the presence of mental patients in the community at large. Hostile responses by American communities to the proposed halfway houses, treatment centers, and group homes is commonplace. The present study suggests that the stigmatization of mental patients may be widespread internationally and includes people educated in psychology at the university level. It is hoped that the magnitude of this problem will lead to investigation into the efficacy of intervention techniques and an eventual reduction in the stigma associated with psychiatric disorders.

Appendix: Twelve Projected Social Distance Items for the Cross-Cultural Study

The dot (sticker) below represents . . .

Practice item:	1. your bed.
Anchor items:	2. another student of the same sex and age as you yourself (*peer*).
	3&4. a female/male person, who is a complete *stranger*, whom you have never met before.
Experimental items:	5&6. a female/male volunteer student who works in the same place where you work.
	6&7. a female/male psychologist working in a hospital.
	8&9. a female/male attendant in a mental hospital.
	10&11. a female/male mental patient.
	12. a mental hospital.

Acknowledgments

The authors would like to thank the following people for their participation and cooperation: Nick Ciaccio, American University in Cairo, Egypt (whose filled-in test booklets were unfortunately lost in a mail embargo before they could be measured and analyzed); John L. M. Dawson and Erik Kvan, Department of Psychology, University of Hong Kong; Morris Eagle, Department of Psychology, York University, Toronto, Canada; Virgilo Enriquez and Divina G. Rabanal, Department of Psychology, University of the Philippines, Philippines; Sol Kugelmass, Department of Psychology, Hebrew University of Jerusalem, Israel; John W. Mann, and his assistant, A. Zimbar, Department of Psychology, University of the Witwatersrand, South Africa; Helmut Morsbach, Department of Psychology, University of Glasgow, Great Britain; and Roger Russell, and Leon Mann, Department of Psychology, Flinders University of South Australia, Australia.

In addition, the authors wish to thank Helmut E. Adler, Department of Psychology, Yeshiva University, and his undergraduate students, Paul Brody, Samuel Schwarzmer, David Seidman, Richard Shefter, and Eli Turkel, for their help in the construction of the test booklets and the measurement of the data. Also, the investigators would like to express their appreciation to doctoral candidates in the Department of Psychology at Adelphi University John Southard and Paula Post, for their help with the computer analyses of the data.

References

Adler, L. L. A plea for interdisciplinary cross-cultural research: Some introductory remarks. In L. L. Adler (Ed.), *Issues in cross-cultural research.* Annals of the New York Academy of Sciences, 1977, *285,* 1–2.

Adler, L. L. The effects of calm and emotional behavior on projected social distances: A cross-cultural comparison. *International Journal of Group Tensions,* 1978, *8*(1 & 2), 49–63.

Adler, L. L., & Graubert, J. G. Projected social distances from mental patient-related items by male and female volunteers and nonvolunteers. *Psychological Reports,* 1975, *37,* 515–521.

Adler, L. L., & Graubert, J. G. Projected social distances from mental patient-related stimuli in cross-national perspective: Four English speaking countries. *International Journal of Group Tensions,* 1976, *6*(3 & 4), 15–25.

Adler, L. L., & Iverson, M. A. Interpersonal distance as a function of task difficulty, praise, status orientation, and sex of partner. *Perceptual and Motor Skills,* 1974, *39,* 683–692.

Adler, L. L., & Iverson, M. A. Projected social distance as a function of praise conditions and status orientation: A comparison with physical interpersonal spacing in the laboratory. *Perceptual and Motor Skills,* 1975, *41,* 659–664.

Aiello, J. R., & Cooper, R. E. The use of personal space as a function of social affect. *Proceedings of the 80th Annual Convention of the American Psychological Association,* 1972, *7,* 207–208.

Ardrey, R. *The territorial imperative.* New York: Dell, 1966.

Barrios, B. A., Corbitt, L. C., Estes, J. P., & Topping, J. S. Effect of a social stigma on interpersonal distance. *Psychological Record,* 1976, *26,* 343–348.

Dosey, M. A., & Meisels, M. Personal space and self protection. *Journal of Personality and Social Psychology,* 1969, *11,* 93–97.

Duke, M. P., & Nowicki, S. A new measure of social learning model for interpersonal distance. *Journal of Experimental Research in Personality,* 1972, *6,* 119–132.

Goffman, E. *Behavior in public places.* New York: Free Press, 1963.

Graubert, J. G., & Adler, L. L. Comparisons between volunteers and nonvolunteers of projected social distances from mental patient-related stimuli. *Proceedings of the 80th Annual Convention of the American Psychological Association,* 1972, *8,* 209–210.

Graubert, J. G., & Adler, L. L. *PSD as a measure of attitudes toward mental patient-related stimulus items; A study of projected social distance.* Paper presented at the 36th annual meeting of the New York State Psychological Association, New York, April 1973.

Graubert, J. G., & Adler, L. L. *Projected social distances as cross-cultural measures of attitudes toward mental patient-related stimuli.* Paper presented at the 5th annual meeting of the Society for Cross-Cultural Research, New York, February 1976.

Graubert, J. G., & Adler, L. L. Cross-national comparisons of projected social distances from mental patient-related stimuli. *Perceptual and Motor Skills,* 1977, *44,* 881–882.

Graubert, J. G., Adler, L. L., & Riva, M. *Projected social distances (PSD) as a measure of female high school students' attitudes toward mental patient-related stimulus items.* Paper presented at the 45th annual meeting of the Eastern Psychological Association, Philadelphia, April 1974.

Hall, E. T. *The hidden dimension.* New York: Doubleday, 1966.

Hayduk, L. A. Personal space: An evaluative and orienting overview. *Psychological Bulletin,* 1978, *85*(1), 117–134.

Horowitz, M. J. Spacial behavior and psychopathology. *Journal of Nervous and Mental Diseases,* 1968, *146,* 24–35.

Horowitz, M. J., Duff, D. F., & Stratton, L. O. Personal space and the body buffer zone. In

H. M. Proshansky, W. H. Ittelson, & L. G. Rivlin (Eds.), *Environmental psychology: Man and his physical setting.* New York: Holt, Rinehart & Winston, 1970.

Jones, K. British experience in community care. In H. P. David (Ed.), *International trends in mental health.* New York: McGraw-Hill, 1966.

Kleck, R., Buck, P. L., Goller, W. L., London, R. S., Pfeiffer, J. R., & Vukcevic, D. P. Effect of stigmatizing conditions on the use of personal space. *Psychological Reports,* 1968, *23,* 111–118.

Kuethe, J. L. Pervasive influence of social schemata. *Journal of Abnormal and Social Psychology,* 1964, *68,* 248–254.

Kuethe, J. L., & Stricker, G. Man and woman: Social schemata of males and females. *Psychological Reports,* 1963, *13,* 655–661.

Lecuyer, R. Psychosociologie de l'espace, II: Rapports spatiaux interpersonnels et la notion d' "espace personnel." *Année Psychologique,* 1976, *76,* 563–596.

Little, K. B. Personal space. *Journal of Experimental Social Psychology,* 1965, *1,* 237–247.

Little, K. B. Cultural variations in social schemata. *Journal of Personality and Social Psychology,* 1968, *10,* 1–7.

Lott, D. F., & Sommer, R. Seating arrangements and status. *Journal of Personality and Social Psychology,* 1967, *7,* 90–95.

Lyman, S. M., & Scott, M. B. Territoriality: A neglected sociological dimension. *Social Problems,* 1967, *15,* 236–249.

Mehrabian, A. Relationship of attitude to seated posture, orientation, and distance. *Journal of Personality and Social Psychology,* 1968, *10,* 26–30.

Patterson, M. L. Personal space: Time to burst the bubble? *Man–Environment Systems,* 1975, *5,* 67.

Pedersen, D. M. Predictions of behavioral personal space from simulated personal space. *Perceptual and Motor Skills,* 1973, *37,* 808–813.

Rodgers, J. A. Relationship between sociability and personal space preference of two different times of day. *Perceptual and Motor Skills,* 1972, *35,* 519–526.

Sechrest, L., Fay, T., Zaidi, H., & Flores, L. Attitudes toward mental disorder among college students in the United States, Pakistan and the Philippines. *Journal of Cross-Cultural Psychology,* 1973, *4,* 342–360.

Swarte, J. H. Stereotypes and attitudes about the mentally ill. In H. Freeman (Ed.), *Progress in mental health,* New York: Grune & Stratton, 1967.

Tolor, A., & Salafia, W. R. The social schemata technique as a projective device, *Psychological Reports,* 1971, *28,* 423–429.

Worthington, M. E. Personal space as a function of the stigma effect. *Environment & Behavior,* 1974, *6,* 289–291.

VICTOR D. SANUA **28**

War Bereavement in
the United States and Israel

ABSTRACT

During the 1973–1974 academic year the author was spending his sabbatical leave in Israel when the Yom Kippur War broke out. He interviewed 30 families who had lost a son or a husband during that short war. Upon his return to the United States he conducted similar interviews with 20 families of soldiers who had died in Vietnam. The interviews assessed their reaction to their loss and how they were coping with their tragedy.

In Israel, a "town major" and a team from the community announce the death to the family and the army takes full responsibility for the burial. In the United States, one or two casualty officers visit the home, make the announcement, and stay with the family until relatives arrive. A telegram is mailed confirming the death and, a few days later, another telegram is sent informing of the arrival of the body. Burial arrangements are made by the family with the assistance of the military. In Israel, Yad Labanim, a semigovernmental organization, provides support to the family. Self-help groups in the United States, such as Gold Star Mothers and Gold Star Wives, were organized well before the war in Vietnam but they never acquired official status. Parents and wives in Israel visit cemeteries rather regularly, and fathers give a free expression to their sorrow. In the United States fathers express their sorrow less openly. More of the soldiers in Israel had young children, and mothers had to cope with children's questions. Loss of a loved one, both in Israel and the United States, did not seem to influence religious attitude. In the United States, a belief in life after death was more commonly held than in Israel. In Israel, death of a soldier was more acceptable because of the security the military provided the rest of the population. Jewish families gave the name of the dead soldiers to the newborns. They could describe in very great detail the events that led to the death of the soldier, information that was not readily available to the American bereaved. Both in Israel and in the United States, pictures of the deceased are displayed, as well as memorabilia. In Israel families print books on the deceased.

CROSS-CULTURAL RESEARCH AT ISSUE

In October 1973, I was spending my sabbatical in Israel working in the psychiatric division at Tel Hashomer Hospital when the Yom Kippur War commenced. Having enjoyed a relatively peaceful existence since the War of Attrition, Israel found herself again in a war with a high number of casualties—almost 3,000 dead and 10,000 wounded. It was a unique opportunity for a visitor to see how a small nation mobilized herself for survival and took steps to cope with the tragedy of bereaved families and maimed youth. What prompted this research on the bereaved was the tragic sight of an old couple, survivors of the Holocaust, who had remarried in Israel and who had lost their son in the Yom Kippur War.

Immediately after the war, I started interviewing psychiatrists, psychologists, social workers, and volunteers who were providing psychological assistance to bereaved families during the critical period. A report on these interviews and a study of the social services mobilized during the emergency are the subject of a monograph (Sanua, 1974). At a later period, I interviewed bereaved parents and widows of soldiers who had died in the Yom Kippur War.

Following my return to the United States, a year later, I decided to interview parents and wives of soldiers who were killed in action in Vietnam. A detailed report (Sanua, 1977) was prepared on the basis of interviews with about 50 bereaved families, in the United States (20 cases) and in Israel (30 cases). This report includes verbatim remarks made by these families in the course of these interviews. The question at issue pertains to the discernible differences in war bereavement emanating from the Vietnam War in the United States and the Yom Kippur War in Israel.

There are important differences in the two situations that could easily result in dissimilar psychological responses. The Yom Kippur War theatened Israel's very existence, and the front was close to the heart of the country. On the other hand, U.S. servicemen were in a war far removed from the United States, and the purpose of the war was not very clear to many families. In Israel, there were also major differences between the 1967 and 1973 wars. In 1967, the Israelis attacked, the war was over in a week, and relatively few casualties were suffered. The mood of the country at that time was one of elation. In 1973, the Israelis were caught by surprise and sustained serious losses over the course of 19 days of fighting. The seriousness of these losses becomes even clearer in light of the fact that an estimated 25% of the casualties were officers.

An exhaustive search of the literature indicates that systematic studies on war bereavement have not been published, or, apparently, ever undertaken in the United States. Studies have been conducted with families of soldiers missing in action and families of soldiers who had been prisoners of war.

Confirmation of the total lack of research on families of the war bereaved was received in a letter from Captain Hamilton I. McCubbin, Head of the Family Studies Branch of the Center for Prisoner of War Studies of the Naval Health Research Center at San Diego, who wrote:

> Our interest in your work stems from, as you might have expected, our work with families of servicemen missing in action and returned prisoners of war. We were, for the most part, functioning in isolation and were unaware of other research. The emergence of your work and the importance of your endeavor touches us because of its similarity both in findings and emphasis.

The efforts to glean information on the war bereaved from the Department of Defense were not successful, as evidenced by the following letter received from the Chief of the Scientific and Technical Information Office: "The MEDLARS (Medical Literature Analysis and Retrieval System) data base contains citations from the more than 2200 journals indexed in the Index Medicus. Only one citation specifically refers to war-related bereavement: . . ." That single reference was Palgi (1974), an Israeli anthropologist already known to me.

In this chapter, I shall delineate some of the major differences between the United States and Israel pertaining to war bereavement. Most of the material has been derived from my interviews with bereaved families in both countries. From the very outset, a major difference was between the ease with which I was able to obtain names of the bereaved in Israel and the difficulties I encountered in obtaining names of the bereaved in the United States, where, for reasons of confidentiality, government agencies such as the Department of Defense and the Veterans Administration, as well as private organizations, were unwilling to provide names. Most of the 20 cases that were interviewed in the United States were obtained through personal contact. In Israel, a complete listing of the bereaved is kept by Yad Labanim, an organization founded after the War of Independence and supported by government funds, whose main function is to take responsibility in handling the interests of the bereaved families. Names were also obtained from the Ministry of Defense in Israel through their Office of Rehabilitation. This office is a repository of papers, monographs, and printed material pertaining to war bereavement in Israel. A list of references is published periodically.

In view of the nonsystematic selection of bereaved relatives, it would not be appropriate to conduct a statistical analysis of the responses for the purpose of generalization. This research was conducted as a pilot study to provide background information on the problems faced by bereaved parents and wives so that a more adequate study could be conducted in the future to provide directions with better instruments. A random sample could be interviewed more systematically. In view of the fact that there are no studies available in this area, it was felt such a pioneering effort could be useful for future research.

In both Israel and the United States relatives were asked to provide information about the soldier who had lost his life in combat—his history and personality, about their reaction when they heard the news of his death, and about the aftermath of the tragedy, particularly their mourning. They were asked to free-associate. At the beginning of the interview, the interviewer asked questions to clarify a number of points in the family's initial statement, and, subsequently, whenever it was felt that important content was left out, specific questions were asked to elicit new information. All answers were recorded verbatim.

In the United States, the bereaved, in general, indicated that the serviceman leaving for Vietnam hardly ever expressed fear or concern about the dangers involved in going to war. The families assumed that the servicemen did not want them to worry. However, many families indicated that in retrospect they remembered a number of incidents that might have reflected the soldiers' fears of not returning. They noted that some went to familiar places before their departure; some revealed their fears to nonfamily members. A few parents and widows felt guilty that they had not tried to elicit the expression of such fears. Even while the soldiers were in Vietnam, letters were more likely to deemphasize the war and present a favorable picture of their situation, expressing optimism about returning home to the United States.

Despite the great controversy surrounding the Vietnam War, there was in general little discussion of its political aspects during the interviews. Relatives concentrated on the loss of their loved ones. However, during the interviews two families who belonged to the Gold Star Mothers for Amnesty expressed very strong feelings about the war. One mother later sent me a seven-page letter in which she expressed in very strong terms her feelings about the war and the significance of the loss of her son. One father, a prominent businessman, began draft evasion counseling after his son's death. Realizing that his son could have benefited before his death from the same counseling nearly destroyed the man with guilt. The sad fact for such parents is their feeling that the war and their loss were meaningless and unnecessary. This is an enormous burden to live with, and each parent struggled to cope with the anger. Most of the families interviewed, particularly the military families, felt that the United States was justified in being in Vietnam. In no interview, however, was there an expression of hate toward Vietnamese as individuals; rather, the anger was directed at the Communists.

In general, the parents were proud of their sons. However, one mother showed concern that the children of the deceased servicemen were negatively influenced by the controversy about the Vietnam War: Whereas children of those who died in World War II had been proud of their fathers, children of those who died in the Vietnam War might try to conceal the information that their father died in Southeast Asia. She wondered about the effects of this inhibition on the children's self-image.

As has already been mentioned, there were differences between the approaches used in Israel and the United States to inform the families. The government of Israel, mindful of the pervasive grief among the families directly involved, and the effect on the morale of the nation as a whole, has developed various services for informing and assisting families. In Israel no telegram is sent to the next-of-kin to inform them that a serviceman has been killed or is missing in action. Instead, the news is transmitted by a team especially selected for this purpose. Teams have been set up in every city, town, and kibbutz. Each is headed by the "town major" (the military representative who handles civilian matters for soldiers). It is to this team that the casualty information is sent. The team's first action is to determine the state of health of members of the soldier's family. Friends and neighbors of the bereaved are approached in order to evolve an appropriate, personal way of breaking the news that will ease the shock. When medical complications are anticipated, a doctor is included as a member of the team.

In the case of the Yom Kippur War, the families were later seen by volunteers from groups organized by the Ministry of Defense to provide psychological assistance during the emergency. In contrast to procedures in the United States, the army takes full responsibility for the burial of the deceased soldiers. The practice is to bury the soldier immediately after his death, following proper identification, and later to remove the body and bury it in a military cemetery close to the family's home.

In the United States, procedures also followed a general pattern, although there were differences depending upon which service was involved. One or two soldiers visited the home of the bereaved to notify the family of the death of the serviceman. It was customary that one of these soldiers have a rank the same as or higher than that of the soldier who was killed. Usually, the soldiers had minimum information regarding the circumstances of the death. They remained with the immediate family until other members of the family arrived. A telegram was sent following the initial visit, confirming the death and providing some clarification. A few days later, another telegram was sent, informing the family as to the time of arrival of the body. A casualty officer visited the family to arrange for the burial. The family selected the undertaker, and indicated whether or not they wanted a military funeral.

It should be noted that the time between the actual death and the return of the body depended entirely upon the number of casualties in Vietnam during that particular week, as planes had to carry a full load before they flew to the United States. The usual terminology in the United States is "remains" of the soldier. One father I interviewed strongly objected to this terminology. According to army regulations, telegrams had to be read to the bereaved family. The initial telegram usually read as follows: "Time ——— To: ——— The Secretary of the Army has asked me to express his deep regret that your son (husband) ——— died in Vietnam on ———. Please accept our deepest sympathy ——— (Signed) ———." At a later period, bereaved families received a number of letters offering condolences, including one from the Chief of Staff, which read as follows:

> Dear Mr. & Mrs ———
>
> Please accept my deepest sympathy in the loss of your son (husband) on (date) in Vietnam.
>
> I know that the passing of a loved one is one of life's most tragic moments, but sincerely hope that you will find some measure of comfort in knowing that your son (husband) served his Nation with honor. His devoted service was in the finest traditions of American soldiers who on other battlefields and in other times of national peril have given the priceless gift of life to safeguard the blessings of freedom for their loved ones and for future generations. In Vietnam today brave Americans are defending the rights of men to choose their own destiny and to live in dignity and freedom.
>
> All members of the United States Army join in sharing your burden of grief.
>
> Sincerely,
> s/
> Chief of Staff

Another procedure was to ask the family to designate one or two friends of the deceased in the service who could accompany the body home from Vietnam. If the army was able to locate one of the friends, arrangements were made for him to escort the body, but he returned to Vietnam immediately after the burial.

The casualty officer went with the family to a funeral home to arrange for the burial. Some coffins arrived sealed and could not be seen by the family because of the condition of the body. In all cases the body was embalmed and prepared for burial prior to arrival at the undertaker. Some bereaved parents and widows saw the body; others did not, preferring to remember their loved one as they had last seen him. One mother supplied a friend with a picture of the dead soldier so that he could identify the body. Many expressed some faint hope that there might have been some mistake, but their illusions were shattered when the death of the dear one was confirmed. One mother described her son as an "inflated mannequin with a lot of make-up." One wife was distressed to see that her husband was wearing a uniform of a rather poor quality. She insisted that he be dressed with his regular ceremonial uniform and polished brass buttons. She felt that because her husband was fastidious, he would have wanted to be buried in his best uniform.

In the United States attempts have been made to organize the bereaved through private auspices. Two groups call themselves Gold Star Mothers and Gold Star Wives of America, Inc. Following World War II, widows and parents of deceased servicemen started such organizations for the purpose of helping solve some of their problems. One objective was to pressure the government to pass legislation in the interest of the bereaved. However, such organizations never acquired official status and tended to be primarily paper organizations.

In short, it appears that the war bereaved in Israel are of serious concern to the Israeli government, whereas the war bereaved in the United States are very much on their own, except that they receive pensions and education for the children. This lack of concern with the war bereaved was reflected in a letter received from a widow who had consented to be interviewed. She wrote: "I know that research cannot be done without cooperation, and to the best of my knowledge, it is the first time that anyone has shown an interest in the families of those killed in action."

Surprisingly, very few families in the United States seem to visit the cemetery on a regular basis. One mother who was interviewed stands out in this regard; she has continued to visit the burial site every other week for the last 9 years. In contrast, the bulk of the families visit on special days, for example, on Memorial Day or on a birthday.

In Israel, the bereaved tend to visit the cemeteries more frequently. One father said that he would continue visiting his son's grave until such time as his legs could no longer carry him. In general, the bereaved in Israel gave a much freer rein to their grief than in the United States. The following comments were made by Israeli parents during the interviews:

It is very hard; every minute I have souvenirs. After the younger died, the older consoled me. I can't say, God, Why did you do this to me? Like pigeons, both were taken away. We are left impotent, infirm, loss of a child is the greatest loss in the world. It is better for a mother to die; otherwise, she dies ten times a day. A child can live without a mother, but a mother cannot live without her child.

The first time I went out of the house, everything was the same, but it was so different for me. I could not move with the world. Life goes on as usual; I resented it. I wanted to stand on the top of the mountain, so that I could say, "My son is dead, everybody should hear it."

A father who had not been able to work since the death of his son expressed his grief in the following way:

> I cannot explain in any language or book, how I feel about my son. Nobody can describe it in any language. We live in an undescribable pain, the mind cannot conceive. We speak and this is not natural. My son was the eyes of the family and they are gone with his death.

Another expressed his grief in the following words:

> I have died a million deaths since I lost my son. My wife had greater inner strength than me, she had the ability to concentrate on her two daughters. I still need my son; nothing will ever replace him. The mother's reaction may be deeper but who can assess pain.

The two fathers who expressed such deep sorrow came from totally different cultural and educational backgrounds. The former was a policeman, the latter was an intellectual.

Whereas Israeli fathers, as well as Israeli mothers, expressed great sorrow, fathers in the United States seem to have been more in control of themselves during the agonizing moments. However, two fathers in the United States died shortly after the death of their sons, and these deaths may have been precipitated by grief. An Israeli bereaved mother who had helped me contact the families in Eilat emphasized the general sorrow in Israel in a letter which she mailed to me in the United States, and which reads as follows: "I hope your work goes well, and it will help us all, in our work with bereaving people. Sometimes, I really stand and do not find the way to go to the heart of my fellow-people. The grief grows with the time going on. . . ."

In Israel, the announcement of the death of a soldier is complicated by the presence of young children. Approximately 75% of the Israelis who died were married and had children. The percentage was much smaller in the United States, as the servicemen were younger.

During these interviews I discussed religion and the belief in life after death, to examine how these factors interacted with bereavement. The expectation was that the loss of a loved one would instill a stronger religious feeling in the family. However, it seems that the effect of the loss depended more or less on the family's attitude toward religion prior to the tragedy. Those who were religious would tend to remain so, or become more religious. In general, in contrast to Israeli families, most families in the United States felt that there is life after death. Some who questioned this possibility prior to the tragedy indicated that they had changed their minds. One parent pointed out, "Could not make up my mind, so I stopped worrying about it. Now I believe in life after death since it makes the mourning easier."

One American mother pointed out that her son is spiritually present because she could not "make it" otherwise. One mother whose husband had died 2 years after their son, stated that when their son was killed her husband had bemoaned the fact that he would have to wait 20 years to see his son, so firmly did he believe in life after death. The mother assumed that in his eagerness to see his son in the next life, he pushed himself to hasten his death.

In the Jewish tradition, it would appear that very little is said about the existence of a soul after death; there does not seem to be a formal religious belief in this area. I asked all of the bereaved relatives in Israel whether they believed in life after death. Reflecting probably the religious tenets of their group, practically all of the bereaved indicated that there is no life after death. Practically all of the bereaved families interviewed in Israel indicated that they were not religious and did not believe in life after death. One mother, however, indicated that it would have been easier if she believed in life after death, and she was jealous of those who did.

In Israel, there were efforts on the part of the bereaved to make the death more acceptable. They felt that their loved ones had lost their lives for a good cause. As one mother said, "We are alive because they are dead." Another mother pointed out that it is easier when a son dies in war than in an accident. In a number of instances, in keeping with the Jewish tradition, the name of the deceased was given to a newborn baby in the family, as if he were reborn symbolically.

In the United States, parents and wives could not provide detailed description as to how their sons or husbands had died. Probably the distance of the theater of war would have made such efforts difficult. Furthermore, none of the families I interviewed had received visits from other soldiers who might have witnessed the death of their loved one, and this might have been primarily a function of the size of the United States as compared to Israel. Israeli families, on the other hand, were quite familiar with the events leading to the death of their loved one, and some had even detailed maps of the area where they had fallen. One father showed me an album with specific details of the battle movements in which his son had been killed. Obviously, it was very easy for some of these parents to visit the very ground where their loved one had fallen.

Families in the United States displayed in the home pictures of the deceased and in some cases the flag that had covered the coffin. A few families had prepared albums of pictures taken during basic training in the United States. In Israel, the bereaved had many more memorabilia on exhibit to perpetuate the memory of the deceased. One way to perpetuate the memory of the fallen is to write a small commemorative book about him. A bereaved family in a kibbutz displayed books which were published, not only for those who died in the war, but also for those who died in accidents or of natural deaths. Some were quite elaborate and professionally bound. The Ministry of Defense provides the funds to the families who wish to prepare a commemorative book for their son and maintains an up-to-date directory of such books. In some Israeli homes there were displays of army insignia, medals, and pictures, sometimes with a permanent light. In a few instances the room of the deceased was left intact. Most kibbutzim and moshavim have a special room set aside to memorialize their dead.

Summary and Conclusions

Originally, we had some misgivings regarding our interviews since they would bring back unpleasant memories. However, as we proceeded, we noted that both in the United States and Israel, parents and wives appeared to derive some solace in discussing their bereavement; the discussion seemed to have a cathartic effect. Often interviews lasted longer than expected and there were invitations to return if need be. One Israeli mother indicated that she wished she had the opportunity to talk about her son everyday.

The purpose of this chapter was to provide a number of impressions derived from interviews with 50 war-bereaved families in the United States and Israel. The death of a serviceman represents a great ordeal to the family, and a study of this ordeal, at least in the United States, has not been undertaken. In this chapter we included only some of the highlights of the tragedy these families have endured and the manner in which the news of the death was communicated. The mourning process—"initial guilt, anger, pain, emancipation, relief, anxiety, reactivation of all conflicts, helplessness, somatic complaints, denial and absence of emotion [Siggins, 1967]"—tends to be quite individual and is heavily influenced by cultural, educational, religious, and socioeconomic variables as well as political outlook. With one single exception, all families interviewed had been able to work through their grief and to proceed with the business of living. It is evident that more data is greatly needed; in particular a larger population should be surveyed, controlling for education, cultural background, religion, and socioeconomic status to determine how these variables affect the mourning process.

There is no question of the need to mitigate the acute suffering of the bereaved and to deal with long-term problems encountered by the surviving relatives—such as bringing up children without fathers. This chapter has been a modest attempt to study the aftermaths of wars, which rarely receive headlines, as they affect individuals who find themselves caught in a treadmill of ever-alternating war and peace.

References

Palgi, P. Socio-cultural expressions and implications of death, mourning, and bereavement in Israel arising out of the war situation. *Israel Annals of Psychiatry and Related Disciplines*, 1973, *2*, 301–329.

Sanua, V. *War stress and bereavement: A report on the social and psychological services in Israel during the Yom Kippur War*. Mimeographed report. (Summary in *New York State Psychologist*, 3 issues, Dec. 1973, June 1974, Aug. 1974.)

Sanua, V. *Coping with war bereavement in the United States and Israel*. Paper presented at the convention of the World Federation for Mental Health, Vancouver, Canada, August 1977.

Siggins, L. D. Mourning: A critical survey of the literature. *International Journal of Psychiatry*, 1967, *3*, 418–432.

Epilogue
An Exaltation of
Cross-Cultural Research:
The Nature and Habits of
the Hyphenated Elephant

When Leonore Loeb Adler invited me to write an epilogue for this book, the time of reckoning was just far enough away for me to agree to do it. Since that time, I have had some second thoughts. I looked up the exact meaning of the word *epilogue* in the dictionary and discovered that it is a "speech, usually in verse, delivered by one of the actors after the conclusion of a play." Right then and there I knew my epilogue could not be verse. I took some solace in discovering, while passing other entries in the dictionary, that I was not going to deliver myself of an epidemic either, but solace was not enough.

I therefore turned to examine the diverse chapters that make up this book and realized that it would be a long time before such a galaxy of stars in this field would be seen together again. I know that while the cross-cultural research presented here was exalted, the problems of integration of the different approaches are truly formidable. Hence my title. Let us look at it in some detail.

First, *exaltation*—I am using that word as a venereal term. I refer here not to sexual activity or disease, but rather to its meaning as a collective, employed by noblemen early in the seventeenth century to refer to the game they hunted. These terms of venery are collectives that refer to groups of animals. For example, a group of larks is called an "exaltation of larks," which provided the title of a book on the subject of venereal terms, *An Exaltation of Larks*, by James Lipton. So I thought that, just for a lark, I might use that term to describe a collection of chapters on cross-cultural

CROSS-CULTURAL RESEARCH AT ISSUE

research. Happily, the term *exaltation* also means an uplifting and so I hope that there will not be too many objections. I am aware that the term *cross-cultural* is perhaps even more in need of definition than the term *exaltation*, but clearly my attempt to mediate in that sea of contradictory statements is more than any reader would care to see.

That brings us to the term *elephant*. Now everybody is aware of what an elephant is, and many probably much better than I. Nevertheless, I must point out that my elephant is not to be taken literally, but figuratively. I am referring to the elephant and the blind people who are examining it in an effort to describe it. As most know, one of the blind people finds the elephant to be a snake, one a wall, one a pillar, and so on.

My object in portraying the elephant as hyphenated is to call your attention to the fact that the cross-cultural elephant is still more difficult to describe than the simple single-word elephant. And, of course, my blind investigators find the elephant to be a hyphen.

So while all of the accredited experts in the area of cross-cultural research have discussed the elephant as pillar, snake, and wall, I intend to describe the cross-cultural elephant as connective tissue. What is this connective tissue? For me it is a body of theory necessary to integrate the interesting but as yet splintered body of research.

I find behavior theory stemming from Skinner's work admirably suited for integration. Most important in this theory is the concept of the reinforcement contingency. This concept states that much of our behavior, if not all (technically we call it operant behavior), is of the nature of being controlled by its consequences. The formula is the following: Behavior occurs on particular occasions with specific consequences. Thus, on an occasion when I am asked to give a talk, I speak into a microphone and my response is strengthened by avoiding the shouts from the audience of "louder" or "speak into the microphone, you dummy," as well as by the positive reinforcers given to me by some members of the audiences (who are not my mother) for previous talks. Essentially I am suggesting that much of people's behavior, like that of other animals, is controlled by the classes of stimuli that precede and the classes of stimuli that follow that behavior. We need to add to this that behavior too is conceived of in terms of classes.

The usual definition of a culture is to describe it as consisting of the behavior patterns of people at a particular time and place that distinguishes their behavior from the behavior of other groups. Furthermore, the behavior in question includes both what people do, and what people say they do or say they ought to do. For all these classes of behavior (verbal and nonverbal) the same triumvirate of concepts relates: the occasion for the response, the response itself, and the consequence of the emission of the response on the particular occasion.

To examine behavioral patterns in different cultures, we must view them in the context of the preceding and the following events. Thus, in our society, whereas it is considered quite normal to get undressed in a bathroom before taking a shower, one is likely to be sent for an extensive psychiatric examination if found getting undressed, in exactly the same way, on Times Square in the middle of New York City; furthermore, taking a shower with one's clothing on will also make people suspect one's sanity.

Let us look at an example of the cross-cultural problem presented in a chapter of this book. Gurland and Zubin (Chapter 26) describe their work on diagnosis of dementia versus functional disorder in the aged, in the United States and the United Kingdom. In earlier work along the same lines, they found that hospitals in the United Kingdom admitted twice as many patients with affective psychoses as with schizophrenia, whereas hospitals in the United States admitted twice as many schizophrenics as patients suffering from affective psychoses. Zubin and Gurland investigated whether the cause of this difference is ascribable to the behavior of the patients or of the psychiatrists. Their analysis showed that the difference inheres in the psychiatrists' behavior.

A reinforcement-contingency analysis would ask, first of all, about the kinds of behaviors that bring patients into the hospitals, for example, violent behavior committed against persons in the public light as opposed to such behavior against relatively unknown persons. Second, it would ask what kinds of behaviors in the patients would elicit certain diagnoses from different psychiatrists, for example, the patient's inadequacy in terms of problem-solving ability as opposed to feelings expressed. Third, it would ask about the stimuli that the psychiatric interviewer presents to the patient to respond to, and thus to be classified in a particular way. Furthermore, for each of these behaviors (on the part of the patient as well as on the part of the psychiatrist), it would ask what the varying consequences of the behaviors are. The patient whose aberrant behavior (whether it is depression or hallucinations) is followed by hospitalization and the cessation of further responsibility for having brought about, say, the bankruptcy of a business, would show control by a different kind of contingency than the patient whose bizarre behavior appears to be caused by ingestion of a drug. One question about differences in diagnosis might then be rephrased in terms of the role that hospitals play in providing safety valves in each culture for "leaving the field," as it were.

The pay-off of different behaviors in the culture at large may not be the same as in the psychiatric culture, or for that matter in the legal-system culture. Thus the reinforcement-contingency analysis would also tell us about the differential pay-off of different behaviors vis-à-vis psychiatrists. Will the psychiatrist most likely keep a patient in the hospital if the patient threatens suicide or if he or she expresses delusions? An interview with a patient is, of course, a situation in which the psychiatrist is collecting data to arrive at a judgment. How that is done will depend on the consequences of that psychiatrist's judgment. In its relatively benign form, the influence of others over the judgment made by an individual psychiatrist takes the form of coinciding with a particular theoretical predilection of one's superior. A more malignant form of influence arises when diagnoses are given for political purposes, as is suggested from time to time. Yet before we smugly state that this does not happen, we must evaluate the effect, on the diagnostic procedure, of a state policy that asks that the population of hospitals be markedly reduced within short periods of time and that uses the hospital census as one index for the promotion of those arriving at diagnoses or supervising the process.

The concept of reinforcement contingency has still other advantages in cross-cultural research. As a tool for the analysis of behavior, it calls attention to the fact that the naked count of behaviors is never enough; it calls for the kind of information that good studies of cross-cultural comparison already collect. Coming as it does from learning theory, reinforcement contingency provides a dynamic concept that allows one to analyze for change in a culture as well as for its status at a given time. Thus to the extent that a culture tolerates greater variation in dress and reduces the correlation between dress and socioeconomic class, to that extent such "symptoms" can no longer be considered to be discriminative stimuli or occasions for psychiatric intervention.

It might be of interest to trace such changes in the general reinforcement contingencies as they become translated into hospital-census and prison-census figures.

The reinforcement-contingency analysis would allow us to examine such important questions as the effect of changing environments on the learning behavior of children in schools. In our society, the setting for learning is made everywhere the same irrespective of the nature of the children's cultural background: Some backgrounds, for example, might prepare children for sitting still for a long time under some circumstances, and for running around or flitting from subject to subject at other times; other backgrounds, on the other hand, may not prepare children for quiet activity at all. The ill fit between the environment or the school procedures employed and the learner, in any given place or time, might well be the source for the fluctuation in such diagnostic categories as hyperkinesis.

The area of cross-cultural testing is replete with problems that would be solved by taking into account the reinforcement contingencies acting on the children when they are tested by different people and under different circumstances. The result that children may know the right answer under so-called "natural" conditions, but not in a strict test situation, is not a good enough analysis of the testing situations. One must analyze the different situations in terms of the variables specified by the reinforcement contingency, namely, that particular behaviors are reinforced (positively or negatively) on particular occasions, and that these contingencies are learned.

What then can we say about the elephant as a hyphen? We can analyze it by using a behavior theory concept that has elucidated not only the behavior of animals but also the behavior of human beings. I submit that in cross-cultural research, where conceptualization is so important because there is so much data to be looked at, this concept will prove even more useful.

Index

A
Actualization, 167–169
Adjective Q-sort, 278
Advertising, 209–229
  emotional appeals, 211
Africa, 31, 69, 145, 146, 150, 151, 153, 154
  Algeria, 166
  Baganda, 31, 34–36, 38, 40
  Bantu, 169
  Baoulé, 169
  Berber, 159
  Chagga, 102
  Ghana, 57, 68, 69, 294, 295
  Ivory Coast, 169
  Kalenjiin, 102
  Kenya, 47–54, 57–69
  Kikuyu, 57, 58, 67
  Kipsigis, 47–54, 145–151
  Kokwet, 49, 51–54, 146–151
  Kpelle, 24, 146
  Liberia, 24, 146, 160
  Logoli, 103
  Luganda, 37
  Marakesh, 155–157
  Morocco, 39, 153–162
  Ngecha, 58, 62, 65
  Nigeria, 80, 234, 295
  Rwanda, 166, 167
  Senegal, 146, 154

  Somalia, 118
  South Africa, 335–338, 340–343
  Uganda, 31–43, 118, 119
  Yemen, 154
  Zaïre, 72
Aggression, 104
Altruism, 121, 292
American Peace Corps, 291–300
  evaluation, 291, 294, 298, 300
  selection, 291, 294
  staff, 297
  training, 291, 293, 295, 298, 299
  volunteers, 291, 293–296, 299, 300
Androgyny, 95, 272
Antisocial behavior, 104
Anxiety, 224
Archetypes, 193–206
Asia, 76, 77, 232
  Afghanistan, 118
  East Pakistan, 234
  India, 118, 134, 234, 263–274, 292, 296, 297
    New Delhi, 296
  Indonesia, 154
  Iran, 119, 125, 129, 131–134, 136
    Shiraz, 129, 136
  Israel, 77, 125, 129, 136, 234, 253–260, 335, 338, 340, 342, 343, 349–358
    Jerusalem, 136

Japan, 7, 77, 80, 81, 84, 88, 90, 96, 117,
     231, 234–240, 275, 312, 315–320
     Tokyo, 235
People's Republic of China, 121, 122, 275
     Kwangchow, 121
Philippines, 33, 72, 77, 116, 118, 245,
     335, 338, 340, 342, 343
     Iloco barrios, 118
     Tarong, 116
South Korea, 72, 77, 118
Taiwan, 125, 129, 133, 135, 136
     Taipei, 129, 135, 136
Thailand, 298
Turkey, 106, 129, 136
     Istanbul, 136
Vietnam, 297, 298, 349–358
Aspiration, 243, 106
     achievement, 243, 250, 251, 276
     educational, 106, 244, 251, 257
     levels of, 251
Assessment, 325
Association deficiency theory, 75
Association of ideas, 211, 214
Association processes, 73, 77, 78, 97
Attachment, 119
Attention, 130
Attention deficiency theory, 75
Attitude, 141, 211, 214–219, 231–240, 244,
     245, 335–344, 356
Attraction, 337
     personal, 337
     cross-sex, 337
     –avoidance, 338
Australia, 243–251, 304–308, 335, 338, 340
     Aborigines, 28, 72, 73, 100, 106, 305,
         306, 308
         Fullabo, 72
         Walbiri, 73, 100
     Central, 28, 73
     New South Wales, 243, 245
     Queensland, 243, 245
     South Australia, 345
     Victoria, 243, 245
Authoritarianism, 277, 295

B
Back carrying, 50
Beliefs, 113–118, 120, 122, 147
Bender Gestalt Test, 59, 61, 62, 64, 68
Bilingualism, 137, 153, 161, 338, 340, 344
Binocular disparity, 34

Bisexuality, 314
Breast-feeding, 50

C
Caregivers, 113–115, 118–122
Carey Infant Temperament Survey, 49
Carpentered stimuli, 32
Central America, 23
     Guatemala, 23–29
         Ladino, 24
         Indian, 24
     Panama, 23–29
     West Indies/Caribbean, 103
         Barbados, 101, 105, 106
         Haiti, 125, 129, 130
            Port-au-Prince, 136
         Honduras, 103
         Netherland Antilles, 72
         Childrearing, 48, 116, 122
     methods, 48
     practices, 114, 115
     scales, 243
     techniques, 122
Children's drawings, 71–97
Chronic organic brain syndrome, 329
Classroom behavior, 125, 126, 173
Cognitive functioning, 141, 214
Cognitive tests, 25, 26, 28, 57–69, 133
Competence, 4, 19, 141
Competence-performance model, 163–169
Compliance, 115–117
Concepts, 18
     of listura (smartness), 26
     self, 130
     spatial, 18, 19
Cooperation, 116
Coping, 114
Counterbalanced procedure, 73, 266
Couvade, 99, 100, 103
Crèche, 120
Cross-sectional studies, 138
Crowded quarters, 104
Cultural relativism, 18, 306, 307
Cultural shock, 299

D
Delinquency, 104
Depressive disorders, 325
Development, 2, 3, 164
     cognitive, 3, 9, 68, 100, 163
     mental, 23, 24, 29

ontogenetic, 13, 14, 16, 17, 164
personality, 48
phylogenetic, 164
theories of-, 2–9, 13–20
Deviance, 104
Diagnosis, 329, 330, 333
Differentiation theory, 6, 7, 14–17, *see also*
    Witkin and Berry's theory
Difficult infant syndrome, 48, 54
Digits test, 26, 27
Discipline, 116
Distance, 337
    interpersonal, 335–337, 341, *see also*
        interpersonal relationship
    social, 145–149
        physical, 337
        projected, 335–345
Domain consistency, 19
Draw-a-man test/Draw-a-woman test, 8, 78,
    80, 83
Draw-a-person test, 101

E
Ecological functionalism, 166
Education, 113, 114, 117, 120–122,
    154–162, 172, 233, 244, 247–251
Ego identity, 263–274
Ego Identity Incomplete Sentence Blank (EI-
    ISB), 264, 265, 267
EI-ISB, *see* Ego Identity Incomplete Sentence
    Blank
Embedded figures, 26–28, 59–68
Emic, 18
Epistemology, 14, 163, 164
    genetic, 14, 17
Ethnic groups, 139, 142
    American Indian, 314, 315
    Chicano, 101, 172
    Eskimo, 166–168
    Puerto Rican, 137–142
Ethnocentrism, 13, 17, 18
Ethnographic techniques, 23
Etic, 18, 304
Etiological models, 326, 332, 333
Europe, 72, 76
    Denmark, 76, 90, 91, 125, 129, 132, 136
    France, 76, 86, 87, 93–95, 117, 120, 129,
        134, 214
    Germany, 73, 76, 84, 85, 91, 92, 134,
        214, 226, 231–240, 275–287

Cologne, 277
    Munich, 135, 235
    Great Britain, 121, 125, 129, 134–136,
        292, 323–333, 335–345, 363
    London, 292, 323–333
    Scotland, 338, 345
    Windsor, 136
    Greece, 72, 77
    Italy, 72, 77, 125, 129–136
        Milan, 129, 136
        Palermo, 129, 133, 136
        Sicily, 129, 133, 136
    Netherlands, 336
    Norway, 135
        Bergen, 135
    Poland, 125, 129, 136
        Gdansk, 136
    Spain, 231, 232, 234–236
    Switzerland, 76
    USSR (Soviet Union), 117, 190, 228,
        253–260, 275
    Yugoslavia, 76, 77
Evolution, 14
    cultural, 14
    general, 14
    specific, 15

F
Familiarity hypothesis, 71, 78–80, 95, 97
Family, 99, 106, 151, 244
    control, 245
    extended, 150, 244
    nuclear, 99, 105, 106, 150
    patterns, 100
    structure, 100, 105
Father absence, 99–107
Fathering, 99, 103, 107
Father loss, 105
Father present, 106
Field dependence, 6, 7, 16, 17
Field independence, 16, 17, 243
Figure-placement task, 335, 339
Formal health care system, 326
Franch Drawing Completion Test, 103
Free recall, 2
Fruit tree experiment, 71–97
Functional disorders, 329, 330

G
Generational differences, 238
Geriatric studies, 326–328, *see also*
    psychogeriatric research

Goal, 80, 120
Goodenough–Harris Drawing Test, 101
Grammatical construction, 311

H
Heterosexuality, 314, 315
Homosexuality, 313–315
Hudson Pictorial Depth Perception Test, 35

I
Ideal self-rating, 278–287
Identity, 100
    cross-sex, 100, 101
    sex role, 99, 101, 103, 105, 106
Ideological conflict, 303, 307
Ideological shock, 303–308
Idiosyncratic responses, 336
Illusions, 32 see visual illusions
Illustration, 211
Imagery, 74, 77, 78
Incidental learning, 26, 27, see learning
Industrialization, 232, 244
Infant's niche, 47–54
Information sharing, 294
Initiation rites, 100, 102
Instructional strategies, 171–188
Intellectual functioning, 327
Intelligence quotient, see IQ
Interactional synchrony, 60–62, 67
    experience, 121
    ideas, 121
Intercultural communication gap, 308
Interdisciplinary
    conflict, 303
    gap, 308
    team, 303, 307
    worker, 303
Intergenerational change, 325
Interpersonal relationship, 325, 336, see also
        social distance
Intimacy, 263, 273
IQ (intelligence quotient), 73, 120, 137–142

K
Kagan's Matching Familiar Figures Test, 151
Kibbutz, 105, 257, 259

L
Language, 145, 147, 151, 161, 162, 315
    comprehension, 145, 150
    teaching, 148

Learning, 26, 121, 154, 158–162, 172, 173
    see also Incidental learning
    discrimination, 75
    problems, 126, 128,
Leisure theme, 84, 86
Likert-type scale, 126
Linear perspective, 35
Longitudinal studies, 24, 28

M
Malnutrition, 23, 24, 28, 29
    chronic protein-energy, 23
Marketing, 210
Masculine protest, 100, 101, 104
Matrifocal household, 100
Matrilocal marriage, 198
Memory, 160
    impairment, 328
    recall, 61, 62
    rote memorization, 154, 160
Mental disorder, 325, 331, 332
Mental health ratings, 295
Mnemonic techniques, 160
Mobility, 228, 233, 237, 239, 256
    personal, 231
    social, 228
    of women, 256
Modernization, 80, 93, 97, 231–241, 245,
        246, 249
Monocular depth cues, 31–35, 41
Monolingual (students), 338, 340, 344
Moral judgment, 104
Morpheme, 311
Motivation, 106, 141, 210, 214, 228
    achievement, 100, 106, 142, 217
    affiliation, 217, 219, 224
Msid (preschool or school), 155, 156, 158
Multidisciplinary
    approach, 304
    collaboration, 304
    rapport, 304
    team, 304
    viewpoint, 304
Myths of equality, 254–260

N
Neonatal Behavior Assessment Scale
        (Brazelton), 49
Nonverbal communication, 57, 58, 211, 219
    stimuli, 97
    variables, 61, 62, 67

Nonverbal specificity, 57, 58, 60, 62, 69
  instructions, 181, 182, 184
North America, 25, 315
  Canada, 76, 83, 84, 166, 167, 243–251,
    335, 338, 340, 342, 345
    Baffin Island, 166–168
    Labrador, 243, 245
    Newfoundland, 243–245
  Greenland, 72, 73
  Mexico, 199, 234, 244, 245
  United States, 33, 34, 38, 47–54, 71–79,
    82–84, 89–91, 95–97, 101–107, 117
    119, 122, 125–135, 147, 150, 165,
    171–188, 214, 215, 224–226, 228,
    231–241, 244, 275–287, 291–300,
    316, 318, 323–333, 335–345,
    349–358, 363
  California
    Los Angeles, 50
    San Diego, 172
  Hawaii, 292
  Massachusetts, Boston, 49–50
  New Jersey, Princeton, 135
  New York, New York, 79, 137–142,
    323–333, 363
  Pennsylvania, 33, 38
    Allentown, 235
  Rhode Island, 125–136
Nutrition, 29

O
Obedience, 115, 145, 150, 151
Observation, 2
  experimental, 2
  naturalistic, 2
Oceania
  Guam, 33, 34
  New Britain, 73
    Tolai, 73
  New Guinea, 102
  Pacific Islanders, 33
Oedipal stage, 105
One-parent household, 101
Ontogeny, 15–17, 164
Organic brain syndrome, 325, 330

P
Pagan animism, 196
Paper and pencil tests, 295
Paraphrenic disorder, 329
Parenting, 99

Patrilocality, 102
Pedagogy, 153–162
Perception, 6
  depth, 33–35, 41, 42
  three-dimensional, 31, 34–36, 38–42
  two-dimensional, 31, 34–36, 38–42
Performance, 2–4, 8, 19, 26, 163
  age-related differences, 4
Personal space, 335–337
Phylogeny, 15, 17, 164
Piaget's theory, 5, 8, 18, 121, 163–169
  concrete operations, 5, 18, 19, 163, 165,
    169
    conservation of quantity, 19, 59, 63,
      166–168
    horizontality, 167
  formal operations, 17
  qualitative variations, 18, *see also*
    Epistemology
  quantitative variations, 18
  sensorimotor level, 5, 18
Picture arrangement test, 266
Play, 25, 26
Polygynous marriage, 99, 306
  household, 103
  societies, 100
Power motive, 219, 222–224, *see* Motivation
Programmatic study, 71
Proxemics, 335, 337
Psychiatric ratings, 295
  symptoms, 323
Psychogeriatric research, 323–333
Psycholinguistic theory, 164
Psychopathology, 326, 328, 331, 333
Psychoses, 325
  with cerebro-arteriosclerosis, 325
Psychosocial maturity, 263, 264, 267, 272,
  273
Psychosocial Maturity Questionnaire (PMQ),
  266, 267
Puberty rituals, 99
Punishment, 116

Q
Q-sort, 278

R
Rational will, 277, 283
Rationalism-traditionalism scale, 238–240
Respect, 145, 150, 151, 160
Retinal image, 32

Rhode Island Pupil Identification Scale (RIPIS), 111, 125–136
Rhythmicity, 50
RIPIS, see Rhode Island Pupil Identification Scale
Rorschach Inkblot Test, 266

S
SAT, see Scholastic Aptitude Test
Schema(ta), 336, 338, 344
Scholastic Aptitude Test (SAT), 107
Schools, 25, 120, 121, 153–162, 172
  primary, 25, 121, 137–142
  British, 121
Self-consistency, 7
Self-control, 277, 283
Self-esteem, 337
Semantics, 311, 315, 317
  Componential Analysis of a General Vocabulary, 317
Semi-Structured Interview Schedule (SSIS), 265, 267
Senile dementia, 325, 327, 329, 332, 333
Sexual egalitarianism, 257, 259
Sexual symbolism, 226, 227
SIDS, see Sudden Infant Death Syndrome
Silence, 149
Single-finger movement, 58, 61–63, 65, 67
Single-hand movement, 60–63, 65, 67
Size constancy, 32
Sleep-wake behavior, 49, 50, 53
Social desirability, 80, 95, 97
  roles, 82
Socialization, 106, 122, 145, 146, 149–151, 243, 244, 247
Societal mediators, 325
Society, 82
  advanced, 231–241
  developing, 119, 231–241
  modern, 82
  traditional, 82
  tribal, 304
  Western, 16, 117, 119, 150, 338
Socioeconomic status (SES), 25–27
Spot observations, 50
South America (Latin America), 24, 232, 234, 235, 240
  Argentina, 234

Brazil, 106, 124, 125, 129, 136, 234, 244, 245
  São Paulo, 136
Chile, 231, 232, 234, 235, 237–240
  Santiago, 235
Colombia, 231, 232, 234, 235, 237–240
Bogotá, 235
Peru, 73
SSIS, see Semi-Structured Interview Scale
Stereotypes, 82, 95, 193–206, 304, 308
  sex roles, 82, 224, 228, 254, 259
  occupations, 205
Stigma, 100, 336, 337, 344
  avoidance, 338
  -free stimuli, 335, 341, 343
  -laden stimuli, 335, 341, 343
  -related stimuli, 335, 341, 343
  social, 100
Stigmatization, 314
Stress, 299
Subincision, 100
Sudden Infant Death Syndrome (SIDS), 52, 53
Surrogate, 105
  parent, 105
  father, 103

T
Task relatedness, 60–63, 65, 68
Teaching, 14
  practices, 114, 117, 121–123
Test-retest procedure, 71
Third World, 16, 233
Thinking, 77
  associative, 77
T–M attitudinal scale, 246
Traditionalism, 241–251
  customs, 80
  score, 246
Traditionalism-modernism scale, 243–247
  determinants, 243
  syndrome, 244
Transitional stage, 83
Translation, 129–135, 316
  backward translation method, 278, 286

U
Urbanization, 232, 233

V

Validity, 23, 24, 26, 28, 107
  indigenous, 24, 26, 28
  construct, 24, 26–28
Value hypothesis, 71, 78–80, 84, 97
Values, 83, 106, 114–117, 120, 122, 147,
    211, 214, 217, 228, 240, 243–245,
    247, 249–251
  dominant, 106
  group, 71, 74, 78, 96, 120
Verbal communication, 147, 219
  instructions, 181, 182, 184
  interaction, 147, 149
  productivity, 268
  specificity, 57, 69
  stimuli, 97
  variables, 62, 65
Visual illusion, 31, 32, 34, 37, 39, 41–43
  geometric optical, 42
  horizontal-vertical, 32
  magnitude, 31

Müller–Lyer, 32, 34
  Ponzo, 31–43
Vocalization, 148

W

WAIS, see Wechsler Adult Intelligence Scale
War bereavement, 349–358
Weaning, 118
Wechsler Adult Intelligence Scale (WAIS),
    266
Wechsler Intelligence Scale for Children
    (WISC), 111, 137–142
West Indies, see Central America, West
    Indies/Carribbean
Westernization, 72, 80, 82
WISC, see Wechsler Intelligence Scale for
    Children
Witkin and Berry's theory, 6, 8
Witkin's theory, 5
  of psychological differentiation, 5, 7
Word association test, 76